Great Plains Ethnohistory

STUDIES IN THE ANTHROPOLOGY OF
NORTH AMERICAN INDIANS SERIES

Editors
Rani-Henrik Andersson
Mark van de Logt

Founding Editors
Raymond J. DeMallie
Douglas R. Parks

Great Plains Ethnohistory

New Interdisciplinary Approaches

Edited by Rani-Henrik Andersson,
Logan Sutton, and Thierry Veyrié

UNIVERSITY OF NEBRASKA PRESS, Lincoln

© 2024 by the Board of Regents of the University of Nebraska

Chapter 2 previously appeared in French as "De Deslauriers à Deloria: L'identité française d'une famille sioux," in *Un continent en partage: Cinq siècles de rencontres entre Amérindiens et Français*, ed. Gilles Havard and Mickaël Augernon (Paris: Les Indes Savantes, Rivages des Xantons, 2013), 535–58.

Chapter 13 previously appeared in French as "Personnes au bateau de bois, Esprits, Faiseurs de haches, Poil-aux-yeux . . . Ou comment les Indiens d'Amérique du Nord appelaient les Français," in *Un continent en partage: Cinq siècles de rencontres entre Amérindiens et Français*, ed. Gilles Havard and Mickaël Augeron (Paris: Les Indes Savantes, Rivages des Xantons, 2013), 233–50.

All rights reserved

The University of Nebraska Press is part of a land-grant institution with campuses and programs on the past, present, and future homelands of the Pawnee, Ponca, Otoe-Missouria, Omaha, Dakota, Lakota, Kaw, Cheyenne, and Arapaho Peoples, as well as those of the relocated Ho-Chunk, Sac and Fox, and Iowa Peoples.

Library of Congress Cataloging-in-Publication Data
Names: Andersson, Rani-Henrik, editor. | Sutton, Logan, editor. | Veyrié, Thierry, editor.
Title: Great Plains ethnohistory: new interdisciplinary approaches / edited by Rani-Henrik Andersson, Logan Sutton, and Thierry Veyrié.
Description: Lincoln: University of Nebraska Press, [2024] | Series: Studies in the anthropology of North American Indians | Includes bibliographical references and index.
Identifiers: LCCN 2024008391
ISBN 9781496242099 (hardback; acid-free paper)
ISBN 9781496241757 (paperback; acid-free paper)
ISBN 9781496242105 (epub)
ISBN 9781496242112 (pdf)
Subjects: LCSH: Indians of North America—Great Plains—Social life and customs. | Indians of North America—Great Plains—Ethnic identity. | Indians of North America—Great Plains—History.
Classification: LCC E78.G73 G678 2024 | DDC 305.897/0764809—dc23/eng/20240907
LC record available at https://lccn.loc.gov/2024008391

Set in MeropePonca by K. Andresen.

In honor of Raymond J. DeMallie and Douglas R. Parks

CONTENTS

List of Illustrations................................. xi
List of Tables xiii
Acknowledgments xv

Introduction:
    Ethnohistory in the Twenty-First Century......... 1
    Rani-Henrik Andersson, Logan Sutton, and Thierry Veyrié

1. A Foot in the Field, a Foot in the Archive, and
    a Keen Editorial Eye: The Making of an
    Ethnohistorian................................. 23
    Joanna C. Scherer and Thierry Veyrié

PART 1. CHANGING IDENTITIES IN THE INDIGENOUS
SOCIETIES OF THE GREAT PLAINS

2. From Deslauriers to Deloria: French Identity in a Sioux
    Indian Family.................................. 57
    Raymond J. DeMallie

3. Lakȟóta Modernities and the Ends of History:
    Little Big Man, Crow Dog, and Red Tomahawk in
    Context 87
    Sebastian F. Braun

4. "Although He Had the Ways of a Woman, He Was a
    Great Warrior": Kúsaat in Nineteenth-Century
    Pawnee and Arikara Society.................... 113
    Mark van de Logt

5. Hungry Narratives Turned on Their Head (or Danced on Their Toes?): Toward Decolonial Listening in Ethnohistorical Practice 137
Sarah Quick

6. Paradigms and Poetry: John G. Neihardt's *Cycle of the West*. 165
Francis Flavin

PART 2. SYMBOLS AND CEREMONIALISM

7. From the Litter to the Horse: The Native American Ritual of "Lifting" 193
Gilles Havard

8. Remapping Northern Arapaho Space and Place in Plains Ethnohistory 221
Jeffrey D. Anderson

9. "TiweNAsaakaričI nikuwetiresWAtwaáhAt aniinuuNUxtaahiwaáRA": An Overview of Arikara Spirituality 243
Brad KuuNUx TeeRIt Kroupa

10. "Under the Tree That Never Bloomed I Sat and Cried Because It Faded Away": An Ethnohistory of Black Elk's Visions 265
Rani-Henrik Andersson

PART 3. KINSHIP AND LANGUAGE

11. Comanche Society on the Reservation, 1875–1926, a Patrilineal Hypothesis: The Case of the *Ketahto Yamparika* 293
Thomas W. Kavanagh

12. Linguistic Evidence of Contact between Northern Caddoan and Siouan Languages: Arikara-Pawnee Verbal Classifiers................................315
    Logan Sutton

13. Wooden Boatmen, Spirits, and Bushy Eyebrows: American Indian Names for the French in North America................................345
    Douglas R. Parks

Afterword...369
    Philip J. Deloria

    Contributors 373
    Index 379

ILLUSTRATIONS

1. Margaret Blaker's office in the "Castle" 26
2. Margaret Blaker and Raymond DeMallie........... 28
3. Dorsey catalog card with DeMallie notes.......... 30
4. NMNH summer interns.......................... 31
5. Yellow Bear photograph and catalog card 32
6. Photograph of Red Cloud's family and
    catalog card of DeMallie's gift 34
7. Raymond DeMallie and Joanna Scherer
    looking at photographs 36
8. Raymond DeMallie and James Boon
    looking at a Kiowa drawing 37
9. Raymond DeMallie and Joanna Scherer
    at AAA poster session..........................45
10. Raymond DeMallie and Douglas Parks
    at their residence..............................47
11. Father de Smet being carried 202
12. Collum-Bates wedding 205
13. Ketahto marriages............................. 306

TABLES

1. Yamparika divisional populations, 1869–79 301
2. Ketahto sub-band populations, 1878–92 303
3. Variant forms of the name "French" in
    Algonquian languages 347

ACKNOWLEDGMENTS

This book originated from a symposium held in Bloomington in 2017 titled "Indiana at the Crossroads of American Anthropology and History: Symposium in Honor of Raymond J. DeMallie." Laura Scheiber and Douglas Parks organized the celebration, with the help of the staff and students of the American Indian Studies Research Institute. It was sponsored by the College of Arts and Humanities Institute and the Department of Anthropology at Indiana University, among others. Many of the chapters of the present volume derive from papers given at this event.

We wish to thank Philip J. Deloria for contributing the afterword to this volume and the authors for diligently working on the preparation of their chapters for publication in this volume. We are also thankful to Gilles Havard for sharing the original English-language drafts of the chapters by Raymond J. DeMallie and Douglas R. Parks included here but previously published in French translation. The University of Nebraska Press and especially Matt Bokovoy were indispensable in our work, and we are very grateful that they took on this project. Lastly, our two reviewers, Alice Kehoe and Jennifer Brown, provided constructive feedback and great insights that helped to improve this book.

Great Plains Ethnohistory

Introduction

Ethnohistory in the Twenty-First Century
RANI-HENRIK ANDERSSON, LOGAN
SUTTON, AND THIERRY VEYRIÉ

The anthropological study of the Plains cultural area of North America has been characterized in the last fifty years by the influence of history, linguistics, literature, and other disciplines. This book demonstrates how several disciplinary approaches can be braided into enriched scholarship that better reflects the social life of knowledge. This book is also an homage to Raymond J. DeMallie, anthropologist and ethnohistorian of the Lakȟóta people, and Douglas R. Parks, linguist, anthropologist, and ethnohistorian of the Pawnee and Arikara peoples. Both have been mentors and friends to many scholars and to the editors and contributors to this volume in particular.

Raymond J. DeMallie and Douglas R. Parks

The editors to this volume all knew Raymond DeMallie and Douglas Parks in the last two decades of their prolific careers, when the American Indian Studies Research Institute (AISRI) that they founded had become a venerable institution with a large community of friends and scholars. Their careers were already well accomplished by that point.

DeMallie obtained his PhD in anthropology from the University of Chicago in 1971 with a dissertation on Sioux kinship. At that time he was the youngest PhD in the history of the department. He was subsequently hired by the University of Wyoming in Laramie, where he taught for a year before he joined the Department of Anthropology at Indiana University, Bloomington, in 1973. Ray became a full professor in 1984 and started exploring the possibility of creating a center for American Indian studies. In 1985 he and Douglas Parks cofounded the

American Indian Studies Research Institute, which conducts research, editorial, and community projects to support Native American cultures, languages, and communities.

Parks received his PhD in linguistics in 1972 from the University of California, Berkeley, writing *A Grammar of Pawnee* under the direction of Mary Haas (published as Parks 1976). His first teaching position was at Idaho State University, where he became an assistant professor and acting chair of the Department of Anthropology. After a postdoctoral fellowship at the Smithsonian Institution in 1973–74, Parks was hired as the director of the Indian Languages Program at Mary College in Bismarck, North Dakota (now the University of Mary). In 1983 he joined Indiana University, where he served as a professor in the anthropology department and cofounded AISRI.

Through AISRI, DeMallie and Parks obtained many federal grants, particularly from the National Science Foundation and the National Endowment for Humanities. These projects ranged from editorial projects to language documentation and revitalization. They individually and in collaboration published many important contributions to Native American studies.

In 1980 and 1982, respectively, DeMallie published *Lakota Belief and Ritual*, with Elaine A. Jahner, and *Lakota Society*, two volumes compiling the notes taken by Pine Ridge agency physician James R. Walker, which comprise some of the best sources on Lakȟóta religion and society (Walker 1980, 1982). In 1985, again demonstrating his scholarly commitment to unearth archival sources and present them to the public in well-contextualized fashion, he published *The Sixth Grandfather: Black Elk's Teachings Given to John G. Neihardt*. In 1999 his long collaboration with Vine Deloria Jr. culminated in the two volumes of *Documents of American Indian Diplomacy*, which became an important reference for the study of Indian rights. Two years later his career as an anthropologist was crowned with the publication of the two-part volume of the *Handbook of North American Indians* dedicated to the Plains cultural area (DeMallie 2001).

Parks's contributions to the documentation of Caddoan languages and anthropology are equally impressive. Besides his 1972 dissertation, which described the Pawnee language and was published in 1976, he edited *Caddoan Texts* (1977), containing representative samples of texts from all of the documented Caddoan languages. Parallel to his work in linguistic description and analysis, Doug made contributions to anthropology with *The Ceremonies of the Pawnee*, an ethnography of Skiri and South Band Pawnee ceremonies described by Pawnee anthropologist James R. Murie ([1981] 1989). In 1991 Doug published *Traditional Narratives of the Arikara Indians*, a bilingual opus of Arikara narratives produced from his own collaboration with Native knowledge carriers.[1] In 2008 Doug published *A Dictionary of Skiri Pawnee* (Parks and Pratt 2008), completing in part the Boasian triad of linguistic documentation (grammar, texts, dictionary) for the Pawnee language.

Finally, in 2017 DeMallie and Parks, as one of the last finished projects before their deaths, published in collaboration with Robert Vézina *A Fur Trader on the Upper Missouri: The Journal and Description of Jean-Baptiste Truteau, 1794-1796* (Truteau 2017), an English translation of Truteau's original French writing. This book, decades in its completion, is one more testament to their commitment and dedication to editing and disseminating important, primary historical writings recounting descriptions of Native American cultures from early in the contact period.

DeMallie and Parks initiated many projects across their decades-long careers. Many were completed; some are being completed by their former students and colleagues after their deaths; and, unfortunately, some will have to be taken up and concluded by others who might take interest. Two important contributions in particular should be mentioned: *The Dakota Way of Life* by Ella C. Deloria (published in 2022) is an ethnographic description of Dakota society through the eyes of a woman when many comparable sources came from men. This was an editorial project begun by DeMallie in the 1980s and completed in the last years of his life, published posthumously with the assistance of Thierry Veyrié. "The Roaming Scout Narratives: Teachings of a Pawnee Priest" (working title) by James R. Murie, which Douglas Parks re-transcribed and edited with the assistance of Skiri Pawnee knowledge keeper Lula Nora Pratt in the 1980s–90s, is in its final stages of preparation for publication and will be a vitally important contribution to Pawnee studies: it contains a firsthand extensive cosmology of the Pawnees, in both Pawnee and English.

For all their scholarly accomplishments, DeMallie and Parks were also extraordinary human beings, generous with their knowledge, time, and resources and eager to make meaningful connections with their interlocutors. They were well known in the Native communities that they visited regularly, and they were widely respected, a rare feat for white anthropologists after the Red Power movement. Much of their knowledge and experience came from their Native teachers, some of whom adopted them as their relatives. Nora Pratt, for example, adopted Parks as a son after hundreds of hours of language work on Skiri Pawnee and gave him a name. DeMallie was virtually a member of the Deloria family, knowing everybody and treating the kids with presents. As much as they could, they behaved as functional relatives in the cultures of their teachers. If academic scholarship builds up the myth of the self-made scholar, it was always clear with DeMallie and Parks that their knowledge, expertise, and legitimacy to talk came from real relationships and trust, as well as extensive archival research. They were embedded in a network of relationships and commitments.

Perhaps this is the entryway into DeMallie and Parks's practice and conception of anthropology and ethnohistory. Franz Boas, the father of American anthropology, conceptualized anthropology as a four-field discipline—sociocultural anthropology, linguistic anthropology, archaeology, and physical anthropology—therefore emphasizing its interdisciplinarity. DeMallie and Parks were sociocultural and linguistic anthropologists, but they were also historians. Their mastery of the published and unpublished primary sources was coupled with working relationships with their teachers in Native communities. They thus confronted written documentation with community knowledge, including oral histories. Primary sources were absolutely capital in their research, but they relied on Native people to interpret them, contextualize them, or provide an alternative viewpoint. Their practice of ethnohistorical research was one of placing documents in contact with the cultural knowledge of communities.

The careers and scholarship of Raymond DeMallie and Douglas Parks illustrate the necessity that anthropologists have to complement their expertise with the knowledge and tools characteristic of others. Inherently multifaceted, linguistic and ethnographic description requires a rich set of interdisciplinary skills and interests in order to reflect the complexity of human cultural existences.

Ethnohistory

Interdisciplinarity is not an end in and of itself, but it is an efficient way to enrich a subject matter. It refers to the consecutive or simultaneous use of approaches, methods, or interests from distinct disciplines in the pursuit of a research question. Within the walls of universities and the concepts privy to institutional disciplines, the relevance of academic research sometimes becomes obscure to anyone outside the discipline. Interdisciplinarity offers the opportunity to apply what we know to new realms of understanding. It is at the same time a test of scientific knowledge and the promise of new connections and new understanding.

In the United States the "ethnohistorical" approach, as DeMallie preferred to call it, originated in the works of the Indian Claims Commission. In 1946 the Indian Claims Act passed into law the mandate to examine existing Native American claims against the U.S. government in court. Anthropologists and historians were called upon to testify and to examine and interpret primary documents that supported the claims of the tribes or the defense of the government. Erminie Wheeler-Voegelin was one of the early theorists of American ethnohistory and conducted extensive archival research into government administrative documents to research Indian claims in different regions, including the Great Lakes, the Great Plains, and the Great Basin (Warren and Barnes 2018). Many other anthropologists were called upon to assist the courts or engaged in debates concerning the aboriginal territories of Native peoples. At the University of Chicago, where DeMallie pursued his doctorate, Raymond Fogelson and Nancy Lurie were pioneers in ethnohistorical research. Both Raymond DeMallie and Douglas Parks were also mentored in ethnohistory by Waldo and

Mildred Wedel, who researched historical, including French, sources to provide information on historic Dakota sites.[2] In an article coauthored with Mildred Wedel, DeMallie implied that the definition of ethnohistory was always dynamic and disputed, and that sociocultural anthropologists or ethnologists found in it a way to incorporate oral history in documented history (Wedel and DeMallie 1980, 110). In the plains much of the ethnohistorical research was conducted by archaeologists such as Raymond W. Wood and Waldo Wedel to map protohistoric movements, settlements, and intertribal relations.

At the core of ethnohistory lies the study of primary sources, documents created by contemporary witnesses of colonial processes. These primary sources are defined broadly and include Native accounts and written documents. They can also pertain to different media including photographs, audio recordings, letters, art, treaties, and more. During the work of the Indians Claims Commission, however, written documents were relied upon heavily, and the selection of sources has remained contentious among ethnohistorians.

Defining ethnohistory is complicated. One definition was suggested by Michael Harkin, who argued that ethnohistory in the twentieth century was a gradual move toward collaboration, even harmony, between history and anthropology (Harkin 2010). That may be true, as ethnohistory commonly uses and brings together methods and sources derived from both fields to reach a more in-depth understanding of a given society or its role in historical processes. This definition, however, is not sufficient. Although ethnohistory at first developed from practical approaches more than theoretical, it has over the decades developed its own particular methods that allow and call for multidisciplinary or cross-disciplinary approaches. Ethnohistory does not solely look at a society through an etic, or outside, perspective; rather, it approaches any given society or culture from its own emic, or inside, perspectives. At least that is the goal of any ethnohistorian. This approach, of course, requires an in-depth knowledge and understanding of the society's structures, ontologies, and belief system, and it often requires an understanding of the language. According to Raymond DeMallie, ethnohistorians try to understand culture through its own terms and its own cultural codes (DeMallie 1993). DeMallie continues by defining his approach as being one of "listening" (see Andersson and Quick in this volume).[3] Similarly, Ray Fogelson defines the ethnohistorical approach as one that "insists on taking seriously native theories of history as embedded in cosmology, in narratives, in rituals and ceremonies, and more generally in native philosophies and worldviews" (1989, 134–35).

In the past twenty years, new approaches have emerged for studying and researching Native American or Indigenous people in general. There has been a growing understanding that it is vital to include Indigenous voices and perspectives in research dealing with both the past and the present. Indeed, decolonizing research has become a standard in Indigenous studies. This approach also acknowledges Indigenous traditional knowledge and epistemologies as relevant methodological tools, for example, in using oral histories to understand social structures in historical societies or incorporating place-based knowledge in studies of changing weather patterns (Andersson, Cothran, and Kekki 2021, 1–17). The challenge, as the Maori scholar Linda Tuhiwai Smith has pointed out, has been for academia to accept Indigenous knowledge as a legitimate tool and to merge and apply it within "Western" notions of science (Tuhiwai Smith 2012, 215–26). While the term "decolonizing research" may be a recent "innovation," the methods suggested by Tuhiwai Smith, among others, are not that different from what ethnohistorians have been doing for decades. Ethnohistory has always proposed (but has often failed) to deconstruct and, to some extent, to decolonize or indigenize history, at least in the sources used. DeMallie and Parks, for instance, participated in the movement to center scholarship around the knowledge of Indigenous communities. If ethnohistorians sometimes took sides against Native communities in the courts during the Indian Claims Commission, the intention to interpret through Native lenses was always there. As an example, DeMallie's collaboration with Vine Deloria to present treaties and other documents served Native rights. This was not quite "decolonizing research" since both the works of the Indians Claims Commission and the research on treaties operated within the legal framework of colonial society, but as ethnohistorians, DeMallie and Parks followed research agendas that indeed deconstructed Western epistemologies: they consistently explored events through Native oral histories, visual sources, and Native language documents. That attention to the voices of Native insiders and to understanding the meaning of their testimonies is perhaps where we can connect ethnohistory, as we understand it, and decolonizing research, when history is still dominated by unambiguous administrative written sources. Many of the sources that DeMallie and other ethnohistorians use were and are clearly culturally situated, require interpretation, could be poetic or metaphorical, and, most importantly, need a lot of context to be understood.

Yet, ethnohistorians by and large need to address these new research approaches and methods. For example, in *Towards a New Ethnohistory*, Keith Thor Carlson et al. (2018) suggest that the way forward is in utilizing cross-cultural dialogue and interdisciplinary approaches that aim to collaboratively develop a fresh, decolonized ethnohistory in partnership with Indigenous communities. This transformative ethnohistory genuinely embraces Indigenous epistemologies and addresses the valid criticisms made by scholars who have historically imposed their own research priorities on Indigenous communities. Moreover, it highlights the significance of genuine community-engaged scholarship, which actively involves Indigenous community members in shaping the research inquiries, facilitating researchers during the research process, and meaningfully participating in the analysis of research outcomes (see the introduction to Carlson et al. 2018; Barnes and Warren 2022).

In 1991 Shepard Krech III asked the question "Should ethnohistory cease to exist?" in his article "The State of Ethnohistory" (346), pointing to the changing academic field and new approaches, such as global Indigenous studies that has emerged as a vibrant interdisciplinary field of study (Andersen and O'Brien 2016). At the 2015 Ethnohistory Society Meeting, there were discussions emphasizing the need to include Indigenous voices within the field. In a recent article Alyssa

Mt. Pleasant, Caroline Wiggington, and Kelly Wisecup explore how Indigenous studies can offer new approaches and methods to other fields, including history and literature. They emphasize that new scholarship should go beyond the archives and written records to include oral stories, paintings, images, and Indigenous languages. They also call for increased community-engaged and community-driven research (Mt. Pleasant, Wiggington, and Wisecup 2018). Ethnohistory started out as an interdisciplinary field and continues to demonstrate the strength of interdisciplinary research by finding common ground with these emerging fields (DeMallie 2013).

Ethnohistory first developed in the United States, but in the past thirty years or so it has, like many other fields, experienced what could be referred to as a transnational turn. Ethnohistorians today do research that has a geographical range from South America, Africa, Asia, and Oceania to Northern Europe. But more importantly, scholars are finding common themes and theories that are applicable and useful in different contexts. At times ethnohistory can even operate as a "middle ground" between various fields, as suggested by Jennifer Brown (1991, 113–23; Strong 2015). At the same time as the geographical focus has become more global, the topics that increasingly interest ethnohistorians today have also become more diverse, including feminist studies, gender roles, and sexuality (Silverblatt 1995, 639–50).

Despite the calls for its demise in the 1990s, ethnohistory has "established a niche in academia" that still attracts students and scholars, as DeMallie noted (2013, 233). His assessment a decade ago remains relevant today. The field is changing and adapting to new strands of research, but its core foundation in interdisciplinary approaches remains strong. Ethnohistory and ethnohistorians continue to engage in discourse with countless fields and maybe serve as a "middle ground" or even as an "academic meeting ground" that welcomes the multitude of approaches and methods that has defined it as a field for decades. Despite the calls to dismantle ethnohistory, it has remained a vibrant field of inquiry, and there is still room to "think ethnohistorically," as suggested by Raymond DeMallie (2013, 235).

Interdisciplinary Ethnohistories of the Great Plains

This book centers on ethnohistorical research of Great Plains cultures—particularly Lakȟóta/Dakȟóta, Arikara, and Pawnee, with chapters on Arapaho, Métis, and Comanche, and one on cross-cultural practices extending to the east and southeast—but the contributing authors address many of the above-mentioned new approaches and trends in ethnohistorical research. The chapters presented here certainly bridge history, anthropology, and linguistics, but there are also elements that bring gender and sexuality and Indigeneity and decolonizing research into play, making this volume truly interdisciplinary. In the vein of research traditions promoted by Raymond DeMallie and Douglas Parks, the authors "think ethnohistorically," they "listen," and they (re)visit both the archives and the field.

The first chapter narrates the relationship that Raymond DeMallie built with the National Anthropological Archives and how his career developed from social encounters there, as well as connections made with Native communities. As he explored the materials about the Lakȟóta left by anthropologists before him, he familiarized himself with massive and diverse information about the Lakȟóta culture to such an extent that, with the help of community experts, he started correcting errors and editing primary sources to bring them to the public. He also revisited primary sources about the Lakȟóta through the culturally centered lens of kinship (DeMallie 1971). DeMallie's friendship and collaboration with Vine Deloria Jr. and dedication to preparing the linguistic and ethnographic works of Ella Deloria permeated his entire career (DeMallie 2005, 2006; Deloria 2022). His scholarly engagement included the Lakȟóta language, historical sources, and visual sources, an interest particularly shared with the lead chapter author, Joanna C. Scherer. This review of the development of DeMallie as a scholar allows us to draw a sketch of his model of ethnohistorical scholarship.

The rest of *Great Plains Ethnohistory* is divided into three thematic parts.

Part 1, titled "Changing Identities in the Indigenous Societies of the Great Plains," explores and discusses various identities, Native and non-Native, that exist in historical and contemporary Indigenous societies of the plains. This part fittingly begins with Raymond DeMallie's chapter that illustrates his interest in the Deloria family as well as in historical French sources and identities in Native worlds. The chapter, titled "From Deslauriers to Deloria: French Identity in a Sioux Indian Family," traces the history of the Deloria family from the early nineteenth century onward. DeMallie goes back to the origin of the Deloria family as recounted by Vine Deloria Sr. and Ella Deloria to identify coinciding and competing versions, setting foundational myths with different tones. They all trace back to a French voyageur who married a Yankton woman and had a son named François, who became known as Saswé, the Lakȟóta pronunciation of the French name. DeMallie pieces together Saswé's life: he was recognized as being of mixed heritage, a "half-breed" in the parlance of the time, but received visions and became a holy man afflicted with a prophecy that he would kill four of his fellow Lakȟóta. This chapter reviews the succeeding generations of Deloria family members, expressing this family genealogy within the concepts of traditional Lakȟóta oral tradition marked by kinship and spiritual determination, continuing themes DeMallie has explored elsewhere (2005, 2006, inter alia).

DeMallie's chapter is followed by Sebastian F. Braun's "Lakȟóta Modernities and the Ends of History: Little Big Man, Crow Dog, and Red Tomahawk in Context," which looks at the interpretations of historical figures and how these narratives influence and are influenced by contemporary meanings and needs. As an example, the text takes a look at Crazy Horse, Sitting Bull, Gall, and Spotted Tail. While much of conventional history, anthropology, and ethnohistory focuses on the period before 1890 as history leading to an end, this text attempts to follow the narratives as the beginning of a new period: a history and culture that is often overlooked, not the least because it is sometimes perceived today as a departure from Lakȟóta values and culture. In following how tribal heroes transform history and are transformed by history, it is possible to close the gap between history and anthropology, between narratives and lived identities.

Mark van de Logt then presents a discussion on gender roles in his chapter, "'Although He Had the Ways of a Woman, He Was a Great Warrior': Kúsaat in Nineteenth-Century Pawnee and Arikara Society." Van de Logt's chapter complements Raymond DeMallie's groundbreaking 1983 article "Male and Female in Traditional Lakota Culture" by investigating the position of transgender people in traditional Pawnee and Arikara society. The Pawnees and Arikaras recognized the existence of multiple genders and sexual orientations grouped into a single concept: the Pawnees called men with the "minds" of women *kúsaat* (Arikara *kUxát*)—the focus of this chapter—while they called women with the "minds" of men *ckúsaat* (Arikara *skUxát*). Oral traditions reveal nineteenth-century Pawnee and Arikara attitudes toward *kúsaat* to be ambivalent. Despite the widespread belief that these attitudes were introduced by missionaries and other agents of colonization, it is too simplistic to attribute this phenomenon exclusively to colonial influences; oral traditions suggest that prejudice and homophobia in contemporary Pawnee and Arikara society have antecedents in pre-reservation traditional culture.

Sarah Quick discusses the "art" of listening with her chapter, "Hungry Narratives Turned on Their Head (or Danced on Their Toes?): Toward Decolonial Listening in Ethnohistorical Practice." She takes Raymond DeMallie's (1993) proposal for a conscientious awareness of disciplinary and cultural assumptions in order to adequately undertake ethnohistorical practice and enfolds decolonial listening into his model. His implied critique of the privileging of only certain kinds of historical narratives at the cost of "understand[ing] history as lived reality [and] . . . the perspectives of the actors involved" (DeMallie 1993, 526) remains resonant with a decolonial approach to sound studies (Robinson 2020). How might DeMallie's nuanced and culturally informed understanding of Indigenous languages and texts provide a model for understanding past forms of music making? How might these models work for Indigenous musics in particular? Are there limitations to DeMallie's ethnohistorical practice that a decolonial approach to listening could enhance?

Part 1 concludes with Francis Flavin's chapter, "Paradigms and Poetry: John G. Neihardt's *Cycle of the West*." From the middle of the nineteenth century through the end of the twentieth, a particular representation of American Indians—an archetype of sorts—has become popular around the world: a male Plains Indian, more specifically a Lakȟóta. This image has been shaped and perpetuated through the works of influential writers, artists, showmen, and filmmakers; it has been remarkably pervasive and has influenced notions of Indian identity for both non-Indians and Indians. This article briefly surveys the evolution of this Sioux-inspired image from the mid-nineteenth century through the end of the twentieth century. Image makers such as George Catlin, Francis Parkman, Buffalo Bill, John Neihardt, Dee Brown, and Kevin Costner depicted Indian life not of their day, but of a romantic, nostalgic, and epic past, anchored by the tragic and compelling events of the Battle of the Little Big Horn, the Ghost Dance, and the Wounded Knee Massacre. The chapter argues that Europeans and Anglo-Americans have historically understood the Sioux in terms that reflected contemporaneous European and Anglo-American concerns. Furthermore, it argues that the Sioux became America's most representative Indian group because they embodied the Euro-American "idea" of "the Indian" better than any other Native group.

Part 2, "Symbols and Ceremonialism," opens with Gilles Havard's discussion, "From the Litter to the Horse: The Native American Ritual of 'Lifting.'" This chapter addresses a Native American ritual rarely studied but frequently described in colonial sources and present in intercultural encounters almost as much as the better-known calumet ceremony. It is through this ethnohistorical case study, based on many examples of lifting, that the idea of the colonial encounter is developed: instead of being seen principally as a place of acculturation, it offers a context where cultural features of Indian societies are very clearly laid bare. The Indian pattern of lifting can be connected to the lighting penetration of horse riding in Native North American societies from the eighteenth century onward. Indeed, it is possible to understand the adoption of the horse from a "religious," and not only an "economic," point of view. This adoption may have been favored because it allowed the implementation and the development of ritual elevation practices.

Jeffrey D. Anderson shifts our focus further west in "Remapping Northern Arapaho Space and Place in Plains Ethnohistory." This chapter responds to DeMallie and Havard's (2019) call to open up "Indian Country" to Indigenous perspective, by reconsidering the conventional conceptualization of the Northern Arapaho temporospatial world and critically reexamining the narrative of Arapaho movements and migrations. He refers to Vizenor's (2019) concept of "transmotion" to understand Arapaho locality on the Great Plains as being defined by their movements across and interaction with a vast landscape extending from New Mexico to Canada and from the Missouri River to the western side of the Rocky Mountains. Despite the Arapahos being historically lumped together with "Plains" tribes, Anderson emphasizes the role and status of mountains, hills, rocks, and other elevated features of the landscape within Arapaho cosmology and ethnohistory.

Brad KuuNUx TeeRIt Kroupa discusses Arikara ceremonialism in "'*TiweNAsaakaričI nikuwetiresWAtwaáhAt aniinuuNUxtaahiwaáRA*': An Overview of Arikara Spirituality." Focusing on episodes of Arikara cultural history, this chapter reveals a distinct Arikara narrative of ceremonialism. This case study of the Arikaras shifts the central questions from cultural-historical research to methodological ones, requiring access to oral traditions and multidisciplinary modes of assessment (see Murie 1981; Parks 1991, 1996). Too often, American Indian history is restricted to written tradition or Western epistemology. Scholars need to realize that if they are to understand the historical and cultural experience of the American Indians, they must accept oral traditions as an authentic record of tribal legacy and consider Indigenous narratives as reliable resources. These narratives portray a tribe's conception of the world and the group's history, highlighting how tribal, social, and ceremonial life has developed. Selectively attended to and reinterpreted, oral traditions are a means by which American Indians make sense of, and respond to, changing circumstances. These approaches propose an understanding of history that differs sharply from Western linear concepts, perceiving events from an Indigenous perspective (see DeMallie and Lavenda 1977).

In the final chapter of part 2, Rani-Henrik Andersson delves into the visions of Black Elk, the Oglala holy man. In "'Under the Tree That Never Bloomed I Sat and Cried Because It Faded Away': An Ethnohistory of Black Elk's Visions," Andersson builds on the analysis that Ray DeMallie provided in *The Sixth Grandfather: Black Elk's Teachings Given to John G. Neihardt* (1985). This chapter compares Black Elk's childhood Great Vision to those he received during the Ghost Dance. Andersson lays out a narrative of Black Elk's life, focusing on the changes and evolution of his religious practices and affiliations over the years — from traditional Lakȟóta belief to the Ghost Dance to Catholicism and back — the different visions he had during those years, and how he reportedly related those experiences back to his transcendental and foundational childhood Great Vision that served as the benchmark for all of his other visions (see DeMallie 1982, 1993, 2009a). This chapter places Black Elk's visions in wide cultural and historical contexts, offering an in-depth ethnohistorical analysis of the continuities and changes in Lakȟóta religious practices (for which see DeMallie and Lavenda 1977; DeMallie 1987).

Part 3, "Kinship and Language," begins with a chapter by Thomas W. Kavanagh titled "Comanche Society on the Reservation, 1875–1926, a Patrilineal Hypothesis: The Case of the *Ketahto Yamparika*." Kavanagh contests the conventionally assumed model of pre- and post-reservation Comanche kinship and group membership by surveying the conclusions of historical accounts and anthropological analysis and comparing them to census data. By closely examining census data from the late nineteenth century, taking particular note of the composition of the *Ketahto*, one group that helped compose the larger *Yamparika* division, Kavanagh observes that there is an overwhelming trend toward patrilocal (living with the father's family) and virilocal (living with the husband's family) patterns of organization and exogamous behavior relative to the Ketahto group but endogamous within the Yamparika division.

In "Linguistic Evidence of Contact between Northern Caddoan and Siouan Languages: Arikara-Pawnee Verbal Classifiers," Logan Sutton illustrates how linguistic analysis can contribute to, and present suggestions for, ethnohistorical avenues of investigation. He proposes that ancestors of the Arikaras and Pawnees had significant enough contact with some Siouan-speaking peoples to have left an imprint in these Caddoan languages. Using conventional linguistic analysis, and taking advantage of the substantive collections of Arikara and Pawnee narratives (Parks 1977, 1991; Weltfish 1937) and the pioneering grammatical descriptions of Arikara and Pawnee (Parks 1976; Parks, Beltran, and Waters 1979, 1998, 2001, 2007; Parks and Pratt 2008; Parks et al. 2013), Sutton summarizes the way that Arikara and Pawnee extend verbs that prototypically express basic human postures such as "sitting," "standing," and "lying" to nonhuman entities and inanimate objects to derive a loose classificatory system, a system noted by Parks (1991, 1:xvii–xviii) but never elaborated on.

This volume concludes with a chapter by Douglas R. Parks, "Wooden Boatmen, Spirits, and Bushy Eyebrows: American Indian Names for the French in North America." This chapter was originally published in French (Parks 2013) but is included here based on Parks's original English-language manuscript. As the title suggests, Parks examines the documented Indigenous language names given to the French across eastern and central North America, finding a small number of widespread patterns of naming. As is typical when encountering a new people, technology, or concept, most Indigenous peoples would use a descriptive expression to label the novelty, which would often become conventionalized as the name for it. Parks elaborates on how early names for the French among some tribes would later shift their reference to white men in general or to the later-arriving English or colonial Americans. This chapter reflects Parks's long interest in onomastics of various types, including personal names, as seen in Parks (2023), a posthumous publication based on unpublished manuscripts, as well as names for tribes, ethnicities, and nationalities, as witnessed by his contribution of the "Synonymy" sections of all of the chapters in the *Plains* volumes of the *Handbook of North American Indians* (DeMallie 2001).

The chapters in this volume follow the ethnohistorical tradition cherished and pioneered by DeMallie and Parks, yet they also touch upon the twenty-first-century calls for decolonizing research and approaches employed by many Indigenous studies scholars. All chapters employ cross-disciplinary methods, use both archival and oral sources, seek an understanding through language and culture, but, perhaps most importantly, are based on active community-engaged research: in short, "listening" to Indigenous voices both past and present.

Notes

1. Parks (1996), titled *Myths and Traditions of the Arikara Indians*, comprises the English translations, without the Arikara language original, of a large subset of these narratives: 58 of the 156 texts originally published in 1991.
2. See also Parks and Wedel (1985) for a treatment of Pawnee sites.
3. For more on the history and evolution of ethnohistory as a field, see, for example, Harkin (2010), Braun (2013b), and Strong (2015). For a useful summary of theories and methods employed by ethnohistorians, see Bronwen and Di Rosa (2020).

References

Andersen, Chris, and Jean M. O'Brien, eds. 2016. *Sources and Methods in Indigenous Studies*. New York: Routledge.

Andersson, Rani-Henrik, Boyd C. Cothran, and Saara Kekki. 2021. *Bridging Cultural Concepts of Nature: Indigenous People and Protected Spaces of Nature*. Helsinki: Helsinki University Press.

Barnes, Chief Benjamin J., and Stephen Warren, eds. 2022. *Replanting Cultures: Community-Engaged Scholarship in Indian Country*. Albany NY: State University of New York Press.

Braun, Sebastian F. 2013a. "Introduction: An Ethnohistory of Listening." In *Transforming Ethnohistories: Narrative, Meaning, and Community*, edited by Sebastian F. Braun, 3–21. Norman: University of Oklahoma Press.

———, ed. 2013b. *Transforming Ethnohistories: Narrative, Meaning, and Community*. Norman: University of Oklahoma Press.

Bronwen, Douglas, and Dario Di Rosa. 2020. "Ethnohistory and Historical Ethnography." Oxford Bibliography in Anthropology Online, accessed March 30, 2023. https://doi.org/10.1093/OBO/9780199766567-0240.

Brown, Jennifer S. H. 1991. "Ethnohistorians: Strange Bedfellows, Kindred Spirits." *Ethnohistory* 38, no. 2: 113–23.

Carlson, Keith Thor, John Sutton Lutz, David M. Schaepe, and Naxaxalhts'i (Albert "Sonny" McHalsie). 2018. *Towards a New Ethnohistory: Community-Engaged Scholarship among the People of the River*. Winnipeg: University of Manitoba Press.

Deloria, Ella C. 2022. *The Dakota Way of Life*. Edited by Raymond J. DeMallie and Thierry Veyrié. Lincoln: University of Nebraska Press.

Deloria, Vine, Jr., and Raymond J. DeMallie, eds. 1999. *Documents of American Indian Diplomacy: Treaties, Agreements, and Conventions, 1775–1979*. 2 vols. Norman: University of Oklahoma Press.

DeMallie, Raymond J. 1971. "Teton Dakota Kinship and Social Organization." PhD dissertation, University of Chicago.

———. 1982. "The Lakota Ghost Dance: An Ethnohistorical Account." *Pacific Historical Review* 51, no. 4: 385–405.

———. 1983. "Male and Female in Traditional Lakota Culture." In *The Hidden Half: Studies of Plains Indian Women*, edited by Patricia Albers and Beatrice Medicine, 237–65. Lanham MD: University Press of America.

———, ed. 1985. *The Sixth Grandfather: Black Elk's Teachings Given to John G. Neihardt*. Lincoln: University of Nebraska Press.

———. 1987. "Lakota Belief and Ritual in the Nineteenth Century." In *Sioux Indian Religion: Tradition and Innovation*, edited by Raymond J. DeMallie and Douglas R. Parks, 25–43. Norman: University of Oklahoma Press.

———. 1993. "'These Have No Ears': Narrative and the Ethnohistorical Method." *Ethnohistory* 40, no. 4: 515–38.

———. 1994. "Kinship and Biology in Sioux Culture." In *North American Indian Anthropology: Essays on Society and Culture*, edited by Raymond J. DeMallie and Alfonso Ortiz, 125–46. Norman: University of Oklahoma Press.

———, ed. 2001. *Handbook of North American Indians*. Vol. 13, *Plains*. Washington DC: Smithsonian Institution.

———. 2005. "Deloria, Ella Cara." In *Encyclopedia of Religion*, 2nd ed., vol. 4, edited by Lindsay Jones, 2264–65. Detroit: Macmillan Reference USA.

———. 2006. "Vine Deloria Jr. (1933–2005)." *American Anthropologist* 108, no. 4: 932–35.

———. 2009a. "Black Elk 1863–1950." In *Encyclopedia of Environmental Ethics and Philosophy*, vol. 1, edited by J. Baird Callicott and Robert Frodeman, 114–15. Detroit: Macmillan Reference USA.

———. 2009b. "Community in Native America: Continuity and Change among the Sioux." *Journal de la Société des Américanistes* 95, no. 1: 185–205.

———. 2013. "Afterword: Thinking Ethnohistorically." In *Transforming Ethnohistories: Narrative, Meaning, and Community*, edited by Sebastian F. Braun, 233–53. Norman: University of Oklahoma Press.

DeMallie, Raymond J., and Gilles Havard. 2019. "Writing the History of North America from Indian Country: The View from the North-Central Plains, 1800–1870." *Journal de la Société des Américanistes de Paris* 105, no. 1: 13–40.

DeMallie, Raymond J., and Robert H. Lavenda. 1977. "Wakan: Plains Siouan Concepts of Power." In *The Anthropology of Power: Ethnographic Studies from Asia, Oceania, and the New World*, edited by Raymond D. Fogelson and Richard N. Adams, 153–65. Studies in Anthropology. New York: Academic Press.

Fogelson, Raymond D. 1989. "The Ethnohistory of Events and Nonevents." *Ethnohistory* 36, no. 2: 133–47.

Harkin, Michael E. 2010. "Ethnohistory's Ethnohistory: Creating a Discipline from the Ground Up." *Social Science History* 34, no. 2: 113–28.

Krech, Shepherd, III. 1999. "The State of Ethnohistory." *Annual Review of Anthropology* 20: 345–75.

Mt. Pleasant, Alyssa, Caroline Wigginton, and Kelly Wisecup. 2018. "Materials and Methods in Native American and Indigenous Studies." *Early American Literature* 53, no. 2: 407–44.

Murie, James R. (1981) 1989. *Ceremonies of the Pawnee*. Edited by Douglas R. Parks. Smithsonian Contributions to Anthropology, no. 27. Washington DC: Smithsonian Institution Press. Reprint, Lincoln: University of Nebraska Press.

———. n.d. "The Roaming Scout Narratives: Teachings of a Pawnee Priest." Edited and translated by Douglas R. Parks. Unpublished manuscript, American Indian Studies Research Institute, Indiana University, Bloomington. Also in part available online: http://zia.aisri.indiana.edu/~corpora/RoamingScout.php.

Parks, Douglas R. 1976. *A Grammar of Pawnee*. New York: Garland.

———, ed. 1977. *Caddoan Texts*. International Journal of American Linguistics, Native American Text Series, vol. 2. Chicago: University of Chicago Press.

———. 1979a. "Bands and Villages of the Arikara and Pawnee." *Nebraska History* 60: 214–39.

———. 1979b. "The Northern Caddoan Languages: Their Subgrouping and Time Depths." *Nebraska History* 60: 197–213.

———. 1991. *Traditional Narratives of the Arikara Indians*. 4 vols. Lincoln: University of Nebraska Press.

———. 1996. *Myths and Traditions of the Arikara Indians*. Lincoln: University of Nebraska Press.

———. 2001a. "Arikara." In DeMallie 2001, 365–90.

———. 2001b. "Caddoan Languages." In DeMallie 2001, 80–93.

———. 2013. "Personnes au bateau de bois, Esprits, Faiseurs de haches, Poil-aux-yeux... Ou comment les Indiens d'Amérique du Nord appelaient les Français." In *Un continent en partage: Cinq siècles de rencontres entre Amérindiens et Français*, edited by Gilles Havard and Mickaël Augeron, 233–50. Paris: Les Indes savantes, Rivages des Xantons.

———. 2014. "La sexualité chez les Pawnees et les Arikaras." In *Éros et Tabou: Sexualité et genre chez Amérindiens et les Inuit*, edited by Gilles Havard and Frédéric Laugrand, 154–240. Québec City: Septentrion.

———. 2023. "Arikara and Pawnee Personal Names." *Anthropological Linguistics* 63, no. 1–2: 1–64.

Parks, Douglas R., Janet Beltran, and Ella P. Waters. 1979. *Introduction to the Arikara Language*. Bismarck ND: Mary College.

———. 1998. *An Introduction to the Arikara Language: Sáhniš Wakuúnu'*. Vol. 1. Roseglen ND: White Shield School District.

———. 2001. *An Introduction to the Arikara Language: Sáhniš Wakuúnu'*. Vol. 2. Roseglen ND: White Shield School District.

———. 2007. *An Introduction to the Arikara Language: Sáhniš Wakuúnu'*. Vol. 3. Roseglen ND: White Shield School District.

Parks, Douglas R., Janet Beltran, Ella P. Waters, and Angela Plante. 2013. *Advanced Arikara Language Lessons: Sáhniš Wakuúnu'*. 2 vols. Roseglen ND: White Shield School District.

Parks, Douglas R., and Lula Nora Pratt. 2008. *A Dictionary of Skiri Pawnee*. Lincoln: University of Nebraska Press.

Parks, Douglas R., and Robert L. Rankin. 2001. "Siouan Languages." In DeMallie 2001, 94–114.

Parks, Douglas R., and Waldo R. Wedel. 1985. "Pawnee Geography: Historical and Sacred." *Great Plains Quarterly* 5, no. 3: 143–76.

Robinson, Dylan. 2020. *Hungry Listening: Resonant Theory for Indigenous Sound Studies*. Minneapolis: University of Minnesota Press.

Silverblatt, Irene. 1995. "Women, Power, and Resistance in Colonial Mesoamerica." *Ethnohistory* 42, no. 4: 639–50.

Strong, Pauline T. 2015. "Ethnohistory." In *International Encyclopedia of the Social and Behavioral Sciences*, 2nd ed., vol. 8, edited by James D. Wright, 192–97. New York: Elsevier.

Truteau, Jean-Baptiste. 2017. *A Fur Trader on the Upper Missouri: The Journal and Description of Jean-Baptiste Truteau, 1794–1796*. Edited by Raymond J. DeMallie,

Douglas R. Parks, and Robert Vézina. Translated by Mildred Mott Wedel, Raymond J. DeMallie, and Robert Vézina. Lincoln: University of Nebraska Press.

Tuhiwai Smith, Linda. 2012. *Decolonizing Methodologies: Research and Indigenous Peoples*. 2nd ed. London: Zed Books.

Vizenor, Gerald R. 2019. *Native Provenance: The Betrayal of Cultural Creativity*. Lincoln: University of Nebraska Press.

Walker, James R. (1980) 1991. *Lakota Belief and Ritual*. Edited by Raymond J. DeMallie and Elaine A. Jahner. Lincoln: University of Nebraska Press.

———. (1982) 1992. *Lakota Society*. Edited by Raymond J. DeMallie. Lincoln: University of Nebraska Press.

Warren, Stephen, and Ben Barnes. 2018. "Salvaging the Salvage Anthropologists: Erminie Wheeler-Voegelin, Carl Voegelin, and the Future of Ethnohistory." *Ethnohistory* 65, no. 2: 189–214.

Wedel, Mildred Mott, and Raymond J. DeMallie. 1980. "The Ethnohistorical Approach in Plains Area Studies." In *Anthropology of the Great Plains*, edited by W. Raymond Wood and Margot Liberty, 110–28. Norman: University of Nebraska Press.

Weltfish, Gene. 1937. *Caddoan Texts, Pawnee, South Band Dialect*. Publications of the American Ethnological Society, vol. 17. New York: G. E. Stechert.

A Foot in the Field, a Foot in the Archive, and a Keen Editorial Eye

1

The Making of an Ethnohistorian

JOANNA C. SCHERER AND THIERRY VEYRIÉ

In the last five decades Raymond J. DeMallie (1946–2021) has contributed in enduring and meaningful ways to the scholarship on the plains of North America by editing primary sources on the Lakȟóta and other Native groups, spearheading the publication of volume 13 of the *Handbook of North American Indians* dedicated to the Plains culture area (2001a), and supporting Native communities in their language reclamation efforts. This chapter examines his genesis as a scholar and an anthropologist. Doing so, we identify traits of his training and intellectual growth that are characteristic of DeMallie's brand of ethnohistory. Ethnohistory can be here defined as an approach that examines a corpus of documents alongside knowledge from a Native culture and draws from both disciplines of anthropology and history.

This chapter is centered at the Smithsonian Institution, where DeMallie and Joanna C. Scherer met. There, at the anthropology archives, he developed his foundation as a scholar and retained important relationships that influenced his career. However, this chapter also radiates out to two other angles of DeMallie's scholarship: the second is the field, that is to say, the Lakȟóta communities where DeMallie regularly traveled for his research. This movement allowed him to confront and often question the information he had found in the archives with Native perspectives and living knowledge. Crucially, he also learned the Lakȟóta language in order to understand the historical written Lakȟóta sources that are kept at the National Archives and other repositories. This experience, methodical and systematic review of archival collections on the one hand, and deep and meaningful engagement with Native communities on the other, constituted an expertise that compelled him to edit primary sources and to make them accessible to the public. Thus, the third angle of the triad that forms DeMallie's exceptional scholarship is the editorial preparation of the work of others, most often insiders or direct witnesses to the life of Native communities who provided key testimonies to the understanding of their culture.

Early Years

Raymond J. DeMallie's interest in Native Americans began early. David Miller (2013), in a biographical article on Ray (as he was known), noted that when he was recovering from an illness at age seven, his mother gave him a children's biography of Crazy Horse by Enid Meadowcroft (1954). Following this recovery Ray began "haunting the public library looking for books on Indians" (Miller 2013, 24). Living in Rochester, New York, and an only child, he was indulged by his parents and taken on frequent trips to local museums as well as Iroquois tourist attractions. He might have been drawn into Iroquois studies because of where he lived, but a series of talks he attended at the University of Rochester in April 1964 by anthropologist Fred Eggan, on "Lewis H. Morgan and the American Indian," turned him to Plains Indians. In the final lecture, "Lewis Henry Morgan and the Future of the American Indian," Eggan spoke about the need for someone to do comparative work on the kinship systems of various Sioux groups, and Ray decided this was a challenge worth pursuing (DeMallie 2001b, 46).

During his years at East High School (1960–64) he helped start a literary magazine called *Mosaic*, for which he was the nonfiction editor. In one poem titled "Mosaic '64" he described himself as "overworked," having had to reject multiple student writings. Thus, as a teen, he was driving himself to look critically at other people's texts, a skill that he honed to perfection and that stayed with him for the rest of his life. He had working-class parents, so his desire to attend the University of Chicago probably would have been impossible without some kind of financial support. An article from the local paper quotes him as advising college-bound students to take out a loan to support themselves, if need be, rather than work while going to school, for a good education was worth it. Always cautious, he noted, "The thought of a big loan would scare me a bit, but if it were going for a good education, it would be worth it" (*Democrat and Chronicle* 1962, 123).

Exploring Siouan Materials in the Archives

In 1961 his parents took him on a vacation to Washington DC, where he visited the National Archives and Records Administration (NARA). The lure of the vast Bureau of Indian Affairs collections as well as the War Department Records in the NARA enticed him, and in 1964, the year Ray graduated from high school, he emptied his savings account and traveled to DC. During that foundational visit he was introduced to Margaret Blaker (Miller 2013:26),[1] the archivist for the Bureau of American Ethnology (BAE) — renamed the Smithsonian Office of Anthropology Archives (SOA) in 1965 and then the National Anthropological Archives (NAA) in 1968, reflecting an increased scope for the acquisition of collections.

Before Blaker's tenure the archive was largely an unorganized repository with oversight provided by one of the Smithsonian anthropology curators. Blaker introduced professional standards to preserving and cataloguing the BAE collection of manuscripts and photographs. The BAE archives were in cramped quarters on four levels of the north tower of the Smithsonian Castle for over fifty years.

In 1967 she oversaw the move of the archives from the Castle to offices in the National Museum of Natural History (NMNH). Blaker saw Ray's serious interest in Siouan materials and gave him access to original field notes and manuscripts that nurtured his growing scholarship. Ray in turn became one of the archives' primary early catalogers, helping organize the many collections and produce finding aids for them. He had a natural instinct for creating order out of chaos and for writing clear descriptions of material. These skills probably came from working as an editor on his high school yearbook.

Upon his arrival at the University of Chicago in 1964, Ray was disappointed to realize he had to take multiple courses associated with a BA and couldn't study just Siouan kinship and history. Ray told Joanna

1. Margaret Blaker's office in the "Castle." Left to right: Blaker, Joanna Scherer (museum technician), Rebecca Chancey (secretary), DeMallie (summer intern). Smithsonian photographer, September 15, 1967. Smithsonian Institution Archives.

that one of his professors, probably David Schneider, had admonished him early in his college days that he had to give up wanting to be an Indian in order to become an anthropologist. He did, however, manage to write a paper each of his undergraduate years for Fred Eggan on some aspect of Sioux kinship and, in 1968, a bachelor's honor thesis on Sioux kin terminologies. The study of kinship was in vogue in anthropology during the 1960s and 1970s, but it was also widely considered as a core foundation both in the training of anthropologists and in the systematic study of culture.

The summers of 1965–68 as a National Science Foundation (NSF) research fellow at the Smithsonian were, according to Ray, the beginning of his professional anthropology career. He was given a ten-week summer appointment, June 17–August 23, 1966, working for the Plains curator John Canfield Ewers (1909–97),[2] researching the Miniconjou Sioux chief Hump, and obtaining archival information on Captain

Ezra P. Ewers, an officer during the Indian wars (for an article the curator was writing) as well as photographic projects in the archives (J. C. Ewers to Richard Woodbury, March 16, 1966, Ewers Papers; Miller 2013, 29). Ray had already introduced himself to Ewers during his 1964 visit to DC when he sought clarification from Ewers regarding the clothing a manikin was wearing in the Plains Indian hall (Miller 2013, 26). Ewers saw the budding of a serious student and appreciated Ray's archival research but was not very enthusiastic regarding Ray's early fieldwork goals. Ewers believed that fieldwork in the 1960s might not be worthwhile, as knowledgeable elders had mostly passed away and significant historical materials were no longer recoverable. In these years American anthropology was in crisis. The changing conditions in Native communities that were now generationally removed from pre-reservation Native culture and knowledge and the emergence of Native activists and spokespeople such as Vine Deloria Jr. raised questions about the very purpose and utility of anthropologists (V. Deloria [1969] 1988). By the 1980s Ewers's opinion of Ray's fieldwork had changed significantly, and in November 1980 he wrote to Ray: "I have found that when going into the field you should allow time to let the discussion drift a bit if it seems to be leading into an area about which little is known.... So allow time to let your work lead where it will. It is important for you to know at what point you are plowing new ground, and not just going over a well cultivated field" (Ewers to DeMallie, November 18, 1980, Ewers Papers). Anthropology had to adapt and find new purpose in its practice.

The first record of Ray as a visitor to the Anthropology Archives is August 16–September 1, 1965 (Blaker Papers, box 2, Annual Report 1966). He reviewed Teton Dakota manuscripts as well as photographs on this visit. It was also during this time that the archives received an accession of the personal papers of James Owen Dorsey (1848–95), ethnologist with the BAE, 1878–95, from Dorsey's granddaughter Virginia MacLean (Blaker Papers, box 1, Annual Report 1966).[3] Dorsey's academic papers dealing with Siouan phonology, grammar, comparative vocabulary, and ethnographic subjects and his correspondence while working with the BAE were already in the archive, and an eighty-one-page

2. Blaker and DeMallie in the cramped archive in the "Castle." Photos of James Owen Dorsey (top) and George Bushotter (Teton) on the file cabinet as well as a reproduction of the Catlin painting of "Ha-won-je-tah" One Horn (Hewáŋžiča), painted in 1832 at Fort Pierre on the Missouri River. Smithsonian photographer, September 15, 1967. Smithsonian Institution Archives.

typed bibliography of Siouan manuscripts had been prepared by Judith Buchanan, under the direction of Edward I. Burkart, of the American University, in January 1964. The new Dorsey accession included diaries, correspondence, autobiographical notes, lectures, and a volume of notes on Siouan ethnography and language. Like his leap-of-faith decision to go to the University of Chicago and became a student of Eggan's, Ray's enthusiasm for Dorsey's work saw him invest the next three years to revising the bibliography and catalog for the Dorsey papers and improving documentation on Santee Dakota photographs.

Ray's admiration for Dorsey included the collection of personal memorabilia. Because of Blaker's connections to Dorsey's granddaughter, he was able to obtain some of Dorsey's personal papers and even the original nineteenth-century Dorsey desk, which finally made it to his Bloomington home in the early 1980s.

Thus, Ray's earliest significant archival achievement was to arrange and catalog all manuscript materials relating to the Siouan tribes and to make accessible to the public documents containing potentially important information about a Native culture. This included the Dorsey papers and texts and stories in Lakȟóta by George Bushotter, whom Dorsey brought to Washington in 1887. In about ten months, Bushotter wrote 258 stories and over 3,000 pages of Lakȟóta texts that describe Sioux social customs. There are over 30 linear feet, or 70 boxes of materials, as well as maps, drawings by Bushotter, and photographs. The detailed work Ray did on the Siouan manuscripts, including materials from the Dorsey collection, remains a permanent contribution to the archive (Dorsey Papers).[4]

In a memo to the chairman of the Department of Anthropology, Saul Riesenberg, for the 1968 Smithsonian Year, Blaker noted, "Descriptions of all of the Dakota ethnographic manuscripts are included in 'A Partial Bibliography of Manuscript Materials Relating to the Dakota Indians,' by Raymond J. DeMallie, Jr., to be published in a volume of Dakota papers edited by Ethel Nurge" (Blaker to Riesenberg, June 6, 1968, Blaker Papers, box 1; DeMallie 1970). In August 1972 the archives personnel were thinking of having Ray write a fifty-page — or longer — introduction to his Siouan catalog and submitting it to the Smithsonian Institution Press, but because of the June 1972 retirement of Blaker, the search for a supervisory archivist upended publication efforts and put the project on hold (Evans to DeMallie, August 14, 1972).

Becoming an Expert

In 1974 the NAA was considering having the Siouan catalog of manuscripts microfilmed, but Ray advised them that "the catalog that I prepared must be edited and revised. . . . I could easily do these [errors and omissions] in a week or two at the Smithsonian. More seriously, the catalog needs an introduction that puts the collection in historical perspective and that discusses the work of J. Owen Dorsey, particularly from a linguistic/phonological perspective so as to make his manuscripts more readily intelligible to potential users. This is a sizable

```
4800          DORSEY, JAMES OWEN.
DORSEY
PAPERS:       Lakota vocabulary extracted from the George Bushotter
DAKOTA:       texts (MS. 4800, pt. 103), entered into interleaved
TETON         bound page-proofs of Stephen R. Riggs, "A Dakota-
              English Dictionary," edited by Dorsey, CNAE VII,
(113)         Washington, D. C., 1890. [(1888.] P. and A. D.   2 v.
                  Transcription by Raymond DeMallie, of the approx.
              700 MS. entries from above v.  Washington, D. C.,
              1966.  Xerox c. of T. D. 182 pp.




RDM/1968; 1/1972
```

3. Catalog card from James Owen Dorsey papers for about seven hundred transcriptions of Lakȟóta words extracted by DeMallie from George Bushotter texts. Created in 1968 and revised in 1972. National Anthropological Archives, Smithsonian Institution.

project but inasmuch as I have already collected much of the relevant data, it could be written in a fairly short time" (DeMallie to James R. Glenn, March 25, 1974, Sturtevant Papers).

Joanna met Ray in August 1966. Ray gallantly opened a heavy door in the Castle for her ungainly, unsteady self. She was near the end of her first pregnancy and on her way to interview with Margaret Blaker for a museum technician position. She had not told Blaker about her pregnancy, as in those days if you said you were pregnant some employers would not interview you. So, she went in and convinced Blaker that although she could not start right away, she would be able to begin in a few months. Blaker offered Joanna the job, her first daughter was born October 3, and Joanna started working in the archive in early December 1966.

Joanna next saw Ray the summer of 1967 when he returned (after a visit to Pine Ridge Reservation) to the Smithsonian on an NSF grant. He was one of a number of anthropology summer students.

4. Summer interns in the National Museum of Natural History Anthropology Department. DeMallie is in the back row, third from left. Thomas Kavanagh is in the middle row, fourth far right; he was a high school volunteer working in the archives. Cheryl Rae Goodman is in the front row, far right; she was a volunteer from the University of Maryland working with Scherer in the archives. Smithsonian photographer, August 8, 1967. National Anthropological Archives, neg. no. 1943, Smithsonian Institution.

Ray and Joanna bonded over historical documents. Joanna had fallen in love with the historical Indian photograph collection: just as Ray knew his calling was Lakȟóta kinship and history, hers was the collections of BAE images. They egged each other on, questioning the source of the information with the photos and fixing errors as they found them. He had gone through all the Plains Indian photos before she got to the archives and corrected identifications on the catalog cards, such as one of Yellow Bear. Ray also added to the Plains Indian images in the archives.

5. Catalog card on Yellow Bear. Left: Yellow Bear or Matozhi (Oglala Teton) cropped image from a larger delegation photo made in Mathew Brady's studio in 1870 during the Oglala visit to Washington DC. Right: Catalog card showing corrected identification by DeMallie. National Anthropological Archives, neg. no. 3215-c, Smithsonian Institution.

6. Left: Three generations of Red Cloud's family (Dakota: Oglala). Left to right: Jack Red Cloud, Red Cloud, and Red Cloud's granddaughter. Postcard by O'Neill Photo Company, O'Neill, Nebraska, about 1900. Right: Catalog card identifying DeMallie's gift in 1962. (Left) National Anthropological Archives, neg. no. 55,896; (right) National Anthropological Archives, Smithsonian Institution.

```
                SMITHSONIAN OFFICE OF ANTHROPOLOGY ARCHIVES  FILE PRINT
                          PHOTOGRAPHIC CATALOG                filed Red Cloud
                                                                    folder
    NO.      55,896
    TRIBE    Dakota: Oglala
    SUBJECT  "Three Generations of the Red Cloud Family": l. to r.,
             Jack Red Cloud, Red Cloud, Red Cloud's granddaughter*
             Copied (8/66) from postcard photograph lent by R. DeMallie,
    SOURCE   who purchased it from the Grey Owl Indian Craft Co. in
             New York about 1962.
    DATE     Not recorded; ca. 1900
    PHOTOGRAPHER  O'Neill Photo Co., O'Neill, Nebraska
    REMARKS  Orig. no.: G
             *Identified by R. DeMallie
```

In 1970 Joanna was selecting photos for an exhibit titled "Indian Images: Photographs of North American Indians, 1847–1928" to open in conjunction with the Smithsonian Folk Festival that year.[5]

Ray worked at the archives from February 24 through May 12, and they pushed each other to get more and more details out of the photographs (Blaker to Evans, May 21, 1970, Blaker Papers, box 1). One of the hallmarks of Ray DeMallie's practice of ethnohistory is the use of diverse media with ample context to identify and enrich primary data. Ray and Joanna shared a pointed interest in research on historical photographs for what they could tell about Native life, culture, and people, as well as the manner in which they were portrayed or misportrayed. There were fellow students of Ray's from the University of Chicago who would also drop into the NAA, such as James Boon.

Ray later reminisced that "James Boon—a fellow Chicago graduate student marooned at the Smithsonian"—wasn't thoroughly enjoying the Smithsonian experience as much as Ray was (DeMallie 2001b, 54).

Because of Ray's prodigious and comprehensive work cataloging and reviewing the Plains material, Margaret Blaker began to use Ray as a consultant for other scholars and graduate students who were

7. DeMallie and Scherer looking at archival photographs for an exhibit Scherer organized for the 1970 Folk Festival. Smithsonian photographer in the National Anthropological Archives' office in the National Museum of Natural History, March 27, 1970. Smithsonian Institution Archives, staff photo 6A.

pursuing archive collections. For example, Ray had already done extensive research on the papers of James Mooney, a BAE ethnologist from 1885 to 1921 (the archives had 90 percent of Mooney's papers). Mooney's research on Plains Indians included Kiowa heraldry, the peyote religion, and the Native American Church as well as the Ghost Dance religion. Ray had also reviewed Mooney's papers in the Field Museum of Natural History in Chicago under the mentorship of James W. VanStone (that repository had about 10 percent of Mooney's papers) and thus was recommended by Blaker as a primary consultant to visiting predoctoral fellow William Colby working on Mooney in the summer of 1972 (Blaker to Davidson, March 13, 1972).

In addition to working on the Siouan catalog, Ray had solicited the help of, and was partially supervised by, Paul Voorhis, a linguist

8. DeMallie and James Boon looking at a Kiowa water-and-ink drawing depicting the story of Red Horse the storm-maker (a supernatural being with the upper body of a horse and a long tail like a snake, which it used to stir up tornadoes). Ledger drawing, National Anthropological Archives MS 2531, vol. 2, by unknown artist. Smithsonian photographer in the National Anthropological Archives' office in the National Museum of Natural History, March 27, 1970. Smithsonian Institution Archives, staff photo 13A.

at the Smithsonian.[6] He wished to understand the technical linguistic aspects of Dorsey's linguistic research. Ray had already taped Lakȟóta narratives from his 1967 visit to Pine Ridge Reservation and wanted to transcribe it. Voorhis admitted to Ray that he didn't know much about Siouan languages but stated, "I'm always ready to learn more." On a document from this period Ray explained what he and Voorhis would do: "The idea is to work backward from spoken language in order to carefully reconsider Dorsey's 'Comparative Phonology of Four Siouan Languages' [written in 1882,] which seems to have been very influential in determining the standard Bureau [BAE] alphabet" (DeMallie to William C. Sturtevant, April 3, 1969, Sturtevant Papers). In addition Ray and Voorhis visited Father Vine Deloria Sr. (Yankton

Episcopal priest), who at that time lived outside Baltimore and taped words, sentences, and some brief texts to practice on. With the help of Mary Natani, a Winnebago speaker, they spent a day or two each week during the summer of 1969 practicing Lakȟóta (Miller 2013, 28). Ray persevered working on understanding the complexity of the Lakȟóta language, but it wasn't until his visit to Cheyenne River in 1970–71 that he started to become more proficient in its use (28). This attention and dedication to the Lakȟóta language in order to understand Lakȟóta people in their own terms became another distinctive trait of Ray's anthropological and ethnohistorical practice. Although Franz Boas had made it an imperative for the training of anthropologists, the level of commitment and time it required to learn a Native language was seldom reached by anthropologists (Boas 1906, 643–44). Ray stood as an exception, and his ability to understand, speak—and even teach— the Lakȟóta language granted him respect in Lakȟóta communities.

In the 1969–70 period, Ray continued his studies at Chicago pursuing his MA under the guidance of David Schneider and Raymond Fogelson, defining and exploring the relationship among the cultural units that comprise Sioux kinship (DeMallie 2001b, 51). He wrote his thesis while at the Smithsonian, where he tapped into the expertise of William C. Sturtevant (1926–2007).[7] As Ray dryly admitted, "Sturtevant's advice never failed to be valuable but also never failed to conflict with Chicago models" (DeMallie 2001b, 52). Sturtevant was an important mentor to Ray. He introduced him to Vine Deloria Jr. at the November 1970 American Anthropological Association (AAA) meeting in San Diego and Vine and Ray became lifelong colleagues and friends. Throughout Sturtevant's career he would write references for the many grant applications that Ray (and Doug) submitted to a wide range of organizations in support of their American Indian Studies Research Institute and Ray's publications (DeMallie to William Sturtevant, September 25, 1980, Sturtevant Papers). Ray's PhD thesis was an ethnohistorical study focusing on sources, many of them at the Smithsonian. It was a hard sell as David Schneider "flatly denied that one anthropologist could use another's field notes in any meaningful way" (DeMallie 2001b, 56). Ray persevered and completed his thesis in December

1971, finishing it in just over two years—a record at Chicago for speed (Fogelson 2013, 224).

The winter of 1972 Ray participated in a survey of American Indian economic development organized by Sam Stanley (1923–2011) of the Smithsonian's Center for the Study of Man (CSM).[8] Sam had come to the Smithsonian in 1968 on the recommendation of Sol Tax, an anthropologist at the University of Chicago. He was involved in a variety of projects aimed at applying anthropology to public interest and included collaborative study of American Indian economic development and urgent anthropology projects. That Ray participated in the CSM study may reflect his close personal ties to Sol Tax. Tax was Ray's first anthropology professor, and his nephew, Tom Tax, was Ray's roommate during his undergraduate years in Chicago (Miller 2013, 28). Ray's first fieldwork for Sam Stanley's study was conducted on the Pine Ridge Reservation in the spring and summer of 1972. He also continued archival studies of Siouan history through a grant from the CSM Urgent Anthropology program during the summer of 1974 in South Dakota.

In the summer of 1972, although he had a permanent position teaching anthropology at the University of Wyoming, Ray sent an application to Clifford Evans, chair of the Smithsonian Department of Anthropology, applying for a position as anthropologist in the NAA. Ray wrote: "It was only after composing my recommendations concerning the future of the Archives, contained in my letter of July 30th, that I realized the extent of my involvement with the Archives, my personal commitment to them, and my own interest in working with them and supervising the completion of a catalog of the entire North American manuscript collection" (DeMallie to Clifford Evans, August 10, 1972, Ewers Papers). At the time, he asked Ewers to be a reference for him as well as Mildred Wedel (1912–95), an ethnohistorian with extensive knowledge of historical French sources on North America with whom he shared numerous interests (DeMallie to John Ewers, August 10, 1972, Ewers Papers).[9] Ray did not get offered the position in the archives, and in the fall of 1973 he joined the anthropology department at Indiana University. But he continued his association with the Smithsonian on many levels, including working with Joanna on various projects. Ray also corresponded with Ewers on topics such as Siouan religion, which Ray told Ewers in 1977 he regarded as a "long-range focus of my work" (DeMallie to John Ewers, November 13, 1977, Ewers Papers).

Ray and Joanna's first formal collaboration was a session organized at the 72nd American Anthropological Association (AAA) Annual Meeting in New Orleans in 1973, titled "Pictures as Documents: Resources for the study of North American Indian Ethnohistory." This was the earliest AAA session that focused on pictorial resources and ways to use pictures as primary sources. Ray and Joanna were both critically reading historical documents: Ray's sources were on kinship and language while Joanna was using nineteenth-century photographs. They both knew that written records as well as visual records are selective and incomplete, but they were determined to dig as much information out of them as possible. She realized that a photograph was influenced not only by the photographer but also by the subject and by the viewer's interpretation. It was critical to document and evaluate these sources in order to get any meaningful information from the image. Several of these papers were published in *Studies in Visual Communication* (Bucher 1975; Scherer 1975b). Ray's paper "Photographic Record of the Sioux Treaty of 1868" was incorporated in DeMallie (1981).

Both Ray and Douglas R. Parks were rising scholars of Plains anthropology in the 1970s, Ray specializing in Lakȟóta ethnology, ethnohistory, and linguistics and Doug on Pawnee and Arikara linguistics and anthropological linguistics. They both contributed to *Anthropology of the Great Plains*, edited by W. Raymond Wood and Margot Liberty, based on a symposium that took place in 1976. They met at conferences and later visited each other: Ray went to Bismarck, where Doug taught at Mary College, and Doug visited Bloomington, where Ray was a professor at Indiana University. They started working on shared projects in the early 1980s: a grant application to the National Endowment for the Humanities awarded in 1982 and a symposium on Sioux Indian Religion in Bismarck in April 1982 from which came an eponymous volume edited by both of them. In 1983 Ray was able to facilitate Doug's hire at Indiana University, and they bought a large house together, which became an outstanding book and manuscript library where friends and scholars of the field liked to come and visit. In 1985 they founded the American Indian Studies Research Institute (AISRI) at Indiana University, which formalized their partnership and drew more scholars, students, and projects.

Examples of Ray's Editorial Scholarship

In 1983 William Bittle resigned as editor of the *Plains* volume of the *Handbook of North American Indians*. Sturtevant, the general editor of this twenty-volume series, recruited Ray to be editor of volume 13.[10] The history of the *Handbook* from the Smithsonian's Department of Anthropology's decision to produce a revision of BAE Bulletin number 30 (see Hodge [1907–10] 1965) spans some fifty years. Joanna presents here one small part of *Handbook* lore as it is relevant to Ray's Smithsonian connections.[11] By the early 1980s, the slow progress of the *Handbook*, funded with Bicentennial money, was of concern to the Smithsonian administration. Sturtevant had written to management that he knew that he himself had become a bottleneck and he wished to back away from his commitment to the project. So, for two days in August 1983, active volume editors, including Warren d'Azevedo, David Damas, Raymond Fogelson, June Helm, and Ray assembled in Washington as part of a review committee to try to find a way to increase the publication rate of the volumes. At the end of the two-day meeting, the volume editors could not agree on how best to move forward. Fogelson proposed that efforts should focus on completing the area volumes while d'Azevedo insisted that the vision for completing the whole project be maintained. Damas suggested a more structured apportionment of Sturtevant's time while Helm felt that a scholar not answerable to the general editor was needed to take over many of his responsibilities. Ray, the newest volume editor, insisted that Sturtevant should remain the guiding light for the *Handbook* and maintain control of its content. Sturtevant, to everyone's surprise, recommended that Ray replace him as general editor of the remaining volumes. This was remarkable in that Ray had strongly supported Joanna's class action, sex discrimination suit in the 1970s. The suit clearly demonstrated that there was a climate of discrimination in the department both in hiring and promoting women and that the *Handbook*, led by Sturtevant, was not exempt from these practices. Sturtevant remained the general editor after the 1983 meeting, but it is an interesting sidebar to *Handbook* history that he recommended Ray for this role.

In 1985 Ray assembled a planning committee for the *Handbook*'s *Plains* volume, and he and Doug Parks revised the outline chapters, selecting many new authors. He worked on the *Plains* volume actively from 1985 to 1987, but then work all but stopped. Ray and Joanna sometimes discussed the administrative short falls of the *Handbook* series, but it is unclear why he put the *Plains* volume on hold except that he was always working on multiple projects at that time. For the remainder of his career, Ray's workload between editorial projects, his teaching at Indiana University, grant applications, and collaboration with Native communities delayed completion of many projects. An observation by Ray Fogelson, editor of the *Handbook*'s *Southeast* volume, may be telling. Fogelson noted that "Ray and I also ran into discouraging delays, organizational obstacles, and editorial incompetence in completing our respective handbooks" (Fogelson 2013, 226). As a staff member of the *Handbook* series for thirty-six years, Joanna can attest to the fact that the administration was way out of its depth in anticipating the production requirements of this twenty-volume series (Scherer 2022, 531–48).

Ray and Joanna would catch up with each other at various AAA meetings and talk about future collaborations but also always about the *Handbook*. They both were involved in multiple projects, but the unpublished *Plains* volume hung over their heads. Ray did not concentrate again on the *Handbook* until 1998, when the final drive to complete it began. The *Plains* volume, number 13, came out in 2001 as two bound books, rather than the initially planned one, because there were just too many pages for a single binding.[12]

One of the projects that Ray and Joanna worked on was the publication of Alice C. Fletcher's *Life among the Indians: First Fieldwork among the Sioux and Omahas by Alice C. Fletcher* (2013). Joanna found this manuscript in the NAA in the late 1960s and transcribed it. Ray joined the project in 1977. Its completion had to wait for Joanna's retirement in 2006 and for Ray to finish the *Handbook's Plains* volume, but if it shows anything it is how fully committed that they both were to getting nineteenth-century first-person voices heard. Written by Fletcher in 1887, it was based on her visits among the Sioux and Omaha in 1881-82. It is an autobiographical memoir, not a literal journal, written in novelistic style with many characters, such as who she was visiting, not identified. Omitting personal names was likely a way of protecting those individuals from possible reprisal by government officials. Ray and Joanna had to tease these identifications out by sifting through historical records. While some of the ethnographic material on the Omaha was later revised and expanded for inclusion in Fletcher's 1911 magnum opus—coauthored with Francis La Flesche—*The Omaha Tribe*, her 1887 manuscript includes stories of human interest remembered by individual Omahas that reveal an understanding of everyday life not found in the 1911 publication.[13] They also planned to make available to scholars Fletcher's original Sioux field journals: Ray considered them to be excellent and critical for publication. This work remains in progress.

Accounts in *Life among the Indians* are all based on firsthand observations and preserve ethnographic accuracy. Fletcher presents herself as an outside observer and was acutely respectful of the Indians' sensibilities. She empathizes with Indian life and expresses a cultural relativism and tolerance far ahead of her time. Had it been published when it was written, it would have been the first work by a female ethnologist based on fieldwork using participant observation. Fletcher was deeply concerned about the precariousness of the Omaha ownership of their lands and, responding to pleas from Francis La Flesche's father, Joseph La Flesche, she became an active agent in helping the Omaha obtain legal protection for their land. Her activist role for Indian land rights was thus pressed upon her by the Omahas with whom she worked. She succeeded in getting a bill passed through Congress providing for allotment of lands; that disastrous land loss by the Omaha resulted is a sad part of her legacy. Her work and contributions are both an inspiration and yet a cautionary tale. More generally, Ray's commitment to editing primary sources that were unfairly treated by their social context and the latent sexism and marginalization of non-white voices, notably with Ella Deloria and Alice Fletcher, is yet another element of his scholarly legacy.

The *Plains* volume was almost completed during the planning of the centennial meeting of the AAA in 2001, so Ray and Joanna volunteered an exhibit and poster session titled "Anthropology in the Funny Papers—Cartoons from the Meggers/Evans Collection."

Clifford Evans (1920–81) and Betty J. Meggers (1921–2012) were both archaeologists at the Smithsonian.[14] They had collected 1,500 cartoons from about 1953 to 1989, and Meggers was happy to share them. In addition, Ray and Joanna accepted cartoons from other AAA members including Susan M. Rigdon (research associate in the Department of Anthropology at the University of Illinois, Urbana-Champaign), who contributed cartoons in Spanish by Oscar Lewis.[15] The exhibit was planned as a poster session to run through the 2002 meeting, which was the official centennial. For the 2002 session they added cartoons by Phil Hughte, a Zuni artist (Hughte 1994). The American Anthropological Association Commission that oversaw the centennial noted that humor was one of the best ways to look at how anthropology sees itself, a point of the centennial (Regna Darnell to Joanna Scherer, January 15, 2001). Many of these cartoons were sent again to Ray by Joanna, after his stroke in 2014, for laugh therapy.

Delays in getting complicated manuscripts transcribed and published is not a new story. Ray and Doug had a shared interest in seeing a manuscript of Jean-Baptiste Truteau's journal published as "The Journal and Description of the Upper Missouri." It was written in seventeenth-century French, and Doug had been told of it by John Ewers when he was a visiting fellow at the NMNH Smithsonian in 1973. Mildred Wedel had an early translation of this manuscript made in the 1950s by Fernand Grenier. Doug and Ray spent many days in the 1980s with both Mildred and Waldo Wedel (1908–96) reviewing the various translations and adding footnotes.[16] Mildred died in 1989 and Waldo in 1990, causing the project to go on hold for the 1990s. It was picked up again in 2000–2001 by Ted Seaman, a graduate student

9. DeMallie and Scherer at the American Anthropological Association Centennial poster session, which they organized, 2002. Scherer personal collection.

in French at Indiana University, and following a trip to France, Ray was able to discover a specialist in North American French, Robert Vézina, who joined the project in 2004. The introduction and footnotes were updated in 2013–14. Because of the complexity of the text, they decided the publication should include both the original French and the English. Only the illustrations remained outstanding, and most had not yet been ordered from various repositories. Joanna felt strongly that this work needed to see the light of day. In the summer of 2015 she visited Ray and Doug with the idea to clarify with them which images were still needed, and she volunteered to complete the project. During her visit, Ray and Joanna worked doggedly on the drawings and place-names to go on the map. On her return to the Smithsonian she ordered the images needed, wrote captions for them, and submitted them to the press. The long-awaited book was published in 2017 and included enhanced images by her husband, Noel P. Elliott (Truteau 2017).

Thierry Veyrié came to study with Ray in 2014, being the last of Ray's graduate students. When Ray suffered his stroke, he became unable to speak and teach, but his mind remained intact. In 2019 Ray showed Thierry the files to *The Dakota Way of Life* by Ella Deloria on his computer. After Ella's death, Ray had promised the Deloria family that he would edit and publish this important ethnographic description of Dakota social life on which Deloria had worked for decades. *The Dakota Way of Life* was one of the many projects that Ray wanted to complete to help repair the injustices made to Ella Deloria's scholarship. Ray and Thierry together copyedited the manuscript, cut out repetitions and redundancies, incorporated appendixes to the text, prepared annotations, and wrote the prefatory materials. Just a few months after the final version of the manuscript was submitted to the University of Nebraska Press, Ray passed away. He left behind an extraordinary legacy of primary sources that he edited and presented to the public. While Ray wrote many academic articles, he never was the primary author of a book. This model of dedicating a life of scholarship to the publication of the work of others is undoubtedly an example of how anthropologists can have a newfound purpose and support Native cultures.

Conclusion

The importance of using primary sources in the study of ethnohistory was a hallmark of Ray DeMallie's contributions to anthropology. In his own words, "My goal has been to publish the most important of these sources in critical editions so that they can be used in the future for large-scale synthesis" (2013, 235). With his mentor Mildred Wedel he wrote: "We suggest that the ethnohistorian has two main tasks: (1) the critical editing and presentation of historical documents relating to Indian cultures and (2) the interpretation of data gleaned from these sources" (Wedel and DeMallie 1980, 118). His work, especially on culture change in the social organization of the Eastern and Middle Dakotas and Lakȟóta, uncovered flaws from misinformed interpretation. He emphasized the importance of knowing the full range of source materials, primary and secondary, published and archival, as well as Native oral traditions. He used such materials to help move the field toward a Native-oriented ethnohistory in which an interpretation of the past can help explain the present.

10. DeMallie and Parks at their Bloomington residence, July 2015. Scherer personal collection.

Several distinctive traits characterize Ray DeMallie's practice of the ethnohistorical approach. The study of kinship that permeated his training as an anthropologist remained a thread in his scholarship to explain Lakȟóta social life. We also emphasize Ray's attention to various media in historical sources, notably contextualized visual documents. It also appears clear that Ray's foundation as a scholar was through a prolonged familiarization with relevant archival collections where he unearthed significant primary sources on Native cultures. In complement to this, his dedication to learning the Lakȟóta language and studying Native documents in their own words allowed for a level of insight in his interpretations that made his work stand apart. Finally, it is his editorial preparation of primary sources and the reparation of injustices made to Native ethnographers and women that helped improve the reputation of the discipline of anthropology.

Ray's reading of primary documents started at the Smithsonian Institution, where he began his tutelage while still a teenager. He was mentored by numerous Smithsonian curators, including William C.

Sturtevant, John C. Ewers, Paul Voorhis, and Waldo Wedel, as well as research associate Mildred Wedel and archivist Margaret Blaker. This chapter spotlights DeMallie's relationship with these individuals as well as his longstanding use of primary documents in the Smithsonian National Anthropological Archives. Ray's study of North American Indians blossomed at the Smithsonian and resulted in not only his major ethnohistorical contributions on Plains Indians but also his significant contributions to a better understanding of Lakȟóta kinship and social system. Doug Parks and Ray DeMallie were tireless researchers who pursued historical, anthropological, and linguistic materials even when health issues slowed them down.

They also trained and fostered another generation of scholars dedicated to the editorial preparation and interpretation of Native American sources and to community-based work serving the interests of Native communities. Their contributions to ethnohistory, ethnology, and linguistics shine in the contents of this volume.[17] It was our great privilege to be students and then colleagues of them both.

Notes

1. Margaret C. Blaker (1924–2008). Margaret Eleanor Contant was born May 28, 1924, in Rochester, New York, and received a BA from the University of Rochester. Her professional career at the Smithsonian began in November 1945 as a scientific aide in the Division of Archeology. The next year she transferred to the BAE as a museum aide in the newly created River Basin Surveys.

In 1953 Blaker was appointed archives assistant in the BAE, rising to the position of archivist in 1958. She retired on June 30, 1972, after serving the Smithsonian for twenty-seven years. A member of the American Anthropological Association since 1948, she was also active in the American Society for Ethnohistory, the Middle Atlantic Anthropological Association, and the Society of American Archivists (Fleming et al. 2009, 2–3).

2. John Canfield Ewers was curator of North American ethnology in the NMNH Department of Anthropology at the Smithsonian from 1946 until he retired in 1979. He specialized in Plains Indians, especially the Blackfeet and the history of the West. He also wrote extensively on Plains

Indian art ("John C. Ewers," Wikipedia, https://en.wikipedia.org/wiki/John_C._Ewers; "In Memory of John C. Ewers" 1997).

3. For a biographical summary of Dorsey, see DeMallie (1988).

4. The finding aid for the James O. Dorsey Papers, MS 4800, was updated in 2014 by Lorain Wang. DeMallie's hand is still evident in entries such as box 9-11, item 113 (see fig. 3).

5. After opening at the Folk Festival, this was made into a traveling exhibit by SITES and duplicated; both exhibits traveled throughout the United States. It was chosen in January 1975 as a U.S. Bicentennial exhibit and circulated through 1976. From 1977 to 1983, it traveled in the state of Nevada through the Northeastern Nevada Museum, and one copy is on permanent display at the Ponca City Cultural Center, Oklahoma.

6. Paul Voorhis was a linguist at the Smithsonian in 1969-70. He earned his PhD at Yale and wrote on the Kickapoo and Meskwaki languages. He taught from about 1972 at Brandon University in Manitoba, Canada, where he gave courses in a number of First Nations languages spoken in Manitoba. He is currently an emeritus professor at Brandon University (Ives Goddard, personal communication, May 28, 2022).

7. William Curtis Sturtevant was a museum curator at the Smithsonian from 1956 in the Bureau of American Ethnology and after 1965 in the NMNH Department of Anthropology until his death in 2007. He specialized in the ethnology of the Mikasuki Seminoles and Iroquois and was the general editor of the *Handbook of North American Indians*. He published extensively on subjects in ethnohistory, ethnoscience, and material culture ("William C. Sturtevant," Wikipedia, https://en.wikipedia.org/wiki/William_C._Sturtevant).

8. Samuel Leonard Stanley came to the Smithsonian as the program coordinator of the Center for the Study of Man from 1968 to 1976. He was tasked with developing international research programs, was involved in the startup of the *Handbook of North American Indians* project, and administered urgent anthropology projects (Link 2021).

9. Also see Miller (2013, 35-36), in which he describes a joint paper that Mildred Wedel and Ray presented at the 34th Plains Anthropological Conference in 1976, which provides an assessment of ethnohistory as a method and describes Ray's emphasis on Indigenous evidence that could be found in nontraditional sources.

Mildred Mott Wedel was one of the first female professionally trained archaeologists. She received her MA from the University of Chicago in

1938, married Waldo Wedel in 1939, and was thereafter associated with the Smithsonian NMNH Department of Anthropology. Several fully credentialed female anthropologists who married Smithsonian anthropologists were "honored" with unpaid research associate positions in the NMNH. Mildred specialized in plains archaeology and ethnohistory and published on French explorers who traveled among the Siouan tribes in the central and southern plains ("Mildred Mott Wedel," Wikipedia, https://en.wikipedia.org/wiki/Mildred_Mott_Wedel).

10. In a letter to Paul Gebhard, chairman of the Department of Anthropology at Indiana University, to support DeMallie's promotion to the rank of professor at Indiana University, Ewers wrote of his long association with DeMallie "since he first came to the Smithsonian as a teenage volunteer to assist in the Anthropological Archives . . . [and his] recent appointment as Editor of the Great Plains volume of the Smithsonian Institution's unique Handbook of North American Indians was in recognition of his rapidly developing expertise in that broad field of research and the confidence of his peers in his ability to develop a reference volume on the archeology, ethnology, history, and present day life of many tribes of that culture area. . . . I rather believe it will be the volume in the entire 20 volume series that will be most often consulted in future years" (Ewers to Gebhard, November 17, 1983, Ewers Papers).

11. Joanna was one of the earliest employees to join the *Handbook* staff in 1970, having worked for several years in the Anthropological Archives—formerly the Bureau of American Ethnology Archives. She was the illustrations researcher for fourteen of the fifteen volumes that were published from 1978 to 2007. Selecting the non-artifact images and writing their captions was her principal responsibility. Joanna traveled to museums, archives, libraries, and special collections to find original visuals, and she created a collection of over one hundred thousand historical and contemporary photographs of Native Americans that are now housed in the National Anthropological Archives. She retired in 2006.

12. This is the mini-history of the twenty-volume *Handbook*, originally scheduled to be completed in 1976 but terminated in December 2007 after having published fifteen volumes. The *Handbook*'s introduction, volume 1 of the series, edited by Igor Krupnik of the Smithsonian's Department of Anthropology, was officially published in December 2022. It includes six chapters on the intellectual and production history as well as updates on research of the culture areas.

13. The 1911 publication was La Flesche's appearance as an ethnologist in his own right and was a prototype of Native ethnography made by one of its own members for the education of future generations. It is the first published work in which a tribal member, raised in a Native community, wrote an extended ethnographic account for a professional anthropological audience.

14. Clifford Evans and Betty J. Meggers specialized in lowland South America, especially the Amazon basin. They got their PhDs at Columbia University and married in 1946. Evans was hired by the NMNH Smithsonian Department of Anthropology in 1951, and Meggers was given a nonpaid research associate position in 1954, as was customary for a professional female spouse at this time. Evans was chairman of the Department of Anthropology from 1970 to 1975. They remained active at the Smithsonian, founding a Latin American archaeology program that Meggers directed. She had considerable impact on the evolution of anthropological archaeology and cultural ecology in Latin America (Stump and Fielding 2015; Arellano and Wilkerson 2012).

15. Oscar Lewis helped found the Department of Anthropology at the University of Illinois, Urbana-Champaign. His writings primarily focused on Mexican village life and the culture of poverty, which he believed transcended national boundaries.

16. Waldo Rudolph Wedel was devoted to the prehistory of the Great Plains area and contributed to the understanding of the cultural links between modern Native tribes and archaeological evidence. He studied at the University of California, Berkeley, receiving its first PhD specializing in archaeology. Married to Mildred Mott in 1939, he began his Smithsonian career in 1936 and retired as archaeologist emeritus in 1976. He was the chairman of the Department of Anthropology from 1963 to 1965 ("Waldo Rudolph Wedel," Wikipedia, https://en.wikipedia.org/wiki/Waldo_Rudolph_Wedel; Wedel and Wedel Papers).

17. This chapter is based on a talk Joanna gave September 16, 2017, at Indiana University in a symposium titled "Indiana at the Crossroads of American Anthropology and History: Symposium in Honor of Raymond J. DeMallie."

References

Arellano, A. Jorge, and S. Jeffrey K. Wilkerson. 2012. "Betty J. Meggers (1921–2021): A Latin American Perspective." *Anthropolog: Newsletter of the Department* of Anthropology, Summer: 2–3. Washington DC: National Museum of Natural History.

Blaker, Margaret C. Papers. National Anthropological Archives, Smithsonian Institution, Washington DC.

Boas, Franz. 1906. "Some Philological Aspects of Anthropological Research." Science 23, no. 695: 643–44.

Braun, Sebastian F., ed. 2013. Transforming Ethnohistories: Narrative, Meaning, and Community. Norman: University of Oklahoma Press.

Bucher, Bernadette. 1975. "The Savage European: A Structural Approach to European Iconography of the American Indian." Studies in Visual Communication 2, no. 2: 80–86.

Deloria, Ella C. 2022. The Dakota Way of Life. Edited by Raymond J. DeMallie and Thierry Veyrié. Lincoln: University of Nebraska Press.

Deloria, Vine, Jr. (1969) 1988. Custer Died for Your Sins: An Indian Manifesto. New York: Macmillan. Reprint, Norman: University of Oklahoma Press.

DeMallie, Raymond J. 1970. "A Partial Bibliography of Archival Manuscript Material Relating to the Dakota Indians." In The Modern Sioux: Social Systems and Reservation Culture, edited by Ethel Nurge, 312–43. Lincoln: University of Nebraska Press.

———. 1981. "'Scenes in the Indian Country': A Portfolio of Alexander Gardner's Stereographic Views of the 1868 Fort Laramie Treaty Council." Montana: The Magazine of Western History 31, no. 3 (Summer): 42–59.

———. 1988. "James Owen Dorsey." In Handbook of North American Indians, vol. 4, History of Indian-White Relations, edited by Wilcomb E. Washburn, 640. Washington DC: Smithsonian Institution.

———. 1993. "'These Have No Ears': Narrative and the Ethnohistorical Method." Ethnohistory 40, no. 4: 515–38.

———, ed. 2001a. Handbook of North American Indians. Vol. 13, Plains. Washington DC: Smithsonian Institution.

———. 2001b. "'Procrustes and the Sioux': David M. Schneider and the Study of Sioux Kinship." In The Cultural Analysis of Kinship: The Legacy of David M. Schneider, edited by Richard Feinberg and Martin Oppenheimer, 46–59. Urbana: University of Illinois Press.

———. 2013. "Afterword: Thinking Ethnohistorically." In Braun 2013, 233–53.

Dorsey, James O. Papers. Manuscript 4800, National Anthropological Archives, Smithsonian Institution, Washington DC.

Evans, Clifford. 1972. Anthropology Department, USNM/NMNH secretary's reading files, 1966–1972, box 26, National Anthropological Archives, Smithsonian Institution, Washington DC.

Ewers, John Canfield. Papers. Box 6, Correspondence, National Anthropological Archives, Smithsonian Institution, Washington DC.

Fleming, Paula Richardson, Raymond J. DeMallie, Carol Mahler, and Joanna Cohan Scherer. 2009. "Margaret Contant Blaker (1924–2008)." *Anthropolog: Newsletter of the Department of Anthropology*, Summer: 2–3. Washington DC: National Museum of Natural History.

Fletcher, Alice C. 2013. *Life among the Indians: First Fieldwork among the Sioux and Omahas*. Edited by Joanna C. Scherer and Raymond J. DeMallie. Lincoln: University of Nebraska Press.

Fletcher, Alice C., and Francis La Flesche. 1911. *The Omaha Tribe*. Vol. 1. Twenty-Seventh Annual Report of the Bureau of American Ethnology to the Secretary of the Smithsonian Institution, 1905–1906. Washington DC: U.S. Government Printing Office.

Fogelson, Raymond. 2013. Epilogue to Braun 2013, 222–32.

Hodge, Frederick Webb, ed. (1907–10) 1965. *Handbook of American Indians North of Mexico*. 2 vols. Bureau of American Ethnology, Bulletin 30. Washington DC: U.S. Government Printing Office. Reprint, New York: Rowman and Littlefield.

Hughte, Phil. 1994. *A Zuni Artist Looks at Frank Hamilton Cushing*. Zuni NM: A:shiwi A:wan Museum and Heritage Center.

"In Memory of John C. Ewers." 1997. *Anthropolog: Newsletter of the Department of Anthropology*, Spring: 1–2. Washington DC: National Museum of Natural History.

Kaupp, Ann, ed. 1986–2012. *Anthropolog: Newsletter of the Department of Anthropology*. Washington DC: National Museum of Natural History.

Link, Adrianna. 2021. "(Re)inventing Urgency: The Case of the Smithsonian's Center for the Study of Man, 1968–1976." In *Berose—Encyclopedie internationale des historires de l'anthropologie*. https://www.berose.fr/article2319.html?lang=fr.

Meadowcroft, Enid Lamonte. 1954. *The Story of Crazy Horse*. Illustrated by William Reusswig. New York: Grosset & Dunlap.

Meggers, Betty J., and Clifford Evans. Papers. National Anthropological Archives, Smithsonian Institution, Washington DC.

Miller, David Reed. 2013. "Borders and Layers, Symbols and Meanings: Raymond J. Demallie's Commitment to Ethnohistory, with Nods to Thick Description and Symbolic Anthropology." In Braun 2013, 23–42.

Scherer, Joanna Cohan. 1975a. "Pictures as Documents: Resources for the Study of North American Ethnohistory." *Studies in the Anthropology of Visual Communication* 2, no. 2: 65–66.

———. 1975b. "You Can't Believe Your Eyes: Inaccuracies in Photographs of North American Indians." *Studies in the Anthropology of Visual Communication* 2, no. 2:

67–79. Reprint, *Exposure: The Journal of the Society for Photographic Education* 16, no. 4, 1979. Reprint, *Working Papers on Photography*, Science Museum of Victoria, Australia, 1980.

———. 2022. "Production of the Handbook, 1970–2008: An Insider's View." In *Handbook of North American Indians*, vol. 1, edited by Igor Krupnik, 531–48. Washington DC: Smithsonian Institution.

———. Papers. National Anthropological Archives, Smithsonian Institution, Washington DC.

Stump, Tyler, and Adam Fielding. 2015. "Guide to the Betty J. Meggers and Clifford Evans Papers." Finding Aid, Collection 2013-01, National Anthropological Archives, Smithsonian Institution, Washington DC. https://sirismm.si.edu/EADpdfs/NAA.2013-01.pdf.

Sturtevant, William C. Papers. Series 1, box 27, Correspondence, National Anthropological Archives, Smithsonian Institution, Washington DC.

Truteau, Jean-Baptiste. 2017. *A Fur Trader on the Upper Missouri: The Journal and Description of Jean-Baptiste Truteau, 1794–1796*. Edited by Raymond J. DeMallie, Douglas R. Parks, and Robert Vézina. Translated by Mildred Mott Wedel, Raymond J. J. DeMallie, and Robert Vézina. Lincoln: University of Nebraska Press.

Wedel, Mildred Mott, and Raymond J. DeMallie. 1980. "The Ethnohistorical Approach in Plains Area Studies." In *Anthropology of the Great Plains*, edited by W. Raymond Wood and Margot Liberty, 110–28. Norman: University of Nebraska Press.

Wedel, Mildred Mott, and Waldo R. Wedel. Papers. National Anthropological Archives, Smithsonian Institution, Washington DC.

PART 1

Changing Identities in the Indigenous Societies of the Great Plains

From Deslauriers to Deloria 2

French Identity in a Sioux Indian Family
RAYMOND J. DEMALLIE

The legacy of France on the American Great Plains is inscribed on the landscape. The names of rivers: Belle Fourche, Chouteau Creek, Frenchman's Creek, L'eau qui cours, Moreau River, Souris River; of land formations: Bijou Hills, Butte Cachée, Coteau des Prairies, Coteau du Missouri, Coteau Hills, Pommes Blanches Hills, Verendrye Hill; and of towns and cities: Belle Fourche, Flandreau, Fort Pierre, La Plant, Pierre. All bear witness to the history of French explorers, traders, and adventurers in this vast region connecting New France and Louisiana.

Even more impressive evidence of French activity on the plains are the dozens of French surnames originating with generations of voyageurs and *engagés* (indentured servants working in the fur trade) who came to trade manufactured goods to the Indians for furs, married Indian women — permanently or temporarily — and thereby founded mixed-blood families. Their children, grandchildren, and great-grandchildren became the interpreters and intermediaries between the tribes and Euro-Americans from the late eighteenth century onward. Names such as Archambault, Bisonette, Bordeaux, Ducheneaux, Dupree/Dupris, Janis, Morsette, Mousseau, Picotte, Pourier, Renville, and Shangrau perpetuate the legacy of their French forebears.

Today, however, most of those families preserve little memory of their ancestors beyond their identity as French. Many of their descendants have forgotten that rather than originating in France, in large part the "Frenchmen" who married Indian women were born either in the St. Lawrence Valley or in the Illinois Country (Upper Louisiana). In short, the history of the French-speaking founders of these families, now prominent among the tribes of the plains, has been largely lost to oral tradition. One exception to this generalization is the Deloria family, whose members have interested themselves in their history.

The Delorias are a large family with many branches, but the lives of a small number of individuals have been recorded, both by the Delorias themselves and others (see Deloria Jr. 1999). These prominent individuals are the focus of the story:

> Deslauriers (dates unknown). Fur trader among the Yankton Sioux.
> François (Francis, Frank, or Saswé) Deslauriers (ca. 1816–76); Dakota name Checháʼ Híŋšma "Hairy Thigh." Medicine man (religious leader) and chief of the Half-Breed Band of the Yankton Sioux.
> Philip Joseph Deloria (1853–1931); Dakota name Thípi Sápa "Black Lodge." Episcopal priest and missionary to the Sioux; inherited his father's position as chief.
> Ella Cara Deloria (1889–1971). Master's degree in education from Columbia Teacher's College; educator, linguist, and ethnographer employed by Columbia University to document Sioux language and culture. (See Picotte 1988; DeMallie 1988; DeMallie and Veyrié 2022)
> Vine Victor Deloria Sr. (1901–90). Episcopal priest and missionary to the Sioux. (See P. Deloria 2001)
> Vine Victor Deloria Jr. (1933–2005). Attended Lutheran seminary before turning to law; activist, writer, and university professor. (See DeMallie 2006)

Originating among the Yankton Sioux (Dakota), the Delorias are among the most widely known of the French-derived mixed-blood families. Because Philip Joseph Deloria served for many years as a missionary to the Lakȟóta (Teton Sioux) on Standing Rock Reservation, his son, Vine Sr., and grandson, Vine Jr., were enrolled there, rather than on the Yankton Reservation. Over the generations a succession of Delorias has been prominent in politics, religion, and education—not only among their own people but nationally. Three family members—Ella, Vine Sr., and Vine Jr.—were honored with Indian Achievement Awards, an annual award presented by the Indian Council Fire of Chicago, one of the oldest national American Indian organizations. The story of the Deloria family is one of change and adaptation that, in microcosm, reflects the entire course of American Indian history over more than two centuries.

My Interest in the Deloria Family

As an anthropologist focused on understanding the Sioux, my interest in the Deloria family began from an ethnographic perspective. I met Ella Deloria in Chicago in 1965, when I was a college student, and learned from her about the vast amount of work she had done in the 1930s under the direction of Franz Boas and Ruth Benedict at Columbia University, founding figures in American anthropology. She had recorded hundreds of pages of texts—traditional stories, autobiographies, conversations—in the Lakȟóta language and painstakingly transcribed and translated them, together with hundreds more pages of historical texts. Most of that work remained unpublished, an invaluable resource for future study. In 1969, at his home near Baltimore, I met Father Vine Deloria Sr., who one afternoon gave me my first lesson in spoken Lakȟóta, tape-recording for me words, sentences, and a couple of brief texts. The next spring I visited with Ella Deloria at her home in Vermillion, South Dakota, on my way to begin my first fieldwork on the Cheyenne River Reservation. She meticulously corrected my pronunciation of Lakȟóta and provided contacts to meet on the reservation. That fall of 1970, at the annual meeting of the American Anthropological Association, I met Vine Deloria Jr., whose popular book *Custer Died for Your Sins* (1969), published in the preceding year, had viciously and effectively satirized anthropologists who study the Sioux. "Why don't you do something useful?" he asked me, beginning a collaboration on historical issues of treaty rights that continued until his death.

One of the collections of historical texts that Ella Deloria re-transcribed and translated was written by George Sword, of the Pine Ridge Reservation, around 1909. It consists of an autobiography and a series of ethnographic accounts of daily life, hunting, warfare, ceremonies, and religious beliefs. I had found additional writings by Sword that Ella had not seen, and I wanted to translate them to supplement hers.

In 1981 I asked Vine Sr. if he would help me with the project; by then he had moved to Pierre, South Dakota. He agreed, so long as we could work at his home. We did, and for some time I became the anthropologist living in the basement. Sword's writings would remind him of some anecdote or custom and frequently he spoke of his personal view of Christianity and the Sioux adaptations to it. This usually led back to stories of his father, one of the first Sioux men to be ordained an Episcopal priest, and of his grandfather, who converted from his traditional religion to Christianity near the end of his life.

I was intrigued by those family stories, some of which I was already familiar with from reading Sarah Emelia Olden's *The People of Tipi Sapa (The Dakotas)* (1918), a book about Vine Sr.'s father, Philip J. Deloria, whose Indian name was Thípi Sápa "Black Lodge." According to family tradition Miss Olden was attracted to Philip Deloria as the most prominent American Indian clergyman in the Episcopal Church and wanted to publicize his mission work, while at the same time telling the story of the Yankton people. Vine Sr. said that the whole family knew that Olden would get everything wrong if she tried to write the book on her own, so his father dictated most of it to her. Indeed, the ethnographic part of the book—the bulk of it, which follows a biography of Philip—reads like oral text, the content of which parallels in many subjects the writings of George Sword.

While tracking down archival material relating to the Sioux, I came across a collection of letters written by Ella Deloria to Virginia Dorsey Lightfoot, daughter of James Owen Dorsey, who had been both an Episcopalian minister and an ethnologist at the Smithsonian Institution's Bureau of American Ethnology.[1] He was the leading student of the Siouan languages during the late nineteenth century. Lightfoot was writing a biography of her father and, after reading Olden (1918), was interested in learning more about the Deloria family because of their prominence in Episcopalian mission work. This was the connection that led to the two women meeting and becoming friends. Ella Deloria's letters document her understanding of the family history.

In April 1982 Vine Sr. came to Bismarck, North Dakota, for the symposium on Sioux religion at Mary College organized by Douglas

R. Parks and myself.[2] The symposium brought together religious leaders representing various forms of traditional religion (the Sun Dance, *yuwípi*, Native American Church) and a variety of Christian denominations with scholars studying Sioux religion. From his youth Vine Sr. excelled as an orator, and his presentation on this occasion was at once powerful, funny, and moving. His talk, in which he spoke in some detail about his grandfather's vision and his father's vocation as a priest, was later published in a volume that resulted from the symposium (Deloria Sr. 1987).

A month later Vine Sr. and I were invited to the annual John G. Neihardt Spring Symposium held at the Neihardt Center in Bancroft, Nebraska. I was to serve as interviewer and prompt him to tell a sequence of stories. On May 7, the day before the symposium, we practiced for some two hours while sitting on a bench in the Prayer Garden, shaded by a beautiful flowering tree, symbolic of the great vision of Black Elk, the Oglala holy man whose life story Neihardt recorded ([1932] 2008). The conversation was filmed by a crew from Nebraska Educational TV.[3] The next day we repeated the conversation, in much shortened form, before an enthusiastic audience. The cornerstone of our conversation was the story of his grandfather, François, and the vision that led him to a life as a religious leader.

In spring 1984 Vine Sr.'s wife, Barbara, called to ask me when I was returning to Pierre. I was puzzled, since we had completed the Sword translations. "He wants you to record his stories now, before it's too late." So once again I moved into the basement and spent the days recording Vine Sr.'s stories and songs, both in Lakȟóta and in English versions. They included versions of stories published in Olden's book and stories Vine had learned during the years he spent as a missionary on various Sioux reservations, but many were stories of relatives, of his grandfather, and of life as it was when he grew up at St. Elizabeth's Mission, near the little town of Wakpala on the Standing Rock Reservation in South Dakota.

Vine Sr. was particularly conscious of the family's French origins. In a 1974 interview he commented: "My father sure used to show his French when he spoke English. The next time you see a movie with

Charles Boyer in it, you listen to that voice. That's my father. His accent was French and that's amazing. Of course, he's part French. He just reflected that French background.... I know my father's voice and I'll tell you, I had a lump in my throat about five years after my father died [when] I happened to see Charles Boyer in a movie—and, my golly, I thought—that's my father talking."

My experiences with the Deloria family, and especially my conversations with Vine Sr., led me to think about the French origins of the family and the special position in which they were placed as mediators between Indian and non-Indian, Christian and non-Christian.

Ella Deloria's Story of the Origin of the Deloria Family

In a letter to Virginia Lightfoot, Ella Deloria wrote that her great-grandfather was named François DesLauriers and was a Frenchman from New Orleans. Apparently he was a fur trader who married a Yankton named Iron Woman. The mother died giving birth to a son who was also named François DesLauriers. The father died when the boy was only five years old. The younger François was called Saswé, the Dakota corruption of his French name. Ella Deloria wrote: "He was brought up by uncles, who trained him in the native ways, so that, for all practical purposes, he was a Dakota purely" (Ella Deloria to Virginia Lightfoot, n.d.).

Vine Deloria Sr.'s Story of the Origin of the Deloria Family

When telling me the family story, Vine Sr. began by crediting an entirely different story to his sister Ella, who, he said, related that their great-great-grandparents had been beheaded, victims of the French Revolution (Deloria Sr., personal communication, 1982). One of the family's wealthy friends saved their two sons—Philip, age seventeen, and Francis, age fifteen—by sending them with a governess to New York City. Apparently dissatisfied there, they soon ran away and settled for a time in the area of present-day Syracuse, New York: "In those days it was just a community of log houses with stockades, and where the people farmed and raised stock." Francis hired out to a farmer, but Philip decided to head west.

Eventually Philip reached the Rocky Mountains, but when he came to realize their vastness he was afraid of becoming lost, so he headed back east, following the Missouri River. "Now that's the way I was told," Vine Sr. said. Philip walked along the river, following it as it turned southward, when he became ill; he had a high fever and at last collapsed on a sandy bank where he lay, passing in and out of consciousness. "In coming to in one instance he found a fourteen-year-old Indian girl, down on her knees, feeling of his forehead, making signs that she was going for help. And he came to an Indian tipi and there they gave him medicine and got him well." They were a band of Yankton Sioux who were returning to their home lower down the river. He joined them, and for four years they traveled, stopping frequently for long periods and making a trip westward to the Black Hills to cut tipi poles. Vine Sr. commented, "Those people were in no hurry."

When they finally returned to their home near present-day Greenwood, South Dakota, Philip married the girl who had saved him, now a young woman. (Although Vine Sr. did not explicitly say it in this telling, his father, Philip Joseph, told Olden that the girl was the daughter of "a noted chief" [Olden 1918, 1]). They had children, and one of the boys was named François, in honor of Philip's brother. Vine Sr. added: "The Yankton people, when they found it was hard to say François, called him Saswé." His Indian name was "Chechá Híŋšma, 'Hairy Thigh'; he was half French, so no doubt he was hairy."

Vine Deloria Jr.'s Story of the Origin of the Deloria Family

In 1999 Vine Deloria Jr. published *Singing for a Spirit: A Portrait of the Dakota Sioux*. It is an unusual book, a multigenerational collaboration that celebrates Yankton culture and history. In it Vine Jr. incorporated the material dictated by his grandfather, Philip, that Olden had published in *The People of Tipi Sapa* (1918), replacing Olden's introductory sketch of Philip's life with a broader account of the Deloria family drawn from a combination of family tradition and historical sources.

As Vine Jr. tells the story, the brothers Phillipe and François were orphaned Huguenots who in the 1750s were brought as youngsters to New England. When they were teenagers, Phillipe decided to make his living in the fur trade and went to Quebec. He joined a trading party that traveled west to Lake Winnipeg, where they were attacked, probably by Assiniboines, and most of them were killed. Only Phillipe and another French boy, who were away from the camp when the attack occurred, survived.

The two boys headed south, hoping to reach St. Louis. Near the Big Bend (South Dakota) the other boy died of starvation, and François collapsed on the bank. There he was found by a band of Lower Yanktonai Sioux, who rescued him, and François remained with them for the rest of his life. A Lower Yanktonai winter count (annual calendar) for 1785 has the entry: "Dakota woman married a white man" (Howard 1976). Vine Jr. writes, "I have always liked to believe that this man was my ancestor" (Deloria Jr. 1999, 8). He had a son named François Xavier who married a Blackfeet Lakȟóta woman; it is possible that he established a trading post at Des Lauriers Island, just below the Big Bend. In 1816 François Xavier's son, François ("Saswé"), was born. Like his father, he, too, married a Blackfeet Lakȟóta woman. In 1853 she gave birth to Thípi Sápa, also known as Philip Joseph. About that time Saswé moved his family south to the Yankton Reservation, across the Missouri from Fort Randall (constructed in 1856). The location, near present-day Lake Andes, South Dakota, became known as White Swan Landing, named after a leading Yankton chief. Deslauriers cut wood and sold it to the steamboats that provided transportation on the Missouri. Although he was a Yanktonai, he soon became recognized as a chief of the Yanktons.

Comparison of the Three Versions

Each of the three versions of the story relates the origin of the Delorias as a prominent mixed-blood family on the Yankton Reservation. The French identity of the family's founder is highlighted in all three, and while the variations are relatively minor, they are significant.

Ella Deloria's is the simplest telling, situating the founding ancestor as a fur trader from New Orleans (as opposed to a French Canadian). With the death of his mother in childbirth and of his father a few years later, François is left to be raised by his mother's people as a Yankton, and although he is of mixed parentage, he becomes for all intents and purposes a Dakota.

Vine Sr.'s telling has a more mythic overtone. It is a story of European savagery—the French people are fighting and beheading the members of their own leading families, forcing the survivors to flee to North America. The orphaned son of a French nobleman proves incapable of surviving on his own in the plains wilderness. He is rescued by the daughter of a Yankton chief, a motif whose parallel to the story of John Smith and his rescue by Pocahontas, daughter of chief Powhatan, is irresistible. In the Deslauriers case, however, the two marry and produce a son who is brought up as a Yankton, but with a distinct half-blood identity. This identity is reflected in his names, Saswé, an approximation of François, and Hairy Thigh, a reference to a physical characteristic revealing his parentage.

Vine Jr.'s telling begins with implied savagery of another sort—the European intolerance for religious difference. The founding ancestor, a Protestant, is presumably sent to North America to practice religious freedom. He fails in his first attempt to profit from the fur trade, proves incompetent to survive on his own, and is rescued by a friendly band of Yanktonai with whom he lives out his years. The story implies that he became a resident trader and that subsequently his son, Francis Xavier, succeeded him in the same capacity. Saswé appears only in the third generation and makes the transition from Yanktonai to Yankton, and even though he is a double outsider (half-blood and Yanktonai), he becomes one of the eight chiefs of the Yankton Reservation, the leader of the "Half-Breed Band."

Despite the variations, these stories serve as prelude to the more important episode—Saswé's vision. The sequence of events in the vision, as related by father and son, is the same, so a single summary suffices (Deloria Sr. 1987, 95–97; Deloria Jr. 1999, 16–20).[4]

Saswé's Vision

Saswé's vision typifies the experience of a Sioux Thunder-being dreamer, a man who was selected by *Wakíŋyaŋ* (the celestial power of Thunder and Lightning, symbolized by the Thunder Bird) and offered powers to destroy and to heal, that is, to take and to restore life. The vision occurred when Saswé was an adolescent. He decided to fast and pray on a high butte, a ritual called Haŋblécheyapi (Crying for a Vision). He passed out, and in his vision he followed a long path that ended at a black tipi in the sky (a tipi of storm clouds, home of the Thunder-beings). He entered the lodge and saw that the path diverged. On the left the path was white and curved around the inside of the tipi to the back where sat a large white owl. Along the path were four skeletons, seated as though they were alive, with their heads down. On the right the path was red and curved around to the back where sat a black hawk. Along that path were four sweat lodges, the conical structures in which Iníkağapi (Making New Life, the ritual of the sweat lodge) was practiced. When Saswé decided to take the path to the right, the hawk said to him, "Come on. We knew that you were going to take that." Saswé reached the back on the lodge, the owl to his left and the hawk to his right. The hawk addressed him again: "You have just passed four purification lodges. That means you are going to kill four men of your own tribe."

The next episode of the vision was not known to Vine Sr.

In the third episode, Saswé found himself on horseback, one of a countless number of horsemen who were embodiments of the destructive power of the Thunder-beings. One of the other horsemen told Saswé that they would race across the clouds all the way to the ocean in the distant east. Along the way, down on earth, they saw a woman who was in distress, watching the clouds appear. Saswé was told that she had violated her promise to the Thunder-beings and that they were going to kill her. As they rode overhead, they hurled down lightning bolts, and the woman fell on the ground, dead. When the horsemen reached the ocean, they all transformed into small yellow birds (goldfinches) and started back west. Flying was a pleasurable experience, the birds flying up and down and around one another. Eventually Saswé headed for the butte where he saw his body lying face down on the ground; he landed just between the shoulder blades and immediately awakened.

The Outcome of the Vision

Philip Deloria, in telling Olden about his father's vision, related only that Saswé went into a black house (*thípi sápa*) filled with "all manner of sickness and all manner of disease." At Saswé's touch the sick revived and many recovered (Olden 1918, 8). As a result of the vision Saswé became a *wicháśta wakháŋ* (holy man or shaman) with the power to heal. He became a practitioner of *yuwípi*, a ritual in which he was bound hand and foot, wrapped in a robe or blanket; then, in a darkened lodge, the spirits came and freed him, giving him information about curing a patient, about finding a lost object, or about foretelling the future. For these rituals he wore a pair of moccasins decorated with porcupine quillwork; both had red backgrounds but the left one depicted a white owl and the right one a black hawk. Indicative of his power, and doubtless giving his patients faith in his abilities, when he moved his right foot a hawk cried out, and when he moved his left foot an owl hooted.

The price of these powers was the prophecy that he would kill four men of his own tribe. Vine Sr. told how, as the years passed, the prophecy came true (Deloria Sr. 1987, 100–104). The first murder occurred when a man married to one of his sisters repeatedly abused her. Saswé warned him to stop, but the man persisted in beating his wife. One day Saswé went to his lodge and shot his brother-in-law dead. The second murder was for the same cause. The husband of one of Saswé's daughters repeatedly abused her; again he was warned, and when he failed to reform, Saswé shot his son-in-law dead.

These two murders were, of course, family matters, but in a larger sense they represent Saswé's responsibility in his role as a chief to maintain harmony among his people. As Vine Sr. told the story, the next two murders were directly related to his leadership role. Both occurred in the aftermath of the war between the Santees (the eastern Sioux) and the whites that broke out in 1862. The Santees tried to enlist their Yankton relatives to join them, but the latter refused. When the U.S. Army accused the Yanktons of harboring Santee fugitives, the ranking army officer demanded that the Yanktons put one of the Santees to death as proof of their loyalty. And so Saswé, who was preordained for the killing, carried out the execution. Later, when a group of Sioux fled from their reservation, Saswé was asked by the army to try to bring them back. When he caught up with them, one man challenged him and tried to kill him; in the ensuing struggle Saswé shot the man with a pistol and killed him.

The Significance of the Vision

Thunder-being visions always balanced the powers to cure with the powers to destroy. Usually the destructive powers were implemented in warfare against enemies. What marks Saswé's vision as unique is the turning of those powers against his own people. Yet that also gave him freedom to act in a way that other Sioux men could not, to kill tribal members for the welfare of the tribe as a whole. Could this special interpretation of the vision powers be related to Saswé's status as a mixed-blood? This might be argued, at least as a latent explanation, since his status as both insider and outsider put him in a special relation to the Sioux spiritual world. Although there are many vision accounts, they are virtually all from full-blood Sioux. During the nineteenth century it must have been extremely rare for a mixed-blood to attain the status of holy man.

Moreover, Saswé was not without remorse for the murders. After the last one, he could never again drink from a cup without seeing reflected in the liquid the face of one of the men he had killed, leering back at him. His gray horse, the one he had ridden during the last two murders, was seemingly bothered by the spirits of the dead men as well, and people remarked how the horse came every night to stand in front of Saswé's house before returning to the herd in the morning (Deloria Sr. 1987, 104–5).

The price of Saswé's sacred gifts, according to family tradition, extended beyond his own lifetime. According to Vine Jr., Saswé's son Philip—presumably repeating his father's injunction—interpreted the four purification lodges to mean that four generations of Deloria men were to serve as religious leaders. Whether this represented multigenerational transfer of the vision powers or expiation for Saswé's deeds is a matter of interpretation.

The Expiation of Sin

Traditional Sioux culture lacked the Christian concept of sin until missionaries introduced it in the mid-nineteenth century. The Dakota word chosen to represent the new concept was *wówaȟtani*, a term that had an earlier range of meaning implying sudden misfortune, perhaps caused by the violation of a taboo or even preordained by a spirit being. Saswé's murders fit within both the Sioux and the Christian concepts.

Since murder of a tribesman was one of the most heinous of crimes among the Sioux, Saswé's sanctioned murders were a psychological burden for him. He continued to practice *yuwípi* and traditional healing rituals after the establishment of the Yankton Reservation in 1859. However, new religious teachings were soon introduced to the Yanktons. Exiled from Minnesota as a result of the 1862 conflict, the Santee Dakotas were moved in 1863 to a reservation at the mouth of Crow Creek, about a hundred miles upriver from the Yanktons. A number of Santees came to work at the Yankton Agency sawmill, one of whom was Paul Mazakutemani, who was a Native deacon. For three months during the winter of 1863–64 he held Sunday services and attracted a following on the reservation (Woodruff 1934, 561).

In 1866 the Santees were moved again, this time downriver to the mouth of the Niobrara, only a day's journey from the Yankton Agency. With them came the Rev. Samuel Hinman, an Episcopalian missionary to the Santees. Some of the Yanktons wanted to have a missionary live among them, too, not only for religious instruction but to open a school for their children. The Yanktons were divided over the subject: some eagerly sought the Episcopalians, others hoped for a Roman Catholic missionary (testimony to the lasting effects of the early missionary work of Father Pierre-Jean De Smet), while a third group was opposed to any Christian missionaries. In April 1868, at a formal council, the latter two groups withdrew their opposition, and emissaries from the Yankton Reservation visited Hinman to ask for an Episcopalian missionary.

In his diary Hinman records a visit on January 21, 1869, from François Deslaurier (whom he calls Dolurio). Deslauriers implored him: "Come and help us. . . . Our people want you. Part of them are very bad. But many long for peace and wisdom . . . you can save our children" (Hinman 1869, 31-32). That fall Hinman was able to send them Reverend Mazakutemani, who had been advanced to the rank of deacon, but this did not satisfy the Yanktons, who wanted a white man as their priest. Finally, in spring 1870, the Rev. Joseph W. Cook came from Wyoming to undertake mission work with the Yanktons and remained with them the rest of his long life (Woodruff 1964, 562–63).

Cook refers to Deslauriers as Francis Deloria, calling him "a powerful friend and helper" (Sneve 1977, 35). Deloria and his family faithfully attended Sunday services. Cook wrote, "Every Sunday or two . . . this man with his immense stature would rise in his place and pour forth the most earnest exhortations to his people to attend closely to our instructions" (Cook 1876, 2). What might account for the sudden attraction of Christianity, powerful enough to turn Deloria away from traditional religious practices to the rituals of the Episcopal Church? The answer can be only speculative, but one possibility lies in the account given by his son, Philip (Thípi Sápa).

Philip told Olden that in 1870 some friends persuaded him to go with them to attend a service at Reverend Cook's church. His world was that of Yankton tradition and even his name, Thípi Sápa, referenced the spiritual universe of the Sioux. But when the congregation sang the Dakota hymn "Guide Me, O Thou Great Jehovah," Thípi Sápa was electrified. He said, "It caught and held me like a rope around a bronco." Three successive Sundays he returned to the church, but the hymn was not sung. Then, on the fourth Sunday, he heard it sung again and memorized the tune and the first verse. He commented, "I felt that I was possessor of a great treasure." The boy was attending day school and soon attracted Cook's attention. When the missionary told him that, to become a minister to his people, he must cut his hair, dress in white men's clothes, and go away for an education, he at first refused, but after much deliberation, in Philip's words, "Going to Mr. Cook I gave myself up" (Olden 1918, 9–12). Cook's story presents a slightly different angle. He was impressed by Philip's "brightness and earnestness in learning" and so went to talk to his father. Cook recalled, "On conferring with Deloria about him he desired to give him to me to be trained up for our work among his people" (Cook 1876, 2).

It seems likely that Philip's attraction to the church was the catalyst for Saswé's decision to support it, not just tacitly, but wholeheartedly. There was an especially strong bond between father and son as evidenced by the family tradition that at age three, Philip died of a fever; however, his grieving father bargained with the Thunder-beings and with their power brought him back to life. For that inexplicable feat his people began to fear Saswé (Deloria Jr. 1999, 37–38). If the father saved the son, then—from the Christian Dakota viewpoint—it might be argued that the son saved the father by leading him to Christianity.

Cook reports that Deloria brought all his children and grandchildren to be baptized and persuaded many of his older relatives to be baptized as well. But he himself hesitated because the Christian Dakotas had agreed that no man who had more than one wife could be admitted to the church. Cook says that Deloria had two wives, but reliable family tradition says three. In 1871, however, Thípi Sápa—now Philip—left to attend Nebraska College, and Deloria sent his second and third wives back to their families. Cook speaks of the anguish this caused Deloria, especially since his youngest wife had recently borne him another son. Finally, on Christmas Day, 1871, he was baptized, the first of the chiefs to embrace the church.

Cook wrote a dramatic account of the event, reporting the speech that Deloria made before being baptized. He told Cook: "I have been a very wicked man. I have done most everything that is bad and detestable. But what I have done I did in ignorance. I knew nothing of God's law, I followed my own will... I am ashamed of my evil deeds; I pray every night and morning, (lifting up his hand), 'Jesus, Saviour, have mercy on me!'" Then, addressing Cook, he stated: "But, my friend, when you baptize people, you are accustomed to pour a little water on them. I have been such an awful sinner that it seems to me you would need to take four or five barrels of water to wash away my sins" (Cook 1876, 3).

Vine Sr. picks up the story by reporting the missionary's reply: "Never mind what you have been. Ask God to forgive you and he will take all your sins away." After the baptism there was a feast, and as Saswé picked up his coffee cup he wondered which of his victims he would see reflected there. In Vine Sr.'s words, "But there was no face, no face at all. For Francis Deloria, his sins were gone" (Deloria Sr. 1987, 105).

After two years at Nebraska College and a year at Shattuck School (an Episcopal school in Faribault, Minnesota), Philip returned to his people as a teacher and catechist. Saswé apparently put aside his traditional religious practices, was confirmed, and admitted to Holy Communion. Cook (1876) commented, "I had not a more devout communicant among either the whites or Indians than he." Members of the non-Christian party reviled and harassed him, killing his livestock and trying to compel him to attend Sun Dances and other ceremonies. According to Cook's account he remained steadfast, "not fearing to lift up his voice in councils to speak for the Church and civilization, and to reproach the madness and folly of the heathen" (2–3).

Toward the Historical Deslauriers

The story of the Deloria family here reaches the turning point where religious change catches up with social change. As a means of support, hunting was a thing of the past. The Yanktons were confined to a small reservation and had to learn to make their livelihood there. For many, the change to the white man's way of life implied the need to embrace Christianity, education, and the English language, leaving traditional culture behind. The Deloria family committed itself to this transformation of their people.

It is reasonable to speculate on the impact that the family's mixed-blood identity might have had on this decision. Many full-bloods made the same transition, of course, but we may look for the historical roots of the Delorias' story in the available written record, meager as it is.

The name Deslauriers, in a variety of spellings, is found throughout the records of the Missouri River country during the late eighteenth and early nineteenth centuries. For instance, in 1797, Delassus de Luzieres recommended that one "Mr de fremont de Laurieres, a very honest and educated immigrant gentleman from Brittany," be hired to teach English and Spanish to the youth of Ste. Genevieve (de Luzieres 1797).[5] In 1840 Father Nicolas Point, S.J., served as pastor of a settlement at Kawsmouth (Westport, near Kansas City), which comprised, in his words, "twenty-three families, most of whom were French *voyageurs*, their Indian families, and their children, who were called *métis*." One of the men was Antoine De Laurier, probably the same "faithful Deslauriers," a French Canadian, who served as muleteer for Francis Parkman's celebrated trip on the Oregon Trail in 1846 (Donnelly 1967, 20; Barry 1972, 419, 581; Parkman 1969, xiii). But the most likely candidate for the ancestor of the Deloria family—although even this must remain speculative—is known only as DesLauriers or DeLaurier. In the employ of the Columbia Fur Company, in 1822 he built Fort Tecumseh on the Missouri River at the mouth of the Bad River, the forerunner of Fort Pierre. When the Columbia Fur Company was bought out by the American Fur Company in 1827, DesLauriers joined the opposition French Fur Company, which built their trading post just across the Bad River from Fort Tecumseh. In 1830 it, too, was bought out by the American Fur Company, which established its monopoly on the Missouri River trade (De Land 1902, 329–30, 334). It seems likely that DesLauriers continued in the trade under the employ of the American Fur Company.

We do not know whether DesLauriers stayed with his wife's people, nor do we know for certain when he died. Ella Deloria, passing on information presumably from her father, stated that DesLauriers died when Saswé was five years old, which would be about 1821 (Ella C. Deloria to Virginia Dorsey Lightfoot, August 29, 1947). We have the missionary Cook's testimony that Francis Deloria (Saswé) spoke only Dakota and that prior to 1870 had no acquaintance with Christianity (Cook 1876, 1).

There are few references to Saswé in the written record. His name appears as "Frank Du la rio" in the list of sixteen Yankton leaders who arrived in Washington DC on February 18, 1867. The photographic portrait taken there shows him resplendent in a quilled buckskin shirt, beaded leggings and moccasins, and an enormous eagle feather war bonnet decorated with tassels of weasel skin. That fall he participated in the council at Yankton Agency called by the Indian Peace Commissioners, who were visiting the tribes along the Missouri River. They wrote his name as "De Lareaux." He told the commissioners, "I was raised in this nation," referring to the Dakota people. "I love the whites. Half of me belongs to this nation, and half to the whites. Since last spring I have been Chief of the half breeds" (Indian Peace Commission 1867–68).

Deslauriers's self-identity as "half breed" in the interpreter's phrasing is less instructive than the Dakota words that Saswé must have spoken. The Yankton designation for half-blood is *wašícuŋ hokšina* ("Frenchman's son"). During the early nineteenth century most of the whites whom the Dakotas met were French speakers; only later was the word *wašícuŋ* (which in precontact times designated a type of spirit-being) generalized to all whites, and the French were more specifically designated as *wašícuŋ ikcéka* ("common whites"). The growing number of mixed-blood families among the Yanktons led to the formation of the "Half Breed Band," one of the eight bands on the reservation. Deslauriers's chieftainship of the band was apparently formalized by the recognition he was accorded when he traveled to Washington DC in 1867 (DeMallie 2001, 741).

Inevitably, the question arises concerning the four murders that Deslauriers was said to have committed. It seems remarkable that a man who had performed such deeds, even though preordained by a sacred vision, would be recognized as a chief. It is tempting to dismiss those killings as myth, but, in fact, there is some historical documentation of them.

At the time of his baptism, Deslauriers addressed Reverend Cook: "My friend, I have been a violent man. I was a scout for Gen. Sully and again for Gen. Harney, in the trouble that followed the outbreak of the Santees in Minnesota. I have killed several persons. I have been a man greatly feared among my people" (Cook 1876, 2–3). Corroborating information was recorded by Frances Chamberlain Holley in a memoir of her experiences with the Sioux. She records that in 1862 General Sully hired fifty Yanktons to pursue the Santees who were fighting the army. When the scouts captured some of the enemy, they brought them to the local army officer, but he refused to take them into custody. In one instance, when the scouts were undecided what to do with a prisoner, Deslauriers took action. As Holley tells the story: "An old Indian, De Luris, called 'Chief-of-the-half-breeds,' rode up and said: 'If you don't know what to do with that Indian, *I do!*' and instantly drew up and shot him dead in his seat." Holley goes on to relate the story of Deslauriers's son-in-law abusing his daughter. The outraged father rode his horse to his daughter's lodge. "He hastily dismounted and walked inside, saying: 'My son-in-law, I have come to kill you!' and without further comment or explanation, shot him" (Holley 1892, 77).

Cook (1876) describes Deslauriers as a man of "immense stature," who at the time of his death at age sixty was "very large and corpulent, weighing about three hundred pounds" (1). He lived in the woods six miles from the Yankton Agency, about forty yards from the bank of the Missouri. Philip Deloria took his son Vine to visit the spot. He showed him where Saswé lived in a large, square house and the locations of three other nearby houses in which each of his wives lived and raised their children (Deloria Sr. 1987, 100). According to family tradition he had twenty-two children.

Supporting multiple wives and a large family reflects Saswé's status as a chief and a man firmly rooted in his people's traditions. But Cook tells us that Francis Deloria "was a progressive man, and for many years, since the game disappeared, he had been a cultivator of the ground. He had an ambition to get cattle and hogs and chickens about him, and as far as possible to become self-supporting. He cut a great deal of wood which he sold to the steamboats and to the whites at the Agency" (Cook 1876, 3). These details set him apart from the reservation norm, perhaps reflecting his self-identity as a half-blood.

The most revealing description of Saswé was written by Ella Deloria, in a letter to Virginia Lightfoot. Although she did not intend it for publication, its importance as a family portrait makes it an invaluable resource. She wrote:

> As regards my grandfather, none of us know much about him. There is nothing written, and we have only what my father and his contemporaries said about him—his great spirituality and insight, his exceptional sensitivity, his remarkable ability to diagnose. . . .
>
> He never accepted a patient if he knew he could not be helped. He never accepted reward if his patient failed to recover. . . .
>
> He grew rich because he was sent for, from distant groups of Dakotas, and, because people valued the lives of their dear ones always more than horses and things, they gave him fees which built up his herd and holdings. But he gave freely, too. . . .
>
> But he was wise enough to accommodate himself to a white economy. . . . He employed men to make cord wood, which he sold regularly to the steam boats that plied the Missouri in those days, and did a thriving business. He had cattle, barnyard fowl, hogs, and was never in want and his children had plenty to eat (Ella C. Deloria to Virginia Dorsey Lightfoot, August 29, 1947).

From Ella Deloria's account we see how Saswé's practice of traditional healing rituals provided him the means to succeed in the new reservation economy. It also suggests the magnitude of the economic sacrifice he made in accepting Christianity. She asserts that after he accepted baptism he turned from the old ways and became "an exemplary Christian to the end of his days."

Philip Joseph Deloria

Philip fulfilled the prophecy of his father's vision by becoming a *wichášta wakháŋ*, a "holy man," not in the traditional sense of a medicine man like Saswé, but as a minister of the Gospel. When he returned from his schooling in 1874, Philip told Emelia Olden, "I became a layreader in the Church and at the same time assumed my duties as chief in place of my father." In time he said, "When I found my way a little clearer, I decided to lay aside my chieftainship and work for the spiritual uplift of my people" (Olden 1918, 13–14). In 1883 he was appointed as a deacon and in 1892 was ordained as a priest.

In 1879 Philip was sent to Rosebud Reservation to teach at St. Mary's School. About this time he collaborated with David Tatiyopa and Baptiste Lambert, also Episcopalian lay readers, to found a self-help organization called the Planting Society. It was modeled on traditional Sioux men's societies, and its intention was to stimulate agricultural activities and promote interdenominational harmony among Sioux. The name was later changed to the Brotherhood of Christian Unity. The organization provided help for those in need and continued to function until the 1980s (Deloria Jr. 1999, 49–54).

In 1890 Philip was reassigned to St. Elizabeth's Church on the Standing Rock Reservation and two years later oversaw the building of St. Elizabeth's School. After his ordination he was given charge of the entire Standing Rock Mission. He remained there thirty-five years (Sneve 1977, 53–55).

Vine Sr. recalled how his father loved to dress in liturgical attire, lead processions, and enact the rituals of the church. As a boy, Philip had often accompanied his father when Saswé performed his ceremonies for the sick, and it is tempting to suggest that for Philip the rituals of the Episcopal Church were a direct replacement—in a sense, the fulfillment of those pre-Christian rituals. As Vine Jr. (1999) remarked, "Philip saw his black clerical clothes as a physical representation of the Black Tipi of Saswé. There were four purification tents so there should be four generations of the family following a religious vocation" (69).

Philip's life was marred by a series of personal tragedies. His first two wives died from complications of childbirth. His third wife, Mary Sully, gave birth to four children, including Ella Cara (1889) and Vine Victor (1901).[6] When Mary died in 1915, Vine was sent away to school in Nebraska at Kearney Military Academy, a diocesan school, where he stayed four years. Next he attended St. Stephen's College (later renamed Bard College), in Annandale-on-Hudson, New York, on a football scholarship. There, where he was known as Pete Deloria, he became a celebrated football champion. After graduation in 1926 he had dreams of becoming a professional football player and took his first job as athletic adviser at Chilocco Indian School, in Oklahoma (Deloria Jr. 1999, 75–59; Gruver 1951, 11–12; P. Deloria 2004).

Philip remarried, and after ill health forced him to retire in 1925, he moved back to the Yankton Reservation and finally to Martin, South Dakota. He was insistent that his son Vine continue the family's religious vocation in accordance with Saswé's vision. Accordingly, with a good deal of hesitancy and uncertainty, in 1928 Vine entered General Theological Seminary in New York. Just before Vine graduated in 1931, Philip suffered a massive stroke. Vine hurried back to Martin and appeared before his father wearing clericals. The old man was overjoyed, and before he died two days later, Vine had promised to commit himself to the life of an Episcopal priest (Deloria Jr. 1999, 81–82).

Philip Deloria's contribution to leading his people to the Episcopal Church was recognized in 1936 when he was chosen as one of ninety men and women whose statues appear in the Ter Sanctus reredos behind the Great Altar of Washington Cathedral in Washington DC. (Deloria Jr. 1999, 83; Gridley 1966).

Vine Deloria Sr.

In November 1931 Vine was ordained a priest at St. Elizabeth's Church on Standing Rock Reservation, where he had been baptized and confirmed and where his father had served so long. He was first sent to Pine Ridge Reservation but soon after was reassigned to All Saints Church, off-reservation in Martin, South Dakota. His new assignment was in Bennett County, an area that had been carved out of Pine Ridge Reservation in 1910, and that was home to large numbers of full- and mixed-blood Sioux families (see Wagoner 2002). In 1939 a tornado struck Martin and destroyed the church. To raise the funds to repair it, Vine went on a national speaking tour that, in the words of his son Vine Jr., "made him the national symbol of Episcopal mission work" (Deloria Jr. 1999, 83, 86).

Vine was appointed superintending presbyter for the eastern half of Pine Ridge Reservation so that in addition to his own church he was responsible for eleven other chapels, representing some eight hundred communicants spread over an enormous area and therefore requiring a huge time commitment for travel. He continued in this work until 1951 when, in a conversation with the bishop in Sioux Falls, he realized that because he was an Indian, he was blocked from advancement within the church in South Dakota. Vine left the mission field, moved to the Diocese of Iowa, and became rector of Trinity Church in Denison, Iowa. In 1954 church authorities appointed him to take charge of Indian mission work on the National Council staff of the Episcopal Church in New York. He resigned from that position in 1958 as a result of a disagreement with church officials over the national policy of termination of tribal relations and relocation of Indians to urban areas. Vine then returned to Iowa as vicar of St. Paul's Parish, Durant, Iowa. In 1961 he was called back to his home state and appointed archdeacon, in charge of the Episcopal Church's Indian missions throughout South Dakota. After retiring with the title "Venerable," Vine moved to the East for a time, then returned to Pierre, South Dakota, where he served as pastor of the small Indian church across the Missouri River in Fort Pierre (P. Deloria 2001, 90–94).

In 1982, at the symposium on Sioux Indian religion held in Bismarck, North Dakota, Vine told the mostly Indian audience: "During my career as a missionary I never questioned the Christian religion as reflected by the Episcopal Church. . . . Since my retirement I have come to look differently on the church." Referring to the church hierarchy he said, "There is too much of Saint Paul in their teaching—the Christ—and not enough at all of Jesus—the man." Having witnessed the dissolution of the mission structure and the abandonment of the small rural chapels that were once its mainstay, he concluded that the revival of "our old religion, the religion of our ancestors, is a sign of the failures of the Christian situation" (Deloria Sr. 1987, 110).

Vine Deloria Jr.

Born in 1933 in Martin, South Dakota, Vine Jr. grew up in a missionary household that centered around his father's pastoral duties. Like his father and grandfather, he attended an Episcopal boarding school, Kent School, in Kent, Connecticut, graduating in 1951. After serving in the

Marine Corps from 1954 to 1956 he enrolled at Iowa State College (now University) and earned a degree in general science in 1958. He entered Lutheran School of Theology in Rock Island, Illinois, and earned an MA in sacred theology in 1963. Rather than choosing a career as a minister, in an unanticipated turn of events he was elected executive director of the National Congress of American Indians and served in that capacity from 1964 to 1968. Subsequently he entered the University of Colorado's School of Law and received a JD in 1970. The next year he was one of the founders of a public interest law firm, the Institute for the Development of Indian Law, in Washington DC, dedicated to the study of treaties and treaty rights and to applying the concept of tribal sovereignty to Indian law.

Vine Jr. became the icon of American Indian activism with the publication in 1969 of *Custer Died for Your Sins: An Indian Manifesto*. In this and subsequent books he drew public attention to American Indians as an ongoing presence in American life and laid the intellectual basis for what came to be called "Red Power," a political movement focused on reasserting the government-to-government rights guaranteed to Indian tribes by the Constitution of the United States. In legal terms, this meant holding the government responsible for fulfilling the promises of the many treaties made with Indian tribes but subsequently broken out of political or economic expediency. In practical terms, however, the anger and frustration of younger American Indian activists resulted in three confrontations: the takeover of Alcatraz Island in 1969, the Trail of Broken Treaties march on Washington in 1972 that ended in the takeover and trashing of the Bureau of Indian Affairs building, and an American Indian Movement intervention at Pine Ridge that ended in the takeover and seventy-one-day standoff between Indians and the FBI at Wounded Knee in 1973. Vine's writings served, at least indirectly, to spark those events, but none of them furthered the political agenda that he envisioned. His writings helped win over mainstream sympathies for solving the problems that led to American Indian poverty and marginalization, but the violent political protests that became rich fodder for the news media only hardened the divide between Indian and white.

Throughout his life Vine continued to be involved as a lawyer and a scholar in American Indian politics and, in particular, to pursue legal action through treaty commitments. *Documents of American Indian Diplomacy*, published in 1999, brings together the primary texts that he amassed over more than twenty-five years, documenting American Indian political relations, including the dozens of treaties and agreements signed by Indian leaders in good faith but that were never ratified by Congress (Deloria Jr. and DeMallie 1999). But more and more his attention turned to the religious and philosophical issues that he first raised in 1973 in his book *God Is Red*. There he called into question the relevance of Judeo-Christian religions for the peoples of the New World and suggested replacing the lineal time dimension so central to Western civilization with a nonlineal spatial dimension more in keeping with American Indian religions. Vine began to force his readers to glimpse the possibility of entirely different epistemologies that, threateningly, laid the basis for a true multiculturalism going far beyond the surface features of differing customs and beliefs. In a series of books and essays he sought to imagine a genuine "planetary metaphysics or epistemology" that would transcend cultural boundaries (Deloria Jr. 1979, 1995, 2002; 2004, 3–11). Such an epistemology would transcend and embrace the dual spiritual realms of his heritage, both Dakota and Christian.

Conclusion

At least five generations have passed since the first Deslauriers fathered a son among the Yankton Sioux. Each generation has interpreted that French heritage in the context of its own time. For Saswé (François) Deslauriers, his status as a mixed-blood enabled him to assume the leadership of the Half-Breed Band of the Yankton Sioux and was doubtless also a factor in his economic success on the reservation. His mixed heritage did not prevent him from being culturally Dakota and becoming a powerful medicine man, though it may have been a factor in his ultimate turn to Christianity. His sacred vision compelled four generations of males in his family to serve as religious leaders. Saswé's son, Philip Joseph, and his grandson, Vine Victor, both fulfilled that duty as missionaries among the Sioux. Both men benefited from their mixed-blood status since they were seen as mediators between the world of the Indians and that of the white men.

In the fourth generation, as the effectiveness of the mission system disintegrated, and even the relevance of Christianity for the Sioux came into question, Vine Jr. turned to academia and a career as a public intellectual as the vehicle for religious leadership, now construed in a much broader way. He firmly identified as a mixed-blood Indian, and his French ancestry was a topic of real interest for him; in his later years he tried to determine the identity of the original Deslauriers from whom he was descended. But few of the voyageurs were literate, and the paucity of records made the task impossible.

In the fifth generation Vine Jr.'s son, also named Philip Joseph, is today a professor of history at Harvard University. Because he never lived on an Indian reservation, and because his mother's side of the family is Swedish American, the question of identity is a trickier business. Growing up, he writes, "I never had to worry about my identity." But being the son of a famous American Indian author in a very public professional position forces the issue. In a thoughtful essay titled "Thinking about Self in a Family Way," he refuses to be pushed into a binary category, Indian or white (P. Deloria 1998; 2002, 25; 2004). The postmodern world does not seem so simple. But whatever other choices there may be, French identity will always be a legacy of the Deloria family.

Notes

1. Later renamed the Bureau of American Ethnology. Ella Deloria's letters to Virginia Dorsey Lightfoot are now in my possession. [Editors' note: These letters are at the time of writing held at Indiana University for digitization before being sent on for archiving at the National Anthropological Archives in Suitland, Maryland.]

2. Now the University of Mary. The presentations given at the symposium were published in DeMallie and Parks (1987).

3. The film was never made publicly available.

4. Although Vine Sr. asserted that Ella knew the full story of the vision, no written version by her seems to be extent.

5. Vine Jr. was not amused when I suggested he might be descended from a school teacher rather than a voyageur.

6. Mary Sully was also a half-blood, the daughter of Gen. Alfred Sully and his Yankton wife, who later returned with her daughter to her people when Sully was reassigned to the East. P. Deloria (2019) provides a recent reflection on Mary Sully's life and career as an artist.

References

Barry, Louise. 1972. *The Beginning of the West: Annals of the Kansas Gateway to the American West, 1540–1854.* Topeka: Kansas State Historical Society.

[Cook, J. W.] 1876. *The Church and the Indians.* New York: Office of the Indian Commission, Protestant Episcopal Church.

De Land, Charles E. 1902. "Editorial Notes on Old Fort Pierre and Its Neighbors." In *South Dakota Historical Collections*, vol. 1, 317–79. Aberdeen SD: New Printing.

Deloria, Ella Cara. Letters to Virginia Dorsey Lightfoot. In the possession of Raymond J. DeMallie.

Deloria, Philip J. 1998. *Playing Indian.* New Haven CT: Yale University Press.

———. 2001. "Vine V. Deloria, Sr.: Dakota." In *The New Warriors: Native American Leaders since 1900*, edited by R. David Edmunds, 78–95. Lincoln: University of Nebraska Press.

———. 2002. "Thinking about Self in a Family Way." *Journal of American History* 89, no. 1: 25–29.

———. 2004. *Indians in Unexpected Places.* Lawrence: University Press of Kansas.

———. 2019. *Becoming Mary Sully: Toward an American Indian Abstract.* Seattle: University of Washington Press.

Deloria, Vine, Jr. 1969. *Custer Died for Your Sins: An Indian Manifesto.* New York: Macmillan.

———. 1973. *God Is Red.* New York: Grosset & Dunlap.

———. 1979. *The Metaphysics of Modern Existence.* San Francisco: Harper and Row.

———. 1995. *Red Earth, White Lies: Native Americans and the Myth of Scientific Fact.* New York: Scribner.

———. 1999. *Singing for a Spirit: A Portrait of the Dakota Sioux.* Santa Fe NM: Clearlight.

———. 2002. *Evolution, Creationism, and Other Modern Myths.* Golden CO: Fulcrum.

———. 2004. "Philosophy and Tribal People." In *American Indian Thought: Philosophical Essays*, edited by Anne Waters, 3–11. Malden MA: Blackwell.

Deloria, Vine, Jr., and Raymond J. DeMallie, eds. 1999. *Documents of American Indian Diplomacy: Treaties, Agreements, and Conventions, 1775–1979*. 2 vols. Norman: University of Oklahoma Press.

Deloria, Vine V., Sr. 1987. "The Establishment of Christianity among the Sioux." In *Sioux Indian Religion: Tradition and Innovation*, edited by Raymond J. DeMallie and Douglas R. Parks, 91–111. Norman: University of Oklahoma Press.

de Luzieres, Delassus. 1797. Report on the District of New Bourbon, Archives General de Indias, Papeles de Cuba, Lego. 2355, copy in Abraham Nasatir Collection, box 3, folder 18, Bancroft Library, University of California, Berkeley.

DeMallie, Raymond J. 1988. Afterword to *Waterlily*, by Ella Cara Deloria, 233–44. Lincoln: University of Nebraska Press.

———. 2001. "Sioux until 1850." In *Handbook of North American Indians*, vol. 13, *Plains*, edited by Raymond J. DeMallie, pt. 2, 718–60. Washington DC: Smithsonian Institution.

———. 2006. "Vine Deloria Jr. (1933–2005)." *American Anthropologist* 108, no. 4: 932–35.

———. 2013. "De Deslauriers à Deloria: L'identité française d'une famille sioux." In *Un continent en partage: Cinq siècles de rencontres entre Amérindiens et Français*, edited by Gilles Havard and Mickaël Augernon, 535–58. Paris: Les Indes Savantes, Rivages des Xantons.

DeMallie, Raymond J., and Douglas R. Parks, eds. 1987. *Sioux Indian Religion: Tradition and Innovation*. Norman: University of Oklahoma Press.

DeMallie, Raymond J., and Thierry Veyrié. 2022. "Presentation of Ella Cara Deloria." In Ella Deloria, *The Dakota Way of Life*, ix–xxii. Lincoln: University of Nebraska Press.

Donnelly, Joseph P., S.J., ed. 1967. *Wildness Kingdom: Indian Life in the Rocky Mountains, 1840–1847: The Journals and Paintings of Father Nicolas Point*. New York: Holt, Rinehart, and Winston.

Gridley, Marion E. 1966. *America's Indian Statues: A Comprehensive Compilation of Facts and Photos of Statues Honoring or Memorializing the American Indian*. Chicago: Amerindian/Towertown Press.

Gruver, Richard O. 1951. "'Pete' Deloria: Prince of His People." In "Alumni News," edited by Clifford W. Burgess. *The Bard College Newsletter* 5, no. 1: 11.

Hinman, S. D. 1869. "Journal Written at the Mission in Nebraska." In *Taopi and His Friends, or the Indians' Wrongs and Rights*, edited by William Welsh, 1–48. Philadelphia: Claxton, Remsen & Haffelfinger.

Holley, Frances Chamberlain. 1892. *Once Their Home: Our Legacy from the Dahkotahs*. Chicago: Donahue Henneberry.

Howard, James H. 1976. "Yanktonai Ethnohistory and the John K. Bear Winter Count." Memoir 11, *Plains Anthropologist* 21, no. 73, pt. 2.

Indian Peace Commission. "Transcript of the Minutes and Proceedings of the Indian Peace Commission." 2 vols. National Archives and Records Administration, Record Group 48, Secretary of the Interior Indian Division, Special Files relating to Negotiations with Indians, no. 3, Indian Treaty Commission 1867–68.

Murray, Jan. 1974. Typescript of interview with Vine Deloria Sr., Pierre, South Dakota, March 12, 1974. American Indian Studies Research Institute, Indiana University, Bloomington.

Neihardt, John G. (1932) 2008. *Black Elk Speaks: Being the Life Story of a Holy Man of the Oglala Sioux*. New York: William Morrow. Reprint, Premier Edition, annotated by Raymond J. DeMallie with illustrations by Standing Bear. Albany: State University of New York Press.

Olden, Sarah Emilia. 1918. *The People of Tipi Sapa (the Dakotas): Tipi Sapa Mitaoyate Kin*. Milwaukee: Morehouse.

Parkman, Francis. 1969. *The Oregon Trail*. Edited by E. N. Feltskog. Madison: University of Wisconsin Press.

Picotte, Agnes. 1988. "Biographical Sketch of the Author." In *Waterlily*, by Ella Cara Deloria, 229–31. Lincoln: University of Nebraska Press.

Sneve, Virginia Driving Hawk. 1977. *That They May Have Life: The Episcopal Church in South Dakota, 1859–1976*. New York: Seabury Press.

Wagoner, Paula L. 2002. *"They Treated Us Just Like Indians": The Worlds of Bennett County, South Dakota*. Lincoln: University of Nebraska Press.

Woodruff, K. Brent. 1934. "The Episcopal Mission to the Dakotas." In *South Dakota Historical Collections*, vol. 17, 553–603. Pierre SD: State Publishing.

Lakȟóta Modernities and the Ends of History   3

Little Big Man, Crow Dog, and Red Tomahawk in Context

SEBASTIAN F. BRAUN

On a warm late summer evening slightly over twenty years ago, I was standing on the lawn outside of the American Indian Studies Research Institute with Joshua Wells, a fellow graduate student at Indiana University. The Mathers Museum across the lawn had celebrated its annual Field Day, and I was helping Joshua fill back in a fake archaeological pit that had been used to demonstrate archaeology to school children. From the institute, somebody approached us, watched us work, and announced himself as a new student of Ray DeMallie's and Doug Parks's. We began to talk, and I told him that I had just returned from preliminary fieldwork on the Cheyenne River Sioux Reservation. He asked me about my project, and when I told him it had to do with tribal bison ranching, he told me that I could not do that. Finding it curious that he felt he had a say in the matter, I asked him why. He said that first, DeMallie, my adviser, was an ethnohistorian, and this project was contemporary, and second, I could not draw any conclusion from the project because it was not historical—it was ongoing, and thus I did not know how it would end.

    It is unfortunately not that uncommon for people to hold the opinion that ethnohistory has nothing to do with contemporary cultures. I assume this is an application of a specific form of history. Obviously, cultures of the past are not the same as cultures of the present. However, both history and ethnohistory draw from and are dependent in many ways on an understanding of contemporary interpretations of the past at the very least. History would also be more or less a strictly academic intellectual exercise without practical use if we could draw its conclusions to the present and, for example, learn from it. Both DeMallie and Parks had an exceptional understanding of Plains ethnohistory; they also were both interested in and had a complementary understanding of present-day situations. One of my last cogent conversations with Parks came on a visit to their house when we discussed the Dakota Access Pipeline protests in conjunction with his efforts to finish the Yanktonai dictionary.

It is with these conversations in mind that I am setting out to write this text, in which I try to expand Lakȟóta ethnohistory to the present, or — perhaps at the same time — to extend the present to the past. Before readers accuse me of engaging in presentism, let me briefly explain that Lakȟóta histories function from a different set of questions than those of academic history. There is no Lakȟóta history as such, apart from a corpus of differing histories, each comprising stories of people important to a specific group of people and interpreted and told by them. The idea that there must be a common interpretation of one set of factual events, anchored in specific and unquestionable dates and places with commonly determined meanings, runs contradictory to this notion. If we impose academic history onto Lakȟóta representations of the past, we are already altering that past. In the following, I try to demonstrate this simple idea with an example: the deaths of historically important Lakȟóta figures (Crazy Horse [Tȟašúŋke Witkó], Sitting Bull [Tȟatȟáŋka Íyotake], and Spotted Tail [Siŋté Glešká]) and the actions of those who were directly involved in their killings (Little Big Man [Wičháša Tȟáŋkala], Red Tomahawk [Tȟačhaŋȟpí Lúta], and Crow Dog [Kȟaŋǧí Šúŋka]), who are not often seen as important historical figures.

The Premise

My interest in this subject is tied to an event. Like most anthropological insights, that event brought on a flash of incomplete sudden revelation. A few years after the conversation around the pit on the lawn in Bloomington, I was teaching an introduction to American Indian studies class at the University of North Dakota, where I had been hired in the Department of American Indian Studies. My work there—as opposed to working in a department of anthropology—allowed and forced me to take a step back from conventional anthropology, and this has deeply affected my perspective on scholarship. In those introductory classes, I always tried to make students think about contemporary representations of Native people, pasts, and presents. I commonly used North Dakota highway markers as an example. State roads in North Dakota are identified with signs that feature the road number inside an Indian head in portrait mode. On this day I was pointing out to my students that the portrait used for the signs was that of Red Tomahawk, who had shot Sitting Bull. Naively, I used this as an example of white/Native relations and as evidence of different interpretations of the past. After all, I assumed, to celebrate the killing of Sitting Bull was an indication of a specific worldview. That day my naivete came home to roost, as one of my students raised her hand and indicated that she was very well aware of this. She was proud of the road sign, she said, as all her family was proud of what Red Tomahawk had done—and that she was his grandniece.

Had I paid attention to the significance of her last name from the class roster, Red Tomahawk, I might have reconsidered interpreting the road signs in that way, but I doubt it. I was so deeply embedded in my assumptions that it took her narrative to shock me out of them. Most anthropological insights depend on such casual yet foundational corrections of assumptions. In this case the student's comment not only opened my eyes to the errors of my assumptions but also led to a long effort to reevaluate some of our most common assumptions of Lakȟóta history.

In the conventional interpretation of Lakȟóta history, Crazy Horse and Sitting Bull are heroes who represented and defended the true Lakȟóta culture, manifested in sovereign pre-reservation bison hunting. Their deaths are significant because they also mark the end of that era. They are usually seen as having been killed in conjunction with the transition to the American imposition of new and different values. Their lives—and deaths—are taken as symbolic for Lakȟóta existence, and Lakȟóta existence is a struggle against everything the United States stands for. In some interpretations the transition is seen as the end of (Lakȟóta) history. There are hobbyists and academics who see Lakȟóta culture and history as being terminated in 1890. For example, Finnish popular historian Pekka Hämäläinen begins his 2019 book on Lakȟóta history by noting, "The Battle of Little Bighorn fixed the Lakȟóta, embodied by Sitting Bull and Crazy Horse, in historical memory and made them an object of enduring fascination" (1). He later notes that Crazy Horse personified "the pure, uncorrupted ideals of what it meant to be Lakȟóta and how to remain Indigenous" (304). The concept of an "uncorrupted" or "pure" Lakȟóta culture existing in the days of bison hunting, and away from the agencies, implies that indigeneity and Lakȟótaness became corrupted upon close contact with American ideas. "Pure," authentic Lakȟóta ideals disappeared; as many Americans and some European hobbyists deem to be the case, there are no more "authentic" Lakȟóta people.

While this kind of historiography thus perceives Crazy Horse and Sitting Bull as icons of Lakȟótaness through their resistance to their deaths, the underlying ideas are also apparent in the portrayal of other Lakȟóta leaders. Red Cloud, for example, is of interest to historians while he is still supposedly uncorrupted Lakȟóta, that is, as the leader in the Powder River war. In contrast, his later life near the Pine Ridge agency is mostly ignored.[1] In some cases, this assignment of Lakȟótaness becomes more blurred, such as with the Brule leader Spotted Tail. Hämäläinen (2019) says that he was killed because of his "defiant traditionalism, persisting popularity, and multiple wives," perhaps as a necessary contrast to Crow Dog, his killer, who is characterized as "a captain of the Indian police" (374). From the perspective of a historiography that creates clear distinctions between those who are and are not culturally Lakȟóta, and that places the distinction in part on continued, pure resistance or closeness to Americans, that narrative interpretation might make sense. However, even Nick Estes, who perceives Lakȟóta history and present as a continuous and continuing war with American settler colonialism, characterizes Spotted Tail as "a reservation leader and 'agency chief'" (Estes 2019, 116), thus opening the door for a blurred line between *wólakȟota* (that which makes something or somebody Lakȟóta), leadership, and collaboration.

Lakȟóta Temporalities and Landscapes

A pure assignment of culture, values, or historical roles relies on a perspective of history characterized by determinacy. Who people were or are is determined by and in their acts; no uncertainty can be allowed. One is either a member of the Indian police or a spiritual leader, Indigenous or a settler colonialist, assimilated or traditional, Lakȟóta or not. Similarly, eras of history are determinate entities. Culture is a determinate entity, and its perceived purity depends on remaining as it was defined. Historical events are determinate entities, defined within time and in turn defining time, and their meanings are clear to historians; they reveal themselves within a study of other events, whose meanings are also clearly defined within a place and time. The most determinate marker in Lakȟóta history according to this historiography is the time between 1876 and 1890: the Lakȟóta were living Lakȟóta culture until the massacre at Wounded Knee and a corrupted version of their culture, at best, since then. Authentic Lakȟóta history and culture, from that perspective, ends at that point.

Here, I am interested in events that are often described as symbolic of the fight between Lakȟótaness and assimilation, if they are not ignored: the fact that the deaths of Sitting Bull, Spotted Tail, and Crazy Horse all involved Lakȟóta men. Sitting Bull was killed by Red Tomahawk; Spotted Tail was killed by Crow Dog; and Crazy Horse was held by Little Big Man before or when a soldier killed him with a bayonet. From the determinate historical perspective, the events that define the era are the deaths of these leaders, and with them supposedly Lakȟóta society and culture. Those who killed or helped kill the leaders are then those who have already crossed the line from being Lakȟóta to no longer sharing Lakȟótaness; the events prove the end of Lakȟóta temporality.

I use "temporality" as a term standing in for the existence within time as well as the organization of time and the perception of history. The organization of time and history according to a determined structure leads to the construction of culturally accepted "times," "periods," or "ages" that organize, guide, and determine our perception of history. As an example, we can think of "the Middle Age(s)." The term, that is, the temporality (and with it the organization of history), was coined by those who lived in "the Renaissance" and saw themselves as near the end of history, in an ever more perfected society. The temporalization of the "middle" ages served their ends of history because it marked their existence as a continuation and evolution of the beginning of time, namely, in this understanding, the Greek and Roman societies. What I am addressing here, then, is the temporalization of Lakȟóta acts by people who try to fit those acts into their own organization of history.

I have argued elsewhere that a determinate perspective of temporalities leads to "procedural landscapes" (Braun 2008, 76–90; 2013a). I see the purpose of ethnohistory as understanding such dynamics and interpreting acts from their own temporalities. It seems that the need for a determinate view of history is strongest in those who are without a clear understanding of their world and feel threatened by such uncertainty (see, for example, Kurkiala 2002; Lyons 2010). Ethnohistory can cut through this paradox. It can withstand and thrive in a multitude of histories and accept multiple local temporalities. In contrast to a determinate perspective, local people often use an indeterminate approach to the world and to events taking place in it, as anthropologist Henry Sharp so wonderfully explains in his study of Dene culture.[2] From this approach, events, people, or historical eras do not carry a determinate meaning, time, or place. Instead, their meanings are revealed only in the context of an event playing itself out through time and space. The meaning of an event is revealed in and through the past and future of its participants, not within the determinate time and space of the present.

In actual, non-procedural reality, neither Lakȟóta society nor Lakȟóta culture died in 1890. I begin this ethnohistorical study by entertaining the notion that it was not the deaths of these Lakȟóta leaders that was significant, but instead the complicity of Lakȟóta men in their deaths. What if the real meaning of these events does not lie in them defining the end of an era, but in their performance of a transition of Lakȟóta temporalities? In fact, neither Red Tomahawk nor Little Big Man acted on their own. They acted in concert with other Lakȟóta people. What if they also acted in concert with wólakȟota?[3]

Upon Crazy Horse's death, Touch the Clouds (Maȟpíya Ičáȟtagya) said, "It is good; he has looked for death and it has come" (Bray 2006, 390). The significance of the event was one that was rooted in the past and in the future. It was rooted in the future because Crazy Horse faced the prospect of living in the shadow of Spotted Tail, who did not really want him around. It was rooted in the past because Crazy Horse was uneasy when pondering an answer to the future the night before his death. After he talked with Touch the Clouds, the latter became convinced that his cousin was "looking to die" (Bray 2006, 373). The event itself, thus, was unavoidable because it had been determined by the future and decided in the past. What happened that day was simply those two temporalities playing themselves out.

There is yet another dimension here, though, this one connecting Crazy Horse with the others mentioned above. Apart from Crazy Horse's own temporalities, broad Lakȟóta temporalities played themselves out. According to Chipps, one of his main supporters and friends, Crazy Horse "was not accounted good for anything among the Indians but to make war; he was expected to do that; he was set apart in their minds to make war, and that was his business" (Jensen 2005, 274). However, the time for war had passed. In the collective meaning of many Lakȟóta, then, Crazy Horse's time had passed. The events were thus also unavoidable on a larger scale. There is, indeed, an element of performance in the accounts given surrounding Crazy Horse's death, just as there is a performative element in the events surrounding Sitting Bull's death. This does not mean that people at the time acted as if on stage. However, once the indeterminacy of these events was cleared (in Crazy Horse's case immediately upon his death, or before the events began through Touch the Clouds's determination that Crazy Horse had been looking to die), everybody could be seen as performing their role in a ritual. The—never named—guard who thrust his bayonet into Crazy Horse is thus reduced to an extra, a nonactor. His action is mechanical, not intentional; anybody could have fulfilled the role.

There can also be no doubt that these performances were based on Lakȟóta values and played themselves out according to a Lakȟóta script, in a Lakȟóta "procedural landscape" (Braun 2013a). The American procedural landscape did not reach much further than the agencies and the military posts. This becomes clear with the American attempts to get Crazy Horse to turn himself in during the days before his arrest and killing. Short of military violence, the American landscape could not be enforced. Lakȟóta negotiations brought Crazy Horse to Fort Robinson on Lakȟóta terms. It was when it became clear that the Lakȟóta terms were being replaced by American terms—when Crazy Horse saw that he was to be incarcerated—that he tried to resist. At that moment, though, even the fort became Lakȟóta procedural landscape. It took the intervention of American Horse to prevent a clash between the Lakȟóta sides; William Garnett described this as a successful deception, but it remains a fact that this was a Lakȟóta intervention (Bray 2006, 387–88; for William Garnett's version, see Jensen 2005, 72).

What is important, what provides the meaning to the events is the transition from one Lakȟóta temporality to another: from war to peace, from traditional life to life with reservations; from largely nomadic seasons to largely settled ones; from hunting and gathering to agriculture; from before to after (on this issue of transitions between temporalities, see Ssorin-Chaikov 2017, 79–82).

It is the participation of Lakȟóta actors, holding agency, in the events that make this transition a Lakȟóta transition. This is not the end of Lakȟóta temporality. It is not the end of Lakȟóta traditional culture. Instead, it is the transition of that culture into a new form, a new time. The full determination of that meaning at that time becomes even clearer when the event is seen in the context of other events.

It bears emphasis that this meaning has changed from a contemporary perspective. However, I want to first get to a clearer understanding of this earlier determination of Lakȟóta realities before addressing this change. If we want to understand Lakȟóta lives in the early twentieth century, we need to approach them from their contemporary understandings of these events and their meanings. "Culture and culture change are, in effect, the same phenomenon," as Ray DeMallie put it

(1993, 533). As such, cultures are expressed in different temporalities over time, and each temporality creates and follows its own landscape of meaning. The work of ethnohistory is not just to uncover what events took place; it is to mentally get into the relevant temporality and landscape to be able to find their meanings.

Transitions

I argue above that the transition to reservation life—the transition, arguably, to "modernity"—was, as exemplified in the iconic events surrounding the deaths of Crazy Horse and Sitting Bull, a Lakȟóta transition. Two necessary amendments to this statement need to be made.

First, contrary to others, I do not think that it is these events that best mark this transition, nor is it the massacre at Wounded Knee. Instead of understanding these events as defining the era, we should understand the era—that is, an accumulation of "non-events" (Fogelson 1989), each drawing in itself meaning from the temporalities in which it is embedded—as defining the events (see Braun 2013b). If we define Native/non-Native relations through events of conflict, we define the history as one of conflict and the events of collaboration (now determined as non-events) as exceptions. This is obviously a possible interpretation of history, shared by Native and non-Native people. This view of history, like any other, is a choice, not a given. This choice, in turn, determines the meaning of events and of history represented in events. If history or an era is violence, collaboration can be treason. If, on the other hand, coexistence is the determined expectation, violence is a transgression. If we replaced Wounded Knee as a defining event with, say, the founding of Flandreau (First Presbyterian Church 2003), Sioux history and American history would be fundamentally different.

Second—and not in spite of the above, but as a necessary part of it—this transition to "modernity," as defined by those deeming themselves to be "modern," was not voluntary. This transition, as Nikolai Ssorin-Chaikov (2017) lays out for Siberia, was a Hobbesian gift. Transitions between temporalities are usually ruptures, especially when they are initiated by outsiders, and the refusal of a gift leads to a rupture, and potentially warfare. However, in the face of an offer that cannot be refused, there are still several options, and usually several of these options are explored. Which one succeeds culturally cannot be known beforehand. The meaning of present events can only be determined by future events (see Sharp 2001). The transition to an American-imposed (but not yet necessarily American-defined) modernity was a gift to be accepted or refused. As time went on during the second half of the nineteenth century, it became clear to many Lakȟóta leaders that the gift could not be refused because refusal would mean destruction. Refusal definitely meant conflict; acceptance, however—and this is the Lakȟóta intervention—did not mean surrender.

If the transition is seen as one that is only imposed, we see these events as a time of loss—for example, the loss of culture or the loss of sovereignty. If, however, we provide Native actors the agency to model events and meaning—to shape the temporality—this is not only a timeline of loss but also one of creation (see, for example, Lyons 2010). In my experience, in listening to contemporary stories and in my reading of historical stories, I actually see a strong emphasis on creation. Lakȟóta culture and history has not been lost; it has transitioned, changed, and perhaps reinvented itself. This transition, this creation, was laced with violence—physical, mental, political, and cultural. Yet, this was a Lakȟóta transition, a Native transition. To explain this perspective more, perhaps another story might help.

About ten years ago, I was working with the late Marilyn Hudson on a text about another transition, the Bakken oil boom and its impacts on the Three Affiliated Tribes (Hudson and Braun 2013). In thinking about these contemporary events, it was hard not to compare them to past transitions such as the flooding of the Missouri to form Lake Sakakawea, which resulted in large-scale removals of people on the Fort Berthold Indian Reservation, including Marilyn's family. Like others, they had to move from the bottomlands of the Missouri River to a barren allotment on the uplands. I sent Marilyn a draft, outlining how in return this had been both a consequence and an affirmation of the partial loss of sovereignty. In her reply she scolded me and insisted that the tribes had never lost any of their sovereignty. This assertion, going far beyond a defense of inherent tribal sovereignty, was difficult to reconcile with the taking of the land for Lake Sakakawea, for example. It was one of those difficult moments when we have to "have ears" to stop and listen and actually hear what somebody tells us (DeMallie 1993; Braun 2013b; see also Levi-Strauss 1997). Hers was not a story of reclaiming sovereignty or retaining agency. Foundationally different from those approaches, this history was about an ongoing agency and sovereignty, transforming and being transformed through different temporalities, while none of these transitions impacted the fact that these temporalities and landscapes were and remained fundamentally Native.

What I am proposing is to look at the transition to modernity—defined as reservation life, wage labor, schools, health care, hygiene, literacy, and (American) law—not as a surrender nor a loss of Lakȟóta culture. Although imposed by the outside in its foundational elements, Lakȟóta people made this transition theirs. They did so, in part, through their actions in the events surrounding the deaths of Crazy Horse and Sitting Bull. The era of nomadic freedom and military warfare against the United States was ending. A new era was beginning, but just as much a Lakȟóta era.

The fact that this was a transition on Lakȟóta terms can be gleaned from the events predating Crazy Horse's death. I specifically avoid calling these events leading up or building up to his death, or using similar language, because his death, although seen as the climax of the story by many American accounts, might have simply been the unavoidable consequence of what happened before and was to happen in the future. In the unfolding of these events, several people interpreted why Crazy Horse behaved as he did, why he did not submit to the leaders.

Oglala leaders, upon deciding that Crazy Horse's northern village had to be brought under control, said that Crazy Horse had "no ears," that he "would not listen to them" (Bray 2006, 361). When their forces confronted the village, American Horse defused an imminent fight between his Oglalas, trying to bring Crazy Horse back to Pine Ridge, and Black Fox's men, who were trying to protect Crazy Horse's getaway from his camp. After presenting the charging Black Fox with a pipe, the two leaders sat down, and Black Fox said that Crazy Horse "listens to too many bad talks" (William Garnett's interview with Ricker in Jensen 2005, 64).⁴ When Black Crow told Crazy Horse that he had to come to Camp Sheridan on the Spotted Tail agency, he said that he knew Crazy Horse never listened, but that now, "You must listen to me" (Bray 2006, 368). Spotted Tail himself told Crazy Horse that there was no trouble at his agency, and that, "If you stay here you must listen to me" (Bray 2006, 370; see also Louis Bordeaux's interview with Ricker in Jensen 2005, 294). Crazy Horse, on the other hand, complained that he could not listen because there had been too much talk; his head "was in a whirl" from it, and his "brain ha[d] turned" (Bray 2006, 369, 371). He acknowledged that he had made peace, and he was intent on keeping the peace.

Why was Crazy Horse killed, and why were other Lakȟóta ready to kill him if he did not "surrender" (which he already had, as he pointed out to them)? As his friend Chipps noted in the quote above, his purpose was war, and it might have been seen so much as his purpose, as the meaning of his existence, that people could not reconcile him with being at peace. The meaning of his life had been decided, and "his speech of unprecedented length" (Bray 2006, 371) to the officers Burke and Lee, to Spotted Tail and Swift Bear, the day before his death, when he tried to convince them that he could live at peace, might have been a last step to affirm his meaning over the meaning decided by the people, and simultaneously a first step to bring clarity to himself. However, Spotted Tail, Red Cloud, and American Horse, and with them many Lakȟóta, could not reconfigure the meaning of his life. It had been decided, and no protest by Crazy Horse himself could shake the determination that he represented war, chaos, and trouble. It was after his meditation the same night of his defense that he seemed to be looking to die to Touch the Clouds. Perhaps he had found clarity from the whirl in his head. It seems that Touch the Clouds came to that conclusion.

Through all these events, nobody wanted Crazy Horse to die. His death was either an accident or the regrettable but unavoidable consequence of the past and the future converging in his person. Everybody exhorted him to listen, while at the same time, through the fact that they told him to listen, they already precluded that he would actually be able to do so. His death was, perhaps paradoxically, as much determined as that of the other people who had died because they had no ears a year before: Custer and his men. In a similar fashion, Sitting Bull's death followed his reputation and determined meaning as the leader of "hostiles" who held out on taking action to show that he was listening to the new needs. In situations of crisis or rupture, the meaning of events needs to be determined quickly; there is no time to wait for things to play out. Older meanings are therefore reinforced and applied. Both Sitting Bull and Crazy Horse were seen to be resisting—or having to resist—the new temporalities and realities.

Spotted Tail and Sitting Bull

I have already mentioned how the death of Spotted Tail is often characterized. The "last traditional leader of the Sicangu [Sičháŋǧu]" (Marshall 2001, 222) was killed by Crow Dog, who was the chief of the Indian Police at the agency. This alone might lead some people to see in him a traditionalist. Indeed, Dee Brown wrote that according to Spotted Tail's friends, his murder was "the result of a plot to break the powers of the chiefs and transfer it to men who would bow to the will of the Indian Bureau's agents" (Brown 1970, 420). George E. Hyde (1961) wrote that in 1880 "Spotted Tail stood for freedom and the old Sioux way of life" (274). However, as mentioned, Estes (2019) sees him as an "agency chief," and he had indeed lived around and worked with agents for many years. His role in Crazy Horse's arrest and death four years before his own death certainly makes clear that the two did not see eye to eye.

In his 2019 biography of Spotted Tail, Richmond L. Clow suggests a complex picture. In his 1880 conversations with the visiting Carl Schurz, secretary of the interior, for example, Spotted Tail argued for an English education for Sičháŋǧu children, agricultural training, and more milk cows. He had successfully organized a tribal freighting operation. While he opposed the Episcopalians on the agency, it was mainly, Clow argues, because they taught school in Lakȟóta or, more frequently, in Yankton/Yanktonai. As an "agency chief," Spotted Tail was not advocating for modernity to appease the Americans or because he had surrendered to them. Clow points out that he wanted to create an independent tribal community that was economically self-sufficient and politically sovereign. To do that, he could not rely on American rations (204–7).

Although Spotted Tail saw a need for a Lakȟóta modernity, and had taken the role of an "agency chief" since before Red Cloud, his interpretation of what that meant caused trouble. He was unwilling to share authority. He told Crazy Horse that should the latter wish to live at Spotted Tail's agency, he had to listen to him. Even Hyde (1961), who portrays Spotted Tail in a very positive light, says that when confronted with different ideas, "the Chief said good humoredly that these men had no ideas worth listening to" (275). He fought with the agents over his authority to choose those serving in the Indian Police to cement his authority; in other instances, when challenged, he reportedly did not hesitate to kill those challenging him (Clow 2019, 217). Political violence was not uncommon in leadership disputes at this time of rupture and crisis. However, it seems that, increasingly, other influential men saw Spotted Tail as not listening to anybody. Hyde implies that Crow Dog ambushed Spotted Tail, as does Dee Brown, who writes that "Red Cloud believed that a cowardly assassin was found to remove Spotted Tail because he stood strong for the improvement of his people" (Hyde 1961, 300; Brown 1970, 420). Clow tells a different story (2019, 254–55).

Regardless of Crow Dog's personal motivations, however, this does not seem like an Indian Police officer assassinating a traditional leader or killing a chief on orders of the agent. Rather, it seems that Spotted Tail, while arguing for Lakȟóta modernization, was not giving up traditional life in key aspects that benefited him, but at the same time he reserved this privilege for himself. He also put his opinion above that of everybody else. It was the latter, the refusal to listen, that made him a target of increasing anger. He was advocating for Lakȟóta ways of modernity but exempted himself from the rules. He was doing so by insisting on a system of traditional authority and by living with his four wives and taking wives from others; he exempted himself from the old rules by seemingly abusing the authority to his benefit and not listening to others. In this way he stood in the way of the transition of temporalities.[5]

Sitting Bull's situation was very different: he was not an agency chief, but a symbol of the resistance. However, after his surrender, he had engaged with American (and global) society. This engagement, however, was not seen as a full commitment. Perhaps, as with Crazy Horse, his meaning had been determined to lie on the side of opposing change, and whatever his efforts, they could not break this determination. His remaining social and therefore political influence was seen, in this sense, as a threat by the American institutions, whether rightfully or not. It was also a threat, of course, to those Lakȟóta leaders on Standing Rock who advocated for a Lakȟóta modernity, primarily John Grass and Gall. As with Spotted Tail, Sitting Bull's death can be seen as a consequence of personal jealousies and past grievances or the planned assassination of a powerful Lakȟóta leader at the hand of the Indian Police. However, it also fits into the larger argument presented here: without a full commitment to a new temporality, he represented a temporality that was no longer a solution. When he did not distance himself from the Ghost Dance movement, keeping in mind his previously determined status of a resistance leader, he came to represent a problem of ambiguity. In order to relate to something or somebody, ambiguity has to be resolved. This is all the more important in times of actual or potential crisis.

Native peoples had and have specific ceremonies to resolve such ambiguities or relations — pipe ceremonies make relatives out of ambiguous strangers or eliminate the ambiguity of statements by rendering an unquestionable truth. Ambiguity can result in violence if it is not clarified toward relationship, and thus the law and respect. Both Crazy Horse and Sitting Bull were accused of being cowards in the moment of their arrest; both resisted arrest at the last moment. In their efforts at resistance against arrest, they clarified their already determined ambiguous positions in moves against the new temporality, against the law, and thus reinforced the determinations of meanings surrounding them. In those brief moments, violence was unavoidable.

Wounded Knee and Sitting Bull

As long as the main focuses in Lakȟóta history are the American presence, American actions, and American agency, we cannot understand this history beyond the dualism of assimilation and resistance. Lakȟóta people, it is assumed under that perspective, acted around this seemingly central question of how to react to American demands. They thus split into two groups opposed to each other, but that split really mirrored the relative opposition to the Americans, which are the focus of the story. Thus, Lakȟóta people are either resisting oppression or collaborating with the oppressors. What if we take the Americans out of the center of the story, however? If we deny the Americans that place in dominating Lakȟóta history, if we truly decolonize Lakȟóta history, the dualism will be irrelevant. We can then begin to understand Lakȟóta history and Lakȟóta historical actions beyond this imposed dichotomy of assimilation and resistance.

Up to the establishment of the Great Sioux Reservation after the Bozeman Trail War (Red Cloud's War), Lakȟóta communities thrived through military expansion and resistance against the United States. After 1868 this solution became ambiguous; the successful way into the future was undetermined. Several alternatives were open: an attempt to continue the old ways in the unceded territories, followed by Crazy Horse, Sitting Bull, Gall, and others, and an attempt to consolidate Lakȟóta communities that were no longer in military resistance, on the reservation, followed by Red Cloud, Spotted Tail, and others. After 1876 that debate was over; ambiguity was resolved, and the future course had been determined. For Lakȟóta communities to thrive, peace had to prevail. As always, when people acted against the now determined interests of the community, they had to be brought to listen.

This might be a rather provocative approach. After all, it might seem to take the side of the oppressor. I hasten to disagree. Fundamentally, this approach to history relegates the oppressor to the side line, where they belong for the moment. Handing the Lakȟóta the agency to determine their own course of action means that the Americans lose their dominant position. This does not get rid of the oppression—the Lakȟóta, in broad terms, had to come to grips with the imposed American notion of modernity—but it frees the Lakȟóta, as agents of their future, from the imagined ubiquitous oppressor. It allows them the space and the agency to determine this future, not to have it determined for them. These events largely play out on Lakȟóta terms, and there are two (or, actually, more) Lakȟóta perspectives, all different from the American perspective.

The death of Sitting Bull and the massacre at Wounded Knee Creek, for example, are temporally related, but analyzing them as if they were events of the same category ignores that one took place as a Lakȟóta event and the other as an American event. This becomes clear, for example, through the involvement of the Lakȟóta working for the government. Standing Soldier, first sergeant of the Indian scouts, was sent out to bring in the people who had fled from Standing Rock and from Cheyenne River after the Sitting Bull fight and as part of Big Foot's band. He, or Crazy Thunder under his command,[6] was able to convince a band to come to the agency, and he insisted that "if he had succeeded in reaching Big Foot he should have brought his band round as he did with the others and they would not have been killed" (Standing Soldier's interview with Ricker in Jensen 2005, 243–45). The massacre was immediately recognized as that by all Lakȟóta people. This was not an event that had any remote bearing on the internal discourse over Lakȟóta temporalities. As Ricker notes during his interview with William Garnett, "<u>Slaughter</u> is too dignified a name for this killing. <u>Butchery</u> is a fitter word" (Jensen 2005, 100, emphasis in original).[7] From a Lakȟóta perspective—from the perspective of Lakȟóta people who worked as Indian Police or scouts for the agency—no fighting was necessary; the people were seeking refuge and posed no threat. Standing Soldier even let the people he was bringing into the agency keep their guns. As Justin Gage describes, Lakȟóta letter writers expressed concern but also "hope that the crisis might end peacefully," even after Sitting Bull's death (Gage 2020, 208).

Stanley Vestal included in his biography of Sitting Bull an excerpt from the December 17, 1890, edition of the *New York Herald*, in which it is reported that there was, "cruel as it may seem, a complete understanding from the Commanding Officer to the Indian Police" that should Sitting Bull or any of his people resist his arrest, the chief would have to be killed. Because he would continue to "be a source of great annoyance," if arrested, "nobody would know precisely what to do with him" (Vestal 1989, 308). This is sometimes seen as proof that the Indian Police were simply agents of the federal government, who were intent on killing the Lakȟóta leader. I propose instead a different reading. The federal government and its agents, on the one hand, and the Indian Police and the Standing Rock leadership opposed to Sitting Bull, on the other, had a very different understanding of the situation. There might have been some implied agreement on how to deal with resistance, but this seeming agreement existed based on two different agendas. The Americans were intent on imposing their supposedly civilizing agenda onto the Lakȟóta. The Lakȟóta were intent on carving out their own modernity.

None of the Lakȟóta actors involved in these events were in favor of abandoning or surrendering Lakȟóta sovereignty or agency. However, for all involved the stakes were high. For some, like Crazy Horse and Sitting Bull, a life as proposed by those favoring a different temporality was no longer a Lakȟóta life. "There are no Indians left but me," said Sitting Bull after many on Standing Rock decided to support the 1889 measure to further reduce and split the Great Sioux Reservation (Larson 2007, 208; see also Brown 1970, 430–31). For others, the way to protect Lakȟóta life was to change it; that change, however, would ensure its continuation, not its end. This would be a Lakȟóta solution. In one letter right before Wounded Knee, Sky Bull, a headman at Rosebud, "blamed both the hostiles and the soldiers for the disorder there" (Gage 2020, 208). On Standing Rock, Gall and John Grass had come to the decision that Lakȟóta had to build a new temporality.

The fact that this new Lakȟóta temporality was of necessity complex, yet undetermined in its details, and therefore sometimes defined by contradictory moments can be seen by a change in stance toward the proposed split of the reservation. In 1888 Grass and Gall both vehemently opposed the proposal, effectively shutting down negotiations. Both, however, stood in opposition to Sitting Bull and in favor of a Lakȟóta modernity. Yet, the issue was a Lakȟóta issue, not a question of political or cultural assimilation or surrender. Grass, in a seemingly paradoxical metaphor mirroring Sitting Bull's statement about Indianness a year later, said that anybody voting for the bill would "be considered white people." Gall, on the other hand, complained that he was kept from working his fields during the long negotiations (Larson 2007, 203-4). Finally, John Grass informed the commission that "the Indians would sign neither paper and that they would now return to their farms."[8] Yet, a year later agent McLaughlin convinced both Gall and Grass to vote for the revised bill because he felt that it was the best deal they would get and that the government would take the land anyway (Larson 2007, 207-8). Those leaders who advocated for a Lakȟóta modernity, in other words, were neither puppets of the government nor advocating for complete assimilation. They were trying to resist the theft of their land or, if that was impossible to achieve, at least to be compensated for it.

Lakȟóta Modernities

In present times, those who advocated for Lakȟóta modernities are often seen as antiheroes. Changes in culture are seen, by those who take an essentialist view of culture, as the destruction of culture (see, for example, Lyons 2010; Kurkiala 1997). From that perspective, Crazy Horse, Sitting Bull, and others indeed personify "the pure, uncorrupted ideals of what it meant to be Lakȟóta and how to remain Indigenous," as Hämäläinen puts it (2019, 304). To remain Lakȟóta and Indigenous, according to these notions, means to live these pure, uncorrupted ideas—which those advocating for Lakȟóta modernities corrupted and spoiled. Based on the perspective of hardened, essentialist notions of ethnic identity and of "conceptual separatism" (Lyons 2010, 136), this notion of history presents stark, predetermined choices to historical actors: those who "counseled that survival necessitated learning to live like the whites," as Joseph M. Marshall III (2001) describes Spotted

Tail, Red Cloud, and American Horse (219), would have to be seen as actively working against Lakȟóta culture. Yet, Marshall adds, these were obviously not "the Last Days of the Sioux Nation" (220). Lakȟóta *thiyóšpaye* ("extended family")—communities, bands, tribes—and wólakȟota itself lived and live on.

The assertion that historical Lakȟóta acted on premises of highly determined, pure meanings based on current assertions of political identity should be self-evidently objectionable. The fact that it is not says more about contemporary discourses than ethnohistorical realities.[9] Scott Richard Lyons (2010) writes about the constructed dichotomies that these assertions create: the choice presented is between returning to "thinking, acting, and being like our ancestors" or living "as modern-day Tontos" (137). This dichotomy, then, rules out a change in temporalities, on punishment of losing one's culture and no longer being Lakȟóta or even Indigenous. The very idea of a Lakȟóta modernity is precluded. Yet, the reality is and has been that all those Lakȟóta who have been living in Lakȟóta communities have been living in, struggling with, building, resisting, and debating Lakȟóta modernities. There was an American vision of modernity, which included total cultural assimilation with the goal of terminating Lakȟóta existence, or "complete abandonment of Indian custom" (MacGregor 1946, 35). There was a Lakȟóta vision of modernity, which included partial social acculturation with the goal of ensuring the continuation of Lakȟóta existence. To collapse the two is politically useful, but historically misleading.

Native peoples across the plains and elsewhere determined their own futures as much as they could. They continued to occupy and to create their own procedural landscapes. As scouts, as policemen, as community leaders, as farmers, as cowboys, as sewers, as educators, as priests—as Lakȟóta men and women—they expanded their notions of wólakȟota. They took charge of proceedings and events, in and against the presence of Americans. Those who personified "pure, uncorrupted ideals," those who could not or would not listen, could not change, or were perceived as such, became obstacles to this vision because they were not pragmatic and thus endangered the future of the community.

It has been a fundamental value of Lakȟóta culture that those who endanger the future of the community cannot be allowed to stay within it. That value has been enforced by *akíčhita* ("camp police") and those resisting it were severely punished until they listened.

An ethnohistorical investigation, premised on the cultural meanings deployed by the historical actors, not only helps us understand the past, but it also helps us understand the present. Distinguishing between American and Lakȟóta modernities and allowing for changing Lakȟóta temporalities can explain other events, especially in times of crisis. I am thinking, for example, of the Dick Wilson administration on Pine Ridge and their conflicts with traditional people. Neither side wanted to give up Oglala sovereignty, but they disagreed on the path to be taken to the future. Here, then, at the end of the Termination period, arose another moment of indeterminacy for Lakȟóta meanings, and people worked to determine the meanings of events through their actions. Now, those arguing for a more traditional path were able to circumvent those arguing for a Lakȟóta modernity—which often dominated the tribal councils—in part because the American public by now was open to a moral appeal based on ethnic grounds.[10] What propelled this Lakȟóta discourse—which included limited Lakȟóta violence as people tried to establish the determination of meaning on the ground—into a civil war–like situation was the involvement of outside forces who tried to impose non-Lakȟóta temporalities (see Braun 2013a, 215). With that, the Lakȟóta became the projected battleground between modernity and anti-modernity, and sovereignty, culture, and history became symbols of these two concepts in pure form because they were now no longer tied to Lakȟóta values.[11]

A few years earlier, then chairman Frank Ducheneaux of the Cheyenne River Sioux Tribe argued that what was needed for a better future for the tribe was, among other things, more capital for economic development, better education, better health-care facilities, and a falling rate of Lakȟóta-only speakers (Ducheneaux 1956). With the exception of the last point, this list is still more or less a mirror of needs. Ducheneaux argued that because over 50 percent of children starting reservation schools could not speak English, they needed special attention and "must first be taught to think in English." He mentioned that "this problem will work itself out" as more and more parents used English at home (24). Today, people would give an arm and a leg for having 50 percent Lakȟóta speakers in the population.[12] Far from advocating for total assimilation, however, Ducheneaux was seeking a Lakȟóta modernity. He was at the same time vigorously advocating against Termination and for tribal sovereignty (Ducheneaux 1976). His argument was in line with Lakȟóta temporality until the 1970s.[13] That many tribal government leaders still work toward a Lakȟóta modernity (although of course based on contemporary situations) can be seen, for example, by tribal government responses to the 2007 idea of the Republic of Lakotah. Although they supported many points made by those advocating for the proposed republic, none of the tribal governments supported the concept of returning to a temporality from before the 1868 treaties.

If we look at present events without the ethnohistorical background, we can easily misinterpret these discussions. I am arguing that if we decolonize Lakȟóta histories of the assumed dominant presence of Americans—if we look at Lakȟóta histories not as reactions or extensions of the American presence, but give Lakȟóta people the agency to act on their own—we gain a much better understanding of past and present events. The deaths of Crazy Horse, Spotted Tail, and Sitting Bull were Lakȟóta events that came out of Lakȟóta discourses about the future of Lakȟóta people. Little Big Man, Crow Dog, and Red Tomahawk acted upon Lakȟóta values and principles. The Lakȟóta and their histories, in short, are only "puzzling" (Hämäläinen 2019, 3), only seem contradictory, if we apply our determined meanings to events that were seeking to determine meaning based on Lakȟóta perspectives. The value of "thinking ethnohistorically" (DeMallie 2013) is that it allows us to decolonize histories by avoiding false dichotomies.

Notes

1. See, for a recent example, Drury and Clavin's 2014 book. Purportedly telling "the untold story of Red Cloud," its narrative ends for all intents and purposes with the Treaty of 1868.

2. Sharp (2001) rightfully constrains the detailed explanation of indeterminacy to the Mission Dene; on a structural level, however, very similar views can be found in most local societies around the world, including Lakȟóta communities.

3. I am using "Lakȟótaness" and "wólakȟota" in different meanings in this text—Lakȟótaness to indicate an assignment of (mostly historical) Lakȟóta values from the outside, wólakȟota to indicate living (changing) Lakȟóta values through time.

4. The bad talk Crazy Horse listened to, according to Black Fox, might have been the influence, condemned by Garnett, of Helen Laravie, Black Elk, and John Provost (Jensen 2005, 58–61).

5. The difficulty with assigning labels such as "progressive" or "traditional" is extremely evident in this narrative. Spotted Tail worked toward formal education and economic wage work, for example, but also retained traditional ideas, such as beliefs about marriage and power. Crow Dog, the chief of Indian Police, would later become an ardent defender of the Ghost Dance. In this transitional phase, the meanings of events were still undetermined, and the narratives to make meaning were written in the act. In temporalities without clear timelines, decisions have to be taken within the moment that constitutes the event. None of what I write is a general labeling; in this moment of his assassination, Spotted Tail was acting as an impediment to the future of his people (from Crow Dog's perspective).

6. On Crazy Thunder's involvement, see William Garnett's interview with Ricker in Jensen 2005, 99–100.

7. It is unclear whether these are Ricker's words or if they echo a sentiment from Garnett—probably both, as one does not exclude the other.

8. In a sign of the transitional nature of the times, the same 1888 issue of the *Army, Navy Journal* that carried this report from Standing Rock on the negotiations with Pratt over the diminishment and division of the Great Sioux Reservation also announced the death of General Sherman and the start of work on the battleship *Maine*, of later Cuban infamy.

9. See Kurkiala (2002) on contemporary hegemonic discourses and counterdiscourses and actual traditional notions of historical narratives.

10. See, for example, Meinhardt and Payne (1978) on the establishment of treaty councils, which had some success in being recognized as official representations of Lakȟóta and other tribes.

11. I am writing this in the third month of the Russian war on Ukraine, and without trying to establish parallels between the two actual situations,

it strikes me that this war, too, is projected to be a conflict fought by a country (Russia) that has rejected modernity—democracy, rules of war, civilization—and is instead trying to force another country (Ukraine), which has chosen modernity, to renege on that choice. Such conflicts are not uncommon within the United States, either. The country has been in a conflict (the "culture wars") about modernity for at least thirty years (see, for example, Gribben 2021), and to pretend that this is not a discourse about American temporalities that is as of yet undetermined would be to deny reality.

12. I will always remember visiting the last truly fluent Yanktonai speaker in Cannonball with Doug and Ray. Doug was trying to finish his Yanktonai dictionary. The woman was very ill and passed away a few months later. The efforts of Douglas Parks have enabled communities on the northern plains to begin a restoration or conservation of languages, although they are nowhere near the 50 percent first-language speakers that Ducheneaux mentioned for Cheyenne River in 1956.

13. See, for example, the series of reports by Wagner reprinted in the *Congressional Record* in 1969 on request by Senator George McGovern.

References

Army, Navy Journal. 1888. Department News, Dept. of Dakota. *Army, Navy Journal* 25, no. 55 (August 11): 1095.

Braun, Sebastian F. 2008. *Buffalo Inc.: American Indians and Economic Development.* Norman: University of Oklahoma Press.

———. 2013a. "Against Procedural Landscapes: Community, Kinship, and History." In Braun 2013c, 201–21.

———. 2013b. "Introduction: An Ethnohistory of Listening." In Braun 2013c, 3–21.

———, ed. 2013c. *Transforming Ethnohistories: Narrative, Meaning, and Community.* Norman: University of Oklahoma Press.

Bray, Kingsley M. 2006. *Crazy Horse: A Lakota Life.* Norman: University of Oklahoma Press.

Brown, Dee. 1970. *Bury My Heart at Wounded Knee: An Indian History of the American West.* New York: Henry Holt.

Clow, Richmond L. 2019. *Spotted Tail: Warrior and Statesman.* Pierre: South Dakota Historical Society Press.

DeMallie, Raymond J. 1993. "'These Have No Ears': Narrative and the Ethnohistorical Method." *Ethnohistory* 40, no. 4: 515–38.

———. 2013. "Afterword. Thinking Ethnohistorically." In Braun 2013c, 233–53.

Drury, Bob, and Tom Clavin. 2014. *The Heart of Everything That Is: The Untold Story of Red Cloud, an American Legend*. New York: Simon and Schuster.

Ducheneaux, Frank. 1956. "The Cheyenne River Sioux." *American Indian* 7, no. 3: 20–30.

———. 1976. "The Indian Reorganization Act and the Cheyenne River Sioux." *American Indian Journal* 2, no. 8: 8–14.

Estes, Nick. 2019. *Our History Is the Future: Standing Rock versus the Dakota Access Pipeline and the Long Tradition of Indigenous Resistance*. London: Verso.

First Presbyterian Church. 2003. *An Experiment of Faith: The Journey of the Mdewakanton Dakota Who Settled on the Bend in the River. A Brief History of the Organization and Construction of the First Presbyterian Church Flandreau, South Dakota*. Flandreau SD: First Presbyterian Church.

Fogelson, Raymond D. 1989. "The Ethnohistory of Events and Nonevents." *Ethnohistory* 36, no. 2: 133–47.

Gage, Justin. 2020. *We Do Not Want the Gates Closed between Us: Native Networks and the Spread of the Ghost Dance*. Norman: University of Oklahoma Press.

Gribben, Crawford. 2021. *Survival and Resistance in Evangelical North America: Christian Reconstruction in the Pacific Northwest*. Oxford: Oxford University Press.

Hämäläinen, Pekka. 2019. *Lakota America: A New History of Indigenous Power*. New Haven CT: Yale University Press.

Hudson, Marilyn, and Sebastian Braun. 2013. "Boom! The Mandan, Hidatsa and Arikara People and Sustainability in the Face of Bakken Oil." *Community Connect: The Journal of Civic Voices* 6: 6–9.

Hyde, George E. 1961. *Spotted Tail's Folk: A History of the Brule Sioux*. Norman: University of Oklahoma Press.

Jensen, Richard E., ed. 2005. *Voices of the American West*. Vol. 1, *The Indian Interviews of Eli S. Ricker, 1903–1919*. Lincoln: University of Nebraska Press.

Kurkiala, Mikael. 1997. *"Building the Nation Back Up": The Politics of Identity on the Pine Ridge Indian Reservation*. Acta Universitatis Upsaliensis. Uppsala Studies in Cultural Anthropology 22. Uppsala, Sweden: Uppsala University.

———. 2002. "Objectifying the Past: Lakota Responses to Western Historiography." *Critique of Anthropology* 22, no. 4: 445–60.

Larson, Robert W. 2007. *Gall: Lakota War Chief*. Norman: University of Oklahoma Press.

Levi-Strauss, Claude. 1997. *Look, Listen, Read*. Translated by Brian C. J. Singer. New York: HarperCollins.

Lyons, Scott Richard. 2010. *X-marks: Native Signatures of Assent*. Minneapolis: University of Minnesota Press.

MacGregor, Gordon. 1946. *Warriors without Weapons: A Study of the Society and Personality Development of the Pine Ridge Sioux*. Chicago: University of Chicago Press.

Marshall, Joseph M., III. 2001. *The Lakota Way: Stories and Lessons for Living*. New York: Penguin Compass.

Meinhardt, Nick, and Diane Payne. 1978. "Reviewing the U.S. Treaty Commitments to the Lakota Nation." *American Indian Journal* 4, no. 1: 2–12.

Sharp, Henry. 2001. *Loon: Memory, Meaning, and Reality in a Northern Dene Community*. Lincoln: University of Nebraska Press.

Ssorin-Chaikov, Nikolai. 2017. *Two Lenins: A Brief Anthropology of Time*. Chicago: HAU Books.

Vestal, Stanley. 1989. *Sitting Bull: Champion of the Sioux*. Norman: University of Oklahoma Press.

Wagner, Bill. 1969. "'Anpo Wicharpi'—Teton Sioux See the Dawn of a New Day." *Congressional Record—Senate* 115, pt. 3 (February 17): 3466–78.

"Although He Had the Ways of a Woman, He Was a Great Warrior"   4

Kúsaat in Nineteenth-Century Pawnee and Arikara Society

MARK VAN DE LOGT

In 1904 White Sun, a Kitkehahki Pawnee, sat down with Pawnee ethnographer James Rolfe Murie to share an old tradition about a fine-looking but tragic young man. Although he did not care for women, one night a young female entered the young man's bed, and they had sex together. After intercourse the boy sent the girl home, got up, and washed himself in a nearby spring. Later that night Spider Woman appeared to him in a dream. She was displeased. She told the boy that because he had washed himself in her spring immediately after having sex with a woman, he, too, should be like a woman. The next day the boy felt sick. A Pawnee doctor who examined him discovered that he was transforming into a woman. To cure the boy his relatives had to collect green moss from the bottom of creeks, springs, or other streams of water. The boy's relatives searched everywhere, but Spider Woman had caused all the moss to disappear. When the boy heard that the doctor could not do anything for him, he was so ashamed that he committed suicide. He preferred death rather than be half woman and half man (Dorsey 1906, 138–39).

Only a year before White Sun told the story of the boy who committed suicide, Murie had recorded a very different tradition from Skiri Pawnee priest Roaming Scout. It also involved Spider Woman and a "half-man–half-woman." In this story a group of Pawnee fighters found themselves trapped on top of a hill. Enemy Indians had blocked off their escape and were patiently starving to death the Pawnee warriors. For days the men on the hill suffered from thirst. Some began to drink their own urine. Among the Pawnees was Táhipirus ("whip" or "dance whip"), a man "with the ways of a woman." He dressed like a woman, but he had a wife and was an accomplished warrior. When the situation became most desperate, Táhipirus had a vision of Spider Woman climbing down a rope hanging from the moon. Spider Woman showed Táhipirus how they could escape by tying a number of lariats together and descending from the steepest—and unguarded—side of the hill. Not only did the Pawnees escape that day, but they managed to capture many enemy horses as well. Ever since, this hill—which is located in present-day Kansas—has been known as "Pawnee Rock." The story of this event has been passed down over the generations and remains one of the most popular Pawnee war stories to this day (Dorsey 1904, 199–203).

Both the boy who turned into a woman and Táhipirus are examples of Pawnee *kúsaat*: people who did not fit binary gender categories and heterosexual orientations. They included a whole range of identities and sexualities beyond those that we today call gay, lesbian, bisexual, two-spirit, transgender, queer, and so forth. The Pawnees grouped all of these alternative genders and sexualities together in a single category: *kúsaat*, "men with the 'minds' of women," or *ckúsaat*, "women with the 'minds' of men." This chapter deals primarily with kúsaat.

Although the Pawnees generally respected kúsaat, sometimes these individuals met with fear and rejection. The above stories illustrate these contradicting attitudes among the Pawnees. This chapter seeks to explain the contradiction.

Some scholars have suggested that present-day negative attitudes (including homophobia, transphobia, and other forms of discrimination) toward nonbinary individuals among Native Americans were the result of colonization, Christianization, and assimilationist policies aimed at eradicating Native cultural expressions. They take a rather romanticized view of Native American societies that idealizes past attitudes toward such individuals (Williams 1992; Gilley 2006; Jolivette 2016; Smithers 2022). However, the ethnohistorical record suggests that negative attitudes antedated colonization. Pawnee oral traditions and ethnohistorical sources indicate that degrees of prejudice existed before missionaries and other agents of colonization set out to transform the Pawnee people. If so, colonization, Christianization, and assimilation may have merely intensified existing prejudices.

This chapter argues that the ambiguous position of kúsaat in nineteenth-century Pawnee society depended on the context in which the behavior of such individuals was viewed. Because the Pawnees believed that kúsaat were under the influence of some mysterious supernatural power (usually Moon and her alternative manifestation as Spider Woman), they were both feared and respected. When kúsaat displayed exemplary behavior and used their spiritual powers for the common good, they earned the appreciation of the community even though they challenged Pawnee ideals of masculinity. In such cases they were valued for working hard as gardeners and domestic workers, their success as doctors, their skills at arts and crafts, and so on. They were especially valued if they went to war and performed bravely in battle. Indeed, such kúsaat could achieve high social status. However, when kúsaat displayed personal flaws or weaknesses, such as greed, selfishness, immodesty, or cowardice, their behavior met with disapproval. In short, it was not necessarily their sexuality or gender identity that Pawnee people judged, but rather their observance—or lack thereof—of Pawnee values. Incidentally, the Pawnees judged all individuals, whether kúsaat or not, in a similar manner.

Much of this article is based on oral traditions as well as previously unpublished documents. However, because kúsaat are rarely mentioned in Pawnee ethnohistorical sources, this paper also uses data from the closely related Arikara Indians. The Arikaras and Pawnees share a common ancestry and culture despite separating from each other in the sixteenth century. Cultural and linguistic differences between the two are minimal, thus allowing for cross-cultural references.

The ambiguous status of two-spirit people was not limited to Pawnee society. Raymond J. DeMallie discovered that life was rarely happy for so-called *wiŋktés* among the Lakȟóta. According to DeMallie, there never were many wiŋktés, and one individual even committed suicide by hanging. In fact, DeMallie observes, although homosexual relationships were recognized, people also disapproved of them. Young men were told to stay away from wiŋkté men: "For the Lakota boy, fear of becoming winkte was the ultimate incentive to make him strive to be manly." Yet, at the same time, wiŋktés were considered to be *wakháŋ* ("holy" or "mysterious"), respected for their skills in arts and crafts, and sometimes brought along for luck during war expeditions (DeMallie 1983, 244, 247; see also Deloria 2022, 382–85, endnote 3).

"He Has a Vulva for an Anus": Problems of Definition and Explanation

The Pawnees and Arikaras made clear gender distinctions between males and females. According to Skiri Pawnee cosmology, this order was established at the beginning of creation when the universe was divided into male and female camps. These two groups were brought together by cosmic warrior-chiefs Morning Star and Sun, who overcame a series of challenges to prove their worthiness as partners to the leading female beings, Evening Star and Moon. Out of the union of these celestial powers originated the first humans who were placed on earth. Here history repeated itself: men and women occupied different camps until they were united in a story similar to that of Morning Star and Evening Star.

Although the Pawnees and Arikaras strongly adhered to this binary gender arrangement, there were people who did not fit these categories. The terms "ckúsaat" and "kúsaat" covered a wide range of alternative genders (including agender, androgyne, bigender, butch, gender-fluid, transgender, two-spirit, queer, intersexual) as well as alternative sexual orientations (including gay, lesbian, bisexual, and asexual). The closely related Arikaras had identical categories. The female Arikara form was *skUxát*. The male Arikara form was not recorded, but it almost certainly was *kUxát*, because the prefix *s-* was usually added to the male word to make it female.[1]

During the nineteenth century, non-Indians used several terms for ckúsaat or kúsaat that today are considered inaccurate and offensive, including "hermaphrodite" and "berdache" (Jacobs, Thomas, and Lang 1997, 21–43; Smithers 2022, 20–32). Currently the term "two-spirit" is sometimes used as a blanket term to describe nonbinary

Native Americans. This term, too, is problematic because it incorrectly implies that these people represented two spirits at the same time. Some Native people object to the term because they associate spirits with ghosts. More recently the term applies only to those nonbinary individuals who cherish a (sometimes idealized and romanticized) link to their Native culture. The problems of terminology have become a bit of a political and cultural minefield. For present purposes, therefore, this chapter prefers to use the Pawnee and Arikara words "ckúsaat"/"kúsaat" and "skUxát"/"kUxát" whenever possible (Jacobs, Thomas, and Lang 1997; Gilley 2006).

When Pawnee scholar James R. Murie recorded the term "kúsaat" around 1900, he translated it as someone who "has a vulva for an anus" (Dorsey and Murie 1907). When linguist Douglas Parks compiled his Pawnee and Arikara lexicons in the late 1960s and early 1970s, his Pawnee collaborators indicated that the term "kúsaat" not only meant "homosexual" or "transvestite" but could also mean "sissy," "good-for-nothing male with low morals," or "coward."[2] This fact introduces the scholar to the problem of ambiguous attitudes toward kúsaat. Pawnee (and Arikara) sources imply both tolerance and respect for kúsaat while at other times such individuals were viewed negatively. Despite claims that the negative definitions are of recent origin, ethnohistorical sources imply that nineteenth-century Pawnee attitudes were ambiguous. How can one explain this ambiguity?

It is tempting to view prejudices toward kúsaat as resulting strictly from white influences during the reservation era, when missionaries and other agents of Euro-American civilization introduced prejudice and homophobia among reservation Indians. For example, Randy Burns argued that present-day American Indian homophobia is the result of the "efforts of Indian agents, missionaries, and boarding schools to suppress all forms of traditional Indian culture" (Burns in Roscoe 1988, 3). Roger M. Carpenter concluded that by the beginning of the twentieth century "Christian missionaries and government educators had achieved a great deal of success in imposing European notions of gender on native societies" (Carpenter 2011, 161). Gregory D. Smithers writes that two-spirit people were an essential part of the "social fabric of sovereign tribal nations before colonizers invaded and tried to destroy them" (Smithers 2022, xviii). Because linguists did not systematically study the Pawnee and Arikara language until the 1930s, the negative meanings of the Pawnee and Arikara words mentioned above may actually reflect this change toward kúsaat-phobia. While possible, this observation ignores the fact that oral traditions usually stretch back deeper into the past. It would be too simplistic to blame prejudice and homophobia exclusively on European colonization. In fact, it is possible that assimilation policies merely *reinforced* already existing prejudices among the Pawnees and Arikaras.

Another theory is that kúsaat, especially, violated Pawnee gender ideals. Heteronormative gender and sexual divisions, according to this theory, intensified as a result of the militarization of Great Plains societies following the influx of mostly nomadic nations in the seventeenth and eighteenth centuries (Midnight Sun in Roscoe 1988, 32–47). As warfare became more common and intense—taking on internecine and even genocidal features—the emphasis on males as warriors reached new heights. With male kúsaat, the tribe potentially lost fighting power that was not replaced by reproductive power. Because warfare was so prevalent in the nineteenth century, especially after the arrival of the Lakȟóta and Cheyennes on the plains, the Pawnees and Arikaras prepared their sons for their future life as hunters and warriors: cowardice was unacceptable. Men were only allowed to avoid battle if they had had a vision or dream predicting misfortune. Cowardice, however, affected not only the individual but also reflected poorly on his entire family. Thus, for a man to be labeled a "woman" or kúsaat was one of the gravest insults other Pawnees and Arikaras could heap on a man. However, as the example of Táhipirus shows, some kúsaat distinguished themselves in war.

A third explanation is that kúsaat were feared because they were under the influence of a mysterious sacred power. The Pawnees and Arikaras spent much time searching for and acquiring spiritual power through vision quests, inheritance, or apprenticeships. Sacred power allowed individuals to become successful doctors, hunters, warriors, and craftsmen or to be successful at a whole range of activities.

However, these sacred powers were sometimes mistrusted because they could also be used for evil. Thus, whereas doctors were appreciated for their power to cure, they were feared for their potential ability to bewitch and injure people as well. Of a different order here were the "scalped people" (*kicahúruksu'* in Pawnee or *tshunúxu'* in Arikara). These were people who had "died" (possibly lost consciousness) in battle, had been mutilated by their enemies, but who then were brought back to "life" by some animal or other power. These individuals were no longer considered human but rather seen as spirits who could no longer live among the people. They were forced to live a lonely existence far removed from loved ones because they were feared for the mysterious and potentially dangerous power they now possessed. In some cases the Pawnees and Arikaras even killed such people when they were discovered (van de Logt 2008).

Though they were not witches or scalped men, kúsaat were imbued with spiritual or mysterious power (*waaruksti* in Pawnee) and, consequently, were potentially dangerous. Here, quite literally, the negative view was driven by phobia. But it was not so much fear of the individual as such, but for the potentially harmful power that he or she possessed.

This chapter, however, argues that Pawnee views of kúsaat referred not to the nature of these people but to whether they contributed to Pawnee society within their roles as kúsaat. In short, acceptance or rejection depended on context. Like everyone else, the Pawnees expected kúsaat to develop a skill and work hard, be generous, and be a productive member of society. Thus, being kúsaat was not a reason for rejection and disapproval, but violations of the tribal moral codes were. Greed, selfishness, promiscuity, unrestrained behavior, self-gratifying lust, cowardice, and any other "deviant" behavior were the real standards by which people (kúsaat and non-kúsaat alike) were judged.

Conflicting Sources

References to kúsaat are rare in the ethnographic literature. This might already be an indication that binary gender and sexual roles were the ideal. Research on this issue is further hampered by the social and political context of the time in which early ethnographers did their work. In many cases sociocultural circumstances affected scientific objectivity. Both John Brown Dunbar, the son of a Presbyterian missionary to the Pawnees, and James Murie, the son of a white man and a Skiri Pawnee woman, maintained a nineteenth-century Victorian-era aversion toward this topic. In contrast, later scholars such as Gene Weltfish viewed human sexuality in its many variations more favorably and called for society's acceptance of nonbinary people. Indeed, as discussed below, Weltfish may have somewhat idealized the position of kúsaat in Pawnee society.

The bonds of male friendship, brotherhood, and affection were often forged on the warpath. John Brown Dunbar, who had lived among the Pawnees as a child, recorded the words to a Pawnee song that showed the intensity of such friendships:

> They two who are traveling. (repeat six times)
> They two who are traveling with each other.
> A young woman is said to have queried
> "I wonder if they two are [always] true to each other?"
> They two who are traveling with each other. (Dunbar 1882, 747)

The song was inspired by a young woman who noticed two young men who were "inseparable" while traveling, hunting, and war. It is uncertain whether these friendships indicated more than a platonic friendship, but James Murie, the aforementioned Skiri Pawnee who conducted fieldwork for ethnologist George Amos Dorsey between 1900 and 1924, specified that these bonds were not of a homosexual nature, but merely forms of brotherhood forged during perilous war and hunting expeditions. "Many Skiri tales bear witness to an unusual form of friendship which often bound two young men or two young women together for life," Murie wrote, "In such an attachment it was said *sirawari*, 'they go together.'" Although these individuals shared joy, grief, and rights, such friendships "never extended to each other's wives" (Dorsey and Murie 1907, n.p.).

Roaming Scout, a Skiri Pawnee priest who was Murie's most important source of ethnographic information, provided Murie with a more detailed description of a kúsaat: "According to my informant only one berdache has been known among the Pawnee for many years, although he has heard of others. Such an individual, known as *ckusat* ('has a vulva for an anus'), was said to have the ways of a woman. He was supposed to have been influenced by Moon, directly or through the intervention of a witch or some other evil spirit acting through a deer or some other animal" (Dorsey and Murie 1907, n.p.; 1940, 108).

In his unpublished autobiography, Mark Evarts (ca. 1861–1938), Gene Weltfish's Pawnee collaborator, mentioned the presence of an Omaha "woman" who was out hunting buffalo with the Pawnees. The presence of this kúsaat did not surprise Evarts, even though he did think that it was worthy of mention: "On my way I met an Omaha woman. She used to be like a man, she had a white handkerchief tied around her head, and she had a rifle on her shoulder. She said, my boy where's the buffalo[?] I just pointed back to the place I was coming from" (Evarts n.d, n.p.).

Anthropologist Gene Weltfish, who wrote the classic study of Pawnee culture based on her fieldwork conducted in the 1930s, concluded that Pawnee attitudes toward kúsaat were remarkably tolerant. "Although homosexuals or lesbians were rare," Weltfish wrote, "these relationships were not regarded as a serious social anomaly but as a personal inclination which the Pawnee thought people had a right to have" (Weltfish 1971, 37). Weltfish based her findings mostly on information furnished by Mark Evarts, but Weltfish's own social and political outlooks probably affected her perspective as well.

In contrast, Garland Blaine (1915–79), a Pawnee who had been raised by deeply traditional grandparents, argued that the Pawnees believed "that no same-sex physical attraction should exist": "Although homosexuality was accepted as normal behavior by some tribes, to Garland Blaine's knowledge Pawnees discouraged it. In one family, a man [who was] told of his brother's homosexuality threatened to kill him [his brother] but was persuaded not to do so. Although this might not have been a universal reaction, other present-day examples of negative Pawnee attitudes toward it are known" (Blaine 1997, 136, 250).

It is possible that the attitudes recorded by Weltfish and Blaine reflect twentieth-century sensibilities rather than nineteenth-century ones. Weltfish was deeply committed to the ideal of human equality and rights for women and minority populations. Blaine, meanwhile, was raised in Oklahoma in a time when agents of civilization had already brought about many changes in Pawnee culture.

Still, like Blaine, contemporary Pawnee historian Roger Echo-Hawk believes that prejudices existed against kúsaat among pre-Christian Pawnees. In the third book of his series, *The Enchanted Mirror*, Echo-Hawk relates the story of a nineteenth-century encounter between a kúsaat and a heterosexual man that at first glance indicates a negative attitude:

> In 1986 one of my relatives told me a story handed down from a Kitkahahki named Frank Young Eagle. When Frank was a boy, he sat listening with others as a Pawnee Scout veteran spoke about the exploits of the Scouts. As a former Scout named Tom Walking Sun approached, the man fell silent. Walking Sun urged him to continue, so the man said, "Okay."
>
> He pointed at Walking Sun, "I hate this man here. Because one time when we were out scouting, Walking Sun rode up. As is normal for military life, he offered to put his blanket with mine so we could both keep warm in the cold night. That night as we were sleeping, I awoke. I had my back to Walking Sun, and I felt his hand trying to move my g-string to one side!" This story reproved Walking Sun primarily for indulging a rather rude presumption, but it is difficult to discern anything like relaxed toleration of homosexuality. (Echo-Hawk 2018, 213–14, and email communication, July 31, 2023)

Thus, twentieth-century scholars provide conflicting viewpoints on the position of kúsaat in Pawnee society. Perhaps we should first understand Pawnee gender concepts before tackling the ambiguous views of kúsaat.

Male Gender Roles in Pawnee and Arikara Society

Roaming Scout, a Skiri Pawnee priest who provided invaluable information on Skiri Pawnee culture, explained that gender roles were dictated by "the Heavens." Men and women fulfilled different socioeconomic roles because the creator thought it was good: "Now, brother, I am going to tell you what he planned for our tribe while it was living here on earth—about the ways that the women had. When the Heavens gave them their ways, the things that the women did were good. I am going to tell you about them. Our Father above did not intend that men among us should work the way they do among your people, but that is the way He gave to women" (Murie n.d.).

Male and female gender roles, then, were sanctioned by the sacred powers. Although each was different, there was no inferior or superior role for men and women. Instead, they complemented each other (for a similar code among the Lakȟóta, see also DeMallie 1983, 238–40; Andersson and Posthumus 2022).

Women and men performed different tasks in society. Women's tasks were often associated with the forces of life: they gave birth to children, acted as midwives, raised crops that sustained the people, and owned and kept the house. Men, in contrast, sometimes had to cross into the terrain of death. Men killed animals for food and, to protect their people, might at some point be called upon to kill enemies or sacrifice their own lives in defense of the people. Arikara women were taught from childhood that they should honor a husband "because he will suffer so much for you. He must fight to defend the home and the fields, and he will very likely die in battle," an Arikara informant told Reverend Aaron McGaffey Beede (Beede 1915, 185–86). For the Pawnees, the birth of a boy was welcomed with joy but also sadness. Effie Blaine recalled her father saying:

> For a man life is not a happy thing. When a man is born and they say it's a boy, everyone says regretfully that it would have been better had it been a girl. For it is the proper destiny of men that they should go out on the warpath and be killed. It is a bitter thought that this child will some day have to lie dead on the open plain. My father would say that these old men spoke bitterly about life. They would say, "For those of us that are men it is unworthy to be buried in a regular grave. It is far better to lie in the open and be eaten by the birds." (Weltfish 1937, 18)

One must not apply these binary gender roles too rigidly. In reality these roles were flexible. Women could be warriors and doctors (although they never seemed to have been priests), and there were some esteemed female doctors among the Pawnees and Arikaras in the nineteenth century. A few women even distinguished themselves in battle, and it is said that in the nineteenth century, the Sioux actually feared Arikara women (Beede 1915, 185–86). Husbands frequently helped their spouses in clearing and maintaining the garden and in doing household chores. Men, in fact, maintained gardens of their own albeit to grow the tobacco that they used for ceremonial purposes. And if necessary, a woman might take up a weapon to defend her family and loved ones in case of an attack.

Still, although a woman might show her bravery in battle and a man might show his talents as a gardener or cook, each was still valued first for the qualities associated with their gender. Thus, a woman was valued first for her qualities as a worker, her spirituality, and as a guardian of her chastity, while a man was judged primarily for qualities such as bravery, generosity, and spiritual power. Both genders fulfilled important, but very different, roles.

These ethics were instilled in children from an early age. "You were told that when you grew up, a boy will be a man and a girl will be a woman," said Garland Blaine, a Pawnee (Blaine 1997, 136). In the 1920s Melvin R. Gilmore's Arikara informant explained that "[a] boy prayed that he might grow up to be a brave, generous, useful and honorable man [while] girls prayed to grow into kind, quiet, hospitable and useful women." In addition, children of each gender were taught "reverence, respect for wisdom and age, deference to old persons, helpfulness to the needy, the sick and afflicted, [and] kindness to all" (Gilmore n.d., n.p.).

"Mother Moon"

Men and women did not choose to become ckúsaat and kúsaat. It was not, as anthropologist Ruth Benedict once incorrectly suggested, a "life-style choice" for certain males to avoid the demanding life of men (Medicine 1983, 268). The Pawnees believed that ckúsaat and kúsaat were simply under the influence of one of the sacred powers. According to Roaming Scout, it was "Mother Moon" who was responsible for giving some men the "minds" of women and some women the "minds" of men:

> And, brother, this story I am telling about the women—this story that I am telling about the women—this Moon is the source of these ways for a woman after the Heavens created her—after woman was created.
>
> And right there She [Mother Moon] made the way for some men—right there she made the way for some men when She thought, "Let this man who is living—let me make you a berdache—and yet he is a man."
>
> Brother, long ago it was that way. There would be a male among the people who had a woman's ways and he would grow up. Sometimes after She made a man that way, so that he would act that way, She gave him power so that he would not be poor. He was given the power to be successful as a warrior and yet he was a man who acted like a woman. And this Moon—this Moon was the cause of it, brother, when she put the mind of a woman in this man! Let me put the mind of a woman in him even though he is a man! (Murie n.d.)

As Roaming Scout pointed out, supernatural forces caused the sexual and behavioral orientation of some men and women. Roaming Scout also implied that the Pawnees did not shun these people but viewed them as equals who were fully accepted into society. Still, Roaming Scout's views may not represent those of all Pawnees at the time. Just as there are many expressions of sexuality, there may be just as many different opinions and sentiments (both positive, negative, or indifferent) about them. Pawnee attitudes varied (Echo-Hawk, personal communication, July 31, 2013).

So, what were Pawnee (and Arikara) attitudes toward kúsaat and opinions about other genders? The ethnohistorical record, especially Pawnee oral tradition, provides some insights. Most of these stories were collected by Pawnee interpreter James R. Murie and published by anthropologist George A. Dorsey. It is to these sources that we turn our attention to now.

Kúsaat in Oral Traditions

The story at the beginning of this chapter, of the boy who committed suicide ("The Hermaphrodite"), does not clarify whether he physically turned into a woman with the mind and heart of a man, or if he turned into an actual hermaphrodite with both male and female genitalia, or if he remained a man physiologically but with the "mind" of a woman (Dorsey 1906, 138–39). Although the story sounds quite Victorian with its emphasis on guilt and shame, it is unlikely that the boy felt guilty about having illicit sex or because of a latent homosexual orientation (after all, the boy displayed no interest in women before this incident). If the story was indeed "Victorian," it would support the theory that prejudices were introduced by Europeans. But the story does not provide any clues as to when the events happened.

Rather than Victorian sexual shame, and more in line with Pawnee culture, the boy likely felt ashamed for having offended a sacred power. His transformation was punishment for the violation of a taboo. Indeed, Dorsey's footnote that accompanies the story clarifies the nature of the taboo violation: "The teaching of the story is the warning given to young men not to bathe in springs after sexual intercourse—that is, while unclean. Not only must this be done for the good of the tribe, but also because spider-woman [who created such springs], must be treated with a certain amount of respect" (Dorsey 1906, 139).

Another oral tradition, recorded around 1901, tells of another boy who was "cured" from "womanish" ways. The story, titled "Scabby-Bull, the Wonderful Medicine Man," was told by Wonderful-Sun, a Skiri Pawnee, and published by George Dorsey in 1904. The hero of the story is Scabby-Bull, who was lured into the animal lodge of Pahuk and there obtained power from the deer that enabled him to cure people and perform sleight-of-hand tricks in the medicine lodge ceremony. One day Scabby-Bull was called to cure a boy with feminine ways:

> There was one family where a child had been born, and the child was an idiot when it was born. The people called him "Half-Man-and-Half-Woman," and he acted that way as he grew up. About this time he was ten years old. The parents of the boy, on hearing of the wonders of

Scabby-Bull, sent for him, promising him many presents of robes, leggings, buckskin shirts, and several ponies, if he would cure the boy. The boy, as he grew up, was getting to be like a woman. Scabby-Bull, with Warrior [his friend], went to the lodge of this young man. They placed their medicines on the west side of the fireplace in the lodge, and sat down. They placed the boy on the east side of the fireplace, facing west, where Scabby-Bull and Warrior were sitting. Scabby-Bull told the people to sweep out the lodge and then to leave it. Scabby-Bull and Warrior stayed in the lodge with the boy, and at night, when the man was out, Scabby-Bull and Warrior sang some deer songs. They danced and hopped around in the lodge, so that the boy was soon imitating them. The boy followed Scabby-Bull and Warrior out of the lodge, and they circled around in an open space, and when they entered the lodge again, this young man had many white spots upon his back, with a background of black, all together representing a fawn skin, and also the heavens. These marks upon the young man were to show Scabby-Bull that the deer and the moon had left him and the womanish feelings had gone out of the boy. (It seems that Scabby-Bull had power through the deer, which, it seems, was under the influence of the moon, and thus Scabby-Bull helped the boy.) Now Scabby-Bull, Warrior, and the boy, after entering the lodge, sat down, Scabby-Bull and Warrior singing deer songs all night, while the boy sat by them.

As the sun was about to appear in the east, Scabby-Bull sang one of his deer songs about the sun, at the same time telling the young man now to walk out of the entrance of the earth lodge, and stand facing the east, and look at the sun as it should come up. When the sun was high, Scabby-Bull called the boy into the lodge again, seating him in the west by himself. Scabby-Bull looked upon the forehead of the boy, and there he saw a picture of one half of the sun, which was done by a ray from the sun touching upon his forehead. Scabby-Bull was glad of this, for he knew that his powers had worked, but that the sun had not yet given the boy a man's feeling, for only a part of the sun was pictured upon his forehead. Scabby-Bull had now done with the boy. He sent for the boy's relatives and they came in. They saw the paintings on the boy's forehead and upon his back. Scabby-Bull told them that the boy would never be made entirely well, but that the process of becoming a woman had been checked. The boy was now told to go out of the lodge and to play. The decorations on his back and on his forehead were to remain until the paint itself came off. (Dorsey 1904, 237–38)

The story allows us to draw a few important conclusions. First, deer (and elk) had the power of transformation. They derived this power from Moon. Although Moon determined the sexual and gender orientation of an individual, the story makes clear that this orientation could be manipulated through the intercession by the deer or a doctor with deer power. In fact, there are many Pawnee stories in which deer women transformed men into deer. However, in none of these stories did deer turn men into women.

Second, the role of Sun in the process of transformation is significant. In Skiri Pawnee theology, Sun was a male. He was the warrior who accompanied Morning Star on his epic journey across the sky to the village of the female stars. Sun eventually married Moon, whereas Morning Star married Evening Star. An interesting detail is that whereas Morning Star and Evening Star's child was female, Sun's child was male. The timing of the "curing" ceremony is also significant. Scabby-Bull and Warrior performed their rite during the night (when Moon is visible in the sky), but it ended at sunrise, when Sun dominates the sky. In short, the ceremony itself symbolizes this transformation, or rather "rebirth," of the child into a man.

Third, despite Scabby-Bull's success in "curing" the boy, the transformation was not quite complete. The child remained different (the text says "awkward"). Unfortunately, we do not know what this means exactly.

Finally, the story also reveals that Scabby-Bull lived during the reservation era, because white people interfered at the end of the story. When Scabby-Bull died from what appears to be tuberculosis, his brothers believed a jealous medicine man—a witch—had caused his death. In Pawnee society this amounted to murder, and in line with Pawnee custom, Scabby Bull's brothers planned their revenge, probably to execute the suspected murderer. "The other medicine man was not killed," the story concludes, "for the white people told the chiefs that the disease of which Scabby-Bull died was lung trouble" (Dorsey 1904, 238).

This last observation might be important because it does show that white people were influencing Pawnee behavior at this time. If these white people prevented Scabby-Bull's brother from seeking revenge against the jealous medicine man, perhaps they were also the driving forces behind the anti-kúsaat prejudices that caused the boy's parents to seek Scabby-Bull's services in the first place.

In both stories, the transformation from male into female almost seemed punishment in the eyes of the Pawnees. In another story, "The Chief's Son Who Received the Animal Power," told by White-Sun, it was a witch who transformed a boy into a woman. The story is significant for two reasons. First, the process of transformation from male into female was blocked by the animal powers. Second, the witch, who was attracted to the boy (he was, in other words, unable to control his own sexual desires), was executed for using poisonous magic. Because the story is too long to be included here, a synopsis will have to suffice.

The chief's son was a handsome and kind young man. The witch became very fond of the boy and suggested that they should travel together to the sacred Pawnee site of Pahuk. During the journey the boy became pregnant. At Pahuk the witch told the boy that they should collect some eagle and woodpecker feathers. He tied a lariat around the boy's waist and suspended him from a steep bank to gather the feathers. Once the boy was thus suspended helplessly, the witch ran away so that the boy would die. Fortunately, the animals from the sacred animal lodge took pity upon the boy because he had been bewitched. The Elk and Buffalo jumped over the boy and ended up with blood in their mouths. The Bear used one of his claws to open the boy's belly and removed the bones of the child. He threw the bones away and then healed the boy's wound. The Snake gave the boy a different kind of bone with which he could kill his enemies. The Buffalo gave him a whistle so that he could call the animal powers if he ever was in trouble. The Bear gave him paint with which he could cure people. The Eagles taught him how to fly, and the Ducks taught him how to swim and dive. And so, each animal gave the boy power. Meanwhile, Crow, Beaver, Otter, and Hawk were sent out into the cardinal directions in search of food for the boy. Then one of the animals spoke: "We know what the man did to you. He tried to poison you. He tried to make you like a woman. We have taught you great mysteries. If you desire, you can bewitch him" (Dorsey 1906, 313; see also Elledge 2002, 125–27).

With the help of Owl, Buffalo, and two Crows, the boy returned home. Everyone was happy to see him again. Then one day the boy invited the witch to his home and suggested that they should go to the river for a swim. The boy jumped in. The man followed him, but as soon as he touched the water he was pulled down. He disappeared and was never seen again. When the boy came up, he explained to the people that the man he had killed was a witch and that they would not be bothered by the witch ever again.

Although the story implies that the animal spirits drowned the witch, it seems more likely that the animals gave the boy the power with which to kill the man who had made him pregnant and had left him to die. The undertone of the story is obvious: the witch was attracted to the boy and lured him away; then he impregnated him and had left him to die; therefore, the boy was justified in killing the witch. In short, the witch epitomized immorality as defined by the Pawnees: licentious sex, disloyalty, and attempted murder of the boy, as well as, incidentally, his own offspring.

"Although the Leading Man Had the Ways of a Woman, He Was a Great Warrior"

Whereas the kúsaat described above were shunned or considered to be social "misfits" (in the minds of Pawnee audiences), there are also stories in which they appear as heroes. In fact, Roaming Scout mentions men with the "minds" of women who were highly respected if they went to war:

> And the one who was really a man—that one, brother—the kind of man who was made to act like a woman—he would also go out on the warpath and sometimes he would get married. And he was a man, and he would get

married. And here Moon would think meanwhile, "Go off on the warpath!"

I saw ones who were girls, who seemed they were really girls, and here they would in fact be boys. When one was still immature—what we call a young woman [a girl approximately eight to fifteen years of age]—and here he would be a boy and I thought, "You must be a girl." (Murie n.d.)

One of these kúsaat who earned high honors among the Pawnee people was the aforementioned Táhipirus ("whip" or "dance whip"). Interestingly, Táhipirus wore the dress and had the manners of a woman, but he was nonetheless married to a woman. The story, titled "The Moon Medicine," was told by Roaming Scout. In the story Táhipirus was still a boy when he fell into a trance while playing out on the prairie. When his friends found him, they saw two black streaks running down from the corners of his mouth. The boys took him to a Pawnee doctor, who concluded that the boy was under the influence of Moon and that he would have mysterious powers. After the boy regained consciousness, "he always acted like a woman and had womanish ways." Although he became a warrior who led many successful war parties, his womanly ways grew stronger (Dorsey 1904, 199–203).

One of Táhipirus's greatest feats, the escape from Pawnee Rock, was already described at the beginning of this chapter. After this event, Táhipirus became famous for his powers with ropes. During one performance in the medicine lodge ceremony, he was tied up and hung over a blazing fire. When he was let down from the rope, he had the mysterious black streaks coming from the corners of his mouth again, and "a black stream of fluid began to pour from his mouth," but he was unharmed. The markings around his mouth were physical manifestations of the power he had received from Moon. This was only one of many mysterious acts of this man (Dorsey 1904, 199–203).

While doing research in Oklahoma in the mid-1930s, Gene Weltfish also recorded information on Táhipirus. In her research notes Weltfish wrote:

> Ben White's father, At-sa-wi, acted like a woman and talked like it, tried to embrace men, some were afraid of it, some not. Long ago was a man

of Skiri like that, was a warrior and leader, had Buffalo ways, a Ta-hi-pi-rus, he talked like a woman in voice, ways like woman, fixed moccasins, he had a woman as wife, this man died great. The way he acted was through the moon or the spider. Cheyenne and Arapaho were attacking, old man and others sat high up on a rock. several days, there was only one way on North they could go through, but still they got down (maybe because old man was "Spider" power) and finally he tied a rope to a rock then they were marooned there several days and then they decided to escape. He told the others to dress up as they did for buffalo dance at home (about 5 of them) they went thru the performance as the Moon came up from East, they began to sing: "Now we're going to try to get down." The moon was coming and about midnight there was a shadow over the North side, he tied all the ropes together to the rock. He tried it himself first, then came back up. They [sic] one got down and shook rope, then next, then next, then he himself Each stood close to rock so they wouldn't see their shadows. Then they went between the 2 enemy camps, each took a little drink. There were a lot of horse, 6 or 7 went who were brave. He went with others West, and all got away home before they were discovered. (Weltfish 1935, n.p.)

Weltfish's sources provided us with important insights. First, some Pawnee men were "afraid" of transsexual men such as Ben White's father, At-sa-wi, while others were not. This did not necessarily indicate homophobia—or rather transphobia—but may have instead reflected the Pawnee attitude that any kind of supernatural power was potentially dangerous and, thus, was treated with respect . . . or suspicion.

Second, Táhipirus may have been under the influence of as many as three powers: Moon, Buffalo, and possibly Spider. In fact, Weltfish speculates that it was this Spider power that enabled Táhipirus and his followers to escape by a rope. Third, although he dressed, talked, and acted like a woman, he was nevertheless married to a woman. This implies that even though his gender orientation was female, his sexual orientation was heterosexual.

Finally, Táhipirus was not only a warrior but a war *leader*. He accompanied many war parties and on this one occasion saved all from death.

His prowess as a warrior not only allowed him to live in relative luxury but also afforded him great social status.

But was it his military success that separated Táhipirus from the despised kúsaat in the other stories? Or was it the fact that his sexual orientation was heterosexual? After all, he seems to have been happily married to a woman. Or was the different attitude caused by the way he became a kúsaat? Unfortunately, it is impossible to answer these questions with certainty, but the fact that he was courageous and successful in war certainly helped his reputation.

Conclusion

Although the ethnohistorical record provides only fragmentary insights into the issue of Pawnee ideas about sexuality and gender, I attempt to draw some (admittedly tenuous) conclusions. The Pawnees recognized a range of different genders and sexualities that they included under a collective term, *(c)kúsaat* in Pawnee. These ckúsaat and kúsaat had been created under the influence of some mysterious power, usually Moon, but sometimes by other powers as well. The Pawnees did not consider the nature of (c)kúsaat shameful. Indeed, as the example of Táhipirus shows, some ckúsaat and kúsaat were held in high esteem and respected for their mysterious powers if these were used for the general welfare.

Still, the sources also indicate a certain unease with (c)kúsaat. The argument that this unease was the result of Euro-American influences during the reservation era is not entirely persuasive when applied to the Pawnee bands. Undoubtedly, the reservation era witnessed the intensification of prejudices in Pawnee communities. Indeed, during the reservation era, Roaming Scout observed a noticeable "decline" in the number of ckúsaat and kúsaat among the Pawnees, which may have been the direct result of the activities of white agents. "What Moon did, brother—this way that I am telling you about—no longer occurs among us. This that I am talking about. There are no berdaches among us anymore, and there are no women who have the ways of a man among us anymore, but I only saw them further back. I am referring to the place there (in Nebraska) where we used to live. These ways must have ended when all of the ways that the Heavens made for our tribe passed away" (Murie n.d.).

Still, to attribute Native prejudices toward ckúsaat and kúsaat exclusively to missionaries and Indian agents may be incorrect. Current streaks of homophobia in Pawnee communities today may have antecedents in pre-reservation history and culture. Although many of the sources used in this article were recorded during the reservation era, they often referred to a time before agents of civilization did their destructive work. As Pawnee oral traditions imply, the position of (c)kúsaat was already ambiguous before agents of white civilization arrived among the Pawnees and Arikaras.

It appears that the Pawnees and Arikaras did not object to the existence of ckúsaat and kúsaat as such, but they did judge individuals on how they composed themselves in daily life. Just like men and women were judged not for their gender but on how they behaved within those roles, so did the Pawnees judge (c)kúsaat. Thus, when ckúsaat or kúsaat made positive contributions to Pawnee society, they were well-respected if not valued. However, when a kúsaat in particular did not live up to Pawnee ideals (industry, modesty, chastity, etc.) and was lazy, gossipy, or promiscuous, he was considered a deviant. Similarly, kúsaat such as Táhipirus, who displayed bravery in war, were respected. However, because kúsaat possessed powers that could be used for selfish and evil purposes, they were often viewed with suspicion, perhaps even fear, by other people.

Notes

Acknowledgments: This chapter honors the work of my mentors Raymond J. DeMallie and Douglas R. Parks. Ray wrote an influential article on gender, including *wiŋkté* identity, among the Lakȟóta, and I am indebted to Doug for his invaluable work recording and transcribing Pawnee and Arikara oral traditions. In their personal lives Ray and Doug experienced many of the ambiguities and contradictions faced by the kúsaat described in this chapter.

1. For a prototype online dictionary of Pawnee (Skiri and South Band) and Arikara compiled by Douglas R. Parks of Indiana University, see American

Indian Studies Research Projects, AISRI Dictionary Portal, http://zia.aisri.indiana.edu/~dictsearch/.

2. See AISRI Dictionary Portal.

References

Andersson, Rani-Henrik, and David C. Posthumus. 2022. *Lakȟóta: An Indigenous History*. Norman: University of Oklahoma Press.

Beede, Aaron McGaffey. 1915. Journal 4, Aaron McGaffey Beede Papers. Elwyn B. Robinson Department of Special Collections, Chester Fritz Library, University of North Dakota, Grand Forks.

Blaine, Martha Royce. 1997. *Some Things Are Not Forgotten: A Pawnee Family Remembers*. Lincoln: University of Nebraska Press.

Carpenter, Roger M. 2011. "Womanish Men and Manlike Women: The Native American Two-Spirit as Warrior." In *Gender and Sexuality in Indigenous North America, 1400–1850*, edited by Sandra Slater and Fay A. Yarbrough, 146–64. Columbia: University of South Carolina Press.

Deloria, Ella C. 2022. *The Dakota Way of Life*. Edited by Raymond J. DeMallie and Thierry Veyrié. Lincoln: University of Nebraska Press.

DeMallie, Raymond J. 1983. "Male and Female in Traditional Lakota Culture." In *The Hidden Half: Studies of Plains Indian Women*, edited by Patricia Albers and Beatrice Medicine, 237–65. Lanham MD: University Press of America.

Dorsey, George A. 1904. *Traditions of the Skidi Pawnee*. Memoirs of the American Folk-Lore Society, vol. 8. Boston: Houghton Mifflin.

———. 1906. *The Pawnee Mythology*. Washington DC: Carnegie Institution.

Dorsey, George A., and James R. Murie. ca. 1907. "The Pawnee: Society and Religion of the Skidi Pawnee." Unpublished manuscript, Field Museum Archives, Chicago.

———. 1940. *Notes on Skidi Pawnee Society*. Edited by Alexander Spoehr. Anthropological Series, Field Museum of Natural History 27, no. 2 (September 18).

Dunbar, John Brown. 1882. "The Pawnee Indians: Their Habits and Customs." *Magazine of American History* 8, no. 11 (November): 734–54.

Echo-Hawk, Roger. 2018. *The Enchanted Mirror: The Seven Brothers*. N.p.: CreateSpace.

Elledge, Jim, ed. 2002. *Gay, Lesbian, Bisexual, and Transgender Myths: From the Arapaho to the Zuñi; An Anthology*. New York: Peter Lang.

Evarts, Mark. n.d. "Biography of Mark Evarts, Pawnee." Edited by Alexander Lesser. Unpublished manuscript, American Indian Studies Research Institute, Indiana University, Bloomington.

Gilley, Brian Joseph. 2006. *Becoming Two-Spirit: Gay Identity and Social Acceptance in Indian Country*. Lincoln: University of Nebraska Press.

Gilmore, Melvin R. n.d. "Religious Teaching and Training of Arikara Children." Unpublished manuscript, copy at the American Indian Studies Research Institute, Indiana University, Bloomington.

Jacobs, Sue-Ellen, Wesley Thomas, and Sabine Lang, eds. 1997. *Two-Spirit People: Native American Gender Identity, Sexuality, and Spirituality*. Urbana: University of Illinois Press.

Jolivette, Andrew J. 2016. *Indian Blood: HIV & Colonial Trauma in San Francisco's Two-Spirit Community*. Seattle: University of Washington Press.

Medicine, Beatrice. 1983. "'Warrior Women'—Sex Role Alternatives for Plains Indian Women." In *The Hidden Half: Studies of Plains Indian Women*, edited by Patricia Albers and Beatrice Medicine, 267–80. Lanham MD: University Press of America.

Murie, James. n.d. Roaming Scout Collection. Text 32A, "Skiri Narratives, Thirty-Two." Edited and translated by Douglas R. Parks. Unpublished manuscript, American Indian Studies Research Institute, Indiana University, Bloomington. http://zia.aisri.indiana.edu/~corpora/RoamingScout.php.

Parks, Douglas R. n.d. "AISRI Dictionary Portal." American Indian Studies Research Institute, Indiana University, Bloomington, accessed 2018. http://zia.aisri.indiana.edu/~dictsearch/.

Roscoe Will, ed. 1988. *Living the Spirit: A Gay American Indian Anthology Compiled by Gay American Indians*. New York: St. Martin's Press.

Smithers, Gregory D. 2022. *Reclaiming Two-Spirits: Sexuality, Spiritual Renewal & Sovereignty in Native America*. Boston: Beacon Press.

van de Logt, Mark. 2008. "'The Powers in the Heavens Shall Eat of My Smoke': The Significance of Scalping in Pawnee Warfare." *Journal of Military History* 72, no. 1 (January): 71–104.

Weltfish, Gene. 1935. "Pawnee Field Notes, Summer 1935." Unpublished notes, electronic copy at the American Indian Research Institute, Indiana University, Bloomington.

———. 1937. *Caddoan Texts, Pawnee, South Band Dialect*. Publications of the American Ethnological Society 17. New York: G. E. Stechert.

———. 1971. *The Lost Universe: The Way of Life of the Pawnee*. New York: Ballantine Books.

Williams, Walter L. 1992. *The Spirit and the Flesh: Sexual Diversity in American Indian Culture*. Boston: Beacon Press.

Hungry Narratives Turned on Their Head (or Danced on Their Toes?)   5

Toward Decolonial Listening in Ethnohistorical Practice

SARAH QUICK

Narratives are the stuff of much ethnohistorical analysis. This chapter reflects on how we listen to narratives describing music and dance while also understanding the social, cultural, and political contexts for such practices. I consider the familiar issue of representation for those often, but not always, seen as "Other" with a focus on an Indigenous group currently known as the Métis during a particular period (1890s–1930s) in which they were largely silent or, perhaps more aptly, were silenced. In the more recent narrative for the Métis Nation, this period overlaps with the "forgotten years," those years after their resistances when they were forced to leave their homeland(s) and faced continued strife at the hands of the Canadian government and incoming settlers before they begin to reemerge as a political entity.[1] Nonetheless, Métis and, of course, many other Indigenous folks *were* performing music and dances in public settings during this period, sometimes separately from the settlers largely dominating such spaces but also alongside them. What are we able to learn about the performers and what they perform through such (largely outsider) narratives? Heeding Raymond DeMallie's model to critically engage with such past narratives, this chapter grapples with how to listen to past source materials often lacking in their modalities as well as in the cultural perspectives of the peoples they are representing.

"These Have No Ears": Cultural Symbols for Listening and Disciplinary Practices

DeMallie (1993) characterizes how narratives are created through disciplinary filters and particular cultural perspectives. He aptly accused historians of having primarily paid attention to Euro-American sources when reconstructing Lakȟóta history, stemming from "travelers, traders, colonial administrators, military officers, missionaries, Indian agents" (515), while the many translated speeches from Lakȟóta leaders had largely been ignored. He then expanded to other Lakȟóta literary traditions that could be springboards for better understanding Lakȟóta perspectives, ones that would prove to be contrary to many mainstream historical interpretations.

DeMallie also spoke to Lakȟóta-specific metaphors for listening. As he explained, open, closed, or no ears were the symbols for whether or not individuals were prone to fully listen to others' perspectives. Young Lakȟóta men often had no ears—nor did Euro-American settlers—meaning they were not listening to the perspectives of elders or, in the case of Euro-Americans, to Indigenous peoples more generally. In addition, he explained that this capability was conjoined with honesty. As he wrote: "Semantically, it appears that piercing, opening, or mere acknowledgement of possessing ears expressed a willingness to listen to and accept a significant message, and served, moreover, as a pledge that the parties involved were speaking truthfully. To have open ears was to be adult, sensible, and responsible" (1993, 520).

This ear symbolism was also an effective metaphorical device that he used to craft one of his main points. In sum, he portrayed historians' interpretations as relying on the recounting of events in narrative form often within a specific chronology. In contrast, he characterized anthropologists as trying to understand social structures and interpret cultural meanings, often outside a particular set of events. Ultimately, DeMallie argues that ethnohistory's challenge is to bridge these two disciplinary paradigms, and not listening to each other—keeping the status quo—when accounting for past Indigenous experiences would be paramount to a failure in analyzing and understanding their cultural contexts (for historians) and in realizing the dynamics of cultural *change* (for anthropologists). DeMallie's emphasis on listening here as well as in his other work (and in his oral teaching methods) also conveyed the importance of reflexivity and perspective-taking in considering the narratives that ethnohistory both analyzes and creates (see Braun 2013 for more on DeMallie's varied approaches).

Until recently these concerns have not been apparent in those fields focusing primarily on music and dance. Dance history and dance studies have largely focused on Western art traditions unless work by anthropologists, ethnomusicologists, and folklorists is included. For scholars focused on music, DeMallie's critique of disciplinary silos could again be launched, with ethnomusicology as anthropology's analog and music history as history's, both fields sitting inside (especially music history) and outside (especially ethnomusicology) musicology. Fifteen years after DeMallie's article, music historian Olivia Bloechl (2008) wrote of the entrenched Eurocentrism in music history, asserting her aim to include Indigenous musics as a part of her purview of colonial musical encounters bridging the Atlantic. Her contention that "at least two distinct cosmologies and ideologies of music were in play" (15) during the early modern period and her purposeful move away from common types of analyses in music history are quite reminiscent of DeMallie's earlier points on narrative.

Indigenous Performance Practices, Decolonial Listening, and the Archives

DeMallie sought to highlight the interdisciplinary requirements for an engaged ethnohistory by bringing together anthropology and history. Yet, he also laid a foundation for considering additional disciplinary perspectives when it comes to music and dance as they are understood and represented. The study of music obviously requires a literal listening-in-action, but what might DeMallie's insights provide for the study of Indigenous musics, musical performers, and musical performances *in the past*? I return to this question later, but first I give some critical attention to what might be called "decolonial" listening for considering past historical sources.

The problems of how and why past Indigenous musics were recorded have been reexamined from many quarters. Most recently these concerns have been taken up in order to redress some of the common assumptions and practices in the past and their colonial holdovers for continuing to understand and engage with Indigenous musics (Deloria 2004; Diamond 2019; Giroux 2021; Levine and Robinson 2019; Ochoa Gautier 2014; Robinson 2020; Samuels 2019). Stó:lō musicologist Dylan Robinson's seminal work *Hungry Listening: Resonant Theory for Indigenous Sound Studies* (2020) inspired this chapter's title, and his phrase "hungry listening" (derived from the Halq'eméylem descriptor for white settlers who came with the gold rush) is meant to convey the extractive manner in which Western (art) music is heard and created, with the formal-aesthetic properties pedestaled. Instead of hungry listening, Robinson proposes a decolonizing consciousness of listening practices. Further, in addition to his many provocations aimed at contemporary composers and other scholars engaging with Indigenous musics past and present, Robinson critically attends to the collection of Indigenous musical instruments, sound recordings, and transcriptions by early anthropologists and nearby disciplinary relatives that often still generally reside in museum settings (149–66). He then highlights some of the approaches that Indigenous activist-artists have used in reviving or repatriating these musics and ultimately asks readers to reflect on their own responsibilities when working with or writing about musics stemming from such collections (167–99).

Ethnomusicologist Monique Giroux (2021) similarly takes up these issues with a specific focus on Métis sound recordings now housed in archives. As she correctly notes, early anthropologists and ethnographers generally ignored the Métis as a cultural entity worthy of study. The liminal or ambiguous status geographically, culturally, "racially," and eventually legally for Métis historically also likely contributed to their erasure in early scholarship (see Andersen 2014), even when their presence was quite obviously on record (in various forms) throughout the nineteenth century and beyond. Starting with Marius Barbeau's recording in 1916 of Pierre Falcon's song tied to the birth of the Métis Nation in the early nineteenth century, Giroux (2021) also highlighted the many Métis fiddle recordings archived in local as well as national archival settings (105–6). She asserted that as scholars continue to reorient their positions on old and new collection practices, they might reenvision their practice through rematriation, "a research orientation [that] asks us to critically address past encounters and calls us to make paramount how our work promotes knowledge creation at the community level, including revitalization and resurgences of musical practices" (117).

Giroux primarily considers audio recordings as fodder for reflecting on our contemporary orientations to both archived recordings and the research recordings that ethnomusicologists commonly create for their own personal use. However, what about other forms of documentation—images, musical notation, and descriptive texts? Besides providing context to the performers and performances recorded in them, how might such historical sources provide insight to our listening analyses? Early audio recordings of Indigenous musics were often seen solely as a means to an end, mainly to provide a method toward transcriptions or notated versions for broader non-Indigenous audiences (including composers) as well as for scholarly interpretation (Deloria 2004; Sterne 2003). Other source materials convey specific information about performers and their audiences that sound recordings may not.

Folklorist-ethnomusicologist Ana Maria Ochoa Gautier also delves into these questions in *Aurality*, her "acoustically tuned exploration of the written archives" (2014, 3) for nineteenth-century Colombia. Here she asserts that while the source materials she analyzes index the construction of (Indigenous and other) identities considered imperfect, as both outside and within "the nation," they are not solely from and about the colonial point of view; they also signal "a contested site of different acoustic practices, a layering of contrastive listenings and their cosmological underpinnings" (4). While reflecting on what she characterizes as sound inscriptions (song, language, and even nonhuman sounds), Ochoa Gautier also probes these sources' limitations; the media themselves as well as their perceived function(s) could also leave their mark on interpretations of listening and Indigeneity.

Ochoa Gautier is also particularly interested in how ideas about modernity correspond to notions of Indigeneity during the periods she examines. As Jonathon Sterne writes considering North America, "the ethos of preservation" permeated early ethnographers' desires to record the Indigenous "Other," in part because of their view of these others as evolutionarily in the past (2003, 311–25). Many have also challenged the assumed binarity between Indigenous peoples and perceptions of modernity, Philip J. Deloria (2004) being perhaps the most influential in his coverage of U.S. Indigenous folks grappling with questions of modernity from the 1890s into the 1930s.

I am also using this period for an analysis here, although with a focus mainly in Alberta. Like Deloria (1998) I am also interested in public performances: although I separate performers into those identifying as nostalgic pioneers or "Old Timers" and those identifying as Indigenous, primarily Métis, there is sometimes blurring between these identities, and often sources do not indicate how these performers identified themselves.

What connect these performers are the fiddle dances they celebrate, the genre that was, and definitely is currently, identified with Métis culture. Further, while my focus is 1890s–1930s, these fiddle dances certainly have much earlier references in the nineteenth century, and these performers were often referencing these earlier periods in their public performances. These performers—both the Old Timers and those who identified as Métis—were joined by their preservationist interests in celebrating these forms. Still, I would like to position the rationale and interests for Indigenous performers as straying from the common narrative presented by the Old Timers.

DeMallie's nuanced reflections are made vivid through the historical source materials he interweaves into his analysis, a goal for me here as well. The sources I analyze vary, but most are written documents with some imagery or photographs, again begging the question of how to "listen" to such documents when it comes to the auditory and the kinesthetic. Furthermore, considering that these past sounds were based on instrumental and bodily practice rather than song (or vocal practice), direct linguistic analysis is not possible.

The Old Timers

At the turn of the twentieth century, Old Timers created organizations in response to the burgeoning cosmopolitanism in the Prairie Provinces. These Old Timer groups celebrated their identities as pioneers and their involvement in the past fur trader/frontier days while also recognizing how much "progress" had been made. In Alberta these groups also sponsored banquets that featured music and dances associated with the earlier fur-trading days. The Edmonton Old Timers officially formed in 1894 (NAPDA 1983, 3), and the Calgary Old Timers in 1901 (SAPD 1993, 218). Under different names, each organization still exists, although they have evolved significantly in their membership requirements and the social events they sponsor.

As the Edmonton Old Timers, the organization included several prominent members (NAPDA 1983, 3), many not entirely friendly to Indigenous interests. The most prominent of them, Frank Oliver, published Alberta's oldest newspaper—the *Edmonton Bulletin*—and was an active politician. Oliver was also a land speculator and one of the leaders in removing and reducing Cree reserves near Edmonton. His friend James Gibbons, who initially came to Alberta as a gold prospector, helped this process of surrender by filling a regional position (through Oliver's pressure) as an Indian agent (Goyette and Roemmich 2004, 96, 156, 175). Before some of these lands were surrendered, however, both Oliver and Gibbons were active in forming the Edmonton Old Timers, Gibbons as the first president in 1894 and Oliver later in 1898 (NAPDA 1983, 51).

The Edmonton Old Timers celebrated annual balls from 1896 to 1905 (NAPDA 1983, 55–58). The early balls included nostalgic decor: fur and buffalo heads on the walls as well as "implements of hunting, trapping, mining, travelling" ("Old Timers' Ball" 1896). The first ball also featured several fiddle-accompanied dances later identified with and celebrated as traditional Métis dances—the Red River Jig, the Duck Dance, the Reel of Four, and the Reel of Eight—although interspersed between cotillions, waltzes, and other couples' dances ("Old Timers' Ball" 1896).

In 1900 the "shanty" again appears in the *Edmonton Bulletin*'s ball descriptions; here musicians were also recognized—one being Lawrence/Laurent Garneau, a prominent Edmonton Métis businessman, on violin.[2] The *Edmonton Bulletin* characterized the dances as an ode to yesteryear and indicated their link to Indianness: "The Ball . . . is in memory of, and, . . . a revival of life in the early days when conditions of settlement and civilization were different. . . . The programme included the Duck Dance and the Red River Jig, with Henry Fraser taking part in the latter, attired in Indian costume" (quoted in NAPDA 1983, 56).

Between 1905 and 1924 the Edmonton Old Timers did not regularly meet, but after reorganizing in 1924, they allowed women to become members instead of being solely guests at events; their annual banquets continued with an Old Timers dance afterward (NAPDA 1983, 11, 17, 52). Again, at the 1924 banquet ball, the Red River Jig was a highlight, as was well-known Métis elder Victoria Callihoo, often the featured performer, in addition to other local Indigenous performers (Dalheim and Kerr 1976, 19; Kells 1928, 7; NAPDA 1983, 100).[3] For example, in 1932 as the Northern Alberta Old Timers and Pioneers Association, they hosted a large-scale event that included "Red River jigs, reels and Duck dances, and other features popular in the early eighties. . . . Two Indian fiddlers, Lawrence and Peter Anderson, accompanied the dancers" ("Old Indian Dances Feature Reunion" 1932).

Calgary's Old Timers formed and held their first annual banquet in 1901, and in 1908 they began having an annual ball with the banquet, which eventually became known as their annual roundup (after 1924 the Edmonton group also called these annual events "round ups"). Here again, the Red River Jig appeared. As the *Calgary Daily Herald* reported for the 1908 event, "The guests of the evening were received by Colonel and Mrs. Walker and from the Grand March and opening dance—a 'Red River Jig'—until the closing waltz, merriment ruled supreme" (quoted in SAPD 1993, 218–19). Both Edmonton's and Calgary's Old Timers' events are easily typed as "inventions of tradition" (Hobsbawm and Ranger 1983) as each organization's members reacted to the growing cosmopolitanism in their midst. However, such celebratory nods to the past were also tempered with an embrace of progress.

These kinds of indulgences within the overarching narrative of progress are not difficult to find for each organization during the 1920s. One example is the *Edmonton Bulletin*'s image-filled full-page call for participation in "Old Timers' Day" in July 1926: "Old Timers, Attention! ... Alberta's first citizens will lead the big parade ... from the days of the packers who brought their own supplies on foot; down through the days of the Red River Carts, the buckboards, and the prairie schooners to the top buggy era, and then to the days of the auto and the airplane, the progress of Alberta and Edmonton will be depicted" ("Alberta's Old Timers' Day" 1926). Two prints balance the corners: a bearded pioneer with a rifle looks across the North Saskatchewan River toward a presumably fledgling Edmonton, while diagonally the modern Edmonton sits atop the riverbanks, a shining city with skyscrapers and smokestacks.

Somewhat confounding considering their reported relationship with the Edmonton Old Timers, the Calgary Old Timers eventually lost their ability to feature the Red River Jig at their gatherings, a dance that remained a fixture at the northern Old Timers' gatherings.[4] By the late 1920s only older woman members remembered the dance, and even then they were unable to teach the men's steps, and they did not have a fiddler who recalled the tune in its entirety (Price 1928b). Thankfully for the Calgary Old Timers, "the discovery of the Kipling family" allowed a mother-daughter piano and dance instruction team to document it as highlighted in at least three nearly identical newspaper features in the *Calgary Herald*, the *Toronto Star Weekly*, and the *Edmonton Journal*—all presumably written by Elizabeth Bailey Price. Each recounted the Calgary Old Timers' dilemma, described the Red River Jig of yesteryear, and recounted how it was recently learned and documented.

Price does not make any direct reference to the Kiplings as Métis: is the reader to presume Indigeneity from the three headshots of the Kiplings (in two of the three features)?[5] Price does characterize the dance as a favorite pastime forty years ago, especially at Christmas when "all the people in the country, natives and whites, would gather at the Hudson bay forts." She then referred to "native sons and daughters," first in reference to those gathering at the academy to learn the Red River Jig; and later, after the initial Kipling family demonstrations, when "the floor was crowded with native sons and daughters, stepping along to the rollicking, strenuous strains" (Price 1928a; 1928b; "Red River Jig" 1928).

In the *Calgary Herald*'s "Red River Jig, Dance of Earlier days, Staging Big Comeback," the Kiplings' headshots sit atop even more information. For example, "Mrs. G. (Grandma) Kipling [is] One of the oldest pioneers in the west, who, at the age of 72 is still young when it comes to dancing the Red River jig." The most information is provided for her son: "Willie Kipling who at the age of 10 learned the music for the Red River Jig by ear on the violin. . . . When the pioneers of the country sought to revive the dance, Mr. Kipling was the only person in southern Alberta able to play the music and from his rendition the music was transcribed"—although much of this information repeats the theme of this music and dance nearly being lost ("Red River Jig" 1928).

These newspaper features do provide details on what Bailey observed of the Red River Jig dance form as well as how it was initially learned by the Kiplings. She described it being performed by men and women couples turn-taking over time and further detailed the women's steps as "easy, three simple kinds" in contrast to the men's "intricate, involving 'double shuffles' and many quick changes—exhilarating yet exhausting." In two of the features, she also elaborated on the "women's part" being similar to "the squaw's in the well known 'pow wow,' when the body is held stiffly and a short step is done," while the "man's part [is] more showy, similar to that of Indian dances, which gives the young bucks every opportunity to show the 'strut of the male'" (Price 1928a; 1928b). Here she seems to be referencing the all-too-common stereotypes for "squaw" and "buck" behaviors via dance forms. She also added to the final newspaper feature that both the men's and women's dancing are principally focused on the feet (Price 1928a). She also highlighted Willie Kipling's memories of learning the "Red River Jig" tune directly from his father (aurally); and, the other Kiplings are also cited explaining that they learned the dance "ever since they could walk" and "that their home had been the dancing centre of the community in the early days; that the old-timers had danced till dawn while their father fiddled" (Price 1928a).

Price's descriptions are still not *that* explicit, especially for the musical features of the "Red River Jig." The fiddle tune is captured with metaphorical language, as in "rollicking, lilting, strenuous strains," and "animated, infectious tune." In addition, while she lauded the documentation efforts of the McDonalds, the mother documenting the dance steps and the daughter learning the tune on piano "one measure at a time" to transcribe it, she provided nothing on how their documentation was to be used and whether it was to be published in some fashion. I have found no other source materials directly resulting from these consultations except for McDonald Academy performances wherein the Red River Jig is referenced as being performed ("McDonald Kiddies" 1929; "Student Revue Is Successful" 1928). Later at a festival sponsored by the Canadian Pacific Railway (CPR), children trained at the McDonald Academy are mentioned as performing "the old cowboy dances" (Holmes 1930, 272–73). With these later performances, I wonder whether their students performed or opted to abstain from performing the Red River Jig since this festival also featured the Métis dance troupe discussed in the next section. Overall, these newspaper features convey that the Kiplings' background and experiences were secondary to the grand goals of the Old Timers' preservation project.

Even more blatant at other Old Timers' events, Indigenous peoples were often placed in a subordinate, yet seemingly harmonious, relationship with settlers. It was often this notion of Indigeneity that the Old Timers promoted: a colorful and nostalgically imagined past recaptured and put on display. While the Old Timers framed the heritage they were celebrating as based on an idealized and imagined yesteryear, this view was likely not shared by all performers in such settings, as indicated in the next section.

Before proceeding, however, I present an interlude on some Old Timers' sheet music made available during this same period that others have already referenced in documenting Manitoba fiddling and fiddlers

(Dueck 2013) as well as instances of the "Red River Jig" circulating through other compositions (Giroux 2021). It is worth considering here in more detail for what it tells us as a different form of documentation, or inscription following Ochoa Gautier (2014), than the previous examples. In 1929 the Old Timers' Association of Manitoba took a role in documenting, and later publishing, two musically notated versions of the "Red River Jig" with piano accompaniment (Johnstone and Genthon 1929). The front cover to this sheet music features a stylized print of a smoking campfire next to a teepee on the shore of presumably the Red River, perhaps indexing one of the common origin stories of this tune as well as its more general association with Métis or general "Indians" of the past (Giroux 2013; Quick 2008). The back cover provides dance instructions for the Red River Jig and "Tapatoe," a composition whose music was included as inspired by the Red River Jig (Smith 1929).

For the Red River Jig's instructions, the narrative starts, "This dance is, we believe, derived from the Pow Wow of the North American Indian, the early inhabitants of the Red River Valley, and was continued by the early settlers" before providing a more detailed description of the dance form and the steps involved (Mulligan 1929). Also emphasized is the dancer's "perfect time to the music with one's toes, with as little body movement as possible" before the two dancers change positions "by crossing over with the shuffle step, a hand clasp, and continue to dance six feet apart until tired, or others take their place." Interestingly, what seems to be missing in this description is the varied stepping in the second part of the dance or the "B section" in the musical structure that from my perspective makes it quintessentially the Red River Jig.

The musical notations of the "Red River Jig" violin versions over piano accompaniment include one attributed to Thomas Johnstone, who according to Giroux (2013, 73–74) likely did not identify as Métis but rather as Scottish, and the other to Fredrick Genthon, a Métis fiddler who would have been in his seventies at that time and who was audio-recorded later in 1940 (Randall 1942; Dorion-Paquin et al. 2001). Both versions align with many features often attributed to this tune. For one, they are asymmetric, meaning their two sections are different lengths; nor do they fit into the standard sixteen-bar tune structure that many fiddle tunes follow. Also consistent across these versions and many other versions are their overall melodic contour. Nevertheless, the Genthon version seems to have a more extended transition from the A section to the B section.

Both versions are notated using a 2/8 meter that remains consistent throughout each. Without an audio recording I am left wondering if this metric consistency stems from the one(s) notating these "Red River Jig" versions rather than the fiddlers' actual renditions. Also unknown is how consistent these fiddlers remained across their repeats of the tune. Metric variability and flexibility (especially during the transitions between different sections) have been major areas of interest for scholars studying the "Red River Jig" as well as Métis music more generally (Dueck 2007, 2013; Gibbons 1981; Lederman 1986, 1988; Quick 2009; Whidden 2007, among others). I am also reminded of the debates in ethnomusicology and musicology surrounding the relative merits of varying transcription methodologies (Herndon 1974; Nettl 2015) as well as the relatively recent reflexivity on the ideological implications that transcription has had in establishing authority for these disciplines (Bohlman 1993; Marian-Bălaşa 2005).

Questions also remain as to the purpose of this sheet music: is it in the same preservationist mindset previously noted for Old Timer nostalgia? Likely so, but what might be made of the commercial angle?[6] Sheet music offered publishers a commercial opportunity, and plenty of other stereotypically "Indian" songs had been marketed by this time (Pisani 2005). This sheet music was based on someone having recorded and transcribed the performances of *actual* fiddlers, lending it an air of authenticity while it simultaneously signaled stereotypical Indian tropes with its cover imagery.

Joseph Francis Dion and the Métis Dance Troupe

In the early 1930s Joseph Frances Dion, an activist in establishing Métis recognition and rights in Alberta, emceed for a Métis dance troupe with members from regions near St. Paul, Alberta. Dion (1888–1960) was Cree (Nēhiyaw) and grew up on the Onion Lake reserve in what is now western Saskatchewan. As someone educated at the Catholic mission, Dion had ties to St. Paul and St. Albert that also brought him into close contact with many Alberta Métis. In addition, he married Elizabeth Cunningham, a Métis from St. Albert in 1912, this year also marking the first glimmers of his longstanding interest in documenting the cultural and historical experiences of Cree and Métis peoples as an amateur historian and writer (Dempsey 1979, v–vi).

Dion encapsulated his life experiences as well as his handwritten recordings of elders' remembrances of nineteenth-century events in short journal accounts and newspaper articles. In some of these written accounts, he reflected on his understanding as well as his support of Métis history, culture, and rights. *My Tribe, the Crees*, published posthumously in 1979, combined many of these accounts into one source, but additional recorded interviews and recollections exist at the Glenbow Archives. For example, early on when he began collecting accounts of nineteenth-century life from elders, Dion recorded at least three Métis elders and their recollections of nineteenth-century fiddling and dancing, noting these recollections in an old school notebook titled "Indian and Halfbreed–Old Time Stories." One account not featured in *My Tribe, the Crees* was the July 1915 record of his wife's grandmother's remembrances of "dancing in the old days." At this time Mrs. Cunningham was in her late eighties, so these recollections extend quite far back into the nineteenth century. Cunningham told Dion that while living near Lesser Slave Lake she remembered participating in "the Red River Jig, Reel of Four, Reel of Eight, Right Away Dance, Double Jig, Rabbit Dance, and the Handkerchief Dance" (Dion n.d.).

Returning to the 1930s Métis dance troupe, Dion likely condensed some of the information that he had collected when he introduced the group. Educating the public about Métis culture seemed to be the major reason he traveled with these dancers. As Hugh Dempsey wrote in his introduction to *My Tribe, the Crees*, "Mr. Dion was convinced that the Métis needed a positive identity which could be communicated to the public to offset any negative stereotypes" (vi). At this time he had also become active in working with others to gain a Métis land base, in part because the opening up of St. Paul des Métis to French Canadians had caused many Métis there to disperse elsewhere.

The dance group toured throughout Alberta and eastern Canada in the 1930s (Dempsey 1979, vi), and this period also coincided with Dion's involvement in the political leadership of the Metis Association of Alberta (Wall 2008). The dance group reportedly formed in 1929, performing in St. Paul des Métis (becoming simply St. Paul in 1936) near where many of its members lived ("Alberta Party" 1930) and performed in the Calgary and Edmonton areas in the summer of 1930. According to Dion's daughter Florence Mitchell (interview with author, August 5, 2004), they regularly performed on the exhibition grounds near the legislative building in Edmonton where the Edmonton Old Timers' Pioneer cabin had been located.

The dance group apparently made quite an impression on the opening night of the CPR-sponsored festival in March 1930, with several reviewers noting their appeal. One review described their dancing prowess at length:

> Climaxing a program of great variety was the last number, dances performed by half-breed Indians from St. Paul de Metis, with dexterity and grace almost indescribable. Two girls of the group in particular seemed actually to skim over the stage in the intricate steps of the reel of eight, double jigs, duck dance, reel of fours, "drops of bandy" and the Red River Jig. One member of the group scarcely touched the stage, so light was her step, and her toe dancing would have put a ballet dancer of the professional stage to shame. Several of the male members, also, were very expert with their footwork. ("Panoramic of Background" 1930)

The group's festival performances continued the next day at an afternoon tea event, which was also reported in a few reviews, again their dancing prowess lauded (Donnelly 1930; "Folkdancing, Handicrafts Attracts Crowds" 1930; Marsh 1930; "Tea Programme Pleases Guests" 1930). Here they included the Rabbit dance as well as the Handkerchief dance in addition to other dances, one reviewer noting their appearance and attire in detail: "Wearing moccasins and bright costume, their long black hair caught up in braids, the women were typical of their race. Reds and orange, black and red, orange and purple and a combination of blue, red and pink fashioned the dresses of the four women dancers, while the men wore vivid neckerchiefs to brighten their costumes" ("Folkdancing, Handicrafts Attract Crowds" 1930). Particularly captivating about the photographs of the Métis dance troupe is their seemingly costumed appearance. They were obviously presenting themselves with a nod to the past. The women wore traditional calico dresses and aprons, the men sashes and capotes, all wore moccasins, and it appears some may have also worn wigs, possibly to convey their "Indianness" and old-fashioned hairstyles.[7]

Initially the dance troupe was inconsistently identified. For example, in covering them at the CPR-sponsored festival, the *Calgary Herald* described them as "French Canadians from St. Paul des Metis" in a promotional advertisement and later review of their opening performance (Broder 1930), while another review of the opening (quoted above) described them as the "half-breed Indians from St. Paul de Metis" ("Panoramic of Background" 1930). The next day at the afternoon tea event, they were the "dancers from St. Paul des Metis, of Indian extraction" ("Tea Programme Pleases Guests" 1930).

The *Manitoba Free Press* also reported on their Calgary festival performance in March, designating them as "halfbreed... down from St. Paul de Metis" and quoting them as declaring that "We are not French-Canadians!... We are of French and Indian blood" ("Folk Song–Folk Dance Festival" 1930); while a later July *Edmonton Journal* article explained that the dancers corrected the program that had described them as "French-Canadians," stating that "this was not to their liking, for on their first appearance it was announced that they wished it to be known that they were not French-Canadians—they were native Canadians, halfbreeds" ("Will Recall Dances" 1930, 10). Such inconsistencies did not appear in the later sources outside of Alberta, which leads me to believe that Dion (and others in the group) had become more cognizant of controlling the discourse surrounding their identity. The *Toronto Star* noted that "the Metis of the Far West will demonstrate the Red River Jig" in one advertisement for the Quebec festival, and in a list of all the performers in another, they appeared under "Folk Dances of the North West" as "Metis (half-breeds), from St. Paul de Metis, Alberta" ("Folkdance, Folksong, and Handicrafts Festival" 1930).

The *Montreal Gazette* interviewed Dion about the troupe, where we learn that besides being their "mouthpiece," Dion also called for some of the dances. Here again Dion made a statement of their ancestry: "We are true Canadians... most of us come from St. Paul, Alta; about 125 miles northeast of Edmonton. We are of mixed blood: Cree and French, Irish, English and Scotch, so we have in our veins strains of the foundation bloods of Canada" ("Alberta Party" 1930). Some of the performers later moved to the Métis settlements that Dion was instrumental in establishing (Miller 1984, 16; May and Horstman 1982, 10).

Reflecting on how Dion represented this group and their Métis identity, I am reminded of similar discourse surrounding the Métis heritage performance I began observing directly at the turn of the twenty-first century nearly seventy years later. For example, identifiers of Métis as "mixed blood" or multicultural at their origins were often invoked. I have also asserted that these sites for Métis heritage performance still offer some play as sites where self-awareness, commentary, and social relationships are not under the complete control of the standard narratives (Quick 2009, 286–93, 320–25). Similarly, I see the 1930s Métis dance troupe as providing a counternarrative to what the early Old Timers' associations were generally representing in their performances as well as to what Henderson (2005) described as "the spectacle of difference" represented by the CPR folk festivals.

While both the Old Timers and the Métis dance troupe promoted the celebration and preservation of these music and dance forms, the Old Timers framed the heritage they were celebrating as an idealized and imagined yesteryear. In contrast, the Métis dance troupe represented themselves as a *Métis* dance troupe, not as a group performing nineteenth-century dances solely from the past. While their dress and, presumably, Dion's introductions alluded to "a past" and the celebrated cultural practices of their ancestors, they were also representing themselves as a cultural group, comparable to the other nationalities featured at the larger-scale CPR folk festivals. Stuart Henderson saw the CPR folk festival's opening program in Calgary and its featured performers (a mix of "pioneers" from the west) as primarily reinforcing the hegemony of certain folk—"the primacy of a white, anglo- (and, to limited extent, franco-) supremacy in the west" (2005, 162)—yet the Métis dance troupe also performed this opening night. In addition, although they were misrepresented as French Canadians in the *Calgary Daily Herald* review of their performances, Dion sought to correct such misrepresentations directly at this opening performance as well as in the later press coverage. He conveyed that they were Métis and as such were foundational to Canada's cultural history. His "mixed-blood" statement quoted above reinforces a narrative that conflates race with culture yet also highlights Métis as foundational, not marginal.

While part of the troupe's intent was to celebrate and preserve performances stemming from an idealized past, similar to the Old Timers, they did so, in part, so that a larger public could see them as also deserving benefactors of future policy. Instead of celebrating the days of old whereby the past was neutralized and controlled, the Métis dance troupe conveyed a different story. Besides trying to provide these audiences with entertaining performances, ones with which they could relate, I speculate that Dion and the Métis dance troupe sought to perform in conjunction with their political goals of establishing Métis as a cultural group deserving of recognition and rights.[8]

Cultural Change, Cultural Filters, and Decolonial Listening

A question I left hanging above was what might DeMallie's insights provide for an analysis of these past performance practices? For one, his recommendation to anthropologists in particular, that cultural change is relevant to understanding the dynamic aspects of culture, is quite relevant. In thinking about this period against others previous to and after it, the discourse surrounding these music and dance forms continues to associate with Indigeneity (sometimes Métis-specific, sometimes not) from the mid-nineteenth century until now. Nevertheless, the association becomes even more emphasized later in the period under review (1930s) as it continued to do so thereafter. As I have asserted previously, however, their association as *solely* Métis-specific cultural forms emerged later (Quick 2008, 2009).

Also useful is having additional source materials referencing the range of dances being performed at the turn of the century into the

1930s, even while the Red River Jig had, and continues to have, the most notoriety. Some of these dances are now no longer performed and have been dwindling in the social dance repertoire while other types were added. Therefore, it is useful to realize which of those dances considered older were still being performed into the 1930s. Further, during this period Indigenous-style square dancing was not mentioned together with these dances, although occasionally quadrille *is* mentioned, and Dion was noted as a caller. Later, however, events began featuring square dance contests alongside Red River Jigging contests rather than the other types of dances.

In addition, changes to the Red River Jig dance form are better understood through a close review of this period in comparison to others. While elders with whom I have worked once highlighted the various couples' forms they had danced and seen, instances of couples dancing the Red River Jig have become a rarer occurrence of late, most especially in staged settings. Instead, nowadays the Red River Jig is often danced as a solo dance. Further, only some elders and those who might be called traditionalists emphasize the gendered differences for the ideal movements for men versus ideal movements for women performing this dance. Clearly, the dance form has changed, these changes in part due to changing gender ideals as well as the Red River Jig's prevalence in contest and staged settings. Further, such performances are often digitally recorded for YouTube, TikTok, or Instagram audiences.

DeMallie also emphatically asserted that ethnohistorians should recognize that cultural perspectives are built into the source materials they are examining. He was also obviously encouraging *all* scholars to work with materials created more directly with Indigenous peoples involved, while understanding that these may also be filtered through the non-Indigenous mediators. While DeMallie's point seems simple, it is easy to forget its significance, especially when attempting to forge a more decolonial consciousness toward past "inscriptions" (following Ochoa Gauthier), that is, through the use of writing to document sounds and varied types of human voices.

In most of the source materials under review here, there is little attention to Indigenous perspectives. These representations (or inscriptions) were mainly through a settler's lens. The written descriptions of these music and dance forms are celebratory yet also patronizing, sometimes ridden with stereotypes. The language is also almost uniformly English, with occasional French flourishes, except in Dion's notes in his journal accounts of the dances; and Dion accommodated to settler languages in his public pronouncements as an emcee when the newspaper reporters even attempt to quote him or other Indigenous performers.

The one example of an inscription that includes musical notation is no different. While such notation provides much more detail on the musical qualities of the "Red River Jig" as a fiddle tune with an indication of some variation between these past fiddlers, it leaves many questions unanswered as to the variability of this music (and dance) in practice. If you have been trained to read this type of notation, you are then able to replicate "the sounds" of this tune on an instrument (or in your head). But what does this experience *really* tell you about how Indigenous fiddlers (and other performers) experienced this music? Generally, fiddlers in the past (Indigenous or otherwise) did not read music; and fiddlers today, even if they happen to read music, do not find musical notation especially helpful for conveying the feel of this style (and others). Much is missing, such as the accents, the percussive bowing qualities, and the phrasing subtleties emphasizing danceability.

Overall, these inscriptions provide little indication of the value these fiddle dances had from a perspective of Indigenous performers. It is difficult to know what these past audiences learned in listening to and watching these performers. I believe Dion purposefully shifted the common narrative that the Old Timers often forged for these dances as quaint practices of yesteryear by highlighting their worthiness as cultural practices in their own right. Still, I am left wanting more in my attempts to understand past Indigenous performers' perspectives on these fiddle dances. While I was once able to talk with one of Dion's daughters, I believe the next steps would be to pay even more attention to the direct descendants of these past performers, listening to their perspectives.

Notes

Acknowledgments: As a graduate student at Indiana University, I learned from both Raymond DeMallie and Douglas Parks. I had four semesters of Lakȟóta language under Parks's instruction, while I took many cultural anthropology-related courses under DeMallie, including an independent readings course focusing on my doctoral research interests in Métis history and culture. I am much more likely to see DeMallie's influence as a mentor since he was on my dissertation committee and because he was more aligned with how I saw myself, and continue to see myself, as a cultural anthropologist. Nevertheless, thinking back to their instruction and mentorship, which for me was usually with each separately, I have begun to see them as more merged in their intent to expand students' skills in listening—literally in terms of the listening required to hear, mimic, and document languages and their nuances, as well as more metaphorically in terms of their open-mindedness to source materials and methodologies. Listening to Indigenous collaborators and key consultants as a part of their linguistic and cultural-historical inquiries was one method of many in DeMallie and Parks's research toolkit, so obviously they promoted a methodological insistence on listening. But at a more metaphorical level, *what* listening means has also been addressed by DeMallie when it comes to historical sources, most obviously in "'These Have No Ears': Narrative and the Ethnohistorical Method" (1993).

1. The Métis political reemergence also overlaps with the tail end of this (1890–1930) period (see Dorion and Préfontaine 2001 and Quick 2009 for more discussion on this periodization; see also Hogue 2020 on the lack of attention that historians have given this period in Métis historiography). The term "Métis" first referred (among other terms) to the progeny of European settler men and Indigenous women largely within the fur trade system. The Métis Nation currently refers to a collective political entity recognized by the Canadian government, although exactly what Métis means in terms of rights and recognition is still being negotiated at national, provincial, and more local levels (Andersen 2014). While Métis are not recognized as a separate Indigenous group in the United States, historically the Métis from the Red River settlement (what became Winnipeg) in Manitoba were also known to live and travel south, and

these Métis have often been seen as the prototypical models for Métis national and cultural identity. Further, Manitoba, Saskatchewan, and Alberta have been seen as the eventual primary home places for those Métis communities that scattered after their late nineteenth-century diaspora, although Métis presence and dispersals are known in places beyond these Canadian provinces (Hogue 2015).

2. Garneau does not appear in the Old Timers' early membership list (NAPDA 1983, 4–7). He had been involved with the Red River resistance in 1870, moved to Edmonton in 1874, and late in his life, in 1901, moved to what was then called St. Paul des Métis, the short-lived colony northeast of Edmonton initially designated for Métis settlement by the Catholic Church that later opened up to French Canadian settlers (Dorion et al. 2001, 105–7; Brady 1952). See Anacker et al. (2020) for more on the history of this colony and the continued legacy of its expansion to settlers for Métis.

3. Victoria Callihoo née Belcourt (1861–1966) was a respected Métis elder who lived most of her life in the Lac Ste. Anne region of Alberta. She periodically performed the Red River Jig at Old Timer events, and her memories of nineteenth-century life were later published in the *Alberta Historical Review* (Petten 2004).

4. After the Edmonton Old Timers reorganized in 1924, they were communicating with the Calgary Old Timers, even exchanging tickets for representatives of each organization to attend their respective banquets in 1925 and at later events (NAPDA 1983, 18).

5. Perhaps this ambiguity or lack of identification was out of politeness since the stigma of the 1885 "North-West Rebellion" in relation to Métis identity was still in recent memory for Canadians, and this period is also often framed as the forgotten period for Métis. However, through online genealogical open-source materials, this family is easily attributed to Métis ancestry (WikiTree FREE Family Tree 2021).

6. In a search of these newspapers for "Red River Jig" references, the advertisements for this sheet music also appeared several times.

7. Seeing their appearance as "costumed" may be in part because of the reviewers' framing of them in this way since wearing sashes, for example, was still common for some Métis men at this time (Weselake-George, conversation with author, December 9, 2022).

8. This statement is driven by Dion's writings (1979) and actions (Wall 2008). Indigenous scholars have also recently critiqued this recognition

and rights discourse as having problematic impacts and as only going so far in addressing the continued control of the settler state (Andersen 2014).

References

"Alberta Old Timers' Day." 1926. *Edmonton Bulletin*, May 20, 12.

"Alberta Party on the Way to Festival, Unique Group of 'Metis' to Sing and Dance in Quebec." 1930. *Montreal Gazette*, October 15, 7.

Anacker, Caleb, Tanya Fontaine, Megan Tucker, Pierre Lamoureux, Goddy Nzonji, and Roy Missal. 2020. *Restoring the History of St. Paul des Métis: Understanding Métis Perspectives*. St. Paul AB: Independently published.

Andersen, Chris. 2014. *"Métis": Race, Recognition, and the Struggle for Indigenous Peoplehood*. Vancouver: UBC Press.

Barkwell, Lawrence H., Leah Dorion, and Darren R. Préfontaine, eds. *Métis Legacy: A Métis Historiography and Annotated Bibliography*. Saskatoon SK: Gabriel Dumont Institute.

Bloechl, Olivia. 2008. *Native American Song at the Frontiers of Early Modern Music*. Cambridge: Cambridge University Press.

Bohlman, Philip. 1993. "Musicology as a Political Act." *Journal of Musicology* 11, no. 4: 411–36.

Brady, J. P. 1952. Letter to Ella May Walker. Ella May (Jacoby) Walker fonds, MS-52, box 1, item 20. City of Edmonton Archives, Edmonton. https://archivescanada.accesstomemory.ca/letter-from-laurent-garneaus-grandson-1952-description-of-garneau-plaque-erected-on-saskatchewan-drive-1952.

Braun, Sebastian F. 2013. "Introduction: An Ethnohistory of Listening." In *Transforming Ethnohistories: Narrative, Meaning, and Community*, edited by Sebastian F. Braun, 3–21. Norman: University of Oklahoma Press.

Broder, Anna Glen. 1930. "Programme of Unusual Quality Opens Festival." *Calgary Daily Herald*, March 20, 20.

Dalheim, K., and M. Kerr. 1976. *Calahoo Trails: A History of Calahoo, Granger, Speldhurst-Noyes Crossing, East Bilby, Green Willow, 1842-1955*. Calahoo AB: Calahoo Women's Institute.

Deloria, Phillip J. 1998. *Playing Indian*. New Haven CT: Yale University Press.

———. 2004. *Indians in Unexpected Places*. Lawrence: University Press of Kansas.

DeMallie, Raymond J. 1993. "'These Have No Ears': Narrative and the Ethnohistorical Method." *Ethnohistory* 40, no. 4: 515–38.

Dempsey, Hugh. 1979. Introduction to *My Tribe, the Crees*, by Joseph Frances Dion, v-viii. Calgary: Glenbow-Alberta Institute.

Diamond, Beverly. 2019. "Purposefully Reflecting on Tradition and Modernity." In *Music and Modernity among First Peoples in North America*, edited by Victoria Levine and Dylan Robinson, 240–57. Middletown CT: University of Wesleyan Press.

Dion, Joseph Frances. 1979. *My Tribe, the Crees*. Edited by Hugh Dempsey. Calgary: Glenbow-Alberta Institute.

———. n.d. "Indian and Halfbreed–Old Time Stories and Programme of Old Time Dances." Joseph Dion fonds, M-331-30, Glenbow Archives, Calgary.

Donnelly, Ann. 1930. "Calgary Festival Folk Dance Teas Enchant Guests." *Edmonton Journal*, March 21, 18.

Dorion, Leah, and Darren R. Préfontaine. 2001. "Deconstructing Métis Historiography: Giving Voice to the Métis People." In Barkwell, Dorion, and Préfontaine 2001, 13–36.

Dorion, Leah, R. D. Garneau, Margaret Gross, and Lawrence Barkwell. 2001. "Alberta Métis Leaders." In Barkwell, Dorion, and Préfontaine 2001, 105–14.

Dorion-Paquin, Leah, Trent Bruner, David Kaplan, and Lyndon Smith. 2002. *Drops of Brandy: An Anthology of Métis Music*. Saskatoon SK: Gabriel Dumont Institute.

Dueck, Byron. 2007. "Public and Intimate Sociability in First Nations and Métis Fiddling." *Ethnomusicology* 51, no. 1: 30–63.

———. 2013. *Musical Intimacies and Indigenous Imaginaries: Aboriginal Music and Dance in Public Performance*. Oxford: Oxford University Press.

"Folkdance, Folksong, and Handicrafts Festival." 1930. In "Star's Younger Readers," *Toronto Daily Star*, September 20, 13, and "News," *Toronto Daily Star*, October 4, 23.

"Folkdancing, Handicrafts Attract Crowds of People." 1930. *Calgary Albertan*, March 21, 5.

"The Folk Song–Folk Dance Festival." 1930. *Manitoba Free Press*, March 28, 13.

Gibbons, Roy W. 1981. *Folk Fiddling in Canada, A Sampling*. Ottawa: National Museums of Canada.

Giroux, Monique. 2013. "Music, Power, and Relations: Fiddling as a Meeting Place between Re-Settlers and Indigenous Nations in Manitoba." PhD diss., York University, Toronto.

———. 2021. "Music Research and the Sound Archive: A Meditation on Ethno-Musicological Engagement with Collection-Oriented Research and Re(p)(m)atriation." *Yearbook for Traditional Music* 53: 103–26. Cambridge Core, Cambridge University Press, https://doi.org/10.1017/ytm.2021.3.

Goyette, Linda, and Carolina Jakeway Roemmich. 2004. *Edmonton in Our Own Words*. Edmonton: University of Alberta Press.

Henderson, Stuart. 2005. "'While There Is Still Time . . .': J. Murray Gibbon and the Spectacle of Difference in Three CPR Folk Festivals, 1928–1931." *Journal of Canadian Studies* 39, no. 1: 139–74.

Herndon, Marcia. 1974. "Analysis: The Herding of Sacred Cows?" *Ethnomusicology* 18, no. 2: 219–62.

Hobsbawm, Eric, and Terence Ranger. 1983. *The Invention of Tradition*. New York: Cambridge University Press.

Hogue, Michel. 2015. *Metis and the Medicine Line: Creating a Border and Dividing a People*. Chapel Hill: University of North Carolina Press.

———. 2020. "Still Hiding in Plain Site?: Historiography and Métis Archival Memory." *History Compass* 18, no. 7: e12618. Wiley Online Library, https://doi.org/10.1111/hic3.12618.

Holmes, Clara L. K. 1930. "The Great West Festival at Calgary." *Canadian Geographical Journal* 1, no. 3: 268–75.

Jamison, Phil. 2015. *Hoedowns, Reels, and Frolics: Roots and Branches of Southern Appalachian Dance*. Urbana: University of Illinois Press.

Johnstone, Thomas, and Frederick Genthon. 1931. "The Red River Jig." Transposed by W. E. Delaney. Old Timers' Association of Manitoba. Winnipeg MB: A. Mulligan.

Kells, Edna. 1928. "Mrs. Louis Calihoo Won Honor in Red River Jig Competition." *Edmonton Journal*, June 5.

Lederman, Anne. 1986. "Old Native and Metis Fiddling in Two Manitoba Communities: Camperville and Ebb and Flow." MA thesis, York University, Toronto.

———. 1988. "Old Indian and Metis Fiddling in Manitoba: Origins, Structure, and Questions of Syncretism." *Canadian Journal of Native Studies* 8, no. 2: 205–30.

Levine, Victoria, and Dylan Robinson, eds. 2019. *Music and Modernity among First Peoples in North America*. Middletown CT: University of Wesleyan Press.

Marian-Bălașa, Marin. 2005. "Who Actually Needs Transcription? Notes on the Modern Rise of a Method and the Postmodern Fall of an Ideology." *World of Music* 47, no. 2: 5–29.

Marsh, D'Arcy. 1930. "St. Paul de Metis." In "Fits and Starts," *Calgary Albertan*, March 21, 4.

May, David, and Louise Horstman, eds. 1982. *Tired of Rambling: A History of Fishing Lake Metis Settlement*. Edmonton: Alberta Federation of Metis Settlement Associations.

"McDonald Kiddies to Make 'Whoopee' in Show at Grand." 1929. *Calgary Herald*, May 8, 5.

Miller, Bill. 1984. *Our Home: A History of Kikino Metis Settlement*. Edmonton: Alberta Federation of Metis Settlements.

Mulligan, Barbara Louise. 1929. "Instructions for Dancing the Red River Jig." In "The Red River Jig," transposed by W. E. Delaney. Old Timers' Association of Manitoba. Winnipeg MB: A. Mulligan.

NAPDA (Northern Alberta Pioneers and Descendants Association). 1983. *A History of the Northern Alberta Pioneers and Old Timers' Association, 1894-1983*. Edmonton: Northern Alberta Pioneers and Descendants Association.

Nettl, Bruno. 2015. *The Study of Ethnomusicology: Thirty-Three Discussions*. Urbana: University of Illinois Press.

Ochoa Gautier, Ana Maria. 2014. *Aurality*. Durham NC: Duke University Press.

"Old Indian Dances Feature Reunion." 1932. *Edmonton Journal*, October 29, 12.

"Old Timers' Ball." 1896. *Edmonton Bulletin*, February 3, 4.

"Panoramic of Background of Canadian Life Given in Folk Presentations." 1930. *Calgary Albertan*, March 20, 9.

Petten, Cheryl. 2004. "Métis Woman Painted Vibrant Picture of the West." *Windspeaker* 22, no. 7: 30.

Pisani, Michael V. 2005. *Imagining Native America in Music*. New Haven CT: Yale University Press.

Price, Elizabeth Bailey. 1928a. "Preserve Red River Jig. Old Dance on the Verge of Extinction." *Edmonton Journal*, June 2, 33.

———. 1928b. "Preserving the Red River Jig for Posterity." *Toronto Star Weekly*, April 7. Elizabeth Bailey Price Newspaper Clippings M1002, Glenbow Archives, Calgary.

Quick, Sarah. 2008. "The Social Poetics of the Red River Jig in Alberta and Beyond: Meaningful Heritage and Emerging Performance." *Ethnologies* 30, no. 1: 77-101.

———. 2009. "Performing Heritage: Metis Music, Dance, and Identity in a Multicultural State." PhD diss., Indiana University, Bloomington.

Randall, Walter H. 1942. "Genthon the Fiddler." *The Beaver*, December, 15-17.

"Red River Jig, Dance of Earlier Days, Staging Big Comeback." 1928. *Calgary Daily Herald*, February 11.

Robinson, Dylan. 2020. *Hungry Listening: Resonant Theory for Indigenous Sound Studies*. Minneapolis: University of Minnesota Press.

Samuels, David. 2019. "The Oldest Songs They Remember: Frances Densmore, Mountain Chief, and Ethnomusicology's Ideologies of Modernity." In *Music and Modernity among First Peoples in North America*, edited by Victoria Levine and Dylan Robinson, 13-30. Middletown CT: University of Wesleyan Press.

SAPD (Southern Alberta Pioneers and Their Descendants). 1993. *Pioneer Families of Southern Alberta*. Calgary: Southern Alberta Pioneers and Their Descendants.

Smith, Melba. 1929. "Tapatoe." In "The Red River Jig," transposed by W. E. Delaney. Old Timers' Association of Manitoba. Winnipeg MB: A. Mulligan.

Sterne, Jonathon. 2003. *The Audible Past*. Durham NC: Duke University Press.

"Student Revue Is Successful." 1928. *Calgary Daily Herald*, June 4, 13.

"Tea Programme Pleases Guests." 1930. *Calgary Daily Herald*, March 21, 10.

Wall, Denis. 2008. *The Alberta Métis Letters: 1930–1940 Policy Review and Annotations*. Edmonton: DWRG Press.

Whidden, Lynn. 2007. *Essential Song: Three Decades of Northern Cree Music*. Aboriginal Studies Series. Waterloo ON: Wilfrid Laurier University Press.

WikiTree FREE Family Tree. "Mary-Lucille Lucille (Gladu) Kipling (1850–1949)." Accessed October 20, 2021, https://www.wikitree.com/wiki/Gladu-144.

"Will Recall Dances of Early West." 1930. *Edmonton Journal*, July 7, 10.

Paradigms and Poetry   6

John G. Neihardt's *Cycle of the West*

FRANCIS FLAVIN

By the end of the nineteenth or the beginning of the twentieth century, the Lakȟóta had become the most widely recognized of all American Indian people in the United States. One of the reasons is that many artists, writers, and showmen popularized the Plains Indians — the Lakȟóta, in particular — to broad audiences in the United States, Canada, and Europe.

No one popularized the Sioux more prodigiously than William "Buffalo Bill" Cody. His Wild West show ran from 1883 to 1917 and was attended by tens of millions of people in North America and Europe. The enhancement of lithographic technology facilitated the creation of thousands of posters to advertise each performance, which meant that Cody's Indians were seen by millions of people who never attended an actual show. The Wild West featured almost exclusively Plains Indians, most of them Lakȟóta (see, for example, Moses 1996; Warren 2005; Kasson 2000; Reddin 1999; Rennert 1976; Farnum 1992).

Writers were also important in introducing the Lakȟóta to Europeans and European Americans. James Fenimore Cooper's *The Prairie* (1827) and Francis Parkman's *The Oregon Trail* (1849) each prominently featured the Lakȟóta. Artist and writer George Catlin included graphic depictions and written descriptions of Plains Sioux in his "Indian Gallery," which toured both the United States and Europe in the mid-nineteenth century. In a battle that became enshrined in American myth, the Lakȟóta defeated George Armstrong Custer on the Little Bighorn River in June 1876, a few days before the United States celebrated its centennial. Additionally, it was the Lakȟóta who were the victims of the Wounded Knee Massacre in December 1890, the year that the U.S. Census Bureau declared the "frontier" to be closed. Thus, in the popularized and mythic story of U.S. westward expansion, the nation's *most famous* battle with the Indians and its *last* (and, perhaps, most ignominious) battle (if it even can be called a "battle") with the Indians were with the Lakȟóta. These two events provided authors, artists, showmen, and moviemakers with extraordinarily rich and compelling themes to explore, and they have done so from the late nineteenth century to the present (see, for example, Dippie 1976; Moses 1996; Kasson 2000; Slotkin 1973, 1992; Elliott 2007).

American Indian people have been the subject of many myths that have appeared in popular representations across time. According to Akim D. Reinhardt, they "have been celebrated as the Noble Savage, revered as the mystical medicine man, mourned as the disappearing Red Man, upheld as the harmonious environmentalist, admired as the proud and able warrior, and vilified as the conniving and treacherous barbarian, to name a few of the broad-brush themes that have proliferated" (2003, 184). Important to the popularity of the Sioux is that their historical experience can be presented within a well-established, centuries-old paradigm that frames a dialectic between the "savage" and the "civilized" conditions of human societies. The English word "savage" has its roots in the Old French word *sauvage*, which means "wild, untamed, or uncultivated," which further derives from the Latin word *silva*, which means "woods" or "forest." From the classical antiquity to the colonization of North America, Europeans and European Americans who contemplated the meaning of human history sometimes framed it as a dialectic between simple, close-to-nature societies and complex, advanced, and often urban societies.

When viewing the history of a single people, Europeans and European Americans often imagined that a given group of people began their existence living in a simple, primitive, savage state and, over time, evolved into a robust and vibrant civilization (Morgan [1877] 1907, v–viii, 3–45).[1] A canonical example of this is the esteemed artist of the Hudson River School, Thomas Cole, and his series of five oil paintings, "The Course of Empire," completed between 1833 and 1836.

The paintings depict a triumphal—yet ultimately ruinous—narrative trajectory of human social development from *The Savage State* to *The Arcadian or Pastoral State* to *The Consummation of Empire* to *Destruction* and, ultimately, to *Desolation* (Powell 1990, 62–72; Truettner 1991, 27–32; Cronon 1992, 40–44). In these five paintings the viewer can see the rise and fall of a people, a state, or a civilization, generalized across space and time.

Often, those who viewed human experience as a contest between savagery and civilization perceived themselves in the role of advanced or enlightened civilizers and perceived the other peoples as oppositional figures who were in a less advanced, less enlightened state. During the nineteenth and twentieth centuries, American mythmakers portrayed Indians sometimes as *noble* "savages" and, at other times, as *ignoble* "savages." These are two somewhat contradictory paradigms through which Europeans and Americans had long interpreted American Indians (Pearce 1988; Berkhofer 1978; Dickason 1997; Ellingson 2001; Pagden 1982). The ideas of the "noble savage" and the "ignoble savage" both rest on the idea of "savagism." In the words of literary critic Roy Harvey Pearce, savagism is "a counter-theme [to] civilization" (1988, xix). Savagism was an idea that represented the supposed condition of humankind without the accretions and complexities of "civilization" and, therefore, an alternative—an antithesis—to civilized life.

The idea of societal "progress" from savagery to civilization and the oppositional dialectic between the two conditions are also associated with the concept of "Manifest Destiny." Manifest Destiny is a belief held by many in the United States during the nineteenth century that the nation had a moral and divinely ordained destiny to expand across the continent—spreading European American ideals, beliefs, technology, and institutions; supplanting Native peoples; and incorporating the geographic American West into a national empire.

The "vanishing race" paradigm is another intellectual paradigm within which nineteenth-century and early twentieth-century European Americans viewed Native peoples (Dippie 1982; Norris, Vines, and Hoeffel 2012, 8). This belief held that American Indians were doomed, either lamentably or not, to extinction. One might say that doom was the "answer" to the dialectic: that is, the result of the contest would be that one group vanished. A popular view held that the "vanishing" of Indian people would be existential—that is, American Indians as a "race" would die out and vanish from the continent. Another view held that Indian people might vanish culturally—in other words, over time, people of Indian descent would assimilate to the point at which their culture was no longer recognizably "Indian." This reveals a flawed assumption that Native cultures were static and that Indian cultural borrowings and Indian assimilation were somehow illegitimate. Other people—including missionaries, government agents, and, most notably, Thomas Jefferson—believed that American Indians would, in effect, disappear by intermarrying and assimilating into European American society (Sheehan 1973).

These paradigms, understood among many educated Europeans and European Americans in the nineteenth and twentieth centuries, appeared time and again in artistic and literary depictions of the American West and Indian people, sometimes allegorically and sometimes depicting real events and real people. The rapid, sweeping, and violent process that transformed the Lakȟóta from free-ranging, equestrian buffalo hunters to sedentary tenants of federal Indian reservations provided mythmakers with real historical events and real historical actors—such as Crazy Horse (Tȟašuŋka Witkó), Sitting Bull (Tȟatȟáŋka Íyotake), and Custer. These mythmakers presented tableaus of great battles and doomed heroes that, somehow, epitomized the dialectic between savagery and civilization, the idea of progress, the Manifest Destiny paradigm, and the vanishing race paradigm. Collectively, these tableaus presented an epic narrative so compelling that it deserved a place not solely in the history of the Lakȟóta people and in the history of the United States but, perhaps, in a history of the world.

Neihardt

One of the most celebrated writers of the twentieth century who wrote about American Indian people is John G. Neihardt (1881–1973). His best-known works were about American Indians, about the Sioux, and about the nineteenth century North American West. Neihardt interpreted the nineteenth-century Sioux in a manner far gentler and more poetic than Wild West productions. Yet readers can perceive in his work the tension between savagery and civilization, along with the themes of progress, Manifest Destiny, and the vanishing race paradigm. Furthermore, like other artists, writers, and mythmakers, Neihardt often overlooked the experience of the Sioux who were contemporary to his own life, in the twentieth century. Instead, he memorialized a narrative of the nineteenth-century Sioux and interpreted pre-reservation life as somehow more authentic and meaningful than the reservation experience of the twentieth-century Sioux.

Neihardt was born in Illinois in 1881 and later lived in Kansas, Nebraska, and Missouri. At a young age he developed a deep affection for the North American West and dedicated much of his life to memorializing its history (Aly 1976, 5–7). Neihardt was a prolific author, and he chose the Sioux as principal subjects in his greatest works. *Black Elk Speaks: Being the Life Story of a Holy Man of the Oglala Sioux*, first published in 1932, is Neihardt's most popular work. However, *A Cycle of the West*, which was first published in its complete form in 1949, provides a clearer example of Neihardt writing within the aforementioned paradigms.

A Cycle of the West is a five-part epic poem designed, as Neihardt said, "to celebrate the great mood of courage that was developed west of the Missouri River in the nineteenth century." *Cycle* deals with a period of "discovery, exploration, and settlement—a genuine epic period, differing in no essential from the other great epic periods that marked the advance of the Indo-European peoples out of Asia and across Europe." Neihardt believed it was "a time of intense individualism, a time when society was cut loose from its roots, a time when an old culture was being overcome by that of a powerful people driven by the ancient needs and greeds." For Neihardt, the *Cycle* was wrought from "the richly human saga-stuff" of an era barely past, an era that was a "watershed of history" but "the summit of which" America had "already crossed" when he wrote his *Cycle* in the early twentieth century (Neihardt [1961] 1971, v–vi, xi).

The epic was composed of five poetic "songs," each of which was initially published as a separate piece. The first three songs—*The Song of Three Friends* (1919), *The Song of Hugh Glass* (1915), and *The Song of Jed Smith* (1941)—were poems about white adventurers foraying into the West. The final two songs, *The Song of the Indian Wars* (1925) and *The Song of the Messiah* (1935), were about the Indians of the plains, especially the Lakȟóta. Reflecting the tendency in European American art, history, and literature to cast Indians as oppositional to "civilization" and "progress," Neihardt presented these Indians as representing the "old culture" that "was being overcome" by the advance of Euro-American civilization. Neihardt described *The Song of the Indian Wars* as being about the "last great fight for the bison pastures between the invading white race and the Plains Indians—the Sioux, the Cheyenne, and the Arapahoe." *The Song of the Messiah* "is concerned wholly with the conquered people and the worldly end of their last great dream"; specifically, Neihardt said, "The period closes with the Battle of Wounded Knee in 1890, which marked the end of Indian resistance of the Plains" (Neihardt [1961] 1971, vii).

Using language that calls to mind John Gast's iconic 1872 painting *American Progress, The Song of the Indian Wars* begins in the immediate post–Civil War era, with wagon trains bringing acquisitive white settlers to the Great Plains: "On they swirled, / the driving breed, the takers of the world" (Neihardt [1961] 1971 *Indian Wars*, 2).[2] Set against these interlopers were the Sioux and their Indian neighbors, men who must lose so that others may win.

> But there were those—and they were also men—
> Who saw the end of sacred things and dear
> In all this wild beginning; saw with fear
> Ancestral pastures gutted by the plow
> The bison harried ceaselessly, and how
> They dwindled moon by moon; with pious
>   dread
> Beheld the holy places of their dead
> The mock of aliens.

> Sioux, Arapahoe,
> Cheyenne, Comanche, Kiowa and Crow
> In many a council pondered what befell
> The prairie world. (3)

There came a "clank of hammers" and a "clang of rails" as "hoards of white men" "conjured iron trails" and pushed onto the plains. Euro-Americans, "hungry myriads" of them, poured westward, "pale with greed"—and "whatsoever pleased them, that they took" (4).

In Neihardt's telling, the "Red men groped" in council for a response, "bewildered in the dusk of ancient days." The "wise ones" felt "the end of things, / Inexorably shaping," while the more youthful "hotheads" urged armed resistance. Although it seemed apparent that "ere long whole tribes must take the spirit trail / As once they travelled to the bison hunt," the reigning mood among the Sioux, Cheyennes, and Arapahos was that the tribes should perish gloriously in opposition to the forces of change (4–5).

> Then let it be with many wounds—in front—
> And many scalps, to show their ghostly kin
> How well they fought the fight they could not
>   win,
> To perish facing what they could not kill. (5)

Thus, Neihardt depicts the Sioux, Cheyennes, and Arapahos as exemplars extraordinaire of the vanishing race paradigm. The dwindling of the buffalo and the arrival of the plow made them sense that "the end of sacred things" was close upon them (3). Yet, despite the seeming inevitability of their doom, they would sell their lives dearly, fighting bravely in "the fight they could not win" (5).

The Song of the Indian Wars next describes the councils of the 1860s in which the Sioux, Cheyennes, and Arapahos deliberated as to how they might respond to the flood of European American immigrants.[3] Some proposed to forsake war and seek accommodation because they believed, Neihardt scornfully wrote, that "many presents and the pipe of peace / Are waiting yonder at the Soldier's Town." Reflecting a theme that he would develop in *The Song of the Messiah*, Neihardt wrote that others, "who counselled with a dream," believed that the "Great Spirit made all peoples, White and Red" and "pitched one big blue teepee overhead / That men might live as brothers side by side" (7). Neihardt depicted still others rebutting this, cynically retorting:

> "Their medicine is strong, their hearts are bad;
> A little part of what our fathers had
> They give us now, tomorrow come and take.
> Great Spirit also made the rattlesnake
> And over him the big blue teepee set!" (8)

Neihardt's Indians decided among several strategies. The Indians he depicted as accommodationists were willing to surrender their old ways for an easy peace, the dreamers hoped that the two races could live respectfully as "brothers side by side," and those he depicted as militants rejected peace and scorned brotherhood, preferring instead to fight the invaders, even if the attempt proved futile.

One of Neihardt's central themes in this song is the dichotomy of leadership strategies that developed between Red Cloud (Maȟpiya Lúta) and Spotted Tail (Siŋté Glešká) in the 1860s. Neihardt used Spotted Tail to represent the accommodationist perspective. In his youth Spotted Tail had been a vigorous warrior and an opponent of the Americans; however, after surrendering himself to captivity, Spotted Tail began to grasp the magnitude of American power. He concluded that the Sioux would be best served by seeking accommodation with the Americans rather than by needlessly wasting Indian lives in battle. Neihardt's Spotted Tail "knew old times could never be again" and that the Americans would "take" what they wanted if the Sioux "do not give." Dismissing the militants' solution, he warned, "Not all can die in battle. Some must live" (13).

Neihardt's Red Cloud represents the argument for military resistance as well as the repudiation of accommodation. Red Cloud was "one who never gave despair / A moral mein, nor schooled a righteous hate / To live at peace with evil." He represented righteous opposition.

Neihardt, suggesting the powerlessness of the Indians to alter their own fate and the consequent irrelevance of their deliberations, writes, "all the while / These wrestled with the question, mile upon mile / The White Man's answer crept along the road— / Two hundred mule-teams, leaning to the load" (14–16).

Neihardt describes a great council of Sioux and Cheyennes on the Powder River, in which Red Cloud warned his people that white "hearts are bad and all their words are lies." He asked "Are we cowards? Shall we stand / Unmoved as trees and see our Mother Land / Plowed up for corn?" As he continued his speech of righteous opposition, "smothered wrath . . . mastered him, and 'woke / The sleeping thunder all had waited for. / Out of a thrilling hush he shouted: 'War!'" (27–28).

In response, Neihardt's Spotted Tail arose amid "the blood-lust raging there" and made an eloquent plea for peaceful accommodation. He likened the Sioux to a people whose time was almost past and encouraged them to view their own decline as part of the natural order, "everything begins and grows and ends, that other things may have their time" (29–30).

Neihardt's Spotted Tail told his people that their quest to preserve their old ways was essentially a quest of "trying not to die." He urged them not to war with nature, but to grow old naturally, "as old men should." Alas for Spotted Tail, his council fell on deaf ears, and when he finished his oration a "hostile silence closed, as waters close / Above the drowned" (30).

As if silence were not enough to delegitimize Spotted Tail's argument, Neihardt then had Sitting Bull rise and, like Red Cloud, speak in favor of war. He urged resistance to the rapacious, acquisitive whites:

> "'Twas not many snows ago
> They said that we might hunt our buffalo
> In this land forever. Now they come
> To break that promise. Shall we cower
>   dumb?
> Or shall we say: 'First kill us—here we
>   stand!'" (33)

There was, it seemed, a pause, for "over all the village" Sitting Bull had "cast a spell." Until "like a lean blue flash" a "warrior uttered in a yell" the "common hate" that they harbored for the whites—and throughout the night the men danced and sang their "battle-song" (33–34). With this, in Neihardt's telling, the die was cast: the Sioux—and their Cheyenne allies—chose war over peace, and opposition over accommodation.

The Song of the Indian Wars continues as a series of clashes in which the Sioux and the Cheyennes battled the Americans. As the song progresses, Neihardt repeatedly vilifies Spotted Tail and the accommodationists—they are "beggars at the Great White Father's trough," waiting "to be swilled." As the fight with Custer approached, many of the Sioux sensed an impending doom, but "there were strong hearts yet among the Sioux," and "despite the mumbling of withered gums," the young cast their lot with "Crazy Horse and Sitting Bull and Gall" (Phizí), who remained "contemptuous of alien ways and gods" (109–10).

In depicting the climactic battle on the Little Bighorn, Neihardt wrote that the Lakȟóta and their "faithful brothers," the Cheyennes, met Custer's troops with determination, with Gall urging his followers to "die here today!" and Crazy Horse crying, "*There never was a better day to die!*" (138, 142, 147). Neihardt, as have many historians, grasped the irony of the Sioux victory over Custer: although it was a victory for the Sioux, it sealed and hastened their fate. Their victory became an "irreparable wrong" that spelled ultimate defeat for the recent victors. The free Sioux in *The Song of the Indian Wars* sensed this, too—their drums had "fallen silent" and they knew "all things glorious and old" were "gone forever" (158).

The Song of the Indian Wars closes with Crazy Horse's surrender and death. To friend and foe alike, the holdout Crazy Horse was the "last great Sioux" (169). For Neihardt, Crazy Horse was the "principal hero" of the song (Vine Deloria Jr., quoted in the 1979 edition of Neihardt [1932] 1979, xvi). It was his responsibility to his weaker followers—not a failure of courage—that impelled him to capitulate. He surrendered himself and "twice a thousand beggars" with aloof simplicity: "'I come for peace,' he said; / 'Now let my people eat.' And that was all" (Neihardt [1961] 1971 *Indian Wars*, 171).

For Neihardt, Crazy Horse's surrender brought "long brooding on a birthright lost," the end of the glorious Sioux buffalo culture, and the end of Sioux freedom. Crazy Horse yearned for liberty, as reservation life could never bring satisfaction. Neihardt writes in *The Song of the Indian Wars* that there "wasn't any food the white man had" that could sate Crazy Horse's "gnawing hunger" ([1932] 1979, 172). Neihardt presents that, despite his personal sorrow, Crazy Horse's prestige remained great, and some saw him as "a blood-mad panther in a cage" while others, however, grew jealous and suspicious of him. Fearing trouble, agency authorities led him—unsuspecting—to a prison cell. When Crazy Horse grasped the deception, he struggled to resist and, in the process, received a mortal bayonet wound.

The Song of the Indian Wars ends with Crazy Horse's death, after which, Neihardt writes that "Crazy Horse" became "nothing but a name." His aged parents bore "the last great Sioux" away and secretly, privately buried his body—hidden forever from those who sought to destroy him. "Who knows the crumbling summit where he lies?" (178–79).

A Cycle of the West's fifth and final song is *The Song of the Messiah*.[4] This song is less literal and more mystical than *Song of the Indian Wars*. It is set in 1887, ten years after the death of Crazy Horse, the "one ingloriously slain." And for ten "years had grown the sorrow of the Sioux." Sorrow was not theirs alone, for the "earth was dying slowly, being old." Despair pervaded the northern plains, and it seemed that "it were better nothing had been born." Worse still, there "was no longer magic in the earth" (Neihardt [1961] 1971 *Messiah*, 1–4). In short, Neihardt presented the Sioux as sorrowing over the passing of the old ways while finding little, if any, fulfillment in reservation life and assimilation.

In contrast, when the "old men" of the Sioux contemplated their plight, they found themselves to blame for their misfortune. "There is no hope for us," they said:

"For we have sold our Mother to the lust
Of strangers, and her breast is bitter dust,
Her thousand laps are empty! She was kind
Before the white men's spirit made us blind
   ...We have sinned...
It was the living spirit that we sold—" (6–7)

Into this world of regret and despair came word of a messiah, the Paiute, Wovoka, and his holy and mysterious message that promised a *"new earth and heaven!"* (11). Not surprisingly, the reservation Sioux were receptive to this message of hope. In the spring of 1889, the "dream took root / In hearts long fallow" (12). To some Sioux, the message and its accompanying dance seemed to promise "deathlessness" and immortality, and "Hundreds burned / With holiness" (56). In *The Song of the Messiah*, Neihardt depicts the young Ghost Dancers shouting to their agent:

"Your people tortured Jesus till He died!
You killed our bison and you stole our land!
This dance is our religion! Go and bring
Your soldiers, if you will. Not anything
Can hurt us now. And if they want to die,
Go bring them to us!" (58)

The impassioned opposition once embodied by Red Cloud, Sitting Bull, and Crazy Horse had sprung to life again. Neihardt presented these Sioux as excoriating the whites for their perceived immorality and expressed a willingness to use war to resolve their grievances. Yet, in Neihardt's *Cycle of the West*, there was an important distinction between these Sioux and their forebears. These Sioux Ghost Dancers could not die to defend their pre-reservation freedom and way of life as Red Cloud, Sitting Bull, and Crazy Horse had—because many of the freedoms, lifeways, and autonomy of pre-reservation life had been lost by the time of the Ghost Dance. Neihardt's Ghost Dancers were, however, willing to die to advance a hope that there would be a rebirth of old ways. In other words, the Sioux of Neihardt's *The Song of the Indian Wars* were dying to defend a life that, in reality, had been theirs; in *The Song of the Messiah*, some of Neihardt's Ghost Dancers were willing to risk their lives to realize a religious hope—or dream—of a better future.

Agency Whites became increasingly alarmed by the Ghost Dancers, "who could say / what devilment they hatched against the whites, / what lonely roofs would flare across the nights / to mark a path of murder!" (57). In response, they deployed army soldiers and Indian police to control the potentially volatile situation. This exercise of power angered some of the young Ghost Dancers:

> Youths, burning for the rendezvous with Fate,
> Were loud for battle. "Let us fight and die!"
> They clamored. "Better men than you and I
> Have died before us! Crazy Horse is dead!" (62–63)

Some Ghost Dancers grew confident that their new religion would protect them from the bullets of the whites. Sitting Bull was killed in a scuffle between Indian police and Ghost Dancers when the Indian police attempted to arrest him. The narrative concludes with the Wounded Knee massacre. Neihardt cast Yellow Bird (Ziŋtkázi) as inciting the slaughter:

> The high haranguing voice of Yellow Bird
> Above the lulling murmur: "Foolish ones
> And blind! Why are you giving up your guns
> To these Wasichus, who are hardly men
> And shall be shadows? Are you cowards, then,
> With hearts of water? . . .
>   Stab them, and they bleed
> No blood of brothers! Look at them and see
> The takers of the good that used to be,
> The killers of the Savior! Do not fear,
> The Nations of the Dead are crowding here
> To help us! Shall we shame them? *Do as I!*" (107)

A brief silence followed Yellow Bird's "final spear-thrust of a cry," but then a "gun-shot ripped the hush," and slaughter ensued (107–8).

A proper tragedy reaches an unhappy and sometimes fatal conclusion. A tragic story might have concluded in another, less lamentable way if it had not been for a chance occurrence, a misunderstanding, or a character flaw on the part of the protagonist. For Neihardt the massacre was a tragedy because it was the unhappy and fatal conclusion of the Ghost Dance. Here, Neihardt seems to accept the prevailing belief at the time that some Sioux followers of Wovoka's message interpreted it with a confrontational component even though it was unnecessary, which Neihardt believes is tragic. Neihardt, who developed a deep appreciation for Lakȟóta spirituality through his friendship with Black Elk, believed that a true interpretation of Wovoka's message was one of universal love.[5]

The message of universal love, though muted, was present even in *The Song of the Indian Wars*. From the song's beginning there was a minority of Sioux who were neither accommodationists nor militants, they were "dreamers." The "dream" was that "Red and White . . . could live as brothers side by side" and that all "peoples and the herds / Lived with the winged, the rooted and the finned" in peaceful harmony (Neihardt [1961] 1971 *Indian Wars*, 7; [1961] 1971 *Messiah*, 27). After Sitting Bull's death, Big Foot (Sí Tȟáŋka), the leader of the band who would soon be massacred at Wounded Knee Creek, recognized the true meaning of Wovoka's message, "And even if the soldiers come to kill / The Spirit says that we must love them still, / For they are brothers" (Neihardt [1961] 1971 *Messiah*, 101). He and his followers composed a new and joyous holy song, "'Father, I have seen / The stranger's face! Behold, my heart is green! / The stranger's face made beautiful to see!'" (102).

After Big Foot and his band surrendered to Colonel Forsyth, it seemed that the dream's ideal of universal brotherhood was still alive and growing, "like a father was the Soldier Chief. / Strong-hearted, of the plenty of his beef, / The plenty of his bread, he gave to eat . . . / . . . and he did much to make the children well" (104). It seemed that now "surely was the miracle begun" (107).

At this point Yellow Bird raised his "high haranguing voice" in a manner that precipitated the massacre (107). The dream remained alive for Chief Big Foot until the moment of his death. Amid the melee and fury of the massacre, Big Foot lay on the ground and,

> Then he saw
> One face above him and a gun-butt raised;
> A soldier's face with haggard eyes that blazed. (109)

Though he was face-to-face with hatred, Big Foot saw a "white light" that was the dream. "He strove to rise in vain, / To cry 'My brother!' / And his shattered brain / Went out" (109). Darkness fell, and in the concluding words of the song, a blizzard swept the "bloody field of victory that kept [t]he secret of the Everlasting Word" (110).

Neihardt intimates that the Lakȟóta dream of brotherly love was extinguished with Big Foot's death at Wounded Knee. *The Song of the Messiah* ends violently, leaving the reader shocked with the bloody finality of Big Foot's death. Nevertheless, it ends so abruptly that the reader, after processing the shock of Big Foot's violent death, might be inclined to ask, "and then what?"

Black Elk Speaks, published in 1932, three years before *The Song of the Messiah*, provides insight into Neihardt's thinking. The last chapter of *Black Elk Speaks* is titled "The End of the Dream," again revealing Neihardt's belief that some vital element of Lakȟóta life ended at the Wounded Knee massacre. The last lines in *Black Elk Speaks* are Neihardt's. He presents these lines as Black Elk's, thus using Black Elk as a vehicle for articulating what Neihardt believes to be the significance of Black Elk's life, the Ghost Dance, and the Wounded Knee massacre:

> And so it was all over.
>   I did not know then how much was ended. When I look back now from this high hill of my old age, I can still see the butchered women and children lying heaped and scattered all along the crooked gulch as plain as when I saw them with eyes still young. And I can see that something else died there in the bloody mud, and was buried in the blizzard. A people's dream died there. It was a beautiful dream.

> And I, to whom so great a vision was given in my youth,—you see me now a pitiful old man who has done nothing, for the nation's hoop is broken and scattered. There is no center any longer, and the sacred tree is dead. (Neihardt [1932] 1979, 270)

An "Author's Postscript" to *Black Elk Speaks* describes an episode that occurred shortly after Neihardt interviewed Black Elk in 1931. Black Elk and Neihardt traveled to Harney Peak—renamed in 2016 Black Elk Peak—in the Black Hills of South Dakota, where Black Elk had received a powerful vision in his youth. Black Elk prayed: "A pitiful old man, you see me here, and I have fallen away and done nothing.... Here at the center of the world... here, old, I stand, as the tree is withered." Then, expressing a glimmer of hope, Black Elk continues: "It may be that some little root of the sacred tree still lives.... Nourish it then, that it may leaf and bloom and fill with singing birds.... Hear me, not for myself, but for my people." Then, in the middle of oppressive drought conditions, a rain cloud appeared in an otherwise clear sky, drizzled momentarily on Black Elk and the others, and the sky grew clear again (271–74).

In many ways, as Raymond J. DeMallie indicates, *Black Elk Speaks* "can be characterized as an elegy, the commemoration of a man who has failed in his life's work, as well as of a people whose way of life has passed," and Black Elk's life, as presented by Neihardt, can be seen as "embodying the whole tragic history of defeat" of the Lakȟóta people that Neihardt presented in his *Cycle of the West* (DeMallie 1984, 55–57). However, despite the sincere affection Black Elk and Neihardt had for one another, and despite the seeming fidelity with which *Black Elk Speaks* conveys Lakȟóta culture and Black Elk's sacred vision, Neihardt's presentation of Black Elk is incomplete. Because of Neihardt's zeal to tell the story of the triumph of his own people and the subjugation of Black Elk's, *Cycle of the West* and *Black Elk Speaks* fail to address the significant adaptations that Lakȟóta people made in the twentieth century.

Like the Wild West shows, *The Song of the Indian Wars* and *The Song of the Messiah* demonstrate that the image and the narrative of the nineteenth-century Sioux were very important in the twentieth century. These poems demonstrate that the myths and analytical concepts Europeans and European Americans employed for understanding Indians during the nineteenth century were still important in the twentieth century.[6]

The Song of the Indian Wars and *The Song of the Messiah* are early twentieth-century expressions of the vanishing race paradigm that had become prominent in the nineteenth century. The two songs, when published together as the second volume of *A Cycle of the West*, are called collectively *The Twilight of the Sioux*—a title whose words clearly express vanishing race teleology. In *A Cycle of the West*, the Sioux have two "vanishings," so to speak: the first is the vanishing of their free-roaming, autonomous, pre-reservation way of life; the second is the vanishing of the hope for spiritual renewal and universal love that was present in Wovoka's message.

This first vanishing is symbolized by the death of Crazy Horse, who had come to represent pre-reservation freedom. Neihardt ended his poem upon recounting the death of Crazy Horse because, when Crazy Horse died, Neihardt believed that any hope to regain their pre-reservation freedom died, too.

A second vanishing is present in *The Song of the Messiah*, which contains numerous allusions to the vanishing race paradigm. The languor of reservation life, the brooding of older men who had known life in the glorious buffalo days, and the "dying" earth suggested that much had vanished or was about to vanish. To Neihardt, Wovoka's message of love offered an alternative to cultural, physical, and spiritual extinction. It was both a new beginning in the sense that it promised a "new earth and heaven," and it was a return to older, happier times because it intimated a return of dead ancestors and a return of game animals. However, the song concluded with the Wounded Knee massacre, the end of "the dream." *The Twilight of the Sioux* came to an end, and darkness fell. Just as Neihardt ends *The Song of the Indian Wars* with the death of Crazy Horse, the Lakȟóta chief whose name is synonymous with armed resistance, Neihardt ends *The Song of the Messiah* with the death of Big Foot, the Lakȟóta chief whose name is synonymous with the Wounded Knee massacre. Neihardt never says that the Sioux vanished in the physical sense—although Neihardt does chronicle the demise of many Sioux individuals—but he suggests that very meaningful elements of Sioux culture vanished.

In Neihardt's songs, the Sioux appeared aware that they, as a people, might vanish. Death is a concept that pervades the two songs. In addition to having the death of a prominent Sioux leader close each song, Neihardt depicts Sioux leaders frequently employing the concept of death when trying to shape opinion. Spotted Tail warned his people against militancy—because war could bring about the extinction of the Sioux: "Not all can die in battle. Some must live" (Neihardt [1961] 1971 *Indian Wars*, 13). Other Sioux seemed to prefer death to accommodation. Sitting Bull suggested that the Sioux ought to defy the white interlopers by challenging them, "First kill us—here we / stand!" (33). Gall inspired warriors at the Little Big Horn with the cry "Die here today!" while Crazy Horse urged, "*There never was a better day to die!*" (142, 147). During the Ghost Dance period, young Sioux decided "Let us die today!" rather than stop dancing (Neihardt [1961] 1971 *Messiah*, 58).

Neihardt's two songs also adhere to the long-held tenets of savagism—at least partially. Neihardt's poetry is not a fully developed articulation of savagism because it does not use the Sioux as a tool to critique white society.[7] The majority of his Sioux, in their refusal to surrender their old culture and embrace white customs, are presented within the paradigm of savagism as a people who refuse to surrender their Indigenous ways.

Additionally, Neihardt contrasts Sioux life and European American life in terms of binary opposites. When "bow-grips tightened on the hated plows," Neihardt suggests that hunting was opposed to farming and that the Sioux, who had been nomadic hunters, could not accept farming (Neihardt [1961] 1971 *Messiah*, 3). When Neihardt's whites expressed shock at the "dancing heathen, ludicrously clad," whose Ghost Dance religion spurned "Christian light and progress," Neihardt suggests that late nineteenth-century European Americans saw the Ghost Dance as a primitive counterimage to Christianity (57). When Neihardt's dancers shout that they would rather die than surrender their religion, Neihardt intimates that Christianity and the Ghost Dance are irreconcilably opposed in the minds of some ardent dancers. In their predilection for hunting over farming, resistance over accommodation, and the Ghost Dance over Christianity, Neihardt presents the Sioux as "savage" opposites of European American "civilization," thus following familiar nineteenth-century paradigms.

One cannot say that *The Twilight of the Sioux* expresses complete acceptance of savagism. Neihardt's idea of "the dream" is that the two races could live as brothers, together in harmony with all other living things. In such a dream each race would not be a "counterimage" of the other, and therefore Neihardt's "dream" is implicitly a rejection of savagism. However, despite the author's apparent personal sympathy for the dream, he presents many Sioux as repeatedly acting against it: Neihardt himself is not an adherent of savagism, but he presents some of the Sioux in his narratives as such.

Not all of Neihardt's Sioux were opposed to European American civilization; Spotted Tail and the accommodationists were willing to surrender much to avoid bloodshed, and the dreamers were universalists, believing the two races would share a common future. Both groups envisioned a non-oppositional response to European American immigration. However, in *A Cycle of the West* these were minority factions; militants such as Red Cloud, Sitting Bull, Crazy Horse, Kicking Bear (Mathó Wanáȟtaka), Yellow Bird, and their followers rejected their counsel and instead opted to reject change and to resist the encroaching Americans. Their oppositional, either/or solution to European American immigration matches the dualistic nature of savagism. Furthermore, the idea of savagism suggests that "savages" are actuated more by passion than by reason, and although Neihardt's militants had a logic for resisting Americans by force of arms, in his presentation their passion for war was overshadowed by their rationale for it.

Another important aspect of *A Cycle of the West* is that it links the Sioux to the story of American westward expansion, which is a narrative frequently used in presenting the history of nineteenth-century America. Neihardt, like the historian Frederick Jackson Turner, believed that, at the close of the nineteenth century, an important macrolevel process had ended. For Turner, the European American character-defining frontier experience ended when the U.S. Census Bureau declared the frontier to be closed in 1890. Turner first argued this in 1893 at a meeting of the American Historical Association at the World's Columbian Exposition in Chicago and, later, in other publications (Turner [1920] 1952, 1–38; White, Limerick, and Grossman 1994). For Neihardt, what ended was a "Cycle of the West," a process that he believed was completed with what he perceived as the end of Indian armed resistance and opposition to European American conquest, marked with the Wounded Knee massacre. Thus, each man dated the end of his story to 1890. To Neihardt, the story of European American expansion into the West was a story of "the richly human saga-stuff" (Neihardt [1961] 1971 *Twilight*, v–vi, xi). Turner would have agreed, especially as they both highlighted the importance of vigorous individualism in their interpretations. For Neihardt and Turner, this mythic drama was completed when European Americans and their civilization overspread the continent. In many tellings of the history of the American westward expansion, it was the Sioux who embodied important themes of the story and provided milestones in its telling.

The attraction of non-Indians to this paradigm of Indian history is further evidenced by the success of Dee Brown's *Bury My Heart at Wounded Knee: An Indian History of the American West*, published first in 1970 and considered to be one of the most influential books on the American West. The book describes European American conquest of the Indians of the American West; it is a litany of broken treaties, battles, and confinements of Indian tribes to reservations. *Bury My Heart* ends with the Wounded Knee massacre. Its subtitle implies that, after the Wounded Knee massacre, meaningful Indian history ended. This underscores the propensity of non-Indians to interpret Indian history either partially or wholly within the paradigms of savagism, manifest destiny, and the vanishing race while largely disregarding the lived experience of Indian people after 1890. Like Neihardt's songs, Brown's book underscores how important the historical experience of the Sioux is for non-Indians in interpreting American westward expansion and for assigning meaning to it.

The year 1992 marked the Columbian Quincentenary, commemorating five hundred years since Christopher Columbus landed in the Western Hemisphere. The Quincentenary inspired many artists, moviemakers, scholars, and writers to reconceptualize the consequences of the interhemispheric encounters that followed Columbus's voyages and, of course, to try and better understand the historical experiences of Native people. This process of reconceptualization continues to this day. Numerous authors have made thoughtful efforts to understand Lakȟóta people outside of the paradigms in which Neihardt wrote (see, for example, Hämäläinen 2019; Andersson 2018; Deloria 2004). However, rather than supplanting the paradigms that Neihardt employed, the new paradigms have coexisted with them, as Neihardt's influence continued into the twenty-first century. Many of Neihardt's books are still in print and have received special editions, including a "Premier Edition" and a "Complete Edition" of *Black Elk Speaks* (Neihardt 2008, 2014). Dee Brown's *Bury My Heart at Wounded Knee* is still in print, and it has endured through a special twentieth-anniversary edition and a made-for-television HBO movie (Brown 1991; Simoneau 2007). The cinematic sensation *Dances with Wolves*—which won seven Academy Awards, including Best Picture—used many of the paradigms that Neihardt did (Costner 1990). Although it is too early to know whether, in the twenty-first century, new paradigms will supplant the old, it seems that the old paradigms have endured as popular frameworks for understanding the historical experience of the Lakȟóta people, and that Neihardt remains a revered memorializer of Sioux history.

Notes

This essay is excerpted, in part, from the author's doctoral dissertation, "Red, White, and Sioux: A History of America's Indian" (Bloomington: Indiana University Department of History, 2004).

1. In the United States the person most closely identified with this idea is the ethnologist and anthropologist Lewis Henry Morgan, who studied

kinship systems among the North American Indians. Morgan's studies of American Indian kinship systems led him to develop a theory of social evolution that, he believed, applied generally to human societies (Morgan [1877] 1907, v–viii, 3–45).

2. For more recent interpretations of the conflict on the northern plains in the second half of the nineteenth century, see Hämäläinen (2019); Bray (2006); Ostler (2004).

3. Throughout *The Song of the Indian Wars*, as well as in *The Song of the Messiah*, Neihardt attributes spoken words to the characters in his epic. Often, these characters were real—such as Red Cloud, Spotted Tail, Crazy Horse, Gall, and Big Foot—but the authenticity of their dialog is difficult to establish. In May 1931 Neihardt brought his two daughters to Pine Ridge to record his interviews with Black Elk and other Lakȟóta (Anderson 2016, 168–82; DeMallie 1984, 26–58, 75–296). These two visits occurred after Neihardt published *Indian Wars* but before he published *Messiah*, meaning that the interviews could not have informed *Indian Wars* but could, and did, inform *Messiah*. While it is beyond the scope of this essay to do a comparison between the transcripts and *Messiah*, Neihardt explains that his sources for *A Cycle of the West* transcended his 1931 interviews. When Neihardt described battles, he "depended far less on written accounts than upon the reminiscences of men who fought in them—not only Indians, but whites as well" and that "much of the material" for *Indian Wars* and *Messiah* "came directly from those who were themselves a part of the stories" (Neihardt [1961] 1971, vii–x). Thus, while Neihardt's own explanations reveal several biases, he also presents a plausible claim for fidelity to the events and people he describes.

4. For more recent scholarship on the Ghost Dance among the Lakȟóta, see Warren (2017); Greene (2014); Andersson (2008); Ostler (2004); DeMallie (1984); DeMallie (1982, 385–405).

5. Despite *The Song of the Messiah*'s presentation of the Wounded Knee massacre as a tragedy, both songs suggest the seeming inescapable destiny of European Americans to overspread the continent and marginalize Indian people.

6. Some readers might note that women do not figure prominently in *The Song of the Indian Wars* and *The Song of the Messiah*. Indeed, when they appear at all, Neihardt often depicts them as unnamed background characters. Ella Cara Deloria, a member of the Deloria family prominent among the Sioux, was nonetheless favorable to Neihardt's understanding of the Lakȟóta people (Deloria to Neihardt, March 18, 1932, and May 11,

1932, in the John G. Neihardt Papers, Western Historical Manuscripts Collection, State Historical Society of Missouri, Colombia, as quoted in Anderson 2016, 190–91).

7. One might argue that Neihardt critiques society when he describes the white arrival on the plains in terms that seem to be describing a fantastical monster and when he describes the various "lies" told by representatives of the U.S. government. However, Neihardt's language is supposed to reflect the Indians' perception of the advance of white civilization, not a reflexive critique of American society on the part of Neihardt. His first three songs, after all, are about the glory of America's exploration of the West.

References

Aly, Lucile F. 1976. *John G. Neihardt*. Boise State Western Writers Series 25. Boise ID: Boise State University.

Anderson, Timothy G. 2016. *Lonesome Dreamer: The Life of John G. Neihardt*. Lincoln: University of Nebraska Press.

Andersson, Rani-Henrik. 2008. *The Lakota Ghost Dance of 1890*. Lincoln: University of Nebraska Press.

———. 2018. *A Whirlwind Passed through Our Country: Lakota Voices of the Ghost Dance*. Norman: University of Oklahoma Press.

Berkhofer, Robert F., Jr., 1978. *The White Man's Indian: Images of the American Indian from Columbus to the Present*. New York: Vintage Books.

Bray, Kingsley M. 2006. *Crazy Horse: A Lakota Life*. Norman: University of Oklahoma Press.

Brown, Dee. 1970. *Bury My Heart at Wounded Knee: An Indian History of the American West*. New York: Henry Holt.

———. 1991. *Bury My Heart at Wounded Knee: An Indian History of the American West*. 20th Anniversary ed. New York: Henry Holt.

Costner, Kevin, dir. 1990. *Dances with Wolves*. Los Angeles: Orion Pictures.

Cronon, William. 1992. "Telling Tales on Canvas: Landscapes of Frontier Change." In *Discovered Lands, Invented Pasts: Transforming Visions of the American West*, by Jules David Prown, Nancy K. Anderson, William Cronon, Brian W. Dippie, Martha A. Sandweiss, Susan P. Schoelwer, and Howard R. Lamar, 37–88. New Haven CT: Yale University Press.

Deloria, Philip J. 1996. "Deloria, Ella (*Anpetu Waste*)." In *Encyclopedia of North American Indians: Native American History, Culture, and Life from Paleo-Indians to the Present*, edited by Frederick E. Hoxie, 159–61. Boston: Houghton Mifflin.

———. 2004. *Indians in Unexpected Places.* Lawrence: University Press of Kansas.
DeMallie, Raymond J. 1982. "The Lakota Ghost Dance: An Ethnohistorical Account." *Pacific Historical Review* 51, no. 4: 385–405.
———, ed. 1984. *The Sixth Grandfather: Black Elk's Teachings Given to John G. Neihardt.* Lincoln: University of Nebraska Press.
Dickason, Olive Patricia. 1997. *The Myth of the Savage: And the Beginnings of French Colonialism in the Americas.* Edmonton: University of Alberta Press.
Dippie, Brian W. 1976. *Custer's Last Stand: The Anatomy of an American Myth.* Lincoln: University of Nebraska Press.
———. 1982. *The Vanishing American: White Attitudes and U.S. Indian Policy.* Middletown CT: Wesleyan University Press.
Ellingson, Ter. 2001. *The Myth of the Noble Savage.* Berkeley: University of California Press.
Elliott, Michael A. 2007. *Custerology: The Enduring Legacy of the Indian Wars and George Armstrong Custer.* Chicago: University of Chicago Press.
Farnum, Allen L. 1992. *Pawnee Bill's Historic Wild West: A Photo Documentary of the 1900–1905 Show Tours.* West Chester PA: Schiffer.
Flavin, Francis E. 2004. "Red, White, and Sioux: A History of America's Indian." PhD diss., Indiana University, Bloomington.
Greene, Jerome A., ed. 1994. *Lakota and Cheyenne: Indian Views of the Great Sioux War, 1876–1877.* Norman: University of Oklahoma Press.
———. 2014. *American Carnage: Wounded Knee, 1890.* Norman: University of Oklahoma Press.
Hämäläinen, Pekka. 2019. *Lakota America: A New History of Indigenous Power.* New Haven CT: Yale University Press.
Jensen, Richard E., ed. 2005. *Voices of the American West.* Vol. 1, *The Indian Interviews of Eli S. Ricker, 1903–1919.* Lincoln: University of Nebraska Press.
Kasson, Joy S. 2000. *Buffalo Bill's Wild West: Celebrity, Memory, and Popular History.* New York: Hill and Wang.
Morgan, Louis Henry. (1877) 1907. *Ancient Society, or Researches in the Lines of Human Progress from Savagery through Barbarism to Civilization.* New York: Henry Holt. Reprint, Chicago: Charles H. Kerr.
Moses, Lester George. 1996. *Wild West Shows and the Images of American Indians, 1883–1933.* Albuquerque: University of New Mexico Press.
Neihardt, John G. (1932) 1979. *Black Elk Speaks: Being the Life Story of a Holy Man of the Oglala Sioux.* New York: William Morrow. Reprint, with an introduction by Vine Deloria Jr. Lincoln: University of Nebraska Press.

———. (1961) 1971. *The Twilight of the Sioux: The Song of the Indian Wars and the Song of the Messiah*. Vol. 2 of *A Cycle of the West*. New York: Macmillan. Reprint, Lincoln: University of Nebraska Press.

———. 2008. *Black Elk Speaks: Being the Life Story of a Holy Man of the Oglala Sioux*. "Premier Edition" annotated by Raymond J. DeMallie with illustrations by Standing Bear. Albany: State University of New York Press.

———. 2014. *Black Elk Speaks: Being the Life Story of a Holy Man of the Oglala Sioux*. "Complete Edition" with a new introduction by Philip J. Deloria and annotated by Raymond J. DeMallie. Albany: State University of New York Press.

Norris, Tina, Paula L. Vines, and Elizabeth M. Hoeffel. 2012. "The American Indian and Alaska Native Population: 2010." 2010 Census Briefs, C2010BR-10. Washington DC: U.S. Census Bureau.

Ostler, Jeffrey. 2004. *The Plains Sioux and U.S. Colonialism from Lewis and Clark to Wounded Knee*. Cambridge: Cambridge University Press.

Pagden, Anthony. 1982. *The Fall of Natural Man: The American Indian and the Origins of Comparative Ethnology*. Cambridge: Cambridge University Press.

Pearce, Roy Harvey. 1988. *Savagism and Civilization: A Study of the Indian and the American Mind*. Rev. ed. Berkeley: University of California Press.

Powell, Earl A. 1990. *Thomas Cole*. New York: Harry N. Abrams.

Reddin, Paul. 1999. *Wild West Shows*. Urbana: University of Illinois Press.

Reinhardt, Akim D. 2003. "Native America: The Indigenous West." In *Western Places: American Myths: How We Think about the West*, edited by Gary J. Hausladen, 184–201. Reno: University of Nevada Press.

Rennert, Jack, ed. 1976. *100 Posters of Buffalo Bill's Wild West*. New York: Darien House.

Sheehan, Bernard W. 1973. *Seeds of Extinction: Jeffersonian Philanthropy and the American Indian*. Chapel Hill: University of North Carolina Press.

Simoneau, Yves, dir. 2007. *Bury My Heart at Wounded Knee*. New York: HBO Films.

Slotkin, Richard. 1973. *Regeneration through Violence: The Mythology of the American Frontier, 1600–1860*. Middletown CT: Wesleyan University Press.

———. 1992. *Gunfighter Nation: The Myth of the Frontier in Twentieth-Century America*. New York: HarperCollins.

Truettner, William H. 1991. "Ideology and Image: Justifying Westward Expansion." In *The West as America: Reinterpreting Images of the American Frontier*, edited by William Truettner, 27–32. Washington DC: Smithsonian Institution Press.

Turner, Frederick Jackson. (1920) 1952. "The Significance of the Frontier in American History." In *The Frontier in American History*, 1–38. New York: Henry Holt.

Warren, Louis S. 2005. *Buffalo Bill's America: William Cody and the American West*. New York: Alfred A. Knopf.

———. 2017. *God's Red Son: The Ghost Dance Religion and the Making of Modern America*. New York: Basic Books.

White, Richard, Patricia Nelson Limerick, and James R. Grossman, eds. 1994. *The Frontier in American Culture: An Exhibition at the Newberry Library, August 26, 1994–January 7, 1995*. Berkeley: University of California Press.

PART 2

Symbols and Ceremonialism

From the Litter to the Horse 7

The Native American Ritual of "Lifting"

GILLES HAVARD

Some of them [St. Lawrence Iroquoians], when they saw our people weary, loaded them on them as on horses and carried them.
—JACQUES CARTIER, *RELATIONS*

The sun goes round the earth every day. The old people say it is a great way off, for if it came near it would burn everything up.
—TUCKEBATCHEE MICCO, CREEK, INDIAN TERRITORY, 1842 (IN HITCHCOCK, *A TRAVELER IN INDIAN TERRITORY*)

The bride's maids, we all had horses, you know.
—LOTTIE PRATT, OSAGE, 1936 (IN SWAN AND COOLEY, *WEDDING CLOTHES AND THE WEDDING CEREMONY*)

More than ever, Indian (and colonial) history needs to reconnect with cultural anthropology (DeMallie and Havard 2019). In this contribution, as an illustration, we revisit the theory of the layering of the world, such as Claude Lévi-Strauss has highlighted in his exploration of the Native American theme of the Bird-Nester. This layering, although more or less sophisticated according to Indian groups, basically divides the universe into three levels: the celestial world, the chthonian world, and, between the two, the earth's surface (Lévi-Strauss 1971, 510–58; Lévi-Strauss 1985b, 155–68; Désveaux 2017a, 148). This framework will serve to solve a historical problem. Following Raymond DeMallie's legacy, this contribution is indeed conceived as a historical ethnography or, in other words, as an ethnohistorical case study, as it discusses a Native American practice anchored in historical documents of First Contacts and beyond: the ritual of elevation.

Introduction: The Issue

Two historical sequences from the sixteenth century will introduce us to the matter. In 1535 French navigator and explorer Jacques Cartier entered the Iroquoian village of Hochelaga, in today's Montreal, met its habitants, saluted them, and climbed Mont Royal. Part of Cartier's narrative was inserted a few years later by Venetian compiler Giovanni Battista Ramusio in the third volume of his *Navigationi et Viaggi* (1565). This volume contains seven maps made by Giacomo Gastaldi, including one plan of Hochelaga (*La Terra de Hochelaga nella Nova Francia*), imagined after Cartier's 1535 description (Ramusio 1565, 380; Larouche 1994; Carayon 2019, 172–73).

A detail, in the lower left corner of this engraving, is intriguing. It depicts two Frenchmen who are lifted by two Iroquoians onto their backs. Let us immediately rule out a simplistic explanation, given by Cartier himself: the Frenchmen were not carried because they were exhausted by their journey (Cartier [1535] 1986, 151, 157).[1] A cultural interpretation related to the status given to them by Iroquoians seems more appropriate.

As an echo, a second sixteenth-century vignette describes a setting in what is now South Carolina, when Conquistador Hernando De Soto met a woman chief named Cofitachequi, in May 1540. This chief is carried on a litter, as one Spanish chronicler of the expedition reports: "The cacica, ruler of that land, came, whom the principal [Indians] brought with much prestige on a litter covered in white (with thin linen) and on their shoulders" (Clayton, Knight, and Moore 1993, 82, 278).[2]

There exists a visual illustration of a similar scene in one plate graved by Flemish publisher Theodore de Bry, *Que Pompa Regina delecta ad Regem deferatur*, which is part of his iconographic series dedicated to "French Florida" and the Timucua Indians. In this plate four men are carrying a litter, where a woman chief is sitting on a seat covered "with a rare animal skin." Some other men carry the wooden forks that are placed under the poles at each stop. On each side of the "queen," a man waves an umbrella to protect her from the sun. In addition, some women are carrying flowers, which they probably throw over the woman chief from behind (De Bry 1992, 191; Lankford 2008, 129).[3]

Three remarks here: First, this visual representation obeys European political codes of the time. The bodies meet the naturalistic criteria of Renaissance statuary; but there is more, as the scene echoes one sixteenth-century rite of the French monarchy. During royal funerals a very realistic effigy of the dead king, dressed with all the official signs of power, as if he were alive—because "the king never dies"— was mounted on a military cart, under a canopy, in a similar fashion (Kantorowitz 2000, 934–52; Giesey 1960). It is also possible that, when relating carrying sequences of this kind, Europeans had in mind the raising of the king of the Franks in the early Middle Ages, as, like the Roman emperor of his own era, he was lifted on a shield by soldiers as a means of consecration (Le Jan 2003). Obviously those mental frameworks made observers keener to describe Indian sequences of this kind.

Second, men, not women, are carrying the chief. Thus, the scene has a strong ceremonial meaning. In Native American societies women were supposed to carry objects of everyday life, such as utensils, food, or animal carcasses. In Plains Indian societies, women, in this sense, made and owned the horse travois. When it came to ceremonial or "religious" matters, such as carrying heavy stones during gaming contests or lifting someone special, men were in charge (Désveaux 2013, 42; Ewers 1955, 103).

Third, it is more than tempting to establish a link between the Montreal and the South Carolina sequences. On the one hand, two Frenchmen are lifted; on the other, a (female) chief is carried on a litter. Indeed, this ritual practice is far from isolated, but is part of a widespread North American cultural horizon, from the Southeast to the Great Plains and beyond. Hence, this article addresses a Native American ritual rarely studied although it is quite frequently described in colonial sources, especially French documents from the sixteenth to the eighteenth century.[4] As a matter of fact, this practice is as much present in North American intercultural encounters as the better-known calumet ceremony (Hall 1997; Désveaux 2001, 224) or other adoption practices, such as the feeding ceremonies of newcomers (Havard 2016a, 587–88), weeping greetings (White 1994; Havard 2016b), and sexual hospitality (Kehoe 1970; Havard 2016a, 635–61; Désveaux 2017b). Most of the time the carrying practice emerges when Europeans enter Indian villages: they are lifted by a few Native men, either on their shoulders or on an animal skin.

Methodology

Our ethnohistorical method (see DeMallie 1993) is based on four foundations. First, colonial archives raise a variety of issues related to the observation, understanding, and representation of societies in a cross-cultural context. We are in a situation of documentary asymmetry that makes it very difficult to write history from the point of view of the Natives. Thus, the historian can adopt two positions toward the sources. The first is to disqualify them on the grounds that they paint the Indians as naive and superstitious, that they are mere fables intended to justify the colonial enterprise (Hamlin 1996). In this respect, some historians tend to reject the idea that the Indians perceived the first Europeans they met as separate beings with strange and superior powers, or they prefer to avoid any questioning of these first encounters. In this rationalistic and "secular" setting, the episode of contact with the Europeans is trivial and resembles any other historical episode within the long history of the Indians. The second option, which is ours, highlights our capacity to deal with the sources, which are biased but give us precious information about Native Americans, especially when the chroniclers spent time in their communities or were even able to learn their languages. To interpret the documents, we need to reconstitute the authors' mental universes and deconstruct their writing strategies. In other words, we must decipher the strangeness of Europeans before eventually being able to probe the exoticism of the Natives. But as ethnohistorians, we must also mobilize ethnographic descriptions and anthropological insights to help us decipher what has been recorded in the historical archives. This approach consists of comparing the colonial sources with more detailed ethnography carried out later.[5]

Second, to interpret Native American cultures of the past, attention to cultural details displayed in the colonial documents is crucial. Indeed, there are many details that historians tend to overlook, maybe because they feel this is pure ethnography and not *real* history—movement, fluidity, action, and events. Yet, one must take seriously the slightest or most apparently trivial information and see how the evocation, even fleetingness, of a gesture, how each trace, even seemingly small, can give access to social and symbolic logics. These details must always be contextualized, but they can possibly lead to an understanding of social worlds.

Third, this work draws on Claude Lévi-Strauss's and Emmanuel Désveaux's analyses about Native American cultural transitivity, from Tierra del Fuego to the Subarctic. In this wide cultural area, there exist homogeneous mythological, ritual, and social forms, which are likely to give place to variations.[6] Comparison is a stimulating way of interpreting cultural facts, and, indeed, the colonial sources attest to some of the cultural *continuities* across Native North America, beyond the particular scope of classical cultural areas, as they were drawn a century ago by American anthropologists.

And finally, through this case study, one can stress the idea that the colonial encounter, instead of being seen only as a place of potential acculturation (or destruction), offers a context where cultural features of Indian societies are very clearly laid bare, especially when colonial writers, rightly or wrongly, made connections between European and Indian ritual practices. Rather than acculturation or conquest, we are talking here about intercultural communication as a place of potential "exacerbation" of cultural patterns.

Thus, in this ethnohistorical investigation, we first discuss two received ideas, both of which come from colonial sources. The first equates the lifting of Europeans with deification. The second is that what is at stake in the ritual is the *carrying* proper. This critical discussion finally leads to a proposition that DeMallie would have supported: the Indian pattern of lifting should be connected to the lightning penetration of horse riding in Native North American societies from the eighteenth century onward. In fact, our purpose here is to stress the equivalence between litter and horse as ways of ritual elevation.

Solar Echoes: Nicolas Perrot and Great Lakes Indians

The lifting of Europeans can be analyzed as the necessity for Indians to act properly in the presence of mysterious or sacred people. The case of Nicolas Perrot's experiences among Great Lakes Indians is worth considering on this matter. Born in Burgundy, Perrot was an atypical coureur de bois, as he was literate.[7] His first commercial adventures function as an accelerated apprenticeship in the exoticism of Native worlds, which he apprehended as an educated man of the seventeenth century, understanding them with parallels from his own political culture. When he arrived—in 1667 or 1668—in a Potawatomi village at the bottom of Green Bay, the young trader enjoyed a theatrical reception orchestrated by some "old men" who lit a "solemn pipe" and presented it to him so that he puffed on it. The ritual pipe, an object of mediation, circulates in the assembly, and, in turn, the Potawatomi spread "tobacco smoke" from their mouths, like "incense," on Perrot and his attribute objects (knives, axes). The Indians traditionally used tobacco in the same way when they wanted to contact animal spirits and implore their help and mercy. In the midst of the smoking, chiefs exclaimed, taking the sun as a witness, "You are one of the first spirits, since you make the iron, it is you who must rule and protect all men, *praise the Sun who has enlightened you and made you on our earth*" (La Potherie 1753, 2, 87–88, our translation, our emphasis). The coureur de bois was seen as having supernatural qualities because he was able to produce metallic objects in great quantities.[8]

Certainly Perrot's background led him to see and value certain aspects of Native ritualization rather than others; and no doubt the reported words are doubly distorted, firstly by the translation, secondly by a form of unrealistic glorification of French power. In the rendering of these words, however, Perrot behaved more as an ethnographer than as a storyteller—even if he clearly was not, strictly speaking. In his youth he had been sensitized to representations of the Sun, which can be found, for example, on the coffered ceiling of the *salle des devises* of the Jesuit Collège in Dijon, where he was educated, such as a sun globe darting its rays, both a Jesuit coat of arms and a tribute to Louis XIV, and whose motto was *Lux Totus*, "All the Light." In the seventeenth century, a subject, and even more so a servant of the king, could not be insensitive to the solar ideology at the heart of the monarchical imagination. Not only is Louis XIV's symbol the Sun, but he is himself the Sun: the king's luminous radiance dispels chaos to the end of the earth, thanks to servants such as Perrot. Hence, this familiarity with the Sun favors his own sensitivity to this common motif of Native cosmologies. The Sun is for him a symbol of political power whose resonance is universal, and in the end, it is not a surprise for him if the Sun — called Kiigouké by the Algonquian-speaking peoples — has its place in Native societies' myths and rites.[9]

Among Great Lakes Indians, the Sun or "god of light" is also the pledge of health, which "facilitates the means of finding simples [medicinal plants]." Dogs are "sacrificed to the sun," and the calumet is conceived as "a gift that the sun has sent to men." During the calumet dance, the officiant always presents the pipe to the Sun "as if he wanted to make him smoke" (La Potherie 1753, 2, 13–14, 43). In the ceremony of reception of Perrot, the Potawatomi, after having made him smoke, hoisted him on their shoulders and smoothed out "the paths through which he passed," not daring "to look him in the face," as if he were indeed, in the literal sense, the Sun, or his avatar. This is not a form of deference to him, but rather a ritual expression of the impossibility of sustaining the ardor of the Sun's rays — women and children must even stand very far back, he explains (2, 88–89).[10]

Later on, Perrot went to a large village inhabited by Mascoutens and Miamis, still in the Green Bay area. Accompanied by another trader, he was welcomed by an old Mascouten chief who presented him a calumet "on the side of the Sun" and then swirled it around him in all directions, including toward the ground — the chthonian world — before rubbing with his hands the head, back, legs, and feet of the Frenchman, and then his own body, in order to encourage the capture of a greater spiritual power. This gesture perhaps did not surprise Perrot: civility, in France, taught men to dominate their affects, to put bodies at a distance and to be in control of the representation of oneself for others, but it did not prevent certain expressions of emotional spontaneity such as emphatically kissing the bottom of a great lady's dress or kissing the king's thigh. The two French visitors were then made to sit down on a painted buffalo hide, while the Mascouten officiant tried to make fire with two sticks. However, the humidity prevented him from doing so, and Perrot—self-proclaimed civilizer—began to take out his firebrand to help him, causing "great exclamations" from the chief, who took him for "a spirit." The Mascoutens then offered to carry Perrot on a buffalo hide, but he made his hosts understand "that he knew how to knead iron and had the strength to walk." This could explain why Perrot, called Mandaamineens—Little Corn—by the Algonquians, was given another advantageous nickname: "the one with iron legs" (La Potherie 1753, 2, 105–6, 271).

In the French imagination of the seventeenth century, iron legs could refer to seven-league boots, and the Natives may have considered Perrot an excellent runner. But if this term is indeed a Native neologism—in Ojibwe, its rendering could be *biiwaabikogaade* (Baraga 1878, 1, 146–47; Ives Goddard, personal communication, April 2016)—one can also suppose that such legs were likely to exempt Perrot from being lifted. The Frenchman, thanks to his metallic legs, literally became a Sun on legs, as is shown later. The expression, besides, translates the close relationship maintained by Perrot with the supernatural: iron can appear to the Indians as an improved version of copper, considered as a substance of chthonian origin; and the metallic legs, because they are in contact with the ground, serve as a mediating element with the entities of the lower world (see Lévi-Strauss 2013, 127; Désveaux 2017b, 181).

The Mascoutens then accompany Perrot and his companion to the Miamis, who, at the sight of them, display a calumet (unlit) while "bending their knees alternately, almost to the ground." They present the ceremonial pipe sometimes to the Sun "with the same genuflections," sometimes to Perrot "with many gesticulations." But this time the Frenchman could not deviate from the uprising ritual: a war chief "took him on his shoulders, accompanied by all the Musicians who led him to the village" (La Potherie 1753, 2, 102–9). One must imagine the pride that overwhelms the coureur de bois, who is recognized as having great spiritual power: the political symbolism of the Sun, so strongly anchored in him, finds an almost carnal echo among Great Lakes Indians. But far from being a form of deification in the Greco-Roman fashion, the lifting is a game of mediation: it tells how Europeans were included in, or associated with, a specific ceremonial sphere. Indeed, as demonstrated next, Native carrying was less a goal than a device.

Being above the Ground

In June 1687 Henri Joutel, a companion of explorer Cavelier de La Salle, gave an account of the reception of a few Frenchmen, including himself, in one Kadohadacho community, part of the Caddoan cultural family:

> A band [of Natives] came to join us, and they made us understand that they had to carry us to their village. Our [Indians] made us a sign that this was the custom of the country and that we must submit and let them carry us. Although we were embarrassed by this ceremony, seven of the most hardy ones offered us their backs or their shoulders. The Abbé [Jean Cavelier], as the leader, was the first to be carried, and the others were likewise. As for me, being rather large [. . .], I assuredly weighed more than one bearer could support. As I was taller than he was, *and my legs touched the ground*, two other Indians did carry them. Thus I had three bearers. Other Indians took our horses to lead them and we arrived in the village in this ridiculous fashion. Our bearers, who had gone a good quarter league, need rest. (Margry 1876–86, 3, 405–6, our translation, our emphasis)[11]

What is striking here is that the two additional bearers take great care that Joutel's legs *do not touch the ground*. The prime objective is not carrying people as a means of respect but avoiding contact with the ground.

In 1724 Etienne de Veniard de Bourgmont's journal offered two accounts of ritual carrying, this time among Kansa and Padouca Indians. As soon as his company of explorers arrived in one Kansa village, on July 8, the chiefs delivered speeches, made their guest smoke, and

11. Father de Smet is carried into a Blackfeet camp, 1840. Originally published by Francis P. Harper, 1905 (author unknown).

then spread a large buffalo hide on the ground. They placed Bourgmont on it and carried him "to the cabin of the first chief." The Frenchman was then taken "to the cabins of the other chiefs" where the harangues continued (ANOM, C13C, 4, f. 132v).[12] In October 1724 the Padouca (Plains Apache) reception was even more spectacular. Indeed, after a speech made by their "great chief," the Padoucas "spread a bison robe on the ground and place Mr de Bourgmont on it with his son, accompanied by Mr de St Ange and sieur La Renaudière. They carried them to the cabin of the Padouca great chief, they were fifteen men carrying them and then they had us fest with them" (ANOM, C13C, 4, f. 149, our translation).

At first glance it seems hard to believe that four people could stand on just one bison robe. To our knowledge it is the only example in the colonial archives of a lifting ceremony with more than one European carried on a single bison robe. But as this written account is very detailed and realistic overall, it would be a mistake to simply dismiss it. The ritual of elevation here could be related to a wider ceremonial cycle (games, weddings, etc.), unless the fact of carrying *four* men referred to the importance of cardinal points in this society.[13]

This practice of elevation was used also in the northern plains, as attested by the French trader and explorer of the fabled "Mer de l'Ouest," Pierre de La Vérendrye. In December 1738, accompanied by 600 Assiniboines, 30 Mandans, and 25 Frenchmen, he entered a grand Mandan village of about 1,500 inhabitants, located around the mouth of the Heart River. He explains that he made the entry the French way, with his son Louis-Joseph walking at the head, carrying a heavy white flag, but he had to adapt to a local ritual, as the Mandans indicated that they wished to carry him. He writes, "The Mandan *would not allow me to walk*, but insisted on carrying me, and I had to consent, the Assiniboin begging me to do so and saying that I should displease them greatly if I refused" (La Verendrye 1927, 2, 326). Once again, the imperative was to keep Europeans from touching the ground.[14]

Although we could multiply such examples, let us finish with a famous one, that of Jesuit Father Pierre-Jean De Smet, who received a similar greeting among the Blackfeet, in October 1840:

> Twelve warriors and their chief, in full costume, shortly afterward presented themselves before my lodge and spread a large and fine buffalo robe. The head chief took me by the arm and, leading me to the skin, made me a sign to be seated. I had no idea of the meaning of this ceremony, but I sat down, thinking that it was an invitation to smoke the calumet with them. Judge my surprise when I beheld the twelve warriors seize this kind of carpet by the ends, lift me from the ground and, preceded by their chief, carry me in triumph to the village, where everybody was instantly afoot to see the Black-robe. (De Smet 1905, 253)[15]

In the Great Lakes and Great Plains, as we have seen, the elevation techniques were diverse and the process either individual or collective. Joutel was carried on three men's shoulders, but usually one man was enough, as with Perrot; Bourgmont was lifted on a bison robe by many men, and then with three other Frenchmen, again on a bison robe. Whatever the technique, the ritual imperative was the same: raising those men above the ground.

One of the few anthropologists to have commented on this ritual is the Cheyenne specialist George Bird Grinnell, as he reported on the same custom encountered by Lewis and Clark in 1804 among the Sioux. Grinnell suggests that the practice is traditional:

> The custom of carrying a person who was to be highly honored on a robe or blanket by young men is very old. It was practiced to show honor to aged or brave people, and also if two young people of good family were about to be married, the young girl, as she drew near the home of the bridegroom's parents, riding on a horse led by some old kinswoman, was often met by young men related to the bridegroom, who spread down a robe or blanket, assisted her from her horse, asked her to sit down on the robe, and then carried her to the lodge of her future husband. (Grinnell 1911, 149)

Grinnell had in mind particularly the case of the traditional Cheyenne wedding, which he was able to document (Grinnell [1923] 1972, 1, 144). As this sequence clearly shows, a striking continuity exists between two modes of lifting: the horse and the blanket; we return to this later in the chapter. What also needs to be emphasized is the wedding context. Daniel C. Swan and Jim Cooley showed that the Osage traditional wedding, a sacred form of marriage called Mízhi^n, also contains a lifting sequence, which was still alive in the mid-1930s: the groom's kinsmen or kinswomen carry the bride on a buffalo robe or blanket, after she has ridden a horse to the ceremony (Swan and Cooley 2019). But can the two ritual sequences, that of carrying Europeans and Native maidens, be related?

Carrying the Stars

To understand this pattern, an ethnographic investigation through the U.S. Southeast is necessary. In this region also, from Florida to the Lower Mississippi Valley, Europeans had to adapt to the ancient requirement of lifting special people. In 1729 French officer Régis du Roullet was carried by four Choctaw men, again who made sure his feet did not touch the ground: "The great chief came to greet me with his hat in his hand, followed by the other chiefs, then one of the principal

12. Collum-Bates wedding, Fairfax, Oklahoma, 1916. After having traveled on a horse, the bride is carried in a blanket or a sheet to the wedding site by female relatives of the groom. From Swan and Cooley 2019, 57.

beloved men [*principaux considerez*] presented me a pipe to smoke and another came to stretch out his back to climb on top of me—as soon as I was there, two others each took a foot from me, and four savages held a skin stretched over my head in the form of a canopy" (ANOM, C13A, 15, f. 198, "Extrait du Journal des Voyages faits par le Sieur Régis du Roullet," our translation).[16]

The use of the canopy, as we have seen, is a common feature in the Southeast chief's transportation, and the fact that there were four men lifting the French officer is reminiscent of the *Nahua Teomama*, or "god carriers," in Mexico, who usually numbered four, in relation to the importance of cardinal points in Aztec solar cosmology (Saumade 2008, 256).[17] Governor Kerlerec described a similar sequence in 1754, when he met two thousand Choctaw and Creek Indians in Mobile. During this assembly, the medallion chiefs, singing and "dancing" the calumet, visited Kerlerec's home, and the French governor, as he reported, was "taken away and carried into the shed intended for listening to their harangues and making their presents" (ANOM, C13A, 38: 113, 122–24).

The Natchez, neighbors to the Choctaws, shared with them this ritual dynamic of "raising." Indeed, the Natchez practice of carrying their chief is well known, thanks to rich French sources. In several contexts the chief, the Great Sun, is forbidden to tread the ground. In

1700 Jesuit Paul Du Ru was one of the first witnesses to mention this carrying, which he explained by the disease that overwhelmed the chief. Du Ru also noted the existence of a "parade bed, about 3 feet high," which was to be used on the day of his death (Du Ru [1700], 51–52). As other French chroniclers at the beginning of the eighteenth century related, at the end of the Natchez deer feast in March, the Great Sun also dominated the assembly from the top of his "throne, which is a large four-legged step ladder made of a single piece of wood," and in the same way, at the end of July during the Green Corn festival, he was carried on a litter. Groups of porters, each composed of eight of the most robust men, then took turns carrying it at an astonishing speed on a stretcher with "four red bars" to the ritual space of the festival, a few kilometers from the Great Sun's village. "One might well say that this is a new method of post riding," writes the chronicler Dumont de Montigny, "for myself and several officers were *on horseback*, and we could barely keep up with them." He speaks of this ritual course of high acrobatics as an "airborne route," as if it mimicked the movement of the solar star (see Désveaux 2001, 346, 350; Sayre 2005, 211–16; Le Page du Pratz 1758, 2, 360, 367–70; Dumont de Montigny 2012, 363). In this sequence the horse allows the French to adopt an elevated position that poses them, without realizing it themselves, as avatars of the Sun.

The etiquette surrounding the great Natchez chief is very similar to that which presided over the lives of ritual figures of chiefs in South America and Mesoamerica, as described in Spanish chronicles. The Inca ruler and the ruler of Mexico-Tenochtitlan were individuals apart, endowed with an important domesticity and on whom weighed an imperative of reclusion as well as of elevation. The Inca ruler (Atahualpa), son of the Sun, lived most of the time confined in his royal residence or hidden from the eyes behind a curtain of gauze. His eyes were masked by the royal insignia that encircled his forehead, he was carried on a litter chair upholstered with parrot feathers to avoid any contact with the ground, and all the objects that he had touched, including his clothes and his dishes, were ritually burned (Yaya McKenzie 2017, 120). In the same way, one was not to look in the face nor touch the sovereign of Mexico-Tenochtitlan, Moctezuma, who moved on a palanquin thanks to ritual carriers (see Bernand and Gruzinski 1991, 317, 463–64; Saumade 2008, 254; Lesbre 2014, 1; Bernand 2021, 84–85, 125–26). Thus, social hierarchy is perceived through the mythical framework of the staging of the world.

As Emmanuel Désveaux explains, the Natchez chief was usually carried above the ground as if he were—symbolically—deprived of legs. Is not the Sun, this circular creature, by definition deprived of legs (Désveaux 2001, 346)? Moreover, in the case where it would touch the ground, it would risk setting fire to the whole earth, as attested by the Native American myths dealing with the theme of conflagration (Lévi-Strauss 1985a, 9). Elevation is the means to ward off the risk of a disaster. This ritual motif, significantly, is also found among Native populations where weightlifting contests were held: the men carried large logs or enormous circular stones that could represent the Sun as well as the Moon, by virtue of the same imperative that the stars be carried (Désveaux 2001, 210–14). By nature, the stars are incompatible with the earth's surface because of a risk of conflagration. The Natchez Great Sun must be isolated from the earth, as much as he is isolated from the Celestial World by a canopy: he is both an avatar of the Sun and a mediator between the Sky and chthonian levels of the universe.

Let us now return to Nicolas Perrot and then to the Osage wedding. Perrot was lifted precisely because, as he himself suggested, he was identified with a star, that is to say, a circular creature without limbs. The Mascouten war chief who carries him on his back seems to be an avatar to the *Teomama*, alias Nahua "god carriers" or "sun carriers," studied by Frédéric Saumade, who had some ritual prestige of their own (Saumade 2008, 256). It is therefore tempting to see in the welcome given to Perrot an *actualization* of a cultural pattern shared by many American Indian societies, which requires that special ritual treatments be administered to individuals who are recognized as having singular or unusual qualities. The arrival of coureurs de bois may have revived a cultural practice in the Great Lakes that was less salient or more covert than that of the Natchez or the Nahua.

Among the Osages, if the maiden was carried in the same way, it is because she was not supposed to touch the ground and was assimilated to a star. This prescription offers an echo of isolation rituals that affected women during their time of menstruation, or big men like the Natchez great chief. But more profoundly, this wedding ritual is linked to the motif of celestial weddings analyzed by Lévi-Strauss. Gé Indians from Brazil have many stories where one male mortal marries "Star," who herself connotes in this instance the feminine dimension of the Above (Lévi-Strauss 1964, 173–77, 295). Moreover, Plains Indian weddings can also be seen as an inversion of one widespread trans-American mythical motif highlighted by Lévi-Strauss, that of the "wives of the stars," where female mortals marry celestial bodies, alias Stars (Lévi-Strauss 1968, 170–224; 1971, 520–34; see also Balloy 2023).

Horse Riding as Ritual Elevation

We can now turn to the second aspect of this ethnohistorical investigation, by analyzing the link between elevating oneself and the use of horses—an analogy already at work in the French rendering of Indian rituals because of the central role played by horses in their own culture.[18]

The rise and diffusion of the Plains Indian horse culture is an old anthropological and historical topic, as attested by Clark Wissler's seminal work, "The Influence of the Horse in the Development of Plains Culture" (1914). With great insight Wissler explains that the horse was not really a revolution, because it was totally soluble in the Indian cultural fabric. Pekka Hämäläinen has sought to renew this question recently in a more rationalistic way, insisting on the tremendous effects of this new animal on Indian economies and societies (Wissler 1914; Hämäläinen 2003, 2008). Our analytical framework here is, however, distinct from his, as we seek to value the semantic equivalences between practices.[19]

The analogy between horse riding and elevating can first be illustrated by Omaha chief Blackbird, a big man culturally akin to the Natchez Great Sun, whom Jean-Baptiste Truteau encountered. An educated French Canadian fur trader from St. Louis, Truteau spent the winter of 1794–95 alongside Omahas, in present-day Nebraska, and their famous great chief, Toangarest ("Village Maker"), better known as Blackbird (Truteau 2017, 125-47; Havard 2019, 308-12). Truteau described Plains Indians with a great sense of detail that is sometimes difficult to find in seventeenth-century relations. He offered an incisive description of Blackbird that would contribute to the black legend of this charismatic chief: "the finest, the most cunning savage, and the greatest rascal of all the nations that inhabit the Missouri." Even if Truteau says Blackbird is not fond of war—he may not be a war chief; the Natchez Great Sun was not a war chief either—the fact that he killed competitors made him a warrior. His great influence was not based on warlike exploits but on the use of poisons. Obtaining arsenic from Europeans, Blackbird claimed supernatural powers and intimidated or murdered his rivals, a power of nuisance that made him akin to a sorcerer and a great warrior. Among Plains Indians the bravery of great men inspired respect but also fear. Sometimes these individuals, losing all measure, began to act in a despotic way and to exceed the rules of the group—to the point of being, in return, murdered by their compatriots (Hyde [1937] 1975, 53).

But getting to our main point, Truteau writes: "He [Blackbird] does not travel at all on foot; he is always mounted on one of the finest horses in his village," as if he was forbidden to touch the ground (Truteau 2017, 129). The horse, in this perspective, rather than a convenient means of transportation, becomes a vector of elevation, comparable to a ritual litter, a buffalo robe, or the added shoulders of some men. Taking this analysis further, it is possible to understand the adoption of the horse on the Great Plains, from the eighteenth century onward, from a religious point of view: this adoption may have been favored because it allowed the implementation or the development of ritual elevation practices.[20]

Truteau further revealed that, at night, Blackbird "has one or two attendants or valets who gently rub his legs and feet while he sleeps" and that in the absence of the "ordinary valets" he resorts to the "most important and most brave men among his people." When it is necessary to "wake him," one does it "with caution, taking good care not to shout in his ears or take him by the hand; instead, they use a feather that they pass lightly over his face or gently tickle certain places of his body" (Truteau 2017, 131). The feather is here an object of mediation comparable to the wand used, in some Indian societies, by young warriors or menstruating women to scratch their heads or other parts of the body. In a similar way the Natchez great chief was not supposed to give his plates to anybody with his hands. Before being an authoritarian leader, Blackbird thus evolved in a singular ritual sphere that isolated him from the rest of society. He was a sort of great recluse. Blackbird was also borne on a buffalo skin to go to feasts, and he was later buried (1800) at the top of a mound, sitting on his favorite horse, which was probably sacrificed at his death, so that it continues to carry him in the afterworld. Truteau, interestingly, suggested to his employers that they send a "French saddle" to the Omaha chief (2017, 137).[21]

The link between horse riding and ritual elevation is also suggested by Indian trader Charles McKenzie, a Scottish clerk in the Compagnie du Nord-Ouest. In 1806 he visited a Cheyenne camp and observed a chief welcoming another one, named the Rattle Snake:

> The chief [...] came down from his horse & embraced the Rattle Snake then striping himself as naked as he was the day he came to the world he clothed the Rl. [Rattle] Snake with his flashy war dress & with the assistance of others mounted him on his white horse—This being done the Chief lead the horse by the Tether barefooted & barebodyed to the Camp (Some nations have the custom of carrying the Ambassadour of a neighbouring nation into their camps on their Shoulders but most frequently on a Blanket or a fathom of Cloth; but if none, on a Buffalo Robe between four men) which was 3 good miles off. (Charles McKenzie, in Wood and Thiessen 1985, 281)

McKenzie may have been told this latter remark by other traders. Here Rattle Snake is not carried on a robe, as it was done in the past, but on a horse. This animal clearly serves as an avatar for the more traditional means of carrying and lifting an individual deemed ritually important.

Of course, the horse makes hunting, as well as war, much easier. But the adoption of this animal is not only a story of space and speed.

Havard   210

It also has ritual implications, as it renders elevation accessible to all hunters and warriors, not only to big men such as Blackbird. What is striking is the continuity between the buffalo robe, as a means of elevation, and the horse is that if the horse had so much success, it is because it represented a buffalo robe, but *alive*. As a matter of fact, Indian horse riders often used buffalo skins as saddle blankets, and the trader Alexander Henry even wrote in 1809: "When an Indian is going to mount he throws his buffalo robe over the saddle and rides on it" (quoted in Worcester 1945, 141).

Thus, the domestication and riding of the horse responds in a fascinating way to a cultural convention anchored in American Indian societies: the raising of stars. In this sense we can also offer an alternative analysis to the fact that horses were called "mysterious dogs" or "medicine dogs" by Plains Indians: *xaawaarúxti'* in Arikara, *šúŋka wakháŋ* in Lakȟóta, and so on (Ewers 1997, 207; Douglas Parks, personal communication, October 2009). The usual explanation for this naming is the greater efficiency of horses over dogs in all respects—reducing the distances, facilitating the hunting of bison, which becomes a more reliable resource accessible in all seasons, making it easier for women to transport provisions and utensils, and so forth (Hämäläinen 2003; 2008, 25–28, 246–47, 346–47)—but again, this eludes all religious dimension. A dog drags more than it carries, while the horse, besides being able to drag, has a great carrying capacity, even for long distances—indeed like the Sun.[22] Therefore, one can wonder if the magical character attributed to the horse, which, according to Plains Indians, possessed supernatural powers (Ewers 1955, 290–91), does not have more to do with its capacity to raise above the ground.

Conclusion

There are several ways to approach the study of Native American societies. While rejecting Marxism, it seems that American cultural anthropology, for over a century, has often been dependent on the materialist theory establishing a link between infrastructure and superstructure. In this work, faithful to the lessons of Raymond DeMallie, we have sought to give more space to an interpretation that makes representations of the world a more determining factor in the understanding of Indian societies and practices.

Notes

Acknowledgments: This chapter is based on a paper given at the symposium in honor of Raymond DeMallie, at Indiana University, Bloomington, September 2017. I thank Emmanuel Désveaux, Frédéric Saumade, Bertrand Van Ruymbeke, and Gordon Sayre for their thoughtful comments or their corrections of my English, as well as the three editors for their remarks. A special thanks, also, to Daniel Swan, who allows me to publish the image of the Fairfax wedding.

1. The same observation was made by Jean de Léry, twenty years later, in Brazil, with the Tupinambas: "Au surplus, parce, comme j'ay dit ailleurs, que n'ayans chevaux, asnes, ny autres bestes qui portent ou charient en leur pays, la façon ordinaire estant d'y aller à beaux pieds sans lance: si les passans estrangers se trouvent las, presentans un cousteau ou autres choses aux sauvages, prompts qu'ils sont à faire plaisir à leurs amis, ils s'offriront pour les porter. Comme de fait, durant que j'estois par delà, il y en a eu tels qui nous ayans mis la teste entre les cuisses et les jambes pendantes sur leurs ventres, nous ont ainsi portez sur leurs espaules plus d'une grande lieuë sans se reposer" (Léry 1994, 460).

[Moreover, because, as I have said elsewhere, they have no horses, donkeys, or other beasts to carry or cart in their country, the usual way being to go there on fine feet without a lance: if foreign travelers find themselves weary, presenting a knife or other things to the Indians, quick as they are to please their friends, they will offer to carry them. As a matter of fact, while I was over there, some of them, having put our heads between their thighs and our legs dangling over their bellies, carried us thus on their shoulders for more than a league without resting.] English translation by Logan Sutton and Gilles Havard.

2. The author is Rodrigo Rangel, private secretary of De Soto.
3. See also Laudonnière (1958, 136). On flowers, see Anya Peterson Royce's work on the Zapotec of Southern Oaxaca (Royce 2011).
4. The only exception is George E. Lankford (2008, 127–35), whose analysis is centered on the (Southeastern) Indian concern with purity and pollution. If we share Lankford's concern for North American comparisons, we try to offer here an alternative interpretation to his.

5. In this respect, "upstreaming" is a fruitful method, as used by anthropologists William N. Fenton (1962), Irving A. Hallowell (2010), and Nathan Wachtel (1971).

6. In the wake of Lévi-Strauss, who proposed a vast comparison—synchronic and structural—of the New World myths (see Lévi-Strauss 1964, 1968), Désveaux discusses America as a cultural area in its own right by focusing on rites, social organizations, and kinship nomenclatures (Désveaux 2001).

7. For more details on Nicolas Perrot, see Havard (2019). This section is a translation of some parts of chapter 4 of this latter book (*L'Amérique fantôme*). On Perrot, see also DeMallie (2006, 242–43).

8. On the magical character attributed to manufactured objects, see Désveaux (1992); White (1994). On the debate about "apotheosis" of Europeans, see Haefeli (2007); Havard (2016a, 578–84).

9. On the solar metaphor, see Apostolidès (1981, 47–48). On Kiigouké, see Nicolas ([ca. 1675], 68; 2011, 446–47).

10. For a fruitful comparison with the Natchez, as will be seen below, see Désveaux (2001, 185–87, 332–80, esp. 374). See also Havard (2024). Perrot's case is not isolated: Europeans were indeed often compared to the Sun by Native Americans. See, for example, Cabeza de Vaca ([1542] 1993, 62); Thwaites (1900, 69:228).

11. Cavelier de La Salle died in March 1687, before this episode. "Sauvages" is translated as "Indians" as it is not used in a pejorative way in the document. Here is the original passage put in emphasis: "parce que j'estois plus grand que luy et que mes jambes auraient touché terre, deux autres me les soustenoient."

12. See also ANOM, C13C, 4, f. 135v, Relation du Voyage de Monsieur de Bourgmont, 1724, our translation.

13. During the sacred marriage of the Osages, in the 1930s, a few bridesmaids ride—or, in other words, are carried by—a "buggy" (Swan and Cooley 2019, 54). On cardinal points, see Saumade (2008, 256). A parallel could be established also with the Ojibwe drum, studied by Thomas Vennum (1982): the drum, recognized as having a strong spiritual personality, had to be placed on a blanket or a skin and held on four feet, each adorned with an eagle feather. Above all, it should never touch the bare ground. As a circular entity, the drum can actually represent the Sun.

14. See also the observation by Cabeza de Vaca ([1542] 1993, 37): "Once they saw that we had gained some strength and gotten warmer, they

took us to the next one [fire] so rapidly that our feet scarcely touched the ground."

15. Quoted also in Swan and Cooley (2019, 58). Daniel Swan and I were able to share our observations on ritual lifting during the conference dedicated to Raymond DeMallie in Bloomington in September 2017.

16. See also Le Petit (1730, 47); Cabeza de Vaca ([1542] 1993, 17): "Then a [Timucua] man [encountered in Florida, 1528] appeared before us carrying on his back an Indian cloaked with a painted deerskin. Many people accompanied him and he was preceded by some playing cane flutes."

17. The Nahua are the dominant ethnic group in Mesoamerica, to which the Aztec belonged. See Duverger (1999).

18. See the description of Dumont de Montigny quoted above about "running the post," Jacques Cartier's quote highlighted at the beginning of this chapter, or Jean de Léry, quoted earlier.

19. For a parallel reflection on horse riding and human portage in the Mexican context, see Saumade (2008, 254–59, 370–80). Saumade stresses the Native cultural predisposition for the integration of horses and bulls in their social universe.

20. On the Natchez Great Sun, see Désveaux (2001, 185). On Blackbird, see Bradbury ([1819] 1904, 64); and Say, in James (1823, 1, 223–24). On ritual prescriptions, see Désveaux (2001, 185, 366–67); Lévi-Strauss (1968, 412–22); Havard ([2003] 2017, 127–28). On Natchez plates, see Anonymous ([ca. 1735], 66).

21. Indians were usually fond of European saddles (see Ewers 1955, 93–94; Worcester 1945). On horse sacrifices, see Ewers (1955, 285, 318).

22. Let's note, however, that among Nahua, during funerals the dog of the deceased was sacrificed to carry the soul of his master across the river that separated the world of the living from the world of the dead. See Saumade (2008, 286). Note also that a horse travois could even be used as a litter (Ewers 1955, plate 5).

References

ANOM (Archives nationales d'Outre-Mer), C13A; C13C, Aix-en-Provence.

Anonymous. [ca. 1735]. "Relation de la Louisianne." Manuscript no. 530, Ayer Collection, Newberry Library, Chicago.

Apostolidès, Jean-Marie. 1981. *Le Roi-Machine. Spectacle et politique au temps de Louis XIV*. Paris: Ed. de Minuit.

Balloy, Benjamin. 2023. *Les Indiens Creek au XVIIIe siècle: Mythologie, guerre, hiérarchie*. Paris: Les Indes Savantes.

Baraga, Frederic. 1878. *A Dictionary of the Otchipwe Language, explained in English*. Montréal: Beauchemin & Valois.

Bernand, Carmen. 2021. *La religion des Incas*. Paris: Edition du Cerf.

Bernand, Carmen, and Serge Gruzinski. 1991. *Histoire du Nouveau Monde*. Paris: Fayard.

Bradbury, John. (1819) 1904. *Travels in the Interior of America, 1809, 1810, and 1811*. 2nd ed. London: Sherwood, Neely, and Jones. Reprint in *Early Western Travels, 1748–1846*, vol. 5, edited by Reuben Gold Thwaites. Cleveland OH: Arthur H. Clark.

Cabeza de Vaca, Álvar Núñez. (1542) 1993. *The Account and Commentaries of Governor Álvar Núñez Cabeza de Vaca, of what occurred on the two journeys that he made to the Indies*. Translated by Martin Favata and Jose Fernández. Houston: Arte Público Press. https://exhibits.library.txstate.edu/cabeza/.

Carayon, Céline. 2019. *Eloquence Embodied: Nonverbal Communication among French & Indigenous Peoples in the Americas*. Chapel Hill: University of North Carolina Press.

Cartier, Jacques. (1535) 1986. *Relations*. Edited by Michel Bideaux. Montréal: Presses de l'Université de Montréal.

Clayton, Lawrence, Vernon J. Knight, and Edward C. Moore, eds. 1993. *The De Soto Chronicles: The Expedition of Hernando de Soto to North America, 1539–1543*. Tuscaloosa: University of Alabama Press.

De Bry, Théodore. 1992. *Le Théâtre du Nouveau-Monde: Les Grands Voyages de Théodore de Bry*. Edited by Marc Boyer and Jean-Pierre Duviols. Paris: Gallimard.

DeMallie, Raymond J. 1993. "'These Have No Ears': Narrative and the Ethnohistorical Method." *Ethnohistory* 40, no. 4: 515–38.

———. 2006. "The Sioux at the Time of European Contact. An Ethnohistorical Problem." In *New Perspectives on Native North America: Cultures, Histories, and Representations*, edited by Sergei A. Kan and Pauline Turner Strong, 239–60. Lincoln: University of Nebraska Press.

DeMallie, Raymond, and Gilles Havard. 2019. "Writing the History of North America from Indian Country: The View from the North-Central Plains, 1800–1870." *Journal de la Société des Américanistes* 105, no. 1: 13–40.

De Smet, Pierre-Jean. 1905. *Life, Letters and Travels of Father De Smet among the North American Indians, 1801–1873*. Map and illustrations by Hiram Martin Chittenden and Alfred Talbot Richardson. New York: Francis P. Harper.

Désveaux, Emmanuel. 1992. "Les Oiseaux-tonnerre sont partis." *Recherches amérindiennes au Québec* 22, no. 2–3: 44–46.

———. 2001. *Quadratura Americana: Essai d'anthropologie lévi-straussienne.* Geneva: Georg.

———. 2013. *Avant le genre: Tryptique d'anthropologie hardcore.* Paris: Éd. EHESS.

———. 2017a. *La Parole et la Substance: Anthropologie comparée de l'Amérique et de l'Europe.* Paris: Les Indes Savantes.

———. 2017b. "Le coureur de bois ou l'homme sans filiation." *Grief: Revue sur les mondes du droit* 4: 177–88.

Dumont de Montigny, Jean-François-Benjamin. 2012. *The Memoir of Lieutenant Dumont, 1715-1747: A Sojourner in the French Atlantic.* Translated by Gordon Sayre. Edited by G. Sayre and Carla Zecher. Chapel Hill: University of North Carolina.

Du Ru, Paul. [1700]. "Journal d'un voyage fait avec Mr d'Iberville de la rade de Bilocchis dans le haut du Mississipi." Manuscript no. 262, Ayer Collection, Newberry Library, Chicago.

Duverger, Christian. 1999. *La Méso-Amérique: L'art pré-hispanique du Mexique et de l'Amérique Centrale.* Paris: Flammarion.

Ewers, John C. 1955. *The Horse in Blackfoot Indian Culture with Comparative Material from Other Western Tribes.* Bureau of American Ethnology Bulletin 159. Washington DC: Smithsonian Institution.

———. 1997. *Plains Indian History and Culture: Essays on Continuity and Change.* Norman: University of Oklahoma Press.

Fenton, William N. 1962. "Ethnohistory and Its Problems." *Ethnohistory* 9, no. 1: 1–23.

Giesey, Ralph E. 1960. *The Royal Funeral Ceremony in Renaissance France.* Travaux d'Humanisme et Renaissance, vol. 37. Geneva: Librairie E. Droz.

Grinnell, George Bird. 1911. *Trails of the Pathfinders.* New York: C. Scribner's Sons.

———. (1923) 1972. *The Cheyenne Indians.* 2 vols. New Haven CT: Yale University Press. Reprint, Lincoln: University of Nebraska Press.

Haefeli, Evan. 2007. "On First Contact and Apotheosis: Manitou and Men in North America." *Ethnohistory* 54, no. 3: 407–43.

Hall, Robert L. 1997. *An Archaeology of the Soul: North American Indian Belief and Ritual.* Urbana: University of Illinois Press.

Hallowell, Irving A. 2010. *Contributions to Ojibwe Studies: Essays, 1934-1972.* Edited and with introductions by Jennifer S. H. Brown and Susan Elaine Gray. Lincoln: University of Nebraska Press.

Hämäläinen, Pekka. 2003. "The Rise and Fall of Plains Indian Horse Cultures." *Journal of American History* 90, no. 3: 833–62.

———. 2008. *The Comanche Empire.* New Haven CT: Yale University Press.

Hamlin, William M. 1996. "Imagined Apotheoses: Drake, Harriot, and Raleigh in the Americas." *Journal of the History of Ideas* 57, no. 3: 405–28.

Havard, Gilles. (2003) 2017. *Empire et métissages: Indiens et Français dans le Pays d'en Haut, 1660-1715.* 2nd ed., Sillery/Paris: Septentrion/Presses de l'Université de Paris-Sorbonne.

———. 2016a. *Histoire des coureurs de bois (Amérique du Nord, 1600-1840).* Paris: Les Indes Savantes.

———. 2016b. "Le soleil et les pleurs: Les premiers contacts franco-amérindiens d'après un coureur de bois du XVIIe siècle." *Les actes de colloques du musée du quai Branly Jacques Chirac* 7. https://journals.openedition.org/actesbranly/693.

———. 2019. *L'Amérique fantôme: Les aventuriers francophones du Nouveau Monde.* Paris: Flammarion.

———. 2024. *Les Natchez: Une histoire coloniale de la violence.* Paris: Tallandier/Flammarion.

Hitchcock, Ethan Alan. (1930) 1996. *A Traveler in Indian Territory: The Journal of Ethan Allen Hitchcock.* Edited by Grant Foreman. Cedar Rapids IA: Torch Press. Reprint, Norman: University of Oklahoma Press.

Hyde, George E. (1937) 1975. *Red Cloud's Folk: A History of the Oglala Sioux Indians.* Reprint, Norman: University of Oklahoma Press.

James, Edwin. 1823. *Account of an Expedition from Pittsburgh to the Rocky Mountains, Performed in the Years 1819 and '20.* Philadelphia: H. C. Carey and I. Lea.

Kantorowitz, Ernst. 2000. *Les deux Corps du Roi: Essai sur la théologie politique au Moyen Age.* In *Œuvres*, translated by Jean-Philippe Genet, Nicole Genet, and Albert Kohn. Paris: Quarto Gallimard.

Kehoe, Alice B. 1970. "The Function of Ceremonial Sexual Intercourse among the Northern Plains Indians." *Plains Anthropologist* 15, no. 48: 99–103.

Lankford, George E. 2008. *Looking for Lost Lore: Studies in Folklore, Ethnology, and Iconography.* Tuscaloosa: University of Alabama Press.

La Potherie, Claude-Charles Le Roy Bacqueville de. 1753. *Histoire de l'Amerique Septentrionale.* Paris: Nyon.

Larouche, Pierre. 1994. "'La Terra de Hochelaga' ou le plan de Ramusio de 1556." *Cap-Aux-Diamants* 37: 66–69.

Laudonnière, René de Goulaine de. 1958. "L'Histoire notable de la Floride" [1586]. In *Les Français en Amérique pendant la deuxième moitié du XVIe siècle, tome 2: Les Français en Floride*, edited by Suzanne Lussagnet, 27–200. Paris: PUF.

La Verendrye, Pierre Gaultier de Varennes. sieur de. 1927. *Journals and Letters of Pierre Gaultier de Varennes de la Verendrye and His Sons.* Edited by Lawrence J. Burpee. Toronto: Champlain Society.

Le Jan, Régine. 2003. "La sacralité de la royauté mérovingienne." *Annales: Histoire, Sciences Sociales* 58, no. 6: 1217–41.

Le Page du Pratz, Antoine-Simon. 1758. *Histoire de la Louisiane, Contenant la Découverte de ce vaste Pays; sa Description géographique; un Voyage dans les Terres; l'Histoire Naturelle ; les Mœurs, Coûtumes & Religion des Naturels, avec leurs Origines; deux Voyages dans le Nord du nouveau Mexique, donc un jusqu'à la Mer du Sud; ornée de deux Cartes & de 40 Planches en Taille-douce.* 3 vols. Paris: De Bure.

Le Petit, Mathurin. 1730. Lettre du P. Le Petit (July 12, 1730), La Nouvelle-Orléans, sur les sauvages du Misissipi et en particulier les natchez et relation de leur entreprise sur la colonie françoise, en 1729, D.F.C. Louisiane no. 40. Archives Nationales d'Outre-Mer, Aix-en-Provence.

Léry, Jean de. 1994. *Histoire d'un voyage en terre de Brésil* [1578]. Edited by Frank Lestringant. Paris: Bibliothèque classique.

Lesbre, Patrick. 2014. "I'Impossible Description? Les Funérailles de Moctezuma." *E-Spania* 17. https://doi.org/10.4000/e-spania.23246.

Lévi-Strauss, Claude. 1964. *Le Cru et le Cuit: Mythologiques 1.* Paris: Plon.

———. 1968. *L'origine des manières de table: Mythologiques 3.* Paris: Plon.

———. 1971. *L'Homme Nu: Mythologiques 4.* Paris: Plon.

———. 1985a. "D'un Oiseau l'autre: Un exemple de transformation mythique." *L'Homme* 93: 5–12.

———. 1985b. *La Potière Jalouse.* Paris: Plon.

———. 2013. *Nous sommes tous des Cannibales.* Paris: Seuil.

Margry, Pierre, ed. 1876–86. *Découvertes et établissements des Français dans l'ouest et dans le sud de l'Amérique septentrionale, 1614–1754, Mémoires et documents originaux.* 6 vols. Paris: D. Jouaust.

Nicolas, Louis. [ca. 1675]. "Histoire naturelle des Indes." Manuscrits français 24225, Bibliothèque Nationale de France, Paris.

———. 2011. *Codex Canadensis and the Writings of Louis Nicolas: The Natural History of the New World, Histoire Naturelle des Indes Occidentales.* Edited by François-Marc Gagnon. Translated by Nancy Senior. Modernized by Réal Ouellet. Tulsa OK: Gilcrease Museum; Montreal: McGill-Queen's University Press.

Ramusio, Giovanni Battista. 1565. *Delle Navigationi et Viaggi, Raccolte da M. Gio. Battista Ramusio in tre volume divise.* Venice: I Giunti.

Royce, Peterson, Anya. 2011. *Becoming an Ancestor: The Isthmus Zapotec Way of Death.* Albany: State University of New York Press.

Saumade, Frédéric. 2008. *Maçatl: Les transformations mexicaines des jeux taurins.* Pessac: Presses Universitaires de Bordeaux.

Sayre, Gordon. 2005. *The Indian Chief as Tragic Hero: Native Resistance and the Literatures of America, from Moctezuma to Tecumseh.* Chapel Hill: University of North Carolina Press.

Swan, Daniel C., and Jim Cooley. 2019. *Wedding Clothes and the Wedding Ceremony: A Given Heritage*. Bloomington: Indiana University Press.

Thwaites, Reuben Gold, ed. 1896–1901. *The Jesuit Relations and Allied Documents: Travels and Explorations of the Jesuit Missionaries in New-France, 1610–1791*. 73 vols. Cleveland OH: Burrows Brothers.

Truteau, Jean-Baptiste. 2017. *A Fur Trader on the Upper Missouri: The Journal and Description of Jean-Baptiste Truteau, 1794–1796*. Edited by Raymond J. DeMallie, Douglas R. Parks, and Robert Vézina. Translated by Mildred Mott Wedel, Raymond J. DeMallie, and Robert Vézina. Lincoln: University of Nebraska Press.

Vennum, Thomas. 1982. *The Ojibwa Dance Drum: Its History and Construction*. Folklife Studies 2. Washington DC: Smithsonian Institution Press.

Wachtel, Nathan. 1971. *La vision des vaincus: Les Indiens du Pérou devant la Conquête espagnole (1530–1570)*. Paris: Gallimard.

White, Bruce M. 1994. "Encounters with Spirits: Ojibwa and Dakota Theories about the French and Their Merchandise." *Ethnohistory* 41, no. 3: 369–405.

Wissler, Clark. 1914. "The Influence of the Horse in the Development of Plains Culture." *American Anthropologist* 16, no. 1: 1–25.

Wood, W. Raymond, and Thomas D. Thiessen, eds. 1985. *Early Fur Trade on the Northern Plains: Canadian Traders among the Mandan and Hidatsa Indians, 1738–1818; The Narratives of John Macdonell, David Thompson, Francois-Antoine Larocque, and Charles McKenzie*. Norman: University of Oklahoma Press.

Worcester, D. E. 1945. "The Use of Saddles by American Indians." *New Mexico Historical Review* 20, no. 2: 139–43.

Yaya McKenzie, Isabel. 2017. "L'Emprise des Sens: La Ritualisation du Pouvoir Royal dans l'Empire Inca." *Mythos* 11: 113–28.

Remapping Northern Arapaho Space and Place in Plains Ethnohistory   8

JEFFREY D. ANDERSON

Following the lead of Raymond J. DeMallie and Gilles Havard (2019) to open up "Indian Country" to Indigenous perspectives, the general objective here is to remap some key dimensions of place in Northern Arapaho ethnohistory. Adopting corrective paths that DeMallie paved in his career-long mission to indigenize ethnohistory, one specific aim here is to challenge several ideas that have too long been accepted as facts in the historical record about the Northern Arapaho territory. A second specific aim is to move toward a deeper understanding of the meanings, functions, and power of space and place in Arapaho experiences. Overall, the study opens out to several ways of seeing the thick web of interconnecting relations among natural, human, and sacred beings and forms in the spaces and places of Arapaho "ethnoethnohistory," to use Raymond D. Fogelson's term, for "taking seriously native theories of history as embedded in cosmology, narrative, in rituals and ceremonies, and more generally in native philosophies and world views" (1989, 134–35). Arapaho history was deeper, older, and more embedded in the real landscape than what anthropologists, archaeologists, or historians have been able to reconstruct or frame with their own theories and methods. Specifically, the aims are to at least open inquiry into the long duration of Arapaho presence in the Plains culture area, their sacred connection to the mountains, and their traditional understandings for interconnecting past, present, and future in the movement of historical time.

As in many Indigenous cosmologies at large, Arapaho time and place are not without a sacred overall purpose in the long duration. In that purpose, as Gerald R. Vizenor argues, is a larger sense of motion that transcends "political and judicatory sovereignty" imposed by colonization to include "Native ancestral sovereignty, a sense of motion, the reciprocity of natural motion, or transmotion, a sense of spiritual or visionary motion" (2019, 87). For understanding what "interior spaces" there are beyond outside frames of space and time that have been imposed, it is thus essential to understand traditional forms of motion that define relations among nature, humans, and the other-than-human world. This includes motion in time and how movement of the long duration is phased and directed. For Arapahos, as for other Indigenous peoples, history was more than chronology and land was more than a mapped, two-dimensional, or political-legal space.

Remapping the Misconceptions

Throughout the ethnographic and historical record of Indigenous peoples of North America, there are seemingly countless and irremovable accepted but untrue ideas. DeMallie observes for Lakȟóta peoples that many of these ideas "have been perpetuated in the anthropological and historical literature by simply repeating as fact what earlier writers presented as surmise" (2006, 239). One of his primary concerns in his career as an ethnohistorian was to expunge accepted untruths about Lakȟóta culture and history that had invaded and settled the territory of academic and popular literature. Such misconceptions become rooted in the documented territory while explicitly or implicitly excluding other interpretations, especially those drawn from oral historical or ethnographic accounts.

There are many such misconceptions entrenched in the literature on Arapaho culture and history, as well, some with far-reaching significance about the topic here of space and place, such as territory, migration, and tribal affiliation. In some cases the imperative to fill in gaps in the historical and prehistorical chronology of events outweighed concern for empiricism. One example of primary interest is the long-accepted narrative about Arapaho migration to the Great Plains from western Minnesota in the eighteenth century as paralleling or simultaneous with Cheyenne migration, for which there is evidence. Some works cite this while at the same time mentioning that there is no documentary or archeological evidence to support it. Others claim that it is based on evidence, though without citing the sources. James Mooney's entry in the first *Handbook of American Indians North of Mexico* cites "tradition" without providing the actual source and frames other statements as "apparently" true: "According to the tradition of the Arapaho they were once a sedentary, agricultural people, living far to the N. E. of their more recent habitat, apparently about the Red r. valley of N. Minn. From this point they moved s. w. across the Missouri, apparently about the same time that the Cheyenne (q. v.) moved out from Minnesota, although the date of the formation of the permanent alliance between the two tribes is uncertain" (Mooney 1907, 72–74). While there are some references in Arapaho oral history to a horticultural past, there is absolutely no valid oral historical, archeological, or documentary evidence that places Arapahos in Minnesota or that alludes to a coincident migration onto the plains with Cheyennes. Significantly, Cheyenne and Arapaho history and culture are often melded together into one "tribe," and thus federal officials merged the two tribes' aboriginal territory into one mapping.

As Virginia Cole Trenholm maintains in her challenge to the recent occupancy theory (1970, 8–10), Mooney borrowed from William P. Clark, who interviewed a number of Northern Arapaho elders in the early 1880s through sign language with help from Chief Sharp Nose, who was then the leader of the Long Legs band of Northern Arapahos, and who became principal chief of the tribe in 1892. Clark wrote in 1885: "Very reliable tradition locates this tribe in Western Minnesota several hundred years ago, meeting the Cheyennes as they (the Cheyennes) came out on the prairie, and for many years moving and camping with or near them, so that for all practical purposes they were one people, and the history of one relates very closely to the history of the other" (41). There is no evidence that Arapahos and Cheyennes were once one people. Second, no citation or supporting evidence is given as to what this "very reliable tradition" is, though Clark does assert that Arapahos "met" Cheyennes when they arrived on the plains. Mooney (1896, 954) refers to "ancient traditions" for this narrative but cites neither written sources nor Arapaho oral historical evidence. As DeMallie notes, many such speculative constructions derive from additions and deletions made in translations or editing over time. This is a possibility here given that Clark used sign language only and was not fluent in Arapaho (DeMallie 2006, 242).

It is likely that Arapaho bands were once horticultural societies in the "northeast" somewhere, but when and where remain open questions. And there are Arapaho stories of crossing a frozen Missouri River in the distant past to explain the separation of the Arapaho proper from Gros Ventres or from a legendary lost tribe left on the other side of the river as the ice broke (Scott 1907, 558). Here and there in the existing sources, like Clark, references are made to oral historical accounts to support the migration story, but none provide such accounts or even indicate the names of the consultants. There are also other interpretations that place Arapahos more to the north prior to the move across the Missouri River into the central plains. In *Arapaho Child Life and Its Cultural Background*, M. Inez Hilger explains that at the time of her research in 1936–40, "Old Arapaho men and women today say that they can remember their old people as always saying that the Arapaho moved to the plains from the valley of the Red River of the North, just north of what is now Minnesota, long before their time" (1952, 2).

The implicit function of such constructed migration narratives is to de-anchor Indigenous peoples from the land, as if they too were just recent migrants to their territories. In this case the migration narrative at least clouds the time of Arapaho arrival on the plains. As DeMallie and Havard recognize, colonizing narratives "cast Indian countries as virgin lands or as spaces of little significance" (2019, 15). This applies especially to the plains. Hidden in the master narrative is the settler imagination of the plains as a harsh unoccupied or at least unsettled region until Native peoples experienced the indirect effects of colonization, such as the push of other groups surging westward, forcing Plains peoples to resettle or introducing technology through trade or contact, such as the horse, which made cultural adaptation to the area possible.

Following DeMallie and Havard (2019), mapping of Arapaho "territory" has also been constructed through the Western lens of political and economic functions. As they recognize, treaty boundaries would in time become framed as "ownership" for future land cessions and claims (29–30). Territories mapped in treaties also became the default baseline for academic knowledge. Accordingly, other dimensions of territory have been left beyond the borders of interest and importance. To map the boundaries, the treaty commissioners for the Fort Laramie Treaty of 1851 met over a period of one day with leaders from each of the eight tribes involved and consulted with Father De Smet and various traders and trappers (Fowler 1982, 28–39). From the late 1700s to the mid-1800s Arapaho bands traveled and camped over a wide area well beyond that "territory," from Taos in the south to north of the Big Horns, into eastern Nebraska, and west into Idaho. There were also many areas of shared usage among groups and other sites where even enemy groups could come together for trade. According to Hank Corless, Arapaho bands traveled into Shoshone territory to trade in Pleasant Valley in Idaho (1990, 14). Both accounts of Captain John R. Bell and Edwin James of the Long Expedition of 1819–20 report that Shoshones and Apaches, then enemies, also occasionally came into Arapaho and Cheyenne territory for trade on Grand-Camp Creek, or what is now called Bear Creek, southwest of Denver (Bell 1957, 180; James 1823, 502).

The boundaries for Arapaho and Cheyenne territory demarcated in the first Treaty of Fort Laramie did not include many areas commonly used or claimed by the two nations, whether individually or in combination with other tribes, such as the Old Park region of what later became Rocky Mountain National Park, an area so central in the Northern Arapaho cultural landscape. In the distant past, Arapahos clearly moved over a great expanse long before settler contact. As Clark's consultants hint at in the longer quote below, after creation in the Rocky Mountains, they "gave all their migrations as roamings from this place" (1885, 41). Several Northern Arapaho elders have told me that, after creation, Arapahos roamed the continent following the circuit of the four directions before settling in the center of the Plains culture area.[1] There is a sense that this roaming may have involved a circuit from one to another butte or mountain in the Arapaho conception of the four hills that marked the boundaries of the world and the four ages of human history. Another dimension of this story is that as Arapahos traveled, small groups split off and remained behind in far-off places, speaking languages that remained somewhat intelligible to Arapaho speakers and whom Arapahos encountered from time to time in history. Though it is beyond the scope of the present study to address, it is clear from both Arapaho understandings and documented evidence that in history and prehistory Arapaho bands traveled far and wide in North America, at least from areas in present-day Canada to New Mexico and from the Missouri River in the east to Idaho and Utah in the west (Beyreis 2019, 68; Fowler 2001, 840; Anderson 2003).

Overall, a vast terrain of ethnographic and ethnoethnohistorical evidence has been excluded in accepted mappings of Arapaho "territory," thus often eliding Arapaho centrality in Plains Indian history and culture. One of the starkest examples of exclusion of facts about place and space can be found in the Arapaho and Cheyenne Indian Claims Commission (ICC) report, which accepted the territory of the Fort Laramie Treaty as the only relevant mapping. Speaking for such reports in general, David Agee Horr explains that the range of ethnographic evidence for researchers was confined to topics that "bear upon how rights to property and power were determined within a group and the question of how Indians originally used the land" (Gussow et al. 1974, 10). Thus, the ethnohistorians involved deemed other ethnographic evidence irrelevant. Remarkably, Zachary Gussow, one of the principal researchers for the Arapaho and Cheyenne case, even devalued any oral history that could have been acquired at the time of his research: "The use of present-day native testimony in the determination of aboriginal occupation among the Cheyenne and Arapaho is of little value in the estimate of the writer" (35). The research team thus limited the scope of the ICC report to a time frame extending only from the last quarter of the eighteenth century to the Treaty of Fort Laramie of 1851: "in the determination of aboriginal land occupation we limit ourselves to that period in Cheyenne and Arapaho history at which time they appear on the scene as fully developed, equestrian, buffalo-hunting, nomadic people" (2). Accordingly, the bulk of the evidence brought forth, then, was drawn from published accounts written by non-Indians.

Centering Arapaho Transmotion in Deep Time

According to Arapaho narratives, they originated in what anthropologists define as the Plains culture area, roamed for a time, and then returned to be the first people at the center of Plains cultural developments that Arapahos in turn shared with tribes who migrated into the area later. Clark's (1885) mapping of origins and migration above contradicts a creation story he cites from his Arapaho consultants in which Arapahos generously gave core elements of Plains culture to other tribes that arrived later:

> This Arapahoe was a God. He had a pipe, and he gave it to the people. He showed them how to make bows and arrows, how to make a fire by rubbing two sticks, how to talk with their hands; in fact, how to live. His head and his heart were good, and he told all the other people, all the surrounding tribes, to live at peace with the Arapahoes, and these tribes came to this central one (Arapahoe),—came there poor and on foot, and the Arapahoes gave them of their goods, gave them ponies. The Sioux, the Cheyennes, the Snakes, all came. The Cheyennes came first, and were given ponies; these ponies were "Prairie Gifts." The Snakes had no lodges, and with the ponies they gave them skin tepees. The Arapahoes never let their hearts get tired with giving; then all the tribes loved the Arapahoes. (43)

Clark is joined by others in refuting the Arapaho "mother tribe" narrative, based on what he interprets as a misapplied meaning for the Plains Indian Sign Language sign for their tribe as "mother," which involves tapping the chest. Setting aside what Arapahos told him, he agrees with other tribes' theory that the sign originated with a famous chief indexing the disfigurement smallpox had left on his chest. Hugh Lenox Scott (1907, 557) provided another recurring interpretation of the mother sign as pointing to the tattoos on the chest for which Arapahos were known and from which the verbal exonym "Arapaho" presumably derived, namely the Crow term for them as "tattooed-on-the breast people." Yet, this is also a weakly supported "fact" that dismisses Arapaho interpretations of their own sign language sign in favor of testimony from other tribes.

As DeMallie adds, another source of constructed but accepted historical truths derives from writers' constructions to prove or support some theoretical models (2006, 239). One of the deepest and long unquestioned but often cited constructions about Arapaho history is based in the theoretical orientation of the tree model for origins and separations from an original Algonquian protolanguage and protoculture. The main objective of early and lingering historical linguistics is to map the direction and timeline of separation from an original single so-called protolanguage and associated protoculture mapped to a particular place. In Algonquianist studies from the middle to late twentieth century, the focus followed Leonard Bloomfield's initial study (1946) to trace all innovations to the core languages of the Great Lakes area as a center of Proto-Algonquian language and culture. Ives Goddard (1974) applied this model to Arapaho. The theory held that Algonquian languages in the west on the plains and in California were the result of movement and innovation away from that core. This paradigm lent more credence to the view that Arapaho peoples had recently moved out onto the plains from the east. To support Arapaho ancient occupancy on the plains, Alfred L. Kroeber maintains in *Arapaho Dialects* that the comparison of Arapaho to other Algonquian languages could help establish by glottochronology the time of Arapaho entry to the plains. He estimates that Arapahos separated from the main body of Algonquian languages over a thousand years ago (1916, 73–74). Since the 1980s, too, the paradigm in historical linguistics has been shifting away from mapping a single Proto-Algonquian core in the Great Lakes area. Paul Proulx (1984, 1985, 1988) maintains that the far-western Ritwan Algonquian languages split off from a Proto-Algic parent as early as seven thousand years ago. More recently, even Goddard moved away from the original paradigm in recognizing that Blackfoot, one of

Plains Algonquian languages that remarkably diverges like Arapaho from Central Algonquian languages, can be traced to a Proto-Plains Algonquian parent that split off from Proto-Algic long before the innovations in the Central and Eastern Algonquian languages (Goddard 2018, 101). In all, Blackfoot and Arapaho–Gros Ventre language variations are more likely to have originated in and diverged from a Plains Proto-Algonquian prior to the divergence of Central and Eastern Algonquian languages. At the very least, this suggests a longer separation than just a few hundred years from Central Algonquian languages in the Great Lakes region.

Furthermore, sociocultural fission from a single protoculture was not the only process in prehistory, for cultural fusion and diffusion also occurred. One problem with historical linguistic comparisons across Algonquian languages is that Arapaho itself was not originally a single language. Remarkably, Kroeber's consultants confirmed five original, distinct Arapaho variations, of which only three remained in use by 1900, including Northern Arapaho, Southern Arapaho, and Gros Ventre (1983, 5–6). A few forms associated with the Beesowuunenno' or "Wood Lodge People" survive today. The fifth group was the Hoho'nookeenno', or Rock People, for which little linguistic evidence remained at the time of Kroeber's research. The accepted narrative (Kroeber [1902, 1904, 1907] 1983, 5–8; Fowler 2001, 840–41; Hilger 1952, 3–4) is that there was originally one Arapaho tribe living east of the plains from which Gros Ventres separated, followed by a split of Arapahos between Northern and Southern bands by the mid-1800s. The opposite process seemed also to have been happening, though. Namely, several different groups merged throughout history and prehistory likely blending at least significant linguistic and cultural forms, as is clearly evident in the case of the Beesowuunenno', a people who likely brought some of the most sacred traditions into Arapaho culture and whose descendants can be found in both Arapaho tribes today. In all, the compiled archaeological and linguistic research has yet to offer a definitive picture of the origins, migration, and time line for Arapaho peoples on the plains. This owes largely to the embedded assumption of the tree model in which there were tribes, languages, and cultures splitting off from original proto-entities rather than diverse within themselves over the long duration of history.

The recent migration theory originating with Clark and Mooney is at odds with convincing evidence that they were in the central plains and Rocky Mountains for a very long time. Today, Arapaho elders talk about the "old people" of the early reservation period, including Sherman Sage, who possessed uncanny abilities for both remembering the past and predicting the future. In Oliver W. Toll's report of an expedition organized in 1914 by the Colorado Mountain Club to collect place-names for the opening of Rocky Mountain National Park, Sage offers a story for the Arapaho name "Mountain Smokes" for Specimen Mountain: "In explaining this, he laid some stones out on the ground. The first stone represented Sage's children, the next Sage, the next his father, the next his father's father, and so on. Sage laid out in this way eight stones. 'Now,' he said, pointing to the last of the stones, 'this man, when he was a boy, saw smoke out of the mountain'" (1914, 53). Toll adds that a geologist subsequently confirmed the volcanic history of the mountain as active five hundred to a thousand years ago, though the author doubts that the number of generations Sage offers suffices to extend to that time. This story is remarkable for several reasons. One is that it places Arapaho people in the central plains/Rocky Mountain area in the precontact period. Specifically, contrary to some accepted but questionable accounts, they also were not pushed into the Colorado area by the arrival of other groups, such as Lakȟóta peoples. Even if "generations" are calculated conservatively in the twenty-five- to thirty-year range, the story places Arapahos in the area in the early eighteenth century. On the other extreme, if the geologist's time frame is correct, then Arapahos had at that time been in the Rockies for at least five hundred years, as far back as the fifteenth century. In the same report, Toll notes that both Sage and the older Gunn Griswold identify a mound along a trail they identified as three hundred to four hundred years old, made at a time when Arapahos were using only dogs as beasts of burden. The oldest trail across the divide they identified as the "Dog Trail," or Heʒebóoó in modern orthography, which was so named for a time when Arapahos "used dogs to carry their possessions when they crossed on the trail, especially after snow was on the ground, when dogs could drag a load easily" (Toll 1914, 66–67; Cowell and Moss 2003, 367).

Life Movement through Mountains and Hills

Describing Arapahos as a "Plains" people is thus a partial characterization in need of revision. More generally, the topology in the bulk of the ethnographic and ethnohistorical literature that has emerged around the Plains culture area generally elides the deeply sacred and historical meanings that various mountain ranges have had and still have for "Plains Indian" peoples. Connections to mountains are often framed as only seasonal habitats in the stock of anthropological knowledge about Plains cultures. Mountains, other elevated landforms, and rocks on a smaller scale play a deep and seemingly ancient role in the Arapaho ultimate concern to create and promote life as transmotion at all levels of temporality. Mountains, life, power, and knowledge are bundled together in Arapaho respect for age in human and other-than-human realms. Arapaho age-theocratic hierarchy, central to Fowler's (1982) ethnohistorical analysis of Northern Arapaho survival strategies, extends into the cosmos itself over the long duration of history. The world is an old being in which some other-than-human beings, sacred objects, and places are intermediaries for survival and endurance. Mountains and rocks embody this. The beginning of this world began with the sacred Flat-Pipe (*se'eicoo*) and an other-than-human person together in a pitiable state, either floating on the water or sitting on a mountain above the water that covered all of the earth at that time. The man was fasting, even crying in some versions. He and the pipe were very lonely. Similar to many other Native North American creation myth variations of the earth-diver tradition, animal divers were called to a council of sorts. First, the duck dives below to bring up some dirt, but what he brings up is not enough. Turtle then tries and brings up enough for the man to use the pipe to expand it to create all the land base of this world. Thus, the earth is an elevated landform created from beneath the deluge.

The story of "The Flood and the Origin of the Ceremonial Lodges" told by the tribal historian known as Blindy, described below, Nih'oo3oo, "the Creator," gave Arapahos a place and purpose in the long duration of time:

> Now there was doubt whether the people should all speak one language or whether they should speak many, for they still spoke alike. Then a council was held and it was decided that most of them should change their languages from the original (Arapaho). And Nih'ā^{n}ça^n [Nih'oo3oo] gave the Arapaho the middle of the earth to live in, and all others were to live around them. Since then there have been three lives (generations); this is the fourth. At the end of the fourth, if the Arapaho have all died, there will be another flood. But if any of them live, it will be well with the world. Everything depends on them. (Dorsey and Kroeber 1903, 16)

This world is the fourth hill or generation, which will last as long as Arapahos, their language, and their sacred traditions remain alive. Time and space at all levels are four-phased in traditional cosmology (Anderson 2001, 91–114). It is, in other words, the ultimate practical concern of all Arapaho values, ceremonies, and beliefs. Homologous with the temporal phasing of the human life cycle, seasons, and directions, the history of the Arapaho universe over the long duration is shaped as "four hills of life." Each age, said to be a hundred years, involves ascent to a butte or ridge, then a stable flat period, followed by descent, then ascent to the next phase. In all, Arapaho transmotion in their territory over the long duration follows a sacred path deeply rooted in mountains, buttes, and hills, a landscape unlike that of the area east of the Missouri River.

In Arapaho sacred space, too, there are Four Old Men, each sitting on a butte or hill in one of the four directions at the boundary of the earth, where they serve as sentinels watching over the people and sending life-giving breath-winds to the people in the center (Dorsey 1903, 113). In other contexts they are referred to as former keepers of the sacred pipe and particularly as the first four keepers in consecutive order. As I have presented elsewhere, the Four Old Men sit quietly with extensive vision, thus mirroring the same presence and powers associated with Arapaho men and women in old age, the fourth hill of life (Anderson 2001, 97–103). They can foresee future happenings and thus avert dangers that approach on the horizon. Most important, they are a source of the "life elements" that provide longevity, abundance, and all good things because they themselves have lived long lives and overcome many life-threatening events. Paralleling the traditional roles of elders and ritual leaders as panoptic observers, they have the best and widest vision for the paths that the people and history should follow. Like elders, they connect past, present, and future for life movement, or what is framed from outside as "history."

The Four Old Men are appealed to in prayers and are the "living element of all people," symbolically represented and spoken of as *hiiteeni* (Dorsey and Kroeber 1903, 14–15). This is symbolized in artistic forms, which Kroeber describes as one of the only abstract symbols in Arapaho art ([1902, 1904, 1907] 1983, 149). The life principle it refers to I have interpreted elsewhere as the very concrete principle of "life movement" (Anderson 2001, 26–35). The four hills and Four Old Men are represented as a square or rhomboidal shape, in some cases lined up in a series of four interconnected buttes. For present purposes it could be said that they are keepers of the life movement of history through expanded vision for the long duration of history. As elsewhere, their placement on hills, mountains, or buttes affords great knowledge, power, and permanence.

Beyond cosmological placement, the deep connection between the Flat-Pipe, the most sacred Arapaho object, and the mountains and hills defines transmotion for revitalization, survival, and visionary knowledge. Consistent with the mythical charter above, the Pipe-Keeper Weasel Bear had a dream in 1869 instructing him that the ancient connection between the sacred Flat-Pipe and the Arapaho people could only endure if the Northern Arapaho people found a place for a reservation near the mountains. The dream portended that if this, the fourth world, did in fact come to an end by means of another flood, the future of his people and even the world depended on placement at high elevation. In that event, which will come at some point in time, the creation of the fifth world with a place for Arapahos in it would be possible (Warden and Dorsey 1905, 1–3). It is impossible to determine with certainty what role this prophecy and its advancement by Arapaho elders and chiefs had in the northern band's influence on government officials for their relocation in 1878 to what is now called the Wind River Indian Reservation in west-central Wyoming, but there is other evidence to (re)consider.

By the late 1870s, a place for Northern Arapahos was uncertain. From the late 1860s into the 1870s, no reservation had been officially established for the Northern Arapaho people. For their service as U.S. Army scouts at Camp Robinson, General Crook had apparently verbally promised to advocate for Northern Arapahos to receive a reservation near the Big Horn Mountains in what is now north-central Wyoming. Two options federal agents presented to them included joining Red Cloud's Lakȟóta on the Great Sioux Reservation or joining the Southern Arapaho in Indian Territory. The leaders who visited both places found them impoverished and suffering from illness. Their concern was also a loss of identity if they settled among Lakȟóta. While supposedly awaiting their own reservation to be established, northern bands were sent to the Shoshone Agency in Wyoming in 1878 (Fowler 1982, 63–65). They have remained there ever since.

Connected to Weasel Bear's prophecy is evidence of a more ancient Arapaho connection to the Wind River Mountain Range in Wyoming. While Clark suspected hidden rationalizing intentions behind their claim, the elders maintained that Wind River was the very site of creation as described in their origin story above: "This band was sent to their present agency in 1878, and finding here evidence of their occupying this country long ago, probably soon after their separation from the Cheyennes, they were inclined to think this was the exact spot where they were created, and, moreover, as this would, in their minds, give them a prior claim to the land over the Shoshones, they, in their shrewd and cunning way, endeavored to press this point with me, and gave all their migrations as roamings from this place" (Clark 1885, 41). Clark and others would not take this seriously, given the entrenchment of the migration narrative, assumed separation from Cheyennes, treaty-based mappings of Arapaho territory, and the precarious legal status of Northern Arapahos at Wind River at that time. There are some ways of looking at this outside of these frames, however. Most likely guided by Weasel Bear and the Flat-Pipe, Northern Arapaho bands had camped in the Wind River area before, in 1870 and again in 1874. By 1870 they had made efforts toward an agreement of peace with Eastern Shoshones and non-Indian settlers, with the suggestion of residing at Wind River long term. On both occasions they were forced out by violent attacks. In 1870 a small group traveling to Camp Brown led by Chief Black Bear was attacked by an angry mob just outside Lander. Black Bear and a number of others were killed, and the northern bands left the area. In 1874 a U.S. Army company and an even larger force of Shoshone warriors under the command of Captain E. Alfred Bates attacked Chief Black Coal's camp on Nowood Creek (Fowler 1982, 48–52). The complexities and discrepancies in the accounts of both attacks would require treatment well beyond the scope of the present essay. Suffice it to say that Arapahos were not there in either instance with intentions of attacking Shoshones or settlers (Murphy 1969, 237–38).

The question remains as to why Arapahos were drawn to Wind River. Along with life movement, movement in space was grounded in the same hierarchy based on age. Movement in history, seasonal migration, the life trajectory, rituals, public discourse, and all levels of Arapaho space and time were governed and guided by a social and cosmic theocracy. The oldest and most sacred being-object, the Flat-Pipe, is the moving center for the people: "Among the northern Arapaho, on the occasion of every grand gathering, the sacred pipe occupied a special large tipi in the center of the circle, and the taking down of this tipi by the medicine keeper was the signal to the rest of the camp to prepare to move" (Mooney 1896, 956). To answer the question, then, Northern Arapahos would not have come to the area unless guided by the Flat-Pipe and elders in council. In fact, the band that came to Wind River each time was the band in which the Flat-Pipe was kept.

The theme of a mountain providing refuge from flooding water recurs in a number of Arapaho narrative traditions. In a cosmogonic story called "The Flood," the culture-hero Beaver-Foot makes the lodge for himself and his sister River-Woman rise to the top of mountain above the rising water caused by the water-monster, or *hiincebiit* (Dorsey and Kroeber 1903, 8–12). Beaver-Foot then paints each of his feet with one of the four colors related to the four directions, namely yellow, red, black, and white. Stretching them outward, his power causes the water to retreat, leaving water animals stranded on land, forming indentations for all the lakes and rivers. In another story that combines earth-diver elements and the power to make rising water retreat, a figure named Rock uses his turtle moccasin to save the people from a deluge (16).

Mooney describes a similar process in the Arapaho-envisioned renewal of the world underlying one Ghost Dance song. Crow (*hou*) the central sacred being of the Ghost Dance will, according to prophecy, use his power to create a mountain and a bridge across the water surrounding earth to join the land of the afterlife for spirits above in the west with the world below: "Taking up a pebble in his beak, the crow then dropped it into the water and it became a mountain towering up to the land of the dead. Down its rocky slope he brought his army until they halted at the edge of the water. Then, taking some dust in his bill, the crow flew out and dropped it into the water as he flew, and it became a solid arm of land stretching from the spirit world to the earth" (Mooney 1896, 983). In a manner similar to the creation story and the stories above, Crow provides refuge for Arapaho people during the coming apocalypse predicted in the Ghost Dance tradition.

Rocks as Markers of Transmotion

Similar to and overlapping with mountains, rocks served as condensed symbolic forms for Arapaho transmotion over the long and short duration of time. Rock formations marked mythical events, ancestral oversight, vision sites, and events where life movement prevailed over crisis. For many generations Arapaho people marked history on the landscape in the form of stone monuments to indicate and remember places where various human and other-than-human events occurred. Like most human monuments, cairns called *3i'eyoono'* ("standing up" objects) were points interconnecting past, present, and future. They served the ultimate Arapaho concern for generating life (*hiiteeni*) and connected that forward-looking intentionality to present practice, and enduring forms left by those who had gone before. One kind of *3i'eyoono'* marked trails, but they served much more than that function. As evident in the report of the Toll expedition to Rocky Mountain National Park in 1914, monuments were places for ritually connecting movement on trails to life movement itself. Toll writes: "In following a trail, the Arapahos passed to the same side of all the monuments on the trail. As they passed, it was customary for everyone to put a rock on the monument, and if there were children in the party they would say, 'May this child live as long as these rocks last'" (1962, 29).

As in other Indigenous cultures of North America, rocks and stones are considered alive and powerful in Arapaho language and mythology (Tinker 2004). In the Arapaho language, the term for rock, *hoho'nookee*, is an animate noun, because rocks can move by themselves and have a vital power for endurance. In a variation of the Found-in-Grass story told by an Arapaho narrator named Tall-Bear around 1900, the culture hero's sister-in-law, Crow-Woman, turns Found-in-Grass, the culture hero, to stone along with the ground around him using a power she acquired from gopher. Her motive was to gain revenge for the public shame her brother-in-law brought upon her in response to her inappropriate behavior toward him. As a result, "Now as people passed this monument of Found-in-Grass, they would leave something in mercy for his protection, since he had changed into a stone." George Dorsey adds in an explanatory note: "This changed Found-in-Grass is the symbol of a man watching from the top of a hill, and is called an image (*wahsahk*) of the Supreme Being who has everything in the bag [sacred bundle] for people. The upright figure represents the man, and its body the earth with all its vegetation" (Dorsey and Kroeber 1903, 349–50). In the current Arapaho orthography, it is likely that the name could be rendered "*wox(u)soox*," which simply means "paint bag." The same type of bag is described in the conclusion to another story, titled "The Origin of the Buffalo Lodge and the Sacred Bundle," told by a Southern Arapaho named Black-Horse. The bag contains all of the elements for ritual painting held by men in the penultimate age-grade lodge, called "The Old Men's Lodge," Hinono'oowu'. Members of this lodge directed all the other lodges. The unnamed man in the story brought all the knowledge of the "natural laws" to the Arapaho people. The place of origin and meaning of the sacred bag are described thus: "The place where this man obtained the full mercy from this animal was very picturesque, the tops of the hills and mountains were pointed, like the shape of the sacred bag. This man said that the paint in the bag is for cleanliness, old age, etc. . . . The bag is painted all red, everything that it consisted of pertaining to life. It is the watchful eye of the Giver. This doctrine began about the middle part of the world's Creation" (48). There is thus a deep cultural affinity between old age, monuments on hills or mountains, sacred bags, stone, and the watching eyes of sacred beings from above.

The identification of monuments as persons is also a connection with this mode of placement. It was typical, as Kroeber ([1902, 1904, 1907] 1983) observes, that "people fasting on hills frequently set up piles of stone there. It seems that these monuments are made either to symbolize persons, or are thought to resemble them" (437). Others encountering monuments on mountains or hills would often leave offerings, such as shell gorgets (431). Fasting monuments were also represented in Arapaho art forms as rectangles or pointed marks (121). Arapahos also used and continue to use monuments by the same name, *3i'eyoono'*, as goals for races and as markers outside a sweat lodge.

Arapaho elder Sherman Sage also pointed out in the Toll expedition of 1914 that a collection of stone monuments marked places in the sequence of events for the warrior first killed in a battle with Apaches at some point in the 1840s–1850s. One stone marked where he was shot, the second where he rose and fell, a third where he was shot down with an arrow, and a fourth main pile of stones where he died (Toll 1914, 45–46). Stories of battles were and still are central to Arapaho history and life movement. Arapaho warriors told, and veteran soldiers today tell, war stories in ceremonial contexts to bring the power of overcoming life-threatening situations into the present as a life-giving power. For example, war stories from warriors were often the basis for giving children names, with the power of the names intended to give long life to the children. To echo the same theme for monuments and old age, history as endurance serves as a source of life-giving power in the present and is thus sacred. Things, people, and places that endured cosmological, human, and natural crises in myth or history can generate life movement for the people in the present.

Medicine wheels as circular rock formations also defined Arapaho territory, though much of the evidence is thin given Arapaho reluctance to talk about them. Traditional memory retained evidence of medicine wheels as markers of territory, though this was dismissed in the ICC case study. Citing published evidence from earlier ethnographic works that both tribes [Arapahos and Cheyennes] had well-defined territorial boundaries marked by medicine wheels, Gussow disregards such evidence without hint of further investigation: "The suggestion that these stone monuments represented aboriginal boundary marks is, in the view of the writer, nothing more than a modernized version of their original function, which was, most likely, ceremonial" (Gussow et al. 1974, 34).

Jesse Rowlodge, a Southern Arapaho consultant for most anthropologists who conducted research in the first half the twentieth century, referred to the endurance of rocks in discussing the ways Arapahos perceived the presence of anthropologist James Mooney in the early 1890s. Mooney had advised a group of chiefs to hold together like the elm tree under which they had been meeting, which had seven trunks growing out of one root. A year later a tornado uprooted and destroyed the tree, which weakened the analogy in the minds of Arapahos. In a letter to Julia Jordan dated April 4, 1968, Rowlodge then referred to Cheyenne chief White Antelope's song as he tried to surrender at Sand Creek in 1864 but was killed nonetheless: "When he came out with his nice clothes on, he came out singing. He said, 'I'm going to go. There's no life certain. Only the rocks last longest that are in the mountains'" (Rowlodge 1968).

To conclude, this brief study has sought only to chart suggestive pathways for reexamining misconception and becoming open to other evidence about Arapaho ways of seeing and knowing place and territory in history. This requires a turn from static, political-legal mappings of territory toward what Vizenor calls transmotion, the many ways that Indigenous peoples moved on the land over the short and long duration of history. Life movement as the sacred telos of history in Arapaho transmotion is intimately grounded in the center of the Great Plains, the power of people and other-than-human beings with antiquity and age, and the mountains and rocks.

Notes

1. Two of the principal elders I heard this from were Arnold Headley and William J. C'Hair.

References

Anderson, Jeffrey D. 2001. *The Four Hills of Life: Northern Arapaho Knowledge and Life Movement*. Lincoln: University of Nebraska Press.

———. 2003. "Arapaho." In *Encyclopedia of World Cultures Supplement*, edited by Melvin Ember, Carol R. Ember, and Ian Skoggard, 44–48. New York: Macmillan Reference.

Bell, John R. 1957. *The Journal of Captain John R. Bell: Official Journalist for the Stephen H. Long Expedition to the Rocky Mountains, 1820*. Glendale CA: Arthur H. Clark.

Beyreis, David C. 2019. "Dangerous Alliances in the New Mexico Borderlands: Charles Bent and the Limits of Family Networks." *Journal of the Early Republic* 31, no. 1: 57–80.

Bloomfield, Leonard. 1946. "Algonquian." In *Linguistic Structures of Native America*, edited by Cornelius Osgood, 85–129. New York: Viking Fund.

Clark, W. P. 1885. *The Indian Sign Language*. Philadelphia: L. R. Hamersly.

Corless, Hank. 1990. *The Weiser Indians: Shoshoni Peacemakers*. Salt Lake City: University of Utah Press.

Cowell, Andrew, and Alonzo Moss. 2003. "Arapaho Place Names in Colorado: Form and Function, Language and Culture." *Anthropological Linguistics* 45, no. 4: 349–89.

DeMallie, Raymond J. 2006. "The Sioux at the Time of European Contact: An Ethnohistorical Account." In *New Perspectives on Native North America: Cultures, Histories, and Representations*, edited by Sergei Kan and Pauline Turner Strong, 239–60. Lincoln: University of Nebraska Press.

DeMallie, Raymond J., and Gilles Havard. 2019. "Writing the History of North America from Indian Country: The View from the North-Central Plains, 1800–1870." *Journal de la Société des Américanistes de Paris* 105, no. 1: 13–40.

Dorsey, George A. 1903. *The Arapaho Sun Dance: The Ceremony of the Offerings-Lodge*. Field Columbian Museum, Publication 75, Anthropological Series, vol. 4. Chicago: Field Columbian Museum.

Dorsey, George A., and Alfred L. Kroeber. 1903. *Traditions of the Arapaho*. Field Columbian Museum, Publication 81, Anthropological Series, vol. 5. Chicago: Field Columbian Museum.

Fogelson, Raymond D. 1989. "The Ethnohistory of Events and Nonevents." *Ethnohistory* 36, no. 2: 133–47.

Fowler, Loretta K. 1982. *Arapahoe Politics, 1851–1878: Symbols in Crises of Authority*. Lincoln: University of Nebraska Press.

———. 2001. "Arapaho." In *Handbook of North American Indians*, vol. 13, *Plains*, edited by Raymond J. DeMallie, pt. 2, 840–62. Washington DC: Smithsonian Institution.

Goddard, Ives. 1974. "An Outline of the Historical Phonology of Arapaho and Atsina." *International Journal of American Linguistics* 40, no. 2: 102–16.

———. 2018. "Blackfoot and Core Algonquian Inflectional Morphology: Archaisms and Innovations." In *Papers of the Forty-Seventh Algonquian Conference*, edited by Monica Macaulay and Margaret Noodin, 83–106. East Lansing: Michigan State University Press.

Gussow, Zachary, LeRoy R. Hafen, Arthur Alphonse Ekrich, and the United States Claims Commission. 1974. *Arapaho—Cheyenne Indians*. New York: Garland.

Hilger, M. Inez. 1952. *Arapaho Child Life and Its Cultural Background*. Smithsonian Institution Bureau of American Ethnology Bulletin 148. Washington DC: United States Government Printing Office.

James, Edwin. 1823. *Account of an Expedition from Pittsburgh to the Rocky Mountains, Performed in the Years 1819 and '20*. Vol. 1. Philadelphia: H. C. Carey and I. Lea.

Kroeber, Alfred L. (1902, 1904, 1907) 1983. *The Arapaho*. Bulletin of the American Museum of Natural History. New York: Knickerbocker Press. Reprint, Lincoln: University of Nebraska Press.

———. 1916. *Arapaho Dialects*. University of California Publications in American Archaeology and Ethnology 12, no. 3, 71–138. Berkeley: University of California Press.

Mooney, James. 1896. *The Ghost-Dance Religion and the Sioux Outbreak of 1890*. Fourteenth Annual Report of the Bureau of Ethnology to the Secretary of the Smithsonian Institution, 1892–1893, 641–1110. Washington DC: Government Printing Office.

———. 1907. "Arapaho." In *Handbook of American Indians North of Mexico*, pt. 1, edited by James Frederick Webb Hodge, 72–74. Washington DC: Government Printing Office.

Murphy, James C. 1969. "The Place of the Northern Arapahoes in the Relations between the United States and the Indians of the Plains, 1851–1879." *Annals of Wyoming* 41, no. 2 (October): 33–61, 203–59.

Proulx, Paul. 1984. "Proto-Algic I: Phonological Sketch." *International Journal of American Linguistics* 50, no. 2: 165–207.

———. 1985. "Proto-Algic II: Verbs." *International Journal of American Linguistics* 51, no. 1: 59–93.

———. 1988. "Algic Color Terms." *Anthropological Linguistics* 30, no. 2: 135–49.

Rowlodge, Jesse. 1968. Letter to Julia Jordan, April 4, 1968. Arapaho T235, T-235-30. Doris Duke Oral History Collection, Western History Collections, University of Oklahoma, Norman.

Scott, Hugh Lenox. 1907. "The Early History and the Names of the Arapaho." *American Anthropologist* 9, no. 3: 545–60.

Tinker, George E. 2004. "The Stones Shall Cry Out: Consciousness, Rocks, and Indians." *Wicazo Sa Review* 19, no. 2: 105–25.

Toll, Oliver W. 1914. "Report on Visit of Arapaho Indians to Estes Park." Manuscript from the Collections of the Colorado Historical Society, Stephen H. Hart Research Center, Denver.

———. 1962. "Arapaho Names and Trails: A Report of a 1914 Pack Trip." Manuscript from the Collections of the Colorado Historical Society, Stephen H. Hart Research Center, Denver.

Trenholm, Virginia Cole. 1970. *The Arapahoes, Our People*. The Civilization of the American Indian Series, vol. 105. Norman: University of Oklahoma Press.

Vizenor, Gerald R. 2019. *Native Provenance: The Betrayal of Cultural Creativity*. Lincoln: University of Nebraska Press.

Warden, Cleaver, and George A. Dorsey. 1905. Warden-Dorsey Collection, A-1, box 2. Field Columbian Museum, Anthropological Archives, Chicago.

"TiweNAsaakaričI nikuwetiresWAtwaáhAt   9
aniinuuNUxtaahiwaáRA"

An Overview of Arikara Spirituality

BRAD KUUNUX TEERIT KROUPA

In marked contrast to the nomadic hunters of the plains, the Arikaras' commitment to agriculture required a settled or semi-settled life.[1] Sedentary settlement provided them with the opportunity to develop a self-sustaining local economy. Settled village life also allowed the Arikaras to continuously develop their connection to the spiritual world and its entities. Over time, their spirituality manifested itself in a rich, communal ceremonial organization with intricate practices and complex symbolism, consisting of the sacred *atiná' neéšu'* "Mother Corn," the *karuúxu'* "village sacred bundle," a religious system of *kunahUxwaarúxti'* "holy man, or priest," a distinctive class of *kunaananá* "medicine man, or doctor," and the *kunaá'u' NAhkaaWIhíni'* "Medicine Lodge." The content of this chapter—atiná' neéšu', karuúxu', kunahUxwaarúxti', kunaananá, and the kunaá'u' NAhkaaWIhíni'—provides an ethnographic synthesis that ameliorates knowledge of Arikara spirituality and ceremonialism.

The complexity of Arikara ceremonialism has caught the attention of only a few scholars who have described the uniqueness of Arikara culture (Dorsey 1904; Parks 1991, 2001). Other scholars in several disciplines have recognized the elaborate religious organization of the Arikaras and described their organization in more detail, notably Melvin R. Gilmore (1929, 1931, among others); Preston Holder (1970), who spent six months with the Arikaras in 1938; James R. Murie, a Skiri Pawnee who copublished works with Alice C. Fletcher and George A. Dorsey, as well as writing many unpublished works, from 1889 to 1981; George F. Will (1934) of the State Historical Society of North

Dakota; and, most recently, Douglas R. Parks (1996, 2001, inter alia), who worked with the Arikara community from the 1970s until the early 2000s in language and cultural studies and development. The known work that Edward S. Curtis did with the Arikaras is largely photographic, although he played an important role in reviving the forbidden Medical Lodge culture of the Arikaras ([1907–8] 1970), which is largely unrecorded outside of published photographs and recordings held in the Archives of Traditional Music at Indiana University. There is still much to be explored. Further scholarship investigating the complexity of Arikara spirituality is clearly warranted. This work is a step in that direction as it sheds light on the Arikaras and adds to the previous work of scholars who paved the way.

The Arikaras

Noting the complexity of Arikara ceremonialism, anthropologist Douglas R. Parks ([1981] 1989) concluded, "Of all the American Indian tribes of the Plains, the Pawnee and closely related Arikara developed their religious philosophy and ceremonialism to its fullest; in fact, they may have developed them more than any other group north of Mexico" (1). Other notable scholars have also recognized the elaborate ceremonial organization of the Arikaras (Dorsey 1904; Gilmore 1931; Murie [1981] 1989; Wissler 1916), which has been described as possessing great "variety and complexity," far surpassing all other Plains tribes (Wissler 1916, 644, 858). Arikara culture was based on the ecology of the Missouri River bottom and comprised robust gardening, a complex ideology and worldview, and an intricate ceremonial and philosophical system encompassing the office of *neešaánu'* "Chief," the sacred atiná' neéšu', and the secrets of the kunaá'u' NAhkaaWIhíni'.

The Arikaras were people of the earth lodge culture, as were their relatives, the Pawnees. Migrating from their Caddoan origins in the south to what is now North Dakota, the Arikaras became the northernmost Caddoan-speaking nation (Parks 1996). The northward movement of the Arikaras was, and still is, integral to their identity. According to tribal tradition, this northward movement was not random or without purpose but was instead in fulfillment of the directive given to them by the Creator, Chief Above, through atiná' neéšu' (Gilmore 1929). It is important to recognize this migratory nature as it connects not only to the Arikaras' ceremonialism but also to the science of farming. During this entire northward advance into regions of colder climates and shorter growing seasons, they still bravely retained their horticulture.

The Arikaras' corn culture, based on a highly developed ceremonial organization centered on corn, distinguished them from neighboring tribes on the Great Plains. By maintaining elaborate sets of skills and cultural practices in areas such as horticulture, ceremonialism, and commerce, the Arikaras established themselves as a developed and influential people from an early period (Kroupa 2011). Their advanced horticultural activities and scientific sophistication in the cultivation of corn—as well as other important crops of squash, pumpkins, sunflowers, tobacco, and various varieties of beans—cemented their reputation as cultural pioneers. In addition to written documents of European explorers and traders, traditions of other tribes also lend credence to the idea of the Arikaras as corn pioneers. Neighboring tribes such as the Omahas and Oglala Sioux tell of receiving corn from them as the Arikaras migrated northward. Omaha tradition credits the Arikaras with being the first to have maize and the first to distribute it to other tribes. An Omaha account described one year during the fall: "The Arikara sent invitations to a number of different tribes to come and spend the winter with them. Six tribes came, and among them were the Omaha. The Arikara were very generous in the distribution of the fruit of this new plant among their guests, and in this manner a knowledge of the plant spread to the Omaha" (Fletcher and La Flesche 1992, 78).[2]

In another tribal account by the Oglala Sioux, Black Elk recalls how Mathó Hokšíla "Bear Boy," a holy man among the Sioux, acknowledged the sacred origin of their crop: "The corn that we Sioux now have really belongs to the Ree [Arikaras], for they cherish it and regard it as sacred, in the same manner that we regard our pipe; for they, too, have received their corn through a vision from the Great Spirit. It is the will of Wakan-Tanka [Wakȟáŋ Tȟáŋka] that they have their corn" (Brown 1989, 107–8). These accounts demonstrate the common knowledge among other tribes of the importance of corn and other crops to the Arikaras, not only as a key food source but as a sacred gift and tradition from Father Above and atiná' neéšu' that figured significantly into their ceremonial life.

Moreover, the Arikara communal ceremonial organization was considerably complex and consisted of the karuúxu', a religious system of kunahUxwaarúxti', and a distinctive class of kunaananá that were well known for their healing and ritual skills, as well as feats of magic. The Arikaras also acted as barterers and were central to the trading process within an extensive commercial network. These cultural achievements made the Arikaras an integral part of the Plains peoples, if not placing them at the forefront in certain areas of agriculture, ritualism, and philosophies, including sophisticated star-based cosmology and skywatching.

Tribal organization of the Arikaras was based on village communities that represented subdivisions or bands of the tribe (Parks 2001, 373). In fact, it is not entirely correct to speak of the Arikaras as a unitary people or nation prior to the 1700s. Before European contact and the introduction of epidemic diseases, the Arikaras are more accurately described as a loose confederation of autonomous bands (Parks 1979). Each band was distinct in a number of ways. For instance, every band had a name, largely associated with its physical attributes or landmarks, its own origin story, a unique dialect, and a sacred "bundle-shrine" (karuúxu') whose keeping was inherited and highly coveted. Each group consisted of one or more villages of varying sizes, centered around the kunaá'u' NAhkaaWIhíni' that was central to its origin stories and all worldly and esoteric practices. It is impossible to determine the total Arikara population at any one time prior to 1700, but scholars agree that they were once numerous, numbering in the tens of thousands (Abel 1939; Holder 1970; Moulton 1987; Parks 1979, 2001).

In marked contrast to the nomadic hunters of the plains, the Arikaras' commitment to horticulture required a settled or semi-settled life. Sedentary settlement provided them with the opportunity to develop a self-sustaining local economy, where all the qualities and resources of the lands they occupied and hunted upon were familiar and thoroughly developed. Settled village life also allowed the Arikaras to further refine their spiritual traditions, where the earthlodge itself was a representation and symbolic reflection of the sky and related cosmologies, where stars and planets were considered as gods that formed the life of humans and provided fauna, flora, and all the natural elements for their use. Over time their ceremonial organization manifested itself in a rich religious life with an intricate tradition and complex symbolism, all of which was passed on in oral narratives.

Part of this tradition and symbolism is embodied in the karuúxu', a unique phenomenon that enhanced the distinctiveness of Arikara bands, as well as the Pawnees who shared this custom.³ Each band had a shrine containing sacred objects such as consecrated parts of birds, animals, and other power objects, with designated kunahUxwaarúxti' who conducted the rituals associated with those objects and who kept them secret from community members. The karuúxu' in its function as the key religious shrine symbolized the history of the band or village and was passed down along a line of ancestors. Where karuúxu' keepers were not generally kunahUxwaarúxti', they could not open the karuúxu' for ceremony or other purposes outside of participating in renewing its contents in rituals. The karuúxu' was an important symbol of the chief's office and of the village itself, with hereditary chiefs and a council composed of those chiefs and other leading men who were tasked with protecting the village shrine at all costs.

Arikara Ceremonialism

Several notable scholars in various disciplines have recognized the elaborate ceremonial organization of the Arikaras (Dorsey 1904; Gilmore 1931; Murie [1981] 1989; Wissler 1916). In a collection of studies in *Societies of the Plains Indians*, the contributors focused on tribal ceremonial associations, summarizing the "variety and complexity" of the Arikara ceremonial organization as far surpassing "that of any other tribe we have investigated," features that gave them "great cultural prestige" (Wissler 1916, 644, 858).

The highly developed ceremonial organization of the Arikaras was centered around corn, which occupied an unsurpassed position in

Arikara life. To the Arikaras, the reverence for corn culminated in the personification of the plant as atiná' neéšu', a spiritual manifestation of corn sent to earth as a woman by the Chief Above to give the people their spiritual teachings and cultural institutions. The Arikaras distinguished two separate spiritual institutions: the religious and the medical, also known as healing. Religious life was represented in each village by a karuúxu' and by one or more kunahUxwaarúxti', who alone knew the rituals associated with it.[4] The kunaananá were the healers, possessing the power to cure the sick and to perform magic. Although kunaananá were mostly men, women also learned the trade in conjunction with their husbands and family members who were kunaananá or learning to be kunaananá. In the physical ceremonial structure of the kunaá'u' NAhkaaWIhíni', the religious and medical institutions were united and formed the most powerful element of the tribe (Parks 1996).

Garden of Spiritual Learning

The concept of atiná' neéšu' is thoroughly engrained in every aspect of Arikara life, from horticultural practices to ceremonialism. As Gilmore (1931) commented, "Rituals of all phases of Arikara life, public and tribal, private and personal, are replete with references to the divine gift of corn" (37). The Arikara chief Ščiskoóku'u' Čiití'Iš "Four Rings" described the role of atiná' neéšu' in teaching the people practical skills as well as spiritual observances, which included a deep respect for all creation: "And the lovely visitor, whom now they knew to be Mother Corn, taught them with words of wisdom in matters of religion and of the high and deep things of life, of human beings in their duties to the Chief Above and to all the holy and mysterious beings who are aids and assistants to the Chief Above. She also taught the people right ways of living with respect to one another and to all the living things in the world, the plants and the animals" (Gilmore 1929, 104). Corn thus represented several different levels of connection with the Arikaras. Chiefly, the "cult of corn" coincided directly with the ceremonies that were done on an annual basis, the largest of which—the month-long kunaá'u' NAhkaaWIhíni' ceremonies—took place after first harvest.

Since they first received the plant from atiná' neéšu', who was given the seeds by Father Above with instructions on how to teach their use, the Arikaras practiced and maintained their horticultural traditions carefully. This crop is therefore deeply embedded in the overall cultural fabric of the people. The Arikaras were not exceptional in their reverence for corn, but they were unique in the way they developed their own varieties of corn and the ceremonial complex and traditions they created that was entirely devoted to this crop and its symbolic implications in relation to the favors given by the gods to the people, which they in turn shared with others.

To the Arikaras, corn not only provided them with sustenance and served as a popular commercial item, but it also figured prominently in their spiritual life, in part because it encouraged permanent settlements. These settlements in turn allowed for the development of complex ceremonial seasons based on the yearly corn cycle. Their reverence culminated in the personification of the plant as atiná' neéšu' as deity, a spiritual manifestation of corn sent to earth as the original Woman by the Chief Above to give the people their spiritual teachings and specific cultural institutions.

Indeed, the entire ceremonial cycle is organized around corn culture, and each individual ceremony is but one part of an elaborate ritual systematizing the atiná' neéšu' concept (Murie [1981] 1989). Most of the rituals associated with the sacred karuúxu' occurred in a prescribed order, usually fixed by the occurrence of natural phenomena. The ceremonial calendar was centered around such fundamental life activities as planting, hunting, and harvesting. Throughout the entire crop cycle, ritual blessings were performed at different stages, from preparation to planting to harvesting. In the spring, with the highly symbolic "First Thunder," a powerful being in its own right, the ritual complex began and proceeded in a systematic sequence until the people relocated to the bottomlands where their winter villages were situated (Murie [1981] 1989; Parks 1996, 2001). The ceremonies associated with the karuúxu' addressed and provided for the necessities of Arikara life during the entire year's cycle, as described by Murie: "[It] opens in the spring at the first thunder with preparations for planting the corn, which proceed step by step with its attendant ceremonies until the seed is in the ground and the plants are well developed. Then the people set out upon the buffalo hunt, to return after a time to tend and harvest the crop, after which they again set out upon the hunt and continue until forced into their houses by the winter storms, where they wait the thunder signal for the next cycle to begin" ([1981] 1989, 30).

With the coming of spring and the first thunder, the people immediately held a ritual of welcome, the Thunder Ceremony. Also known as the Renewal Ceremony, it was oriented toward the development of the cosmic universe and world origin philosophy (Murie [1981] 1989, 43). This ceremony ushered in the ceremonial year and was followed by a number of other rituals in order as the seasons progressed. The cycle continued in an almost unbroken sequence until winter, when the gods withdrew from the earth. With the world reawakening in spring, the people along with the karuúxu' were "awakened from their winter sleep," needing the "sun to fertilize them with the magic forces that would lead the village through the coming seasons" (Holder 1970, 47). Emphasizing the significance of the karuúxu' and the rituals attached to them, Holder observed the Arikara view that "unless this ceremony was performed the world would die" (47).

One ritual occurred before planting, when the people gathered at night for a ceremony in which the sacred ancient blade hoes inside the karuúxu' were used. The women would mimic the actions of preparing the ground for planting, moving the hoes back and forth above the ceremonial ground. Another ritual was performed when the corn germinated. To complete the harvest season, when the crops were fully matured, the Harvest Ceremony was performed (Gilmore, 1930). There were other rituals and their variations—especially in reverence of atiná' neéšu'—during the periods of planting, cultivating, harvest, and the final ripe corn harvest of late summer and early autumn (Murie [1981] 1989), when celebrations of the kunaá'u' NAhkaaWIhíni' would begin.

Karuúxu': The Village Bundle

Throughout Arikara history, tribal movement was heavily influenced by spiritual teachings. The items collected in the village karuúxu' represented events in the history of those movements. For example, each time the Arikaras stopped in a given location or an animal helped the people, it was recorded in the karuúxu', which contained numerous sacred items. During a karuúxu' ceremony, the leading kunahUxwaarúxti' stated: "It was our ancestors who placed all these things in this karuúxu' as they were directed. It was not a thing of their own device, but they obeyed divine instruction in the making of it" (Gilmore 1931, 36). Further demonstrating the all-embracing importance of a karuúxu', Gilmore wrote, "The teachings of the unwritten Bible of the Arikaras, which are called to mind by the objects in their proper order in the Sacred Bundles, give an account of the origin and development and mutual interdependence of all living creatures, both plant and animal, and of man's place in that living world as a partner and companion with all other living things on earth" (36). Its sacredness, significance, and community function placed the karuúxu' at the core of the Arikara ceremonial organization.

Village karuúxu' were inherited. The karuúxu' for each village was often kept by the village chief, who was a direct descendant of the original karuúxu' owner, or was passed down through family lines. Inside the chief's lodge (and other lodges) the karuúxu' was hung from a rafter on the west side, and during the band's northward migration, it was pointed in the direction of travel (Murie [1981] 1989, 36). Safeguarding a karuúxu' inside one's lodge placed certain obligations upon the chief and other household residents. Most of the rules were the same for all karuúxu', with few exceptions. Murie described the most important rules for the Pawnees, who had similar traditions: "(1) no bones, feathers, or buffalo horns are to be put in the [lodge's] fire; (2) knives are not to be used in or about the fire, stuck into the ground, or into a boiling kettle; (3) when women are menstruating they must leave the lodge and sleep outside; (4) persons must not lie in the lodge with face upward and must not shout, whistle, spit, or sprinkle water upon the dirt floor; (5) persons from the outside wishing fire must get permission from the bundle keeper; and (6) no one should approach the place where the bundle is hanging" ([1981] 1989, 37). These rules were strictly enforced and acknowledged, and they applied to everyone who entered the chief's lodge. When not in use, the karuúxu' was cared for by the chief's wife or a female relative when available, one who was familiar with some of the important features of the rituals (Holder 1970; Murie 1914, [1981] 1989). In attending to the karuúxu', it was important for her to remember the unique customs and rules pertaining to the karuúxu' in her care. Although women attended karuúxu' ceremonies, and at times performed as singers, dancers, or sponsors, they were not allowed to conduct or preside over them. In fact, the rituals and ceremonies associated with these karuúxu' were the exclusive domain of the kunahUxwaarúxti', who was generally neither the owner nor the keeper of the karuúxu', but he was the only one who knew its secrets and who could perform the prescribed rituals associated with the karuúxu'.

A village karuúxu' contained physical objects used as mnemonic devices and symbols for recalling the history, ceremonies, and tribal traditions of the people. Traveling to the plains region in 1832, Prince Maximilian provided a general description of an Arikara village karuúxu'.[5] Calling them "bird cases," he wrote:

> One of their greatest medicine feasts is that of the bird case [sacred bundle], which they have faithfully retained; they esteem this medicine as highly as Christians do the Bible. It is the general rule and law, according to which they govern themselves. This instrument is hung up in the medicine lodge of their villages, and accompanies them wherever they go. It consists of a four-cornered case, made of parchment, six or seven feet long, but narrow, strengthened at the top with a piece of wood. It opens at one end, and seven schischikues [rattles] of gourds are fixed at the top, ornamented with a tuft of horse-hair dyed red. Inside of the box there are stuffed birds of all such kinds as they can procure; that is to say, only such species as are here in summer. Besides these the box contains a large and very celebrated medicine pipe, which is smoked only on extraordinary occasions and great festivals ([1843] 1906, 391).[6]

Maximilian continues, "this bird case is of special efficacy in promoting the growth of the maize and other plants," adding that the sacred karuúxu' is "likewise a calendar for the Arikkaras [sic], for they reckon the seven cold months by the seven [rattles]" (392–93).

Ethnobotanist and ethnographer Melvin R. Gilmore was present at the ceremonial openings of various karuúxu' during the 1930s, and he also had the rare opportunity to examine their contents. Gilmore (1931) described the contents of three karuúxu' in detail. The presence of corn was common to all the karuúxu', as it was of most significance to the Arikaras. He quoted the kunahUxwaarúxti' Four Rings, stating that the inclusion of "four perfect ears of sacred corn and an ancient hoe" in each karuúxu' is "evidence of the all-important place which agriculture held, for ages had held, in the life and thought of the Arikara people" (36–37). Another similarity among the village karuúxu' was their exterior. Attached to each karuúxu' were five ancient gourd rattles, which were used by the head kunahUxwaarúxti' and his four assistants during ceremonies (Gilmore 1931). These contents tell the story of a nation and peoples engaged in a gradual movement: each village karuúxu' represents a multi-generational history that extends from the far south to what is today North Dakota.

KunahUxwaarúxti': The Religious System

The highly developed religious system of the Arikaras was exemplified by the karuúxu' and the rites of the kunahUxwaarúxti', who were in charge of the rituals connected with these objects and virtually all spiritual initiatives. Focusing on tribal welfare, a kunahUxwaarúxti' worked to improve the well-being of all his people as well as advancing the arts and history of the tribe. He provided guidance and acted as a mediator between the people and the spiritual powers (Parks 1996, 5). As a mediator, the kunahUxwaarúxti' had direct communication with the various spiritual beings that were called upon to "take pity" on humankind and influence the heavenly and worldly elements to act in their favor or even intervene in their fates. In fact, this communication with deity and supernatural beings affecting people's lives and wellness formed an intrinsic part of almost all ritual acts. The kunahUxwaarúxti' can be described as a holy master of ceremonies, possessing an unsurpassed knowledge of the sacred symbols, prescriptions, and uses of his ancestors' religion.

Inside the kunaá'u' NAhkaaWIhíni', the kunahUxwaarúxti' and his assistants conducted rites and formal procedures consisting of prayers, songs, dances, and offerings. Detailing their significant role in ceremonial life, Parks asserts that the rituals of the kunahUxwaarúxti' "were solemn, measured liturgies composed of offerings and sacrifices interspersed with long cycles of songs recounting events in mythological times, when the world was forming, as well as recitations of the moral teachings given to the people by Mother Corn" (1996, 5). The purpose of such ceremonies was to renew bonds with the sacred powers for the continued well-being of the people. These rituals, which involved speeches by the kunahUxwaarúxti', also focused the attention of the people, instructing them regarding their duties and privileges in their relationship to the Chief Above, atiná' neéšu', and other spiritual beings as well as to each other. During ceremonies, the karuúxu' was supposed to reveal itself to the people via the kunahUxwaarúxti', where "the integrating function of the karuúxu' was made manifest to the people" in order that lessons about the power of the Chief Above and the teachings of atiná' neéšu' could be passed on. As described by Holder, "This recurring round of ceremonies and feasts gave the village a continuing integrity in the eyes of the people" (1970, 48).

KunahUxwaarúxti' ultimately held greater authority than other tribal members because they communicated and negotiated with the higher powers for the well-being and advancement of the people as a whole. These kunahUxwaarúxti' may not have had the same obvious powers as the all-important kunaananá and warriors or women who tended to all domestic duties in determining the fate of the tribe, but in a sense their clout was of a higher order because it dealt with the workings of the cosmic universe that affected all living beings, whereas kunaananá operated more on an individual level.

Kunaananá: The Medical Institution

The medical institution of the Arikaras represented a distinctive class of curers, or kunaananá—commonly called "medicine men" and "medicine women," who obtained healing powers from animal spirits who taught the kunaananá their craft, and who participated in month-long rituals in which they displayed their abilities and skills in the kunaá'u' NAhkaaWIhíni'. Although both kunahUxwaarúxti' and kunaananá shared a general concern with the supernatural and attempted to control natural phenomena using all means available, what distinguished them were the differences in their objectives, the powers they invoked, and the means by which they sought to achieve their objectives.[7]

Kunaananá received their dominion from animals associated with the powers of the earth. Arikara kunaananá were influential members of their village because they possessed the three types of power bestowed on human beings by spirits (Parks 1996). The first of these related to curative abilities. The second involved the ability to perform supernatural feats and demonstrate the mysterious powers of the universe, often during the annual kunaá'u' NAhkaaWIhíni' ceremony. Arikara kunaananá also had the ability to cause misfortune, however, as their powers were not assured in their efficacy and could be used for both good or evil ends. The third type of power concerned "bad medicine" or the capability to poison or "shoot the spirit" of an individual, enabling the doctor to command the actions of a debilitated person or even cause death and diseases (Parks 1996, 89). With their commanding abilities, some used their powers malevolently, often for personal reasons or even for hire, rather than for the good of the individual or community. In either case, due to the fact that the kunaananá profession commanded life and death, they aroused both respect and fear from the community, as well as greater profits than any other class. Even the doctor's lessons cost the student at times a good deal in terms of time and resources, along with his or her services.

Kunaananá often became members of the medicine fraternity and joined a society, but such membership was not necessary. They comprised two classes: those who were less established but possessed medicine, and the developed and adept kunaananá who belonged to formal medicine societies (Parks 2001, 381). Admittance into a society was usually only granted after a lengthy process of instruction.

During the nineteenth century, Arikara kunaananá were members of eight organizations.[8] It is well documented that the kunaananá among the Arikaras, as well as those of their Pawnee relatives, possessed significant powers and developed their medicine societies to a level beyond most other nations (Benedict 1922, 20; Holder 1970). These medicine societies comprised distinguished kunaananá, a few students, and a considerable number of attached members who took part in dancing, singing, and some aspects of the ceremonies but were not otherwise acquainted with their secrets (Murie 1914, 600). Every society had its permanent position of seating in the lodge arranged from the entrance from left to right: Ghost, Black-Tail Deer, Buffalo, Cormorant, Duck, Owl, Din of Birds, and Bear (Parks 1996, 6). Each possessed individual bundles, songs, clothing, accessories and body paints, dances, and rites. Additionally, each society had a particular medical specialization based on body parts. These songs and medicine powers were demonstrated annually in the kunaá'u' NAhkaaWIhíni' ceremony.

kunaá'u' NAhkaaWIhíni': The Medicine Lodge

One of the most spectacular ceremonies was the kunaá'u' NAhkaaWIhíni', a combination of various rites that were performed every year, usually during the late summer and early fall, lasting for about four weeks. The central purpose of the ceremony was to gain the attention of the mysterious powers and show reverence and gratitude to the Chief Above, atiná' neéšu', and other spirit beings so that they might bless the tribe. The kunaananá and kunahUxwaarúxti', although representing different spiritual institutions, collectively joined in the kunaá'u' NAhkaaWIhíni', creating the most powerful religious expression and strongest element of the tribe (Parks 2001, 379).

The ceremonial or holy lodge, where all of the important village ceremonies were conducted, was the largest structure in the village, always placed in the center of the village. According to Ščiskoóku'u' Čiití'Iš "Four Rings" and NeétAhkas TiiriwátAt "Rising Eagle," also known as Frank Hart, as recorded by Melvin R. Gilmore in 1926, the floor plan of the ceremonial lodge reflected Arikara cosmology. As such, the kunaá'u' NAhkaaWIhíni' is symbolic of the structure of the world according to Arikara ideology and culture. The entrance always faced east, in the direction of the rising sun. A fireplace was located in the center. On the west wall, directly across from the entrance, was the altar that held the sacred karuúxu' and other ceremonial instruments. The ceiling embodied the infinity of the sky in its shape and function. The foundation of the lodge consisted of the four poles that represented the four quarters of the world: the southeast, southwest, northwest, and northeast. They also represented the four paths from the powers above, acting as aids of the Chief Above to perform his will in the world (Gilmore 1929).

Apart from singing, dancing, and other ritual performances, the ceremony included spectacular and theatrical displays of power and knowledge by each of the kunaananá societies. The feats performed were many and varied. Men shape-shifted to bears, and corn grew from a seed to full bloom in a few minutes, for example. People were buried alive and suddenly arose from the river a few hundred yards away. Many of these performances were done in broad daylight or in a well-lit lodge, in full view of dozens and sometimes hundreds of people, including Europeans and other visitors. These feats made deep impressions on the audiences attending the ceremony. The following stories of the Bear Medicine Society may serve to demonstrate, where ethnographer George F. Will stated: "Another member of the Bear band would dress himself in the skin of a bear and amble around the fireplace imitating a bear in his actions. A second member would take up a rifle and shoot him, often several times. The first man would drop, roll about on the floor, and would bleed profusely. The medicine men would then surround him. Soon he would stand up, cough, and spit the bullets out into his hand, when he would be as well as ever" (1934, 46–47).

Another lengthy narrative of the Bear Society demonstrates the power of animation of inanimate objects. This particular story occurred in the early 1800s and was witnessed and recorded in detail by more than one European traveler:

We accordingly followed our guide to the medicine lodge, where we found six men dressed in bear skins, and seated in a circle in the middle of the apartment. The spectators were standing around, and so arranged as to give each individual a view of the performers. They civilly made way for our party, and placed us so near the circle that we had ample opportunity of detecting the imposture, if any imposition should be practiced. The actors (if I may so call them) were painted in the most grotesque manner imaginable, blending so completely the ludicrous and frightful in their appearance, that the spectator might be said to be somewhat undecided whether to laugh or to shudder. After sitting for some time in a kind of mournful silence, one of the jugglers desired a youth who was near him, to bring some stiff clay from a certain place which he named on the river bank. This we understood through an old Canadian name Garow, (well known on the Missouri,) who was present and acted as our interpreter. The young man soon returned with the clay, and each of these human bears immediately commenced the process of moulding a number of little images exactly resembling buffaloes, men and horses, bows, arrows, &c. When they had completed nine of each variety, the miniature buffaloes were all placed together in a line, and the little clay hunters mounted on their horses, and holding their bows and arrows in their hands, were stationed about three feet from them in a parallel line. I must confess that at this part of the ceremony I felt very much inclined to be merry, especially when I observed what appeared to me the ludicrous solemnity with which it was performed. But my ridicule was changed into astonishment, and even into awe, by what speedily followed.

When the buffaloes and horsemen were properly arranged, one of the jugglers thus addressed the little clay men or hunters: "My children, I know you are hungry; it has been a long time since you have been out hunting. Exert yourselves to-day. Try and kill as many as you can. Here are white people present who will laugh at you if you don't kill. Go! Don't you see that the buffalo have already got the scent of you and have started?"

Conceive, if possible, our amazement, when the speaker's last words escaped his lips, at seeing the little images start off at full speed, followed by the Lilliputian horsemen, who with their bows of clay and arrows of straw, actually pierced the sides of the flying buffaloes at the distance of three feet. Several of the little animals soon fell, apparently dead—but two of them ran round the circumference of the circle, (a distance of fifteen or twenty feet,) and before they finally fell, one had three and the other five arrows transfixed in his side. When the buffaloes were all dead, the man who first addressed the hunters spoke to them again, and ordered them to ride into the fire, (a small one having been previously kindled in the centre of the apartment,) and on receiving this cruel order, the gallant horsemen, without exhibiting the least symptoms of fear or reluctance, rode forward at a brisk trot until they had reached the fire. The horses here stopped and drew back, when the Indian cried in an angry tone, "why don't you ride in?" The riders now commenced beating their horses with their bows, and soon succeeded in urging them into the flames, where horses and riders both tumbled down, and for some time lay baking on the coals. The medicine men gathered up the dead buffaloes and laid them also on the fire, and when all were completely dried they were taken out and pounded into dust. After a long speech from one of the party, (of which our interpreter could make nothing,) the dust was carried to the top of the lodge and scattered to the winds.

I paid the strictest attention during the whole ceremony, in order to discover, if possible, the mode by which this extraordinary deception was practiced; but all my vigilance was of no avail. The jugglers themselves sat motionless during the performance, and the nearest was not within six feet of the moving figures. I failed altogether to detect the mysterious agency by which inanimate images of clay were to all appearance suddenly endowed with the action, energy and feeling of living beings. (Mitchell 1835, 657–58)

Stories such as this demonstrate the mysterious powers of the universe the Arikaras inhabited, their reliance on and unwavering belief in spirits and their powers, and the awe-inspiring and inexplicable powers that were passed onto and characterized the Arikara kunaananá and kunaá'u' NAhkaaWIhíni' activities in the old days.[9]

Conclusion

The examples of spiritual expression I present here offer a restored understanding of both the scope and intensity of the spirituality possessed by Arikara ancestors. Moreover, this chapter is an effort in the spirit of the quotation given in the title: "*TiweNAsaakaričI nikuwetiresWAtwaáhAt aniinuuNUxtaahiwaáRA* (today we remember them, the ways of the old ones who were: the good ways that were ours)," a line from the Arikara song memorial to the Old Scouts.

Unfortunately, only a handful of the old ceremonies have survived into the twenty-first century, and most of these remain today only in altered form. Most disappeared completely during the nineteenth and early twentieth centuries as a result of diseases, warfare, and government policies that discouraged the Arikaras' abilities to preserve and perform traditional forms and culturally destroyed the Arikara people—for example, intensive forced conversion of all Indigenous people to Christianity and severe curtailing or elimination of their traditional culture and practices, including family names. A series of smallpox epidemics and other uncontrollable diseases that struck during this prosperous era was the single most detrimental historical event for the Arikara population and their cultural environment.

Although the numerous cultural upheavals throughout the history of the Arikaras led to tremendous cultural change, they have survived and persisted in the remembrance of their beliefs and traditions. Today Arikara descendants are reaching back to the ancient spiritual expressions and cultural anchors of their forebears and recovering what is salvageable, as well as creating new traditions. These efforts have forged a modern cultural identity for the Arikaras that is built on both previous and novel traditions. This approach—scrupulous observance of relevant ancient traditions and blending of old and new—is facilitating a contemporary reeducational process for the Arikaras by carrying forward the tribe's cultural history and mores into new settings and for ongoing generations.

Notes

1. *TiweNAsaakaričI nikuwetiresWAtwaáhAt aniinuuNUxtaahiwaáRA*: "Today we remember them, the ways of the old ones who were: the good ways that were ours," a line from the Arikara song memorial to the Old Scouts.
2. Hunger and nutrition were recurring winter problems, especially for nomadic tribes.
3. Many non-Caddoan Plains tribes possessed bundles of various kinds serving different purposes. It was specifically the karuúxu', the sacred village bundle, and its sacred contents and the purpose it served that were unique to the Arikaras and Pawnees.
4. In total, there were three types of bundles among the Arikaras: the village bundle, the medicine bundle, and the personal bundle. The karuúxu', discussed in detail below, was considered the most powerful due to its deep cultural, historical, and symbolic significance as the actual source of the Arikara peoples. Of secondary importance were personal bundles. These bundles symbolized the relationship between an individual and his animal power benefactor. Warriors had their own bundles, usually small bags that could be carried on expeditions. Perhaps more important were the bundles belonging to kunaananá, or medicine bundles. In addition to the typical contents, these bundles contained herbs and other medicines. Medicine bundles and their secrets could be inherited or purchased.
5. Maximilian's reference to the karuúxu' as "bird cases" was apparently due to the extensive collection of bird skins included therein.
6. The reference to horse hair in Maximilian's account suggests that the karuúxu' was made after horses were introduced in the Great Plains. This demonstrates that the horse developed into an important cultural symbol and part of the tribe's history. It also raises a central question: if the Arikaras had horses, why did they not become more nomadic like other surrounding tribes?
7. The "powers" invoked by kunaananá were not "gods" as such but rather manifestations of one sacred power. In Arikara spirituality there were graded levels of supernatural power, all of which were manifestations of the higher order.
8. Douglas R. Parks (1996) lists eight medicine societies that composed the Medicine Lodge during the late eighteenth century. Edward S. Curtis ([1907–30] 1970), however, identified nine medicine fraternities. Curtis

included the "Principal Medicine" and had them seated at the altar, separating the southern and northern halves of the lodge where the other societies were seated. He identified "the Principal Medicine, who, four in number and representing respectively Beaver, Otter, Muskrat, and Swamp-owl" (65). George F. Will (1934) disagreed, commenting with respect to Curtis's Principal Medicine his belief that "the place at the altar is given over to the singers of the officiating [kunahUxwaarúxti'] who change with the [kunahUxwaarúxti'] and are selected in turn from the different bands" (17–18).

9. Specifically, in the historical accounts written by European authors, there are many references to "legerdemain" or "sleight of hand" used in the ceremonies. These performances are discussed in journals and early accounts from traders and travelers, and the credibility of these rituals is often challenged. Nonetheless, the Arikaras and other tribes believed in the authenticity of the rituals performed. No matter what position the reader or scholars take as to the credibility of many of the rituals, it does not detract from the elaborate spectacle and deep significance of the ceremonies performed by the kunaananá. To the Arikaras, these feats are displays of supernatural powers, and as in other oral histories, there is no question as to the authenticity.

References

Abel, Annie Heloise, ed. 1939. *Tabeau's Narrative of Loisel's Expedition to the Upper Missouri*. Norman: University of Oklahoma Press.

Benedict, Ruth Fulton. 1922. "The Vision in Plains Culture." *American Anthropologist* 24, no. 1: 1–23.

Brown, Joseph E., ed. 1989. *The Sacred Pipe: Black Elk's Account of the Seven Rites of the Oglala Sioux*. Norman: University of Oklahoma Press.

Curtis, Edward S. (1907–30) 1970. *The North American Indian*. 20 vols. Edited by Frederick W. Hodge. Norwood MA: Plimpton. Reprint, New York: Johnson Reprint.

Dorsey, George A. 1904. *Traditions of the Arikara*. Washington DC: Carnegie Institute of Washington.

Fletcher, Alice C., and Francis La Flesche. 1911. *The Omaha Tribe*. Vol. 1. Twenty-Seventh Annual Report of the Bureau of American Ethnology to the Secretary of the Smithsonian Institution, 1905–1906. Washington DC: Government Printing Press.

Gilmore, Melvin R. 1929. "The Arikara Book of Genesis." *Papers of the Michigan Academy of Science, Arts, and Letters* 12: 95–120.

———. 1930. "A Harvest Home Ceremony of the Arikara." Gilmore Papers, American Indian Studies Research Institute, Indiana University, Bloomington. https://aisri.indiana.edu/research/editorial/gilmore/a_harvest_home_ceremony_of_the_arikara.pdf.

———. 1931. "The Sacred Bundles of the Arikara." *Papers of the Michigan Academy of Science, Arts, and Letters* 16: 33–50.

Holder, Preston. 1970. *The Hoe and the Horse on the Plains: A Study of Cultural Development among North American Indians*. Lincoln: University of Nebraska Press.

Kroupa, Brad K. T. 2011. "Through Arikara Eyes: History of Education as Spiritual Renewal and Cultural Evolution." Paper presented at the Annual Meeting of the Organization of Educational Historians, Chicago, Illinois.

Maximilian, Prince of Wied-Neuwied. (1843) 1906. *Travels in the Interior of North America, 1832–1834*. Translated by Hannibal Evans Lloyd. 2 vols. London: Ackermann and Co. Originally published in German as *Reise in das innere Nord-America in den Jahren 1832 bis 1834*. 2 vols. Coblenz: J. Hoelscher, 1839–41. Reprint in *Early Western Travels, 1748–1846*, vols. 22–24, edited by Reuben G. Thwaites. Cleveland OH: Arthur H. Clark.

Mitchell, D. D. *Extraordinary Indian Feats of Legerdemain*. In the *Southern Literary Messenger* 1, no. 12 (August 1835). Richmond: T. W. White, Publisher.

Moulton, Gary, ed. 1987. *The Journals of the Lewis and Clark Expedition*. Vol. 3. Lincoln: University of Nebraska Press.

Murie, James R. 1914. "Pawnee Indian Societies." In *Societies of the Plains Indians*, edited by Clark Wissler, 543–644. Anthropological Papers of the American Museum of Natural History 11, pt. 7. New York: Order of the Trustees.

———. (1981) 1989. *Ceremonies of the Pawnee*. Edited by Douglas R. Parks. Smithsonian Contributions to Anthropology, no. 27. Washington DC: Smithsonian Institution Press. Reprint, Lincoln: University of Nebraska Press.

Parks, Douglas R. 1979. "Bands and Villages of the Arikara and Pawnee." *Nebraska History* 60: 214–39.

———. (1981) 1989. Introduction to *Ceremonies of the Pawnee*, by James R. Murie, 1–28. Smithsonian Contributions to Anthropology, no. 27. Washington DC. Reprint, Lincoln: University of Nebraska Press.

———. 1991. *Traditional Narratives of the Arikara Indians*. 4 vols. Lincoln: University of Nebraska Press.

———. 1996. *Myths and Traditions of the Arikara Indians*. Lincoln: University of Nebraska Press.

———. 2001. "Arikara." In *Handbook of North American Indians*, vol. 13, *Plains*, edited by Raymond J. DeMallie, 365–90. Washington DC: Smithsonian Institution.

Will, George F. 1934. *Notes on the Arikara and their Ceremonies*. Denver: John VanMale.

Wissler, Clark, ed. 1916. *Societies of the Plains Indians*. Anthropological Papers of the American Museum of Natural History 11. New York: Order of the Trustees.

"Under the Tree That Never Bloomed   10
I Sat and Cried Because It Faded Away"

An Ethnohistory of Black Elk's Visions

RANI-HENRIK ANDERSSON

Foundations: *Black Elk Speaks* and *The Sixth Grandfather*
Oglala *wičháša wakȟáŋ* (holy man) Black Elk (Heháka Sápa, 1863–1950) is one of the best known Lakȟóta individuals, and most certainly the best known wičháša wakȟáŋ. John G. Neihardt's *Black Elk Speaks: Being the Life Story of a Holy Man of the Oglala Sioux* ([1932] 2008) immortalized him and preserved Lakȟóta nineteenth-century religious practices and beliefs for later generations. In 1985 Raymond J. DeMallie published *The Sixth Grandfather: Black Elk's Teachings Given to John G. Neihardt*, which took a scholarly approach to Neihardt's texts using the original shorthand notes that were taken down directly from Black Elk's speech. *The Sixth Grandfather* provides the readers with a far more nuanced understanding of Black Elk and his world by offering extensive commentary and analysis, based on Ray DeMallie's profound knowledge of Lakȟóta culture.[1]

The Sixth Grandfather is a masterpiece of ethnohistorical research and serves as the foundational text for this chapter's discussion on Black Elk's most powerful visions: his boyhood vision that he refers to as his Great vision and his Ghost Dance visions. It is not necessary to detail the vision experiences here; rather, I approach them through emerging themes that were central to Black Elk's beliefs and also at the heart of Lakȟóta culture. While Ray DeMallie explains Black Elk's visions in *The Sixth Grandfather* and in the 2008 annotated edition of *Black Elk Speaks*, he does not offer a full analysis or comparison of these particular visions. Thus, I pick up the story from there to provide a fuller analysis of Black Elk's Great vision and Ghost Dance visions by employing what I would like to call an "ethnohistorical close reading."

The original manuscripts and other materials on which Neihardt based his *Black Elk Speaks* are in the John G. Neihardt Collection, Western History Manuscript Collection at the University of Missouri, Columbia. What is presented in Neihardt's work, however, is his interpretation of what Black Elk said, written in Neihardt's prose. It includes sentences never uttered by Black Elk and omits crucial phrases that are of utmost value for a fuller understanding of Black Elk's teachings. Hilda Neihardt Petri, the daughter of the famed author, who was present during many of the interviews, described the process of trying to understand Black Elk through an interpreter as excruciatingly difficult and slow. Sometimes even the interpreter struggled to comprehend Black Elk's vision experiences in the Lakȟóta language, let alone adequately express his thoughts in English. Thus, she says, what Neihardt published in *Black Elk Speaks* represented Black Elk's ideas as accurately as possible given the circumstances. To achieve a more nuanced interpretation of Black Elk and his wakȟáŋ world, DeMallie began to research the original manuscripts and eventually edited these documents with in-depth annotations as *The Sixth Grandfather: Black Elk's Teachings Given to John G. Neihardt* (1985). Neihardt Petri welcomed DeMallie's work, saying "I commend this book warmly and affectionately as an essay of understanding" (Neihardt-Petri in DeMallie 1985, xviii).[2]

Black Elk and His Wakȟáŋ World

Black Elk lived a long life during which he witnessed the increasing onslaught of the *wašíču* (whites) on Lakȟóta lands. He participated in the Little Big Horn battle of 1876 at the age of thirteen or fourteen, surrendered with his family in 1877, and settled on the Great Sioux Reservation. The most foundational and transformative event of his life took place when he was about nine. At that time he received what he referred to as his Great vision that led him to a path of seeking and interacting with the wakȟáŋ.

Seeking a vision, Haŋblécheyapi, is one of the seven foundational Lakȟóta ceremonies. Each (male) individual sought a vision, which then gave him direction for life. Powerful vision experiences needed to be explained by a wičháša wakȟáŋ, and understanding the vision required also that the person enact his vision through certain ceremonies (DeMallie 1985, 214–26, 232–35). Sometimes a vision could be so powerful that it offered the person the choice to become maybe a great hunter or a warrior, or a holy man or medicine man (pȟežúta wičháša) (DeMallie 1985, introduction; Andersson and Posthumus 2022, 38–39).

In fact, Black Elk's understanding of the Lakȟóta belief system has to be understood through the Lakȟóta concept of wakȟáŋ, the sacred. The Lakȟóta differentiated between the ordinary world and the superhuman, sacred world, but both worlds were equally normal and understandable and were natural parts of the universe. For the Lakȟóta there was traditionally no single God. Instead, the foundation for their religion is the belief in a general spirit force that manifests itself in nature in the visible and the invisible world. This all-encompassing spirit force is known as *Wakȟáŋ Tȟáŋka*, sometimes translated as the great spirit or the great mystery. However, neither of these English terms fully captures the essence of wakȟáŋ or Wakȟáŋ Tȟáŋka. While Wakȟáŋ Tȟáŋka can be considered as a godlike or divine being, it is more complicated than that. On a fundamental level, wakȟáŋ is everything. Everything that is mysterious or causes awe can be wakȟáŋ. Above all things is Wakȟáŋ Tȟáŋka, which encompasses everything wakȟáŋ. Wakȟáŋ also reflects kinship networks, which comprise human-to-human relationships, human-to-nature relationships, and human-to-sacred relationships. The concept of wakȟáŋ and the Lakȟóta system of belief (religion) was constantly evolving and adapting. Each individual could formulate, change, and contribute to the understanding of wakȟáŋ — for example, through visions (Walker [1980] 1991, 68–80; DeMallie and Lavenda 1977; Andersson 2018b, 228–29; Andersson and Posthumus 2022, 22–42). Thus, Black Elk's experiences and his interpretation of Lakȟóta culture and religion need to be understood, not as a final truth, but rather as a part of this evolving individualistic religious world.

Understanding Lakȟóta religion as an ever changing and evolving belief system serves also as a gateway to understanding the Ghost Dance religion and Black Elk's involvement in it. The Ghost Dance or *Wanáǧi Wačhípi kiŋ* swept across the plains in the late 1880s. In 1888 a Paiute Indian, Wovoka, fell into trance and had a vision. In his vision he met the Great Spirit, who gave him instructions for a new religion. When Wovoka woke up, he started to instruct his people in a new dance. Dancing the new dance would bring about a transformation of the earth. There would be a new world where the white man would not hold the Indians down. There would be buffalo and other game, and the dead Indians would be brought back to life. It would, indeed, be an Indian paradise. Wovoka's religion attracted thousands of American Indians around the Great Basin area and beyond, especially on the Great Plains.[3] Soon the Lakȟóta started to hear rumors of this wonderful new religion brought by a Messiah in the west who had come upon the earth to help the Indians. The Lakȟóta, like so many other tribes, wanted to learn more about this religion that the whites called the Ghost Dance. The Lakȟóta of Pine Ridge and Rosebud held the first meetings and ceremonies of the new religion in April 1890. Lakȟóta eagerly participated from the beginning. Scores of Lakȟóta got together to watch the dances, many being drawn into the dance and experiencing powerful visions. In the visions the Lakȟóta met their dead relatives and received messages about the return of happier times. After waking up from trance, people wept from happiness, and many were convinced that a new world was indeed coming (Andersson 2008, 2018a).

The Ghost Dance filled a religious void resulting from years of oppression by the whites. Recent scholarship has shown that the Lakȟóta did not use the Ghost Dance to start a final uprising against the white people as believed by contemporary whites and scholars. For the Lakȟóta the Ghost Dance was first and foremost an expression of religious beliefs. That it led to bloodshed was due to misunderstandings between the whites and the Lakȟóta on both individual and collective levels. The Ghost Dance caused tremendous frictions within Lakȟóta society, and the Lakȟóta found various ways to deal with the situation (Utley 1963; DeMallie 1982; Ostler 2004, 234–360; Andersson 2008, 2018a; Greene 2014; Warren 2017). To understand the significance of Lakȟóta Ghost Dance experiences, one needs to place them not only in the context of reservation life but also in the framework of Lakȟóta history, culture, and religious traditions. Such experiences as meeting spirits in the spirit world were natural in Lakȟóta culture. Things that were revealed in visions were as real as those in the tangible human world. The return of the buffalo is also a common theme in Lakȟóta culture. In the Lakȟóta creation story, the Lakȟóta and the buffalos once emerged together from a cave in the Black Hills. By 1890 the buffalo were gone, but the Ghost Dance promised to bring them back. The Ghost Dance, like the traditional Sun Dance, was a ceremony of renewal. At the center of the dance circle, a sacred tree, *čháŋwakȟáŋ*, was erected as a symbol of the unity and prosperity of the people. The dance circle itself represented the *čhaŋgléška wakȟáŋ*, the nation's hoop or the unbroken unity of the Lakȟóta people. In the late 1880s reservation context, this sacred hoop was broken, and many saw the Ghost Dance as an opportunity to bring the people back into the hoop, where people would again prosper. For no one was this idea more real than for Black Elk.

During his early reservation years in the late 1870s and early 1880s, Black Elk became increasingly interested in the wakȟáŋ world and leaned toward healing and other Lakȟóta sacred ceremonies. He also became interested in Christianity, which, by the early 1880s, was taught on the reservation by both Protestant and Catholic missionaries, but he did not yet adopt it. In the late 1880s he traveled to Europe with Buffalo Bill's Wild West show (DeMallie 1985, introduction; Andersson 2008, 2018a; Andersson and Posthumus 2022). His time in Europe proved to be another formative experience for Black Elk. While in Europe he met a woman he referred to as his girlfriend, and during breakfast one morning, he suddenly fainted and was taken up into the air and transported across the ocean to Pine Ridge. He was watching from above as his mother stood outside the tipi and people were going about their daily business, but they were in despair. When Black Elk revived, his girlfriend's family had called for a doctor, who had pronounced him dead. They had a coffin ready for him. Having seen his people in despair, he could no longer stay in Europe, and after meeting Buffalo Bill in Paris, he asked for funds to return home. He was not only homesick but felt he was losing his power, and his duty on earth was to help his people with this power (DeMallie 1985, 9–11, 245–54). In Europe he learned more about Christianity and the ways of the wašíču, but at the same time he was losing his connections to the wakȟáŋ. To find clarity both in his personal quest and the fate of his people, he needed to go home. When finally back on Pine Ridge, he saw his people in despair, suffering from hunger and disease and facing a cultural crisis, just like his vision told him. "When I came back [from Europe] my people seemed to be in poverty. Before I went some of my people were looking well, but when I got back, they all looked pitiful. There had been quite a famine. I returned in 1889. While I was gone, I had lost my power, but as soon as I returned, I was called out to cure a sick person and just then my power returned" (256).

As a response to this despair, the Ghost Dance (Wanáǧi Wačhípi kiŋ) promised to bring about a better life, and many found this an exciting opportunity. It appealed to Black Elk, who eventually became one of the leading Ghost Dance wičȟáša wakȟáŋ. When witnessing a Ghost Dance ceremony at White Clay Creek on the Pine Ridge Reservation in the early fall of 1890, he felt the ceremony was a real-life enactment of his boyhood vision. In his own words, "[I] went there first to find out what they had heard, but now I changed my mind and was going there to use my own power to bring the people together." He was not sure about the new religion at first, but the ceremony and its foundational principles were so familiar to him that he became a Ghost Dancer (DeMallie 1985, 255–60; Andersson 2018a; Andersson and Posthumus 2022, 204–31).

The Wounded Knee massacre on December 29, 1890, practically ended Ghost Dances on the Lakȟóta reservations. Black Elk participated in a few skirmishes after the Wounded Knee massacre, but like so many Lakȟóta, he experienced a spiritual loss after the Ghost Dance failed to bring about a new way of life. Black Elk married Katie

Warbonnet in 1892 and became a father the year after. Of his three children, only Benjamin survived to adulthood. In 1903 Katie died, and perhaps due to this disaster, Black Elk turned to Catholicism, which he had earlier rejected despite the many efforts by missionaries. Like so many Lakȟóta at the time, he found solace in the Catholic societies and church activities (DeMallie 1985, 11–13; Andersson and Posthumus 2022, 192–96).

Black Elk's conversion to Catholicism was undoubtedly genuine. As a man always interested in and searching for the wakȟáŋ, he wrote in 1909: "When they [priests] [speak?] words from God, we should hold them strongly. There are many Indians in the U.S. but only few belong to God's church; Many are living unhappy lives. For this reason, we should take firmly what the priests tell us: These are God's words and so mankind should benefit from them in the name of our saviour" (DeMallie 1985, 21). Because of his devotion, he was asked by Father Henry I. Westropp to become a catechist in Manderson on the Pine Ridge Reservation, but he was also sent to other reservations for mission work. Black Elk formed another marriage in 1905 to Anna Brings White, who had two daughters from a previous marriage, and together they had three more children. They remained together until Anna's death in 1941 (10–17). Despite being a devout Catholic, in his old age Black Elk turned again to traditional religion, and through Neihardt, he became a symbol of Native resistance and a keeper of cultural traditions (DeMallie 1985, preface).

At the time John G. Neihardt arrived on Pine Ridge, Black Elk was seriously pondering his religious path and the powers he had been given in his youth. Had he followed his vision properly, or was it his failure to act according to his vision that caused the suffering to the Lakȟóta? It was a terrible burden to carry. In Neihardt he found a kindred spirit, a man who could help him relieve his burden, and who could help him save sacred Lakȟóta ways. He told Neihardt that he knew in advance that he would be coming, that it was told to him in a vision. Neihardt too had had a dream, and Black Elk interpreted that as a sign that they were to meet in order to make his vision "go out": "This vision of mine ought to go out, I feel, but somehow, I couldn't get anyone to do it. I would think about it and get sad. I wanted the world to know about it. It seems like your ghostly brother [spirit in a dream] has sent you here to do this for me. You are here and have the vision just the way I wanted, and then the tree will bloom again, and the people will know the true facts. We want this tree to bloom again in the world of true that doesn't judge" (DeMallie 1985, 43). After relating his vision to Neihardt, Black Elk felt that a tremendous burden had been lifted from his shoulders, but at the same time he had given away his power: "I have no power now, but you can take it, and perhaps with it you can make the tree bloom again, at least for my people and yours" (47).

The Six Grandfathers and the Flaming Rainbow

Now it is time to examine Black Elk's original vision more closely. As mentioned, one morning at the age of nine, Black Elk was out with his friends, when he heard a voice calling for him: "It is time, now they are calling you," the voice spoke. Black Elk immediately knew that the spirits had called upon him. He fainted and was taken to his family's tipi, where he lay sick—apparently dead—for twelve days. Yet he was not dead; instead, two men came from the clouds and told him that the grandfathers were calling for him. So Black Elk went out with these men who took him up into the clouds. They were the messenger from *Wakíŋyaŋ*, the thunder beings.

In the clouds Black Elk was shown four rows of twelve horses, all representing the different directions and the powers associated with each. The horses eventually took him to a tipi where he met the six grandfathers, each also representing one direction and certain powers. "Do not fear, come right in," said one of the grandfathers. Hesitantly Black Elk entered through the door that was a flaming rainbow. One of the grandfathers called to him and said, "Younger brother, behold me; a nation's center of the earth I shall give you with the power of the four quarters like relatives you shall walk. Behold the four quarters" (DeMallie 1985, 114–19). Then one by one the grandfathers gave him items that represented the powers that he was supposed to use on earth.

The most important were a cup of water and a bow and arrow. The cup of water represented the powers to heal, and through it, he was going to be a healer for his people. The second grandfather gave him an herb that he was to use to cure the sick. The bow and arrow represented the power to destroy. Traditionally a vision of the thunder beings gave the dreamer two options, to become a healer or a destroyer, that is, a warrior. This option was given to Black Elk too; it was a decision that he found extremely difficult to make, and it affected his entire life. But he was given even more.

Each of the grandfathers represented a direction and the power(s) associated with that particular direction. After receiving powers from all of the grandfathers, Black Elk suddenly realized that he was given *all* the powers of the different directions including the above and the below. As he left the cloud tipi, he understood that he himself was the sixth grandfather, representing the earth.

> Then the sixth grandfather said: "Boy take courage, you wanted my power on earth, so you shall know me. You shall have my power in going back to earth. Your nation on earth shall have great difficulties. There you shall go." . . . I saw him go out the rainbow gate. I followed him out the rainbow gate. . . . I stopped and took a good look at the sixth grandfather, and it seemed I recognized him. I stood there for awhile very scared and then as I looked at him longer, I knew it was myself. (DeMallie 1985, 119)

Black Elk was given not only the powers to heal and to fight but also the powers to decide the fate of his people. He was going to be the intercessor between his people and the wakȟáŋ. As the sixth grandfather he would have great responsibilities, and whenever his people needed him, he would have to act accordingly.

When Black Elk related his vision to Neihardt, several of the old Oglala men present noted that his vision was one of the most powerful visions any of them had heard of. For many years Black Elk was unsure of what to do with this vision. Finally, according to Lakȟóta custom, he told it to a wičȟáša wakȟáŋ, who instructed him to conduct the appropriate ceremonies: first the Horse Dance and later the *heyókȟa* (thunder dreamer, contrarian) to enable him to enact the vision in his life. With this power came also tremendous burdens and responsibilities. Black Elk had to decide which road he would travel in his life: the Red Road of good healing and curing or the Black Road of destruction and war.

After performing the necessary ceremonies, he would become a wičháša wakȟáŋ in his own right, but was also forced take on the power of the Black Road of war and destruction. The grandfathers had given him the power to destroy all the enemies he would face, but Black Elk was reluctant to take on this responsibility and would only rely on these powers when necessary. Black Elk was a young boy during the major wars the Lakȟóta were fighting against the whites who were encroaching on their lands (DeMallie 1985). Yet, instead of fully committing himself to the life of a warrior, he decided it would be his duty to help his people through the powers given to him by the grandfathers of the West and North. Those were the powers of healing (117–35).

It was not until the late 1880s that Black Elk really had to truly decide whether to use his powers to destroy. When he learned that the new religion, the Ghost Dance, had been started on the Pine Ridge Reservation, he was curious enough to go and see the ceremony. What he saw astounded him and affected him profoundly. It was like his childhood vision enacted in the human world. After some hesitation he joined the ceremony and fell into a trance:

> I ascended into the air again and there was a spotted eagle in front of my eyes, and I could hear the shrill whistle and scream of the eagle. I was gliding again prone through the air with my arms out. I was right on a ridge again and as I neared it, I could hear strange noises, [a] rumbling sound. Right below that ridge there was flame coming up. As it began to flame up, I glided right over it. I glided over the fifth circle village and glided over the sixth circle village. I landed on the south side of this sixth village. As I landed there, I saw twelve men coming toward me and they stood before me and said: "Our Father, the two-legged chief, you shall see."

Black Elk went to the center of the circle where he saw a man with outstretched arms, and he could not say if this man was an Indian or white, or if he was the Christ, or if he represented the grandfathers of his vision. "As I looked at him, his body began to transform. His body changed into all colors, and it was very beautiful. All around him there was light. Then he disappeared all at once. It seemed as though there were wounds in the palms of his hands." Then the twelve men told Black Elk: "Turn around and behold your nation, your nation's life is such." Here again the same messengers from his childhood vision appear and ask him to behold his nation, meaning that his duty was to lead them out of difficulty, thus validating to him that the Ghost Dance was true and, similar to his Great vision, asked him to be the intercessor for his people. "The day was beautiful—the heavens were all yellow and the earth was green. You could see the greenward of the earth [the plains].... As they finished speaking to me I heard singing in the west (where the sun goes down).... I prepared myself to come back and before I started the twelve men took two sticks and pounded them into the ground and they said: 'Take these, you shall depend upon them.'" One of the sticks was painted white and the other was painted red (DeMallie 1985, 117–19).

Interestingly, the Ghost Dance vision then continues with twelve women telling Black Elk to "behold his nation" and to take the teachings he was now receiving back to his people. In his childhood vision women did not act as messengers or advisers from the spirit world; perhaps the women represented the Ghost Dance, since women and men danced together in the Ghost Dance ceremony holding hands, and women too received powerful visions during the ceremonies. This was an innovation of the Ghost Dance, thus the women in Black Elk's vision may be a reference to this ceremony.

Then Black Elk went gliding over a dark river with six villages in circles on the other side of the river:

> This was a very fearful, dark river, rushing with foam in it. On this side nobody was living. As I looked down there were men and women. They were trying to cross this river, but they couldn't do it so they were crying

about it. They looked up to me and said: "Help us!" I came on and glided over them. Of course, when I came over the river, I heard the strange rustling and rumbling sounds and the flames also, but I just glided over them. I saw my people again and I just figured that I had brought something good for them. (DeMallie 1985, 264)

The first Ghost Dance vision impressed Black Elk because it repeated many elements from his Great vision and he ascertained that the Ghost Dance would help him act as mediator and aide for his people. The six villages in circles represented for him the six grandfathers and he landed at the sixth village because "in the flaming rainbow of the first vision, I had seen six grandfathers—the powers that the earth got from these six powers. I saw two men first in the vision and now I saw two men in the Messiah vision also. . . . In my first vision I had seen twelve riders and again I saw twelve men in this vision. It represents the twelve moons in the year. This village might represent six generations from the first and perhaps in the sixth generation the tree will bloom as in my vision" (265).

Black Elk took notice of how the twelve men in the vision were dressed, and he "made six sacred shirts according to what these twelve men wore." Then, "I took six copies of the fashion of the twelve women that I'd seen in my vision" (DeMallie 1985, 265). Here Black Elk refers to the Ghost Dance shirts called by the Lakȟóta *oglé wakȟáŋ kiŋ*, sacred shirts. The shirts became central garments used during the Lakȟóta Ghost Dance ceremonies and had their roots in vision experiences, as well as in other Lakȟóta traditions. Shields and other sacred objects, including paintings, could be considered bulletproof. They were signs of the holder's medicine or power. The Ghost Dance shirts served a similar function: as symbols of sacred powers, they helped the Ghost Dancers stay united. They were not "made for war" as maintained by many contemporary white observes and historians alike; rather, they were an expression and innovation born out of Lakȟóta beliefs and traditions where invincibility is not strange or uncommon. The shirt gaining protective features reflects growing Lakȟóta concerns, as the invulnerability feature appeared only *after* the U.S. military invaded

Lakȟóta reservations on November 19–20, 1890. A military intervention had seemed likely, and many Ghost Dancers were scared. There was a desperate need for these protective garments, and the visions by prominent medicine men confirmed that the shirts had the power to protect them from the bullets of the wašíču. The Ghost Dance shirt was wakȟáŋ (Andersson 2008, 67–73, 288–90; Andersson 2018a; Warren 2017).

Black Elk became a leader of the Ghost Dance ceremonies on Pine Ridge and began to interpret visions that others received during the ceremony. He felt dizzy himself several times during the ceremony but never received such a powerful experience that would have matched his boyhood Great vision. In the end he was not sure if the man in his Ghost Dance vision was the Messiah, the Christ, or whether he represented the six grandfathers. This must have left a seed of doubt about the Ghost Dance. He simply was not sure.

In his last Ghost Dance vision, Black Elk again saw the flaming rainbow: "The only thing I saw was toward the west I saw a flaming rainbow that I had seen in the first vision. On either side of this rainbow was a cloud and right above me there was an eagle soaring, and he said to me: 'Behold them, the Thunder-being nation, you are relative-like to them. Hence, remember this.' During the war I was supposed to use this rainbow, and the Thunder-beings but I did not do it. I only depended on the two sticks that I had gotten from the vision. I used the red stick" (DeMallie 1985, 265–66).

Here Black Elk refers to the aftermath of the Wounded Knee massacre, where he fought the soldiers and was wounded in the side. While preparing for the fight and taking revenge for his slain relatives, Black Elk invited his people to gather on a high point where he again prayed for the six grandfathers:

> This day I remembered my six grandfathers, although I had completely forgotten my vision for a spell before this. I had some white paint with me, so I told them to bring their weapons that I might make them sacred [*to do their great damage*]. I put a little bit of white paint on every gun that they brought and when that was done everyone stood facing the west, pointing their weapons toward the west.

Then I thus sent a voice: "Hey-a-a-a-a (four times). Grandfathers, the six grandfathers that I thus will recall to you today, behold me! And also to the four quarters of the earth and its powers. Thus, you have said if an enemy I should meet that I should recall you. This you have said to me. Thus, you have set me in the center of the earth and have said that my people will be relative-like with the Thunder-beings. Today my people are in despair, so, six grandfathers, help me."

About this time we could see a storm coming up (in January, in the middle of winter), but the Thunder-beings appeared with lightning and thunder. The people all raised their hands toward the Thunder-beings and cried. The Thunder-beings followed the White Clay up and went toward Pine Ridge. We were well prepared now and were going out again for revenge. Revenge is sweet. (DeMallie 1985, 280)

Here Black Elk seems to rely on his power vision instead of the Ghost Dance vision, finally making the choice to walk the Black Road asking the six grandfathers and the thunder beings to help him now when he and his people were in despair. The Wounded Knee massacre and the subsequent fighting made Black Elk further doubt the power of the Ghost Dance. Later he lamented that he never should have depended on his Ghost Dance visions, allowing them to override his childhood Great vision. "It seems to me on thinking it over that I have seen the son of the Great Spirit himself. All through this I depended on my Messiah vision whereas perhaps I should have depended on my first great vision which had more power, and this might have been where I made my great mistake" (266).

This mistake weighed heavily on Black Elk, perhaps initiating his conversion to Christianity. The burden that he was bestowed by the six grandfathers was much to bear. When John G. Neihardt returned to Pine Ridge after his initial visit, he was greeted by Black Elk, who had erected a large tipi outside of his house; the tipi door was painted as a rainbow. Through this rainbow Neihardt entered the tipi that in essence was the same tipi in the clouds to which the six grandfathers had invited the young Black Elk. Now Black Elk was the sixth grandfather, representing perhaps not only the earth but all the powers and all the directions that the grandfathers had shown him. This time Neihardt had entered the sacred space to learn from Black Elk. To Black Elk the rainbow symbolized the entryway to this sacred space and all thoughts that were pure and true: like how there is clarity after rain, and the rainbow a symbol of that clarity. Black Elk felt Neihardt was to relate his thoughts and beliefs onward to future generations, to make them "go out." Black Elk named Neihardt Pȟéta Wígmuŋke, "the Flaming Rainbow" (DeMallie 1985, 36–37).

The Tree That Never Bloomed and the Nation's Hoop

The six grandfathers were present in Black Elk's Ghost Dance visions, but not at the center as they were in his childhood vision. This caused him some doubt. Two other elements that were central to his childhood vision and the Ghost Dance vision were the sacred tree and the circle or the nation's hoop. The sacred tree, čháŋwakȟáŋ, was central to the *wiwáŋyaŋg wačhípi* (Sun Dance) that was the most important collective calendrical ritual for the Lakȟóta. It was typically held at the peak of summer, when the bands would come together, as a public celebration of tribal unity. The high point was reached in a dance held around the sacred tree. In the Sun Dance the dancer was attached to the sacred tree with a rawhide thong, which looped around a stick inserted through pairs of slits in the chest or back. The goal was to dance and pull against the thong until the skin tore and the dancer was released. No food or drink was allowed; the pain and suffering helped the dancer reach another world. Self-mortification convinced the spirits of the dancer's sincerity and pitifulness. Originally a warrior's ceremony to obtain power over enemies, it also functioned as a prayer for abundance and increase of both the people and the buffalo (Andersson and Posthumus 2022, 38–39).

In his Great vision one of the grandfathers gave Black Elk a sacred stick, or cane, that represented the center of the earth, and as the stick began sprouting it symbolized the prosperity of the people. Black Elk was to use this flowering stick to make good for his people. Black Elk relates:

> The fourth grandfather had a stick in his hand, and he said: "Behold this, with this to the nation's center all of the earth, many you shall save." I looked at the stick and saw that it was sprouting out and at the top there were all kinds of birds singing. The fourth grandfather said: "With this you shall brace yourself as a cane and thus your nation shall brace themselves with this as a cane and upon this cane you shall make a nation. Behold the Earth for across it there are two roads. Behold the sacred road from where the giant is [North] to where we always face [South]. Behold, this road shall be your nation. from this road you shall receive good." (DeMallie 1985, 118)

In his vision the people were rejoicing at the center of the sacred hoop, and at the center of the hoop the flowering tree was blooming, and the southern grandfather said: "Behold the circle of the sacred hoop, for the people shall be like unto it; and if they are like unto this, they shall have power, because there is no end to this hoop and in the center of the hoop these raise their children." Black Elk clarified: "The sacred hoop means that the people shall stand as one and everything reproduces inside the hoop" (129).

Black Elk continues:

> So they put the sacred stick into the center of the hoop and you could hear the birds singing all kinds of songs by this flowering stick and the people and animals all rejoiced and hollered. The women were sending up their tremolos. The men said: "Behold it from there we shall multiply, for it is the greatest of the greatest sticks." This stick will take care of the people and at the same time it will multiply.... We live under the flowering stick like under the wing of a hen. Depending on the sacred stick we shall walk, and it will be with us always. From this we will raise our children and under the flowering stick we will communicate with our relatives—beast and bird—as one people. This is the center of the life of the nation. (DeMallie 1985, 129–30)

It needs to be remembered here that Black Elk's vision took place at the time when the major fighting against the whites was beginning in the late 1860s, but when he related this vision to Neihardt he had already lived on the reservation for decades and had seen the disruption that war and reservation life had brought to his people. In fact, he lamented to Neihardt that "this tree never had the chance to bloom because the white men came" (130). Still, at the end of the 1880s, the Ghost Dance gave Black Elk one more chance to make the sacred tree bloom.

In the Ghost Dance the sacred tree was erected at the center of the dance circle; no one was attached to it, but offerings hung from it. The dance leaders, wičháša wakȟáŋ, were standing by the tree directing the ceremonies. For Black Elk, people dancing around the tree was a direct link to his childhood vision.

> Then I went to the center of the circle with these men and there again I saw the tree in full bloom. Against the tree I saw a man standing with outstretched arms. As we stood close to him these twelve men said: "Behold him!" The man with outstretched arms looked at me and I didn't know whether he was a white or an Indian. He did not resemble Christ. He looked like an Indian, but I was not sure of it. He had long hair which was hanging down loose. On the left side of his head was an eagle feather. His body was painted red. (At that time I had never had anything to do with white men's religion and I had never seen any picture of Christ.)[4]
>
> They had a sacred pole in the center. It was a circle in which they were dancing and I could clearly see that this was my sacred hoop and in the center they had an exact duplicate of my tree that never blooms and it came to my mind that perhaps with this power the tree would bloom and the people would get into the sacred hoop again. It seemed that I could recall all my vision in it. The more I thought about it, the stronger it got in my mind. Furthermore, the sacred articles that had been presented were scarlet relics and their faces were painted red. Furthermore, they had that pipe and the eagle feathers. It was all from my vision. So I sat there and felt sad. Then happiness overcame me all at once and it got a hold of me right there. I was to be intercessor for my people and yet I was not doing my duty. Perhaps it was this Messiah that had pointed me out and he might have set this to remind me to get to work again to bring my people back into the hoop and the old religion.

Again I recalled Harney Peak in the Black Hills [*the center of the earth*].⁵ And I remembered my vision that the spirits had said to me: "Boy, take courage, they shall take you to the center of the earth." When they took me here, they said: "Behold the universe, the good things of the earth. All this behold it, because they shall be your own." Then I saw people prospering all over. And I recalled my six grandfathers. They told me through their power I would be intercessor on earth for my people. They had told me that I should know everything so therefore I made up my mind to join them. (DeMallie 1985, 257–59)

The next morning Black Elk went to the dance ground and joined the men standing around the sacred tree erected at the center of the dance circle. Black Elk's uncle Good Thunder (Wakíŋyan Wašté), who was one of the main leaders of the Lakȟóta Ghost Dance, took him by the arm and offed a prayer. As Good Thunder prayed, Black Elk became overwhelmed by emotions, thinking about his dead parents and other close relatives. To keep the tears from running he put his head up, but he could not hold his tears any longer:

I was really sorry and cried with my whole heart. The more I cried, the more I could think about my people. They were in despair. I thought about my vision and that my people should have a place in this earth where they would be happy every day and that their nation might live, but they had gone on the wrong road and they had gone into poverty but they would be brought back into the hoop. Under the tree that never bloomed I stood and cried because it faded away. I cried and asked the Great Spirit to help me to [make it] bloom again. I could not stop crying no matter how much I tried. (259–60)

The sacred tree was not blooming, but Black Elk still believed that his duty on earth was to bring his people back to the sacred hoop. In Lakȟóta culture the sacred hoop, čhaŋgléška wakȟáŋ, was a symbol of kinship and belonging. For the Lakȟóta, all people speaking the same language were referred to as *lakȟólkičhiyapi* (allies) and were *wólakȟota* (related). Together they made up the čhaŋgléška wakȟáŋ, which represents the unity of the people. All non-Lakȟóta Native

Americans were seen as outside the Lakȟóta sacred hoop and were related as *tȟókakičhiyapi* (enemies). The Lakȟóta considered themselves to be related to all other lifeforms and to the earth from which they came. Thus, they incorporated the entire universe into the sacred hoop of kinship. There was no sharp distinction between nature and culture or society (Posthumus 2018, 383–84; Andersson and Posthumus 2022, 43–72). Kinship in turn transcended biological relatedness, providing a mechanism for incorporating everyone into the network of relatives. Through kinship the Lakȟóta people were held together in a great network of relationship that extended beyond tribal boundaries outward to the rest of the universe. This all-inclusive sacred hoop of relationship is expressed by the Lakȟóta axiom *mitákuye oyás'iŋ* (all my relatives, we are all related). Through kinship the Lakȟóta maintained civility, good manners, and a sense of responsibility toward all individuals, human and nonhuman (Deloria [1944] 1998, 25; Standing Bear [1928] 2006, 193, 250; DeMallie 2001, 808; Andersson and Posthumus 2022, 43–72; Deloria 2022, 59–75, 195–281).

When camping, the Lakȟóta traditionally formed a large circle, *hóčhoka*. Different *oyáte* (tribes, bands) placed their own camp circles in designated places inside the larger circle, thus creating a sacred hoop of relatives. The Lakȟóta *thiyóšpaye* (extended family) ordinarily stayed together throughout the year and lived in geo-residential units called *wičhóthi* (camps or, literally, "place where humans dwell"). Formal camps were always circular, while informal camps were linear, with tipis typically erected along a creek bed. Lakȟóta camp circles consisted of each family's tipi, all of them facing inward toward the center of the *hóčhoka*, a common area consisting of open space for socializing and ceremonial activities, the *thípi iyókhiheya* (council lodge, "tipis joined together") or *thiyóthipi* ("lodge of lodges"), and the various men's society lodges. Outside of the camp circle stood temporary shelters, sweat lodges, and menstrual lodges (Deloria [1944] 1998, 38–39; DeMallie 2001, 801). Inside the circle everything was Lakȟóta. When Black Elk described the sacred hoop of his visions, he referred to both the camp circle and the sacred hoop, but they both represented the prosperity and unity of the Lakȟóta people and the wholeness and relatedness of the Lakȟóta universe.

The sacred hoop was at the center of Black Elk's Great vision. Through the powers he was given he was to "raise a nation," but it was not certain whether it would be in prosperity or in difficulty. When presenting him with a sacred hoop one of the grandfathers said. "Behold this sacred hoop, it is the people you shall have." He also presented Black Elk with a bow and arrow and a wooden cup of water. With the bow and arrow he could defeat all enemies, and the water would heal and make his people grow, that is, prosper. "The thunder beings have the power to kill and the water the power to heal," noted Black Elk, whose vision was a thunder vision (DeMallie 1985, 123). Thus, through the thunder beings Black Elk received both powers, and he would raise a nation, which meant that people would follow his lead, he would destroy their enemies when necessary, and he would place them at the center of the sacred hoop.

During the Ghost Dance, many people moved away from their log cabins and erected tipis to camp at the dance sites; the traditional camp circle, the sacred hoop, was restored (Andersson 2018b, 11–12). Moving to the dancing grounds meant the strengthening of the camp circle and hence the unity of the nation. This is what Black Elk saw in his vision:

> Then I had a funny feeling of shivering over my body, and this showed that it really was the real thing. Everyone knew my power and with my own will to make that tree bloom, I joined the people there. All I saw was an eagle feather in front of my eyes at first. I felt as though I had fallen off a swing and gone out into the air. My arms were outstretched and right before me above I could see a spotted eagle dancing toward me with his wings fluttering and the shrill whistle he made. I could see a ridge right in front of me and I thought I was going to hit that ridge, but I went right over it. I did not move at all, I just looked ahead. After I reached the other side of the ridge, I could see a beautiful land over there and people were camping there in circle[s] all over. I noticed that they had plenty, and I saw dried meat all over. I glided over the tipi. Then I went down feet first and lighted on the ground. As I was going down

to the center of the hoop, I could see a tree in full bloom with flowers on it.... I could see fat horses all over and the wild animals ranging out over the country and hunters were returning with their meat. (DeMallie 1985, 259–60)

In the vision Black Elk saw a circles of villages, and within those circles people had plenty and they were happy. Yet while he was returning to earth from his vision, his flowering tree was still not blooming: "When I got right above the dance place, they were still dancing the Ghost Dance. I hoped to see that tree blooming [*but the day following it was not blooming*] and it was just seemingly faded. I went down to my body then and I could hear the voices. Then I got up from my vision. When I saw the tree in the vision it was in full bloom, but when I came back the tree was wilted and dead" (261). The Ghost Dance promised to make all this come true, and now the visions by Black Elk and others collaborated with these promises. In many visions a recurring theme was that the people were not yet ready for the return of the spirits, or the renewal of the earth. But by continuing the Ghost Dance and acting properly, they would make way for the things that were seen in the visions (Andersson 2018a). For the Lakȟóta, visions were an inseparable part of life, and for the believers in the Ghost Dance, they were a real reflection of a future that would surely come true. Black Elk put his thoughts into words by lamenting, "If this world would only do as it is told by this vision, the tree would bloom" (DeMallie 1985, 261).

Conclusion

Black Elk's childhood vision was the foundation for his life. The key concepts for his life as a wičháša wakȟáŋ, as a warrior, and as a provider for his people came from his Great vision. He obviously had other visions during his life that had similar themes (DeMallie 1985). His childhood vision made him the sixth grandfather, the one representing the below, the earth, and whose task was to be a mediator between the people in the human world and the wakȟáŋ world. His duty was to help his people with his powers. At the time of great despair, the Ghost Dance provided him the means to act as a provider and spiritual leader to his people again. As I demonstrate in the *Lakȟóta Ghost Dance of 1890* (2008) and *A Whirlwind Passed through Our Country* (2018b), the Lakȟóta approached the Ghost Dance in a variety of ways. Some embraced it wholeheartedly; others denied it for political, personal, or religious reasons. Black Elk's experiences and his visions connect the Ghost Dance to Lakȟóta traditions and religious concepts. Black Elk's life was strongly influenced by his vision experiences, but even for those not so deeply immersed in the world of the wakȟáŋ, the Ghost Dance and its religious concepts were appealing and understandable. While it was in many ways an innovation born out of cultural, religious, economic, and psychical destitution, it looked forward to a better future for the Lakȟóta people (DeMallie 1982; Andersson 2008, 2018a; Warren 2017). For many like Black Elk, it provided a way to get back to the sacred hoop of Lakȟóta life, albeit in a slightly new form. Still, its core concepts were deeply rooted in Lakȟóta culture, beliefs and traditions, in short *Lakȟól wičȟóȟ'aŋ* (Lakȟóta life ways).

Yet, when the Ghost Dance failed to make the tree bloom and bring prosperity to the people, Black Elk turned elsewhere for power and guidance: Catholicism. Later in life he regretted that he had relied on his Ghost Dance vision instead of his Great vision. Despite many similarities the Ghost Dance vision was not as powerful as his Great vision and proved a great disappointment and a spiritual burden to Black Elk.

Finally, through John G. Neihardt, the Flaming Rainbow, Black Elk certainly has helped the Lakȟóta people come back to the hoop, and with the revitalization Lakȟóta language and culture over the past decades, he is making the tree bloom again. Through *The Sixth Grandfather* Black Elk's legacy will continue to "go out" and inspire further generations of readers. Raymond J. DeMallie's work in *The Sixth Grandfather* and his other key works are examples of outstanding ethnohistorical scholarship that provides in-depth analysis and understandings of Lakȟóta culture and history, but that also inspire new generations of scholars to continue research and ask new kinds of questions to reimagine and redefine the field of ethnohistory specifically and Indigenous studies at large.

Notes

1. This chapter is based on the text presented in DeMallie (1985). Those interested in further comparison should consult Neihardt ([1932] 2008).
2. Black Elk's life and teachings have been further explored in, for example, Black Elk DeSersa et al. (2000); Steltenkamp (2009); Oldmeadow (2018); and Sweeney (2020). But it is through *Black Elk Speaks* that Black Elk's understanding of the sacred, wakȟáŋ, has reached a far larger audience than any other accounts collected by anthropologists or historians.
3. Much has been written about the Ghost Dance, starting from Mooney ([1896] 1991). Other works include Utley (1963), Smith (1975), and Hittman (1997). Some of the more recent works are Ostler (2004), Andersson (2008, 2018b), Warren (2017), and Gage (2020).
4. By the time of the Ghost Dance in 1890 Black Elk had actually become acquainted with Christianity. For example, while in Europe he wanted to travel to Jerusalem to see the place where Christ was crucified (DeMallie 1985, introduction).
5. Harney Peak in the Black Hills was considered to be the center of the world and thus very sacred. It was the place where Black Elk was taken in his boyhood vision. See DeMallie (1985, 98).

References

Andersson, Rani-Henrik. 2008. *The Lakota Ghost Dance of 1890*. Lincoln: University of Nebraska Press.

———. 2018a. "In Search of Wakȟáŋ." *Great Plains Quarterly* 38, no. 2: 227–35.

———. 2018b. *A Whirlwind Passed through Our Country: Lakota Voices of the Ghost Dance*. Norman: University of Oklahoma Press.

Andersson, Rani-Henrik, and David C. Posthumus. 2022. *Lakȟóta: An Indigenous History*. Norman: University of Oklahoma Press.

Black Elk DeSersa, Esther, Olivia Black Elk Pourier, Aaron DeSersa Jr., and Clifton DeSersa. 2000. *Black Elk Lives: Conversations with the Black Elk Family*. Edited by Hilda Neihardt and Lori Utecht. Lincoln: University of Nebraska Press.

Deloria, Ella C. (1944) 1998. *Speaking of Indians*. New York: Friendship Press. Reprint, Lincoln: University of Nebraska Press.

———. 2022. *The Dakota Way of Life*. Edited by Raymond J. DeMallie and Thierry Veyrié. Lincoln: University of Nebraska Press.

DeMallie, Raymond J. 1971. "Teton Dakota Kinship and Social Organization." PhD diss., University of Chicago.

———. 1982. "The Lakota Ghost Dance: An Ethnohistorical Account." *Pacific Historical Review* 51, no. 4: 385–405.

———, ed. 1985. *The Sixth Grandfather: Black Elk's Teachings Given to John G. Neihardt*. Lincoln: University of Nebraska Press.

———. 1993. "'These Have No Ears': Narrative and the Ethnohistorical Method." *Ethnohistory* 40, no. 4: 515–38.

———. 2001. "Teton." In *Handbook of North American Indians*, vol. 13, *Plains*, edited by Raymond J. DeMallie, 794–820. Washington, DC: Smithsonian Institution.

DeMallie, Raymond J., and Robert H. Lavenda. 1977. "Wakan: Plains Siouan Concepts of Power." In *The Anthropology of Power: Ethnographic Studies from Asia, Oceania, and the New World*, edited by Raymond D. Fogelson and Richard N. Adams, 153–65. Studies in Anthropology. New York: Academic Press.

Gage, Justin. 2020. *We Do Not Want the Gates Closed between Us: Native Networks and the Spread of the Ghost Dance*. Norman: University of Oklahoma Press.

Greene, Jerome A. 2014. *American Carnage: Wounded Knee, 1890*. Illustrated ed. Norman: University of Oklahoma Press.

Hittman, Michael. 1997. *Wovoka and the Ghost Dance*. Lincoln: University of Nebraska Press.

Mooney, James. (1896) 1991. *The Ghost-Dance Religion and the Sioux Outbreak of 1890*. Fourteenth Annual Report of the Bureau of Ethnology to the Secretary of the Smithsonian Institution, 1892–1893, 641–1110. Washington DC: Government Printing Press. Reprint, Lincoln: University of Nebraska Press.

Neihardt, John G. (1932) 2008. *Black Elk Speaks: Being the Life Story of a Holy Man of the Oglala Sioux*. New York: William Morrow. Reprint, annotated by Raymond J. DeMallie with illustrations by Standing Bear. Albany: State University of New York Press.

Oldmeadow, Harry. 2018. *Black Elk, Lakota Visionary: The Oglala Holy Man and Sioux Tradition*. Bloomington IN: World Wisdom.

Ostler, Jeffrey. 2004. *The Plains Sioux and U.S. Colonialism from Lewis and Clark to Wounded Knee*. Cambridge: Cambridge University Press.

Posthumus, David C. 2018. *All My Relatives: Exploring Lakota Ontology, Belief, and Ritual*. New Visions in Native American and Indigenous Studies. Lincoln: University of Nebraska Press.

Smith, Rex Alan. 1975. *Moon of the Popping Trees. The Tragedy at Wounded Knee and the End of the Indian Wars*. Lincoln: University of Nebraska Press.

Standing Bear, Luther. (1928) 2006. *My People the Sioux*. Edited by E. A. Brininstool. Boston: Houghton Mifflin. Reprint, Lincoln: University of Nebraska Press.

Steltenkamp, Michael F. 2009. *Medicine Man, Missionary, Mystic*. Norman: University of Oklahoma Press.

Sweeney, Jon M. 2020. *Nicholas Black Elk: Medicine Man, Catechist, Saint.* Collegeville MN: Liturgical Press.

Utley, Robert M. 1963. *The Last Days of the Sioux Nation.* New Haven CT: Yale University Press.

Walker, James R. (1980) 1991. *Lakota Belief and Ritual.* Edited by Raymond J. DeMallie and Elaine A. Jahner. Lincoln: University of Nebraska Press.

Warren, Louis S. 2017. *God's Red Son: The Ghost Dance Religion and the Making of Modern America.* New York: Basic Books.

PART 3

Kinship and Language

Comanche Society on the Reservation, 1875–1926, a Patrilineal Hypothesis

The Case of the *Ketahto Yamparika*

THOMAS W. KAVANAGH

11

My father, Albert Attocknie, was Yamparika from both sides, his father and mother.
—FRANCIS JOSEPH ATTOCKNIE (JOE A), 2016

Recent research has shown that pre-reservation Comanche sociopolitical structure was composed of several structural poses in four levels of integration: the nuclear family, the extended family, the residential local band, and the political division (Kavanagh 1980, 1986, 1996; Thurman 1980). The Spaniards and Mexicans generally recognized those levels; Anglo-Americans generally did not, instead addressing, and thus confusing, the range of Comanche sociopolitical organization within the single term "band." While my earlier works focused on the political economy of Comanche divisions, the supra-residential political organizations, there has not been a parallel research emphasis on the local level, mostly because there was little if any detailed information on that level.

Several years ago, as I was preparing a genealogy for *The Life of Ten Bears*, by Francis J. Attocknie (better known to Comanches as Joe A), based on census materials prepared by the Kiowa Agency (Kavanagh 2016),[1] I realized that all—or almost all—of the males in Ten Bears's (Parua Semʉno)[2] reservation period (1867–1901) local group, the Ketahto, were either brothers or patrilateral cousins, while the women were either unmarried daughters or came from somewhere else. Moreover, that "somewhere else" proved to be the Yamparika division. To be specific, close analysis of documents related to the Ketahto local group suggested that it was behaviorally *exogamous*. Moreover, these data also show that during that same period the Yamparika division, of which the Ketahto was one of several local groups, was behaviorally *endogamous*.

That conclusion contradicted the received anthropological wisdom about Comanches, that Comanche "bands" were "composite." Based on his work with Basin Shoshones, Julian H. Steward defined "composite band" as "non-exogamous, bilateral in descent, lacking in rules of residence and consisting of several independent families" (1936, 331). They consisted of "many unrelated nuclear or biological families . . . integrated on the basis of constant association" (Steward 1955, 143). Further investigation revealed that this received wisdom about Comanche "bands" was not based on positive information about Comanches but was deduced from Steward's Shoshone materials.

This contradiction between the received wisdom and the genealogical evidence forms the problematic addressed in this chapter.

The Comanche "Band" in History and Anthropology

Although visited by earlier anthropologists (Ten Kate 1885; Mooney 1898; Lowie [1915] 1916), most twentieth-century discussions of aboriginal Comanche sociopolitical organization rest upon the work of E. Adamson Hoebel (1939, 1940, 1954; Wallace and Hoebel 1952). In the summer of 1933, as a third-year graduate student at Columbia University, Hoebel participated in a six-week ethnographic field school among the Comanches (Kavanagh 2008). That "Field Party," as a group and as individuals, interviewed a total of eighteen middle-aged and elderly Comanches about what they remembered of "aboriginal conditions" (Linton 1933).

In terms of social and political relations, the results of the 1933 summer's work were minimal.[3] They comprised a number of tabulations of ethnonyms—what I call "band-lists"—of varying specificity, and statements about postmarital residence. Those latter were mostly anecdotal, such as Frank Chekovi's comment (August 2) that his married brother lived with his wife's people, "not his own relatives" (Kavanagh 2008, 316); from a female perspective, both Nemaruibitsi

(July 31) (Kavanagh 2008, 294–97) and Herkiyah (August 14) (Kavanagh 2008, 380–86) told of moving from group to group with new husbands and lovers.

There were other, more generalizing statements, such as Herman Asenap (June 30), from the very first day of conversations: "Marriage was within or between bands; families were at liberty to change their band affiliation. Bands were non-exogamous; they were loosely organized. A member might leave at will" (Kavanagh 2008, 36). More extensive were Niyah's comments on July 7, as recorded by Waldo Wedel (Kavanagh 2008, 80):

> When a married young man had living parents, he always [emphasis in original] took his wife to his own people. They lived near the wife's parents only when the man had no living parents.
>
> If the man's parents had accumulated much stock, he stayed and took care of the stock when they died; he remained in the same band. If a father died, his sons must take care of his stock, therefore, he can't be with his wife's folks. If his parents had little or no wealth, he might, at their death, transfer to his wife's band. If a man's father was poor, the above did not hold, and he might move over if he wanted.
>
> If a man had several sons, he tried to keep them and their families near his own lodge.
>
> If there were several boys, one or more might go to live with their wife's people.
>
> After the father's death, the sons usually stayed more or less together and kept their tipis together. As a practice, brothers stay as close together as they can.

The next summer, Hoebel and his wife conducted fieldwork among the linguistically related Seed-Eater Shoshones of Fort Hall, interviewing five individuals—three male, two female (Hoebel 1939). Hoebel also borrowed Julian Steward's unpublished manuscript that became Steward (1938), *Basin-Plateau Aboriginal Sociopolitical Groups* (Hoebel 1939, 440n1). This was a fateful move, for in his later discussions of Comanche sociopolitical organization, Hoebel often first referred to a Shoshonean residence pattern as described by Steward and then stated that the Comanche pattern was "slightly different." For instance, in his 1939 paper comparing Comanche and Seed-Eater Shoshone "Relationship Systems," he wrote: "Shoshone residence was bilocal in extended family households or groupings within the band. Band organization was of the semi-endogamous, bilateral or composite type *as defined by Steward* [1936, emphasis added]. Since marriage was largely within the band, it was easy to shift residence to either parent and back. Comanche residence tended to be more patrilocal, but equally subject to easy change. It was somewhat less intra-band" (Hoebel 1939, 446). Almost immediately, however, he began to hedge on this description. Thus, in his 1940 dissertation, he started to emphasize a "composite" formulation first, not just as "more patrilocal" but as "semi-patrilocal":

> The Comanche band or social group, ranged in size from a single family camping alone, through the small group of related individuals who formed a composite extended family, up to the large band of several hundred persons. . . . Marriage was commonly intra-band when a person was a member of a larger group, but there was no fixed rule of residence. Since marriage seems to have been to a large extent within the band, a couple lived customarily in the same group as their parents. To [his adolescent lodge] a boy brought his wife. In this and in certain other respects, Comanche residence was semi-patrilocal. Children, as a result, usually belonged to the band of the father.
>
> . . . [T]he organization of such groups was markedly similar to that which was characteristic for the aboriginal groups of the Great Basin in the days preceding white contact as summarized by Dr. Julian Steward. (Hoebel 1940, 11–12, 14)

But it is not at all clear to which Shoshoneans Hoebel was referring or which type of Stewardian band he meant. For instance, the phrase "bilateral or composite" from Hoebel (1939, 440) does not directly occur in the cited reference, Steward (1936), although the term "bilateral" was used in reference to both the "Patrilineal" and "Composite" types. While that phrase does occur in Steward (1937, 632), it was used there in reference to eastern Shoshones, those of the Idaho Plateau and Wyoming, not those of the Basin of Utah and Nevada. Conversely, while by 1940 Hoebel was explicitly comparing Comanches to Great Basin peoples, Steward consistently described those western Shoshoneans as not organized in supra-familial bands at all.

Here Hoebel's etic "no fixed rule of residence" directly contradicts Niyah's emic statement of "always" virilocal residence. Moreover, while Hoebel uses the phrases "composite extended family," "extended family band," "large band," "larger group," and "semi-patrilocal," he resists being more specific, adding the disclaimer, "What constituted a Comanche local group is not a problem to be settled by monistic definition" (1940, 12). But while that disclaimer overtly attributed an indeterminacy to Comanche social structure, it covertly served to hide his lack of specific data.

By 1954 Hoebel's emphasis on the Great Basin as model for the Comanches had hardened into a stereotype: "Comanche cultural background was meager it was that of the so-called 'Digger Indians' of the Great Basin. In the tradition of these tribes there was no great social organization. People moved and lived in small isolated family bands. In the Plains the Comanche never wholly shed this heritage. They never forsook band autonomy for tribal government" (1954, 128–29).

Those conclusions had wide ramifications upon the anthropological representation of Comanches, in the form of George Peter Murdock's "Ethnographic Atlas" (Murdock et al. 1962a, 1962b; Murdock 1949). Based on Hoebel's work, the Comanche "Profile of Marital Residence" therein (column 16) was classified as "ambilocal," a variant on Hoebel's "bilocal," "residence established optionally with or near the parents of husband or wife, depending upon circumstances, *where neither alternative exceeds the other in actual frequency by ratio greater than two to one*" (Murdock et al. 1962a, 117, emphasis added). But of course, Hoebel had not provided any "actual frequencies" of residence types.

The Comanche "Band" Revisited

One part of this confusion—that "the Comanche band or social group, ranged in size from a single family camping alone, through the small group of related individuals who formed a composite extended family, up to the large band of several hundred persons" (Hoebel 1940,

11)—could have been resolved as early as 1971, if researchers had bothered to talk to Comanches.⁴ That year Joe Attocknie (Joe A) drafted an introduction to his manuscript, *The Life of Ten Bears*, including this discussion of the "problem":

> The various divisions of the Comanches have proved incomprehensible to non-Comanche researchers and writers. The Yamparika "Rooteater" division of the Comanches (*which in this instance will not be referred to as a "band" because even some present day, i.e. 1971, Comanches confuse the term "band" with family clans and warrior brotherhoods*) [emphasis added]. . . . Many such subdivisions made up the people known as the Yamparikas. To name <u>some</u> [emphasis added] family subdivisions or clans would be to name the Pibianigwai ("Loud Talkers"), the Widyu ("Awls"), the Mootsai ("Mountain People"), the Wo'oi ("Wormy"), Wahkohnuu ("Oyster Shell Ornament"), and the Ketahto ("Don't Wear Moccasins") also known as the Napewat ("No Shoes").⁵ (Attocknie 2016, 4)

Attocknie's use of "clan" to refer to the "family subdivisions" may be anthropologically nonstandard, but it is specific: it referred to the kinship-based residential groups here called local bands.⁶

Recently, the issue of the nature of Comanche "bands" and "clans" has arisen again. In his 2002 book, *Comanche Society: Before the Reservation*, Gerald Betty has asserted that the ethnonyms "Cuchanec," "Jupe," and "Yamparika" were "clan" names, which "allowed individuals to identify co-descendants whose actual birth-link connections have been obscured by tradition and time. Such names also allow the identification of distant co-descendants. Both male and female offspring inherited the clan name of the father, but only males passed along the name to succeeding generations. Thus, it can safely be assumed that [the sons of Ecueracapa] belonged to the Cuchanec family since Ecueracapa had this ancestral name. Ecueracapa's spouse would have belonged to a clan other than Cuchanec" (2002, 19). If we follow Attocknie's usage, Betty's argument may be valid about Comanche "clans" but is on the wrong level of organization: they were local groups not divisions. But Betty offers no direct ethnographic evidence in support of his assertion. Also, the above epigraph from Joe A, "My father, Albert Attocknie, was Yamparika from both sides, his father and mother," explicitly refutes Betty's claim that "[a man's] spouse would have belonged to a clan [division] other than [his own]."

Comanche bands continue to be described as "composite" (Peoples and Bailey 2006, 241), implying that they were made up of "unrelated families" such that intra-"band" marriage was possible. Hämäläinen (2008, 270) explicitly follows Wallace and Hoebel (1952, 140), stating that "marriage took place within rancherías" (2008, 270, 425n58).

Unfortunately, Attocknie did not further expound on the nature of those "family clans." Thus the questions remain: What was their composition? What were their relations to other "bands" and to the wider "divisions"?

The Evidence

It is one thing to say that an author's conclusions are incorrect, invalid, or not backed by evidence. It is another to present evidence in support of one's own position. As noted above, while my earlier works have focused on the political economy of Comanche divisions (Kavanagh 1996), the supra-residential political organizations, there has not been a parallel research emphasis on the local level, mostly because there is little if any detailed information on the pre-reservation local band level.

There is, however, detailed genealogical information from the fifty years 1876–1926 in the form of annual censuses and census-like data. The first twenty-five years, 1876–1901, were within the duration of the Kiowa-Comanche-Apache Reservation in what is now southwestern Oklahoma; the last twenty-five, 1901–26, were after the allotment and the disestablishment of the reservation. Because most of the reservation period census lists were organized by "band" and families within bands, the relationships between them and their descendants can be traced. These constitute a database encompassing some 4,400 records representing all recognized Comanche individuals who were alive between 1876 and 1942, as well as several hundred mentions of individuals alive before 1876.

Objections might be raised that the censuses are the artificial constructs of colonial power, or that aboriginal sociocultural structure and the resultant on-the-ground social organizations were so disrupted by the reservation experience that any and all conclusions about aboriginal conditions made from that data are invalid. However, by maintaining a close control of the lists from one to the next, deviations can be detected. Ultimately, while there were indeed demographic and other disruptions to Comanche social organization such that by the end of the reservation period the Comanche local bands and divisions had lost most of their overt social and political functions, this was a historical process, progressing over time on the reservation. This is not to say that by 1901, if not 1926, local band and division identity categories had become empty labels: those identities continue to influence social behavior.[7]

In addition to the censuses is the "Family Record Book," which was initially compiled in 1903 as part of an investigation of alleged allotment fraud (Leupp 1903, 6–8). Based on the 1900 census, it also gives the names of the parents of every allottee, even for those adults whose parents were themselves never listed on a census, that is, those who had died before 1879. Thus, it allows the discovery of wider connections between individuals not directly linked in the censuses.

The Ketahto, 1865–1926

The Ketahto ethnonym is one of the few, and one of the earliest, recorded Comanche local group ethnonyms, although it has often not been recognized as such.[8] Attocknie (2016) specifically attributed the ethnonym to the local group of Ten Bears, and by extension to himself via his grandmother Querherbitty "Arrives to Capture," the granddaughter of Ten Bears.

Ten Bears was born about 1790 (Attocknie 2016). By the 1840s he was chief of the Ketahto, and from about 1866 until his death in 1872, he was principal chief of the Yamparika division. He had several wives and many children, including sons (stepsons?) Hitutatsi "Little Crow" and Isananaka "Hears the Wolf." One of Ten Bears's daughters—whose name is unknown, as is that of her husband, both having died in the 1849 cholera epidemic—was the mother of Cheevers "Goat" and Querherbitty, born about 1840 and 1841, respectively. About 1870

Querherbitty married a half-Crow man from the Mootsai Yamparika local group named Attocknie (Kavanagh 2016, x). He came to live uxorilocally with her group.

Ten Bears's Ketahto were among the largest Comanche local groups in the immediate pre-reservation period: in September 1866 he was reportedly leading two hundred lodges (McCusker 1866). There were some hints of internal cleavages, whether political (Ten Bears and Cheevers were notable in their efforts at peacemaking, while Isananaka and Hitutatsi were hostile) or demographic (too many people for long-term co-residence) is not known. Whatever the case, the result was that the later Ketahto were listed in multiple entries (Cheevers, Hitutatsi, Isananaka) such that if one did not already know the relations between them, they would remain seemingly independent.

In November 1869 Ten Bears's following was estimated at 120 people; a year later, he and Hitutatsi had 132 people between them (Badger 1869). In March 1874, after his death, his sons Isananaka and Hitutatsi and grandson Cheevers were reported to have 262 people between them (Anonymous 1874). In 1878 Cheevers's band had 115 people, Isananaka had 37, and Hitutatsi had 34, for a total of 186 people (Anonymous 1878) (see table 1).

TABLE 1. Yamparika divisional populations, 1869–79

	November 1869	December 1870	March 1874	June 1878
Paruasemena	120	84		
Cheevers			186	115
Isananaka			100	37
Hitutatsi	48	76	76	34
Howeah	60	84	84	27
Poyawahtoyah	180	102	120	25
Tipenavon			66	
Tabenanaka			100	72
Quitsquip	62	216	100	24

Both Hitutatsi and Isananaka died of unknown causes about 1883; they were both probably in late middle age. Many of Hitutatsi's people had also died by that year, again of unknown causes; the rest dispersed, some to Isarosavit's "White Wolf" Yamparika local group. Of Isananaka's people, some reorganized under Nanaka "Hears It," a surviving member, although his relation to Isananaka is unknown; however, he too died within the year. Others went to Isananaka's nephew-in-law, Attocknie, husband of Querherbitty, granddaughter of Ten Bears.

In 1883 a man named Sohe "Hairy," with his two wives and two children, transferred from Honnetosavit's "White Badger" Yamparika local group to Cheevers's group. His relation to them is unknown. By 1889 Sohe was recognized as band "headman," and a large portion of Cheevers's people—forty of fifty-eight people—had transferred to him; the remainder were Cheevers's immediate family. That major transfer while Cheevers was still alive—he died about 1894, aged about fifty-four—suggests that the motivation for the transfers was not individual, as in a marriage, nor internal succession, as in Isananaka to Attocknie, but was a political schism, although the details are unclear. The political history of the Ketahto leadership, 1867–92, was thus from Ten Bears to Isananaka, Hitutatsi, and Cheevers; then from Isananaka to Nanaka to Attocknie, and from Cheevers to Sohe.

To be sure, there was movement of people into and out of the Ketahto during the period 1879–92 (see table 2). The specific motivations for those movements are not always clear, although since it was usually the women who transferred from their natal bands, most would have had virilocal marital residence. There was one exogamous virilocal marriage transfer of three Ketahto sisters to a sororal polygynous marriage with a Kwaharunʉʉ man—one of the few such cases clearly visible in the records—as well as a virilocal transfer from a Kwaharunʉʉ group and one from a Penateka group. There was one exogamous uxorilocal transfer out from the Ketahto, but still within the Yamparika: in 1883 the daughter of a widow in Cheevers's band married a male in Isarosavit's band. When she transferred, so did her mother and her two younger brothers.

TABLE 2. Ketahto sub-band populations, 1878–92

	1878	1879	1883	1885	1889	1892
Cheevers	115	56		59	13	9
Sohe					40	38
Isananaka	37	35				
Nanaka			11			
Hitutatsi	34	27				
Attocknie				34	38	41
Total	186	118	11	93	91	88

Families and Bands

In the spring of 1878, Commissioner of Indian Affairs Edward A. Hayt returned a census sent by agent James M. Haworth with the following comment:

> I have to say that the roll as furnished by you is not in all respects satisfactory and is herewith returned that necessary corrections may be made. It is the desire of this office to obtain a list of all individual Indians and heads of families, and only one man should appear upon the roll in any one family. Any male or female adults, other than the father or mother or husband and wife, as the case may be, should be entered on the roll as individual Indians. It appears from the roll as furnished by you that in some of the families fifteen, twenty and even thirty adults are included. (Hayt 1878)

This correspondence provides the official, albeit artificial, definition of an Indian "family."

Following Commissioner Hayt's definition, the 118 Ketahto people enumerated in 1879 were listed in 54 "families": 22 of those "families" were single persons, 17 of whom were female. It is unlikely, however, that these single females were actually living alone; unfortunately, their links to others within the Ketahto are unknown. In 1885 the 92 Ketahto were in 44 "families": 21 were single, 4 of whom were females.

While the census lists do not provide clues to relations of "families" to one another, the Family Record Book allows a glimpse of wider connections, at least in the nearest generation, sometimes in greater depth. For instance, in 1885 one "family" in Cheevers's band consisted of a man, his wife (listed in 1879 in Howeah's Yamparika band, with a daughter), and three children. Listed as separate "families" were the man's widowed mother and his wife's unmarried half-brother. That half-brother later married a widow in the band (who was formerly in Coby's "Wild Horse" Nokoni band). On the other side, a brother of that man was listed in 1879 in Howeah's "Gap in the Woods" Yamparika band (with his unnamed wife), but later he transferred via Isananaka to Attocknie's branch of the Ketahto where his wife's parents lived.

Using 1892 as a baseline, as that was the last year the censuses explicitly recognized bands, the Ketahto population of 1879–92 can be charted into between sixteen and twenty sets of relatives—depending upon how the extensions are counted—in up to five generations. These range from a small number of individuals who cannot be linked to any other persons, several husband-wife pairs, ten sets of parents and children, and five sets of ten persons or more. The largest of those latter groups, the Ten Bears–Hitutatsi–Isananaka extended family/core lineages, encompassed some thirty-five persons. Most of these persons also had links to other Yamparika local groups, through the women.

Expanding the data set to the half century between 1879 and 1926, some 375 individuals can be associated with the Ketahto ethnonym, however fleetingly. Dividing these into artificial "generations," the earliest (Generation 1) were born before 1879 (n=134); those of Generation 2 were born on the reservation between 1879 and 1892 (n=61); Generation 3 were born between 1892 and 1926 (n=179). By 1926 many of the older part of Generation 3 had matured and were marrying. Of the 32 Ketahto descendants born after 1892 but before 1908—that is, those who would have been old enough to marry by Anglo law in 1926—only 5 had done so. Significantly, none of those marriages were to another Ketahto descendant.

Discussion and Implications

In a 1965 discussion of Steward's "bands," Eleanor Leacock asked, "What was the exogamous unit, the small fall and spring band [here called the 'local' or 'subsistence band'] or the larger summer band [here called the 'division']?" (Leacock 1969). As none of those thirty-two marrying Ketahto married another Ketahto, it is clear that at least behaviorally Ketahto were exogamous. And except for the very few cases noted above, the overwhelming residential tendency was toward virilocality.

The converse of Leacock's question is, "What was the endogamous group, if there was one?" Figure 13 graphically displays in- and out-marriages of the local groups in the Yamparika division, 1879–93 (the period of "band" recognition), as seen from a Ketahto-centric perspective. Comparing those origins and destinations against their divisional affiliations clearly shows that most of that movement was to or from other Yamparika groups; thus, the behavioral endogamous category for the Ketahto was the Yamparika division. The same pattern holds for the five Nokoni/Noyuka and the four Penateka local groups: most of the marriages were within their division. The data for the newly formed (ca. 1860) Kwaharenʉʉ are ambiguous.

As noted above, many contemporary Comanches have expressed their belief that descendants of the same local band considered themselves cousins, even though they could not specify the relation, and thus should not marry. The censuses support this assertion and add specific details. The Ketahto indeed practiced local band exogamy in reciprocity with other Yamparika groups. Thus, in Herman Asenap's 1933 comment that "Marriage was within or between bands.... Bands were non-exogamous," the "non-exogamous band" part must be interpreted as referring to the wider divisions (Kavanagh 2008, 36).

In his explicit statement, as recorded by Wedel, Niyah (July 13) stated, "When a married young man had living parents, he always took his wife to his own people" (Kavanagh 2008, 80). The few exceptions noted by the 1933 consultants resulted in Hoebel's characterizing the

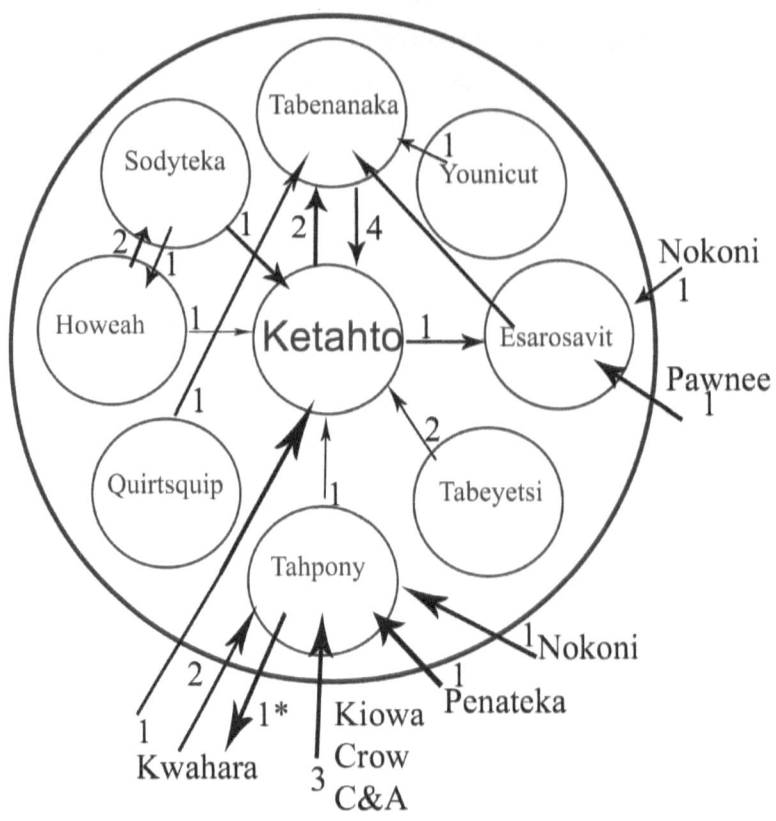

13. Ketahto in- and out-marriages. [*Uxorilocal marriage from Tahpony to Waysee.] Created by Thomas W. Kavanagh.

Comanches as having a "more patrilocal," or "semi-patrilocal" residential pattern (1940, 11–12). But how many particularistic exceptions are enough to make a "composite" behavioral pattern out of a "virilocal" norm? Despite Steward's observation that "certain social practices [that] temporarily introduced unrelated families into the patrilineal band" could nudge a patrilineal band toward the composite pole (1955, 149–50), neither Steward—nor Murdock (1949)—established a threshold at which behavioral uxorilocal residence became a normative bilocal residence, and thus turn a viri-/patrilocal band into a composite band. Only the editors of the "Ethnographic Atlas" provided a standard: "residence established with or near the parents of husband or wife, depending upon circumstances, where neither exceeds the other in actual frequency by ratio greater than two to one" (Murdock et al. 1962a, 117). Thus, determination of one or the other requires actual data with which to establish the "actual frequency." Until this study, no one had provided such data for the Comanches.

As noted above, there were two historical uxorilocal marriages associated with the Ketahto: Cheevers and Querherbity's unnamed father lived with his wife, Ten Bears's daughter, and Attocknie lived with Querherbitty. Can the census data be used to determine descriptively uxorilocal residence? Beginning about 1888 and maintained—with some interruption—through 1926, families (as defined by Hayt 1878) were assigned what came to be called "family numbers." These numbers were assigned to adult males and female heads-of-households. Generally, a male's family number was retained throughout his lifetime. There are, however, a few cases in which an adult male's family number is the one associated with the wife's natal family. I suggest that these cases indicate an uxorilocal move by the husband. As such, there were apparently only two descriptively uxorilocal marriages among the reservation period Ketahto. For the entire adult male Comanche population in 1923 (n=425), 53 (12 percent) are potential examples. By this measure, virilocality is much more than "two to one"—more like eight to one—among the historic Comanches.

One of the features of "composite" bands often emphasized is that membership is based on "free association" and "subject to easy change." However, "free association" and "subject to easy change" do not of themselves indicate frequency of movement. Certainly, based on their life histories as recorded in the Field Notes (Kavanagh 2008), the females Herkeyah and Nemaruibetsi moved around quite a bit. However, most of the Ketahto male population, 1879–1926, remained in the Ketahto: in 1879 there were 30 adult Ketahto males; of the 12 still alive in 1892, 8 (66 percent) were still listed as Ketahto.

Steward (1955, 1970) argued that in the nineteenth century, those Shoshones who adopted a horse-mounted lifestyle underwent a cultural shift away from a patrilineal (patrilocal) base. In this he followed in the footsteps of Lewis Henry Morgan (1877, 472) and John

W. Powell (1899), who argued that the introduction of the horse altered primeval bands away from lineal structures. Although not giving a specific cause, Steward also more generally argued that "the Plains Indians did not develop patrilineal bands" (1970, 147).

The Comanches were the premier horse people of the southern plains, although they probably stole (for trade) more horses than they actually bred. On the reservation, even after the U.S. Army's periodic attempts to "dismount and disarm" them, many Comanches maintained large horse herds and later cattle herds. As shown here, the reservation period Comanches did maintain patri-/virilocal patterns in band organization rather than develop "composite" ones. Indeed, based on the Shoshonean—Comanche continuum, development of a horse-mounted pastoral and raid/trade economy, with significant input of European goods, may have led to the development of more formal social and political structures rather than to their collapse. Moreover, based on Niyah's comment, "If the man's parents had accumulated much stock, he stayed and took care of the stock when they died; he remained in the same band. If a father died, his sons must take care of his stock, therefore, he can't be with his wife's folks," it was not the use of horses in hunting that influenced social organization; it was the need for pastoral care.

Notes

Acknowledgments: Although I was never a formal student of Ray DeMallie, I count him as my first anthropology teacher. In 1967, when he was a sophomore and I was yet a freshman, he taught me the difference between physical and cultural anthropology. He introduced me firsthand to such figures as John Wesley Powell, James Mooney, and James Owen Dorsey. He later gave me my first anthropology textbook; ironically, given the current topic, it was E. A. Hoebel's *Anthropology* (1966). During the fifty years that I knew him, from our days in the National Anthropological Archives to a decade as colleagues across a parking lot, he emphasized the innovative use of original materials to address ethnohistorical problems.

1. The official name of the reservation was the Kiowa-Comanche-Apache Reservation, but the agency itself was commonly known as simply the Kiowa Agency.

2. Most Comanche words herein are spelled according to *Taa Nʉmʉ Tekwapʉ'ha Tʉboopʉ*, "Our Comanche Dictionary," from the Comanche Language and Cultural Committee (2003).

It should be noted that the Comanches were among the few Native groups whose personal names were usually not translated into English in daily usage; the exception here is Ten Bears. Other names are here translated at first usage but retained in Comanche thereafter. However, inasmuch as few of these personal names have not been entered into the dictionary, I have generally followed what I call the "agency spelling." The exceptions are when that spelling is particularly horrific, as with Ten Bears's son Hitutatsi, "Little Crow," which was given as "Hightoastischi." Three other exceptions concern vowels: the names "Esananaka" and "Esarosavit" contain the element "wolf" *isa*—rather than "gray" *esi*—and so should be transcribed as "Isananaka" and "Isarosavit," respectively.

3. All of this information from the 1933 field notes is more thoroughly reported on in Kavanagh (2008).

4. Hoebel never revisited the Comanches (or Shoshones) to check on any possible lacunae.

5. While it may be assumed that all local groups had ethnonyms, it is not always possible to attach such names to particular groups, and vice versa. The censuses discussed below were all organized by local bands under the names of their chiefs or headmen.

6. Independently, the late Melburn Thurman (1980, 1982, 1987) and I (Kavanagh 1980, 1986, 1996, 2001) made parallel distinctions within the range of Comanche "bands," noting a difference between the local residential or "subsistence" bands and wider political "divisions."

Hämäläinen (2008) followed my distinctions—he did not cite Thurman on this—between local group and division but used the Spanish *ranchería* for the former.

7. Over the years many Comanches have expressed to me their contention that their "bands"—once we had straightened out the terminological confusion between the local residential band and the wider regional division—practiced exogamy, that even in modern times descendants of the same local band considered themselves cousins, even though they could not specify the relation, and thus should not marry.

8. Documentary mention of Ketahto apparently dates from *Vocabulario del Idioma Comanche* by Manuel García Rejón (1866), whose information was obtained from an escaped captive: "La nación, que está situada entre el Estado de Tejas y el Nuevo México, en territorio de los Estados-Unidos, se compone de las siguentes tribus ó Pueblos á saber ... *Napuat ó Quetahtore*" (5, emphasis added). (The [Comanche] nation, which is situated in the state of Texas and New Mexico, in the territory of the United States, comprises the following tribes or peoples, namely, ... *Napwat or Ketahto*.) García Rejón did not give translations of these ethnonyms.

García Rejón's comments were quoted (with citation) by Francisco Pimentel (1874–75, 2, 7). In 1884 Bureau of Ethnology linguist Albert Gatschet, working with Comanches, recorded the ethnonym as "Ketahnone" (*ketahto nʉʉ*) (Gatschet 1884). James Mooney, another Bureau of Ethnology collaborator, however, argued that García Rejón's ethnonyms "Napuat ó Quetahtore" referred to "Carrizo" populations in the lower Rio Grande (Mooney 1907, 209); he did not provide a rationale for his assertion. Edward S. Curtis reported, without translation, "Ketáte, a branch of some other band" (1907–30, 19:187). García Rejón's recent translator, Daniel Gelo, commented that "García Rejón's equation of Napuat with Quetahtore has been perpetuated [e.g., via Pimentel in Mooney (1907)] but could not be verified independently" (1995, 67).

References

Anonymous. 1874. Names of Chiefs and Headmen and Numbers in Bands; Delawares, Comanches, Apaches, Kiowas. Oklahoma Historical Society, Kiowa Agency, microfilm reel 1a: 25.

———. 1878. Indian Office, Circular 21: Names of Chiefs and Numbers in Their Bands. June 14. Oklahoma Historical Society, Kiowa Agency, microfilm reel 47: 349.

Attocknie, Francis Joseph. 2016. *The Life of Ten Bears*. Lincoln: University of Nebraska Press.

Badger, N. D. 1869. List of Indians at Fort Sill, IT. November 30. Oklahoma Historical Society, Kiowa Agency, microfilm reel 1a: 857.

Betty, Gerald. 2002. *Comanche Society: Before the Reservation*. College Station: Texas A&M University Press.

Comanche Language and Cultural Preservation Committee. 2003. *Taa Nʉmʉ Tekwapʉʔha Tʉboopʉ*. Lawton OK: Privately printed.

Curtis, Edward S. 1907–30. *The North American Indian*. 20 vols. Edited by Frederick W. Hodge. Norwood MA: Plympton Press.

García Rejón, Manuel. 1866. *Vocabulario del Idioma Comanche*. Mexico: Ignacio Cumplido.

Gatschet, Albert S. 1884. "Comanche Language." Manuscript no. 748, National Anthropological Archives, Smithsonian Institution, Washington DC.

Gelo, Daniel J. 1995. *Comanche Vocabulary: Trilingual Edition*. Austin: University of Texas Press.

Hämäläinen, Pekka. 2008. *The Comanche Empire*. New Haven CT: Yale University Press.

Hayt, Edward A. 1878. Letter to James M. Haworth, March 25. Kiowa H 520, 1878. Oklahoma Historical Society, microfilm reel KA 1: 121, 128.

Hoebel, E. Adamson. 1939. "Comanche and H3kandika Shoshone Relationship Systems." *American Anthropologist* 41, no. 3: 440–57.

———. 1940. *The Political Organization and Law-Ways of the Comanche Indians*. Memoir of the American Anthropological Association 54, no. 4. Menasha WI: American Anthropological Association.

———. 1954. *The Law of Primitive Man*. Cambridge MA: Harvard University Press.

———. 1966. *Anthropology*. 3rd ed. New York: McGraw Hill.

Kavanagh, Thomas. 1980. "Recent Socio-Cultural Evolution of the Comanche Indians." Unpublished MA thesis, George Washington University.

———. 1986. "Political Power and Political Organization." PhD diss., University of New Mexico.

———. 1996. *Comanche Political History, 1706–1875: An Ethnohistorical Perspective*. Lincoln: University of Nebraska Press.

———. 2001. "Comanche." In *Handbook of North American Indians*, vol. 13, *Plains*, edited by Raymond J. DeMallie, 886–906. Washington DC: Smithsonian Institution.

———. 2008. *Comanche Ethnography, 1933: The Field Notes of Gustav G. Carlson, E. Adamson Hoebel, and Waldo R. Wedel*. Lincoln: University of Nebraska Press.

———. 2016. Introduction to *The Life of Ten Bears*, by Francis J. Attocknie, vii–xx. Lincoln: University of Nebraska Press.

Leacock, Eleanor. 1969. "The Montagnais-Naskapi Band." In *Contributions to Anthropology: Band Societies*, edited by David Damas, 1–20. National Museum of Canada Bulletin 228. Ottawa: National Museums of Canada.

Leupp, Francis E. 1903. Report of Francis E. Leupp to the Secretary of the Interior. November 30. Doc. 26, 58, Congress 2d Session.

Linton, Ralph. 1933. Letter to Jesse Nusbaum, June 7. File 89FS 3.013.1. Archives of the Laboratory of Anthropology, Museum of New Mexico, Santa Fe.

Lowie, Robert S. (1915) 1916. *Dances and Societies of the Plains Shoshone.* American Museum of Natural History Anthropological Papers 11: 803–35. Reprint in *Societies of the Plains Indians,* edited by Clark Wissler. New York: Order of the Trustees.

McCusker, Phillip. 1866. Letter to Thomas Murphy, September 7; enclosure in letter from Murphy to D. N. Cooley, September 17, 1877. Letters Received from the Kiowa Agency, NARS microfilm publication M234, 375–90.

Mooney, James. 1898. *Calendar History of the Kiowa Indians.* Seventeenth Annual Report of the Bureau of American Ethnology, for the years 1895–1896. Washington DC: Government Printing Office.

———. 1907. "Carrizo." In *Handbook of American Indians North of Mexico,* edited by F. W. Hodge, Bureau of American Ethnology Bulletin 30, 209. Washington DC: Government Printing Office.

Morgan, Lewis Henry. 1877. *Ancient Society, or Researches in the Lines of Human Progress from Savagery through Barbarism to Civilization.* New York: Henry Holt.

Murdock, George P. 1949. *Social Structure.* New York: Free Press.

Murdock, George P., Fred Adelman, Donald W. Dragoo, John P. Gillin, Peter B. Hammond, Edward A. Kennard, David Landy, Barbara Lane, William P. Lebra, Otto von Mering, Arthur Tuden, Frank W. Young [credited as The Editors]. 1962a. "Ethnographic Atlas." *Ethnology* 1, no. 1: 113–34.

———. 1962b. "Ethnographic Atlas." *Ethnology* 1, no. 2: 256–86.

Peoples, James, and Garrick Bailey. 2006. *Humanity: An Introduction to Cultural Anthropology.* 7th ed. Belmont CA: Thomson Wadsworth.

Pimentel, Francisco. 1874–75. *Cuadro descriptivo y comparativo de las lenguas indigenas de Mexico.* 2nd ed. Mexico: Tip. de I. Epstein.

Powell, John W. 1899. "Report of the Director." Seventeenth Annual Report of the Bureau of American Ethnology, xxv–xciii. Washington DC: Government Printing Press.

Steward, Julian H. 1936. "The Economic and Social Basis of Primitive Bands." In *Essays in Anthropology; Presented to Alfred Louis Kroeber in Celebration of His Sixtieth Birthday, June 11, 1936,* edited by Robert H. Lowie, 331–50. Berkeley: University of California Press.

———. 1937. "Linguistic Distributions and Political Groups of the Great Basin Shoshoneans." *American Anthropologist* 39, no. 4: 625–34.

———. 1938. *Basin-Plateau Aboriginal Sociopolitical Groups.* Bureau of American Ethnology Bulletin 120. Washington DC: Smithsonian Institution.

———. 1955. *Theory of Culture Change: The Methodology of Multilinear Evolution.* Urbana: University of Illinois Press.

———. 1970. "The Foundations of Basin-Plateau Shoshonean Society." In *Languages and Cultures of Western North America: Essays in Honor of Sven S. Liljeblad*, edited by Earl H. Swanson Jr., 113–51. Pocatello: Idaho State University Press.

Tatum, Lawrie. 1870. Nominal List Containing the Name of Each Head of Band in the Comanche and Kiowa Tribes of Indians. December 30. Oklahoma Historical Society, Kiowa Agency, microfilm reel 1a: 865.

Ten Kate, Herman F. C. 1885. "Notes ethnographiques sur les Comanches." *Revue d'Ethnographie* 4: 120–36.

Thurman, Melburn. 1980. "Comanche." In *Encyclopedia of Indians of the Americas*, vol. 4, edited by Keith Irvine, 4–13. St. Clair Shores MI: Scholarly Press.

———. 1982. "A New Interpretation of Comanche Social Organization." *Current Anthropology* 23, no. 5: 578–79.

———. 1987. "Reply [to Gelo]." *Current Anthropology* 28, no. 4: 552–55.

Wallace, Ernest, and E. Adamson Hoebel. 1952. *The Comanches: Lords of the South Plains*. Norman: University of Oklahoma Press.

Linguistic Evidence of Contact between Northern Caddoan and Siouan Languages

12

Arikara-Pawnee Verbal Classifiers
LOGAN SUTTON

Arikara and Pawnee, two closely related Caddoan languages, are characterized in their grammars by a classificatory use of their posture verbs, a feature also highly prevalent among neighboring Siouan languages. This chapter provides a summary description of these grammatical constructions and investigates the possibility of Siouan contact as a source for the Arikara-Pawnee construction.

The term "classifiers," in linguistics, refers to a wide range of constructions in which there is a contrastive choice among two or more linguistic elements determined by coreference with a reference in the clause. Or, as Alexandra Aikhenvald (2000, 13) defines them, herself citing Keith Allan (1977, 285): "Classifiers ... denote 'some salient perceived or imputed characteristics of the entity to which an associated noun refers' ... and are restricted to particular construction types known as 'classifier constructions'" which are "understood as morphosyntactic units (which may be noun phrases of different kinds, verb phrases, or clauses) which require the presence of a particular kind of a morpheme, the choice of which is dictated by the semantic characteristics of the referent of the head of a noun phrase."

Posture verbs are those core verbs that prototypically express a person as "sitting," "standing," or "lying" (among other linguistically specific contrasts). These verbs are highly frequent, being used not only as main verbs to express where someone or something is located, marking the posture they're in, but also as demonstrative modifiers, classifying an entity by the posture it is in. A particularly clear example of this usage is seen here in (1):[1]

(1) t*naáxA-   t*neešá   nuxtaanoóku
    ti-na-*xa*   ti-nee-*xa*
    this.**lying**   here.**lies**   the.one.that.had.been.singing

"Here **lies this [lying]** (old coyote) that had been singing."

Arikara (Dan Howling Wolf in Parks 1991, vol. 2, "Singing Coyote," 1098)

The coyote mentioned in this story is here doubly expressed as lying: once in a demonstrative construction, translated here as "this one [lying]" and again in the main verb, asserting that the coyote was lying in that location as it sang.

When many people think about language contact and "borrowing," they will typically think of lexical borrowings: borrowed words, for example, the thousands of French and Latin words that have become integrated into English, or the fewer but numerous words from Indigenous American languages, such as *moose* and *opossum*. However, language contact may affect all levels of language structure, from the integration of new language sounds (e.g., the introduction of click sounds into the Nguni Bantu languages of southern Africa, such as Zulu and Xhosa, from neighboring Khoesan languages) to new meanings and metaphors, to new grammatical structures (e.g., Croft 2000, 201–9; Kroskrity 1998; Mithun 1999, 311).

Many authors have noted the dearth of recognizable foreign words adopted from any neighboring tribes into their language of study, at least before colonization (Mithun 2020). This can make linguistic contact more difficult to recognize. Douglas R. Parks (2001b, 90) and Parks and Robert L. Rankin (2001, 109) specifically remark for Caddoan and Siouan, respectively, on these languages' resistance to lexical acculturation (see also Goddard 2001, 77, in the same volume for a similar comment on Plains Algonquian languages).

Cecil H. Brown (1996) suggests that lexical acculturation and borrowing is most prevalent in areas where there is widespread bilingualism or a lingua franca that serves as a trade medium. Although Brown's study reflects only the post-contact situation, the same principles would reasonably apply to the prehistoric period as well. On the Great

Plains—the area of relevance for the current study—the dominant trade language until the late nineteenth century was Plains Indian Sign Language (PISL) (Clark [1885] 1982; Davis 2007, 2010), which would not have promoted the diffusion of spoken word forms.[2]

Paul V. Kroskrity (1982, 1993, 1998), in discussing Hopi and Spanish borrowings into Arizona Tewa, emphasizes another aspect of language contact and how lexical acculturation may be managed and filtered to negotiate identity and sociocultural spaces. Speakers can often recognize that a word has been acculturated from another language and may choose to express the concept by other means when they do not wish to identify with the linguistic or cultural associations of that word. But as Kroskrity also describes, there are other linguistic structures, particularly grammatical, semantic, and pragmatic patterns, that can go under the radar, patterns that are acculturated and diffused across language boundaries with little or no conscious awareness by speakers. Across generations such acculturation can lead to major changes in a language without many or any foreign words ever being introduced and integrated (see also Sherzer's 1976 survey of North American languages).

The Caddoan and Siouan Language Families

The Caddoan language family consists of five documented languages: Caddo, Kitsai, Wichita, Pawnee, and Arikara (listing them from south to north, according to their pre-reservation residency).[3] They are readily divided into two primary branches: Southern Caddoan, consisting only of Caddo, and Northern Caddoan, comprising the other four (Lesser and Weltfish 1932; Parks 1979). Within Northern Caddoan, Arikara and Pawnee constitute a clear subgrouping—close enough that much of the literature has considered Arikara to be merely a dialect of Pawnee, although mutual intelligibility studies would contest this (Parks 1979; 2001b; personal communication, 2006). All but Kitsai are attested to have been composed of multiple dialects; however, by the time that extensive linguistic study and recordings were carried out in the twentieth century, only the differentiation between South Band and Skiri Pawnee had been retained enough to allow for detailed documentation of the dialectal distinctions. It is attested that there were, in the eighteenth and nineteenth centuries, Arikara dialects that were impressionistically more similar to Pawnee than other dialects, but the details of those similarities and differences are lost to us.

Within this historical period, the Caddoan-speaking peoples resided largely in riverside semisedentary villages extending from the Red River of the Texas-Arkansas-Louisiana border area through northeastern Texas, central Oklahoma, and Kansas and throughout central and eastern Nebraska to the Missouri River on the South Dakota border. It was only in the nineteenth century that the northernmost Caddoan group, the Arikaras, permanently moved farther up the Missouri to northwestern North Dakota, where the tribe is currently based on the Fort Berthold Indian Reservation, along with the Siouan-speaking Hidatsa and Mandan peoples.[4]

The Siouan language family is a larger, more geographically distributed family, having historically extended both to the east through the Ohio River valley as far as Virginia—the Catawba language has been convincingly argued to be a close sister to the Siouan language family—and both north and south along the Missouri River, including the Biloxi and Ofo languages of Mississippi, to the Assiniboine and Stoney peoples of Alberta and Saskatchewan. It has been argued that Siouan language speakers migrated west roughly along the Ohio River Valley, south of the Great Lakes, from the central Appalachian region before following the Missouri and Mississippi, or their tributaries, northward and southward. This is attested from tribal traditions among Dhegiha-speaking groups, speaking to that sub-group's origin and migration to their historical regions. The antecedent movements that brought the more northerly and southerly Siouan groups to the edge of the plains may have followed different routes in detail but still would have passed through the lower Midwest.

A full summary of the Siouan language family is not given here, this chapter's emphasis being on Caddoan, but for our purposes the family is typically divided into six main subgroupings: the Ohio River Valley languages, such as Tutelo and Biloxi; the Dhegiha languages of the Ozarks and central Missouri areas; the Chiwere-Winnebago languages; the widespread but closely related Dakotan languages of the Great Lakes woodlands and Great Plains; the Missouri River languages, Hidatsa and Crow of North Dakota and Montana; and the Mandan dialect groupings, also of the (central) North Dakota Missouri River area.

Classifiers in Caddoan

In sentences asserting where someone or something is, Arikara and Pawnee most commonly use a verb of posture as the main verb. That is, unlike English and many other European languages that have the option of using a verb such as "to be" to assert location, Arikara and Pawnee must use an appropriate verb of posture: essentially, "sit," "lie," or "stand" (the more specific distinctions are presented below).

(2) iriíratukstaakakaawi   iritúkskaa**waarit**   rihúksiri'.
                                             *irii-ti-uks-kaa-**waarik***
    where.we.used.to.dwell there-IND.3-PAST-inside-**stand**.PL ten
    "In our earthlodge there would **stand** ten [poles]."
    South Band Pawnee (Lottie Fancy-Eagle in Weltfish 1936, "Earth Lodges," 146)

(3) aniné**kUx**   kóstš   niinooNAxeerí**č**I   niinareeká**W**I   aniné**kUx**.
    *ani-nee-**kux***   *niinoo-na-x-i-**ariči***   *ani-nee-**kux***
    there-ASR-sit kettle there.where-PRT-2S-AUX-**stand**.SB   where.the.door.is   there-ASR-sit
    "There **sits** the kettle. It's **sitting** there by the door where you're **standing**."
    Arikara (Ella P. Waters in Parks 1991, vol. 2, "Woman with Red Leggings," 1000)

In and of itself, this use of posture verbs in predicates of location is unremarkable: Leon Stassen (1997, 61) reports, "The large majority of languages in my sample [of 410 languages][5] match these semantic contrasts by formal encoding contrasts to at least some degree" (see also the chapters in Newman 2002). However, it lays the groundwork for extensions from this system.

One outcome of this use of posture verbs is the nascent development of a classificatory system. If there are multiple verbs available to express location, then some principle within the language must determine which verb to use in a given instance. In Arikara and Pawnee, when talking of a human being who is within view of the speaker, the person is asserted to be "sitting," "standing," or "lying" according to his or her actual posture (see example 3 above). When the reference is not present, other contextual factors may dictate which verb is used, although sitting is by far the most frequent in the narrative corpora.[6] With nonhuman animals, the usage reflects a mild classificatory system, the choice among posture verbs determined by cultural conventions. In general, when the animal takes on its prototypical posture (e.g., quadrupeds standing on all four legs), the following patterns prevail: snakes crawling on their bellies—extended or non-coiled—are considered to be "lying," as are fish swimming in the water or birds flying in the sky (example 4); large quadrupeds, namely ruminants such as bison, horses, cattle, and perhaps sheep and goats, are considered to be "standing" (example 5); most other animals, including birds, are viewed as "sitting" (example 6), whether they are standing on all four legs, sitting on their haunches, or perched on a branch.

(4) tat   a   tirakuusuhuhkátа**sa**   ríkucki   kítuu'u'…
                    ti-ra-kusuhur-kata-**sa**
        I am   and   this-PRT-flying-against-**lie**.SB   bird   all

"I am with all of these birds flying [**lying**] in the sky."

Skiri Pawnee (Roaming Scout in Murie n.d., *Paahukaatawa*)

(5) táku   te**rit**   aruúsa'
                 ti-**arik**
        there   IND.3-**stand**   horse

"There **stands** a horse there."

South Band Pawnee (Effie Blaine in Weltfish 1937, "Pawnee Biographies," 17)

(6) nooWIšitiihuuwiraáWA   tišinaákUx   xaátš   nii'AhnaraanoótA.
                            ti-ši-na-**kux**
    then.they.two.ran   this-DU-PRT-   dog   where.they.live
                            sit

"Both of the dogs [**sitting**] ran there where they lived."

Arikara (Alfred Morsette in Parks 1991, vol. 1, "Crazy Dog Society," 369)

These basic conventions may be overruled whenever the animal takes on a non-prototypical stance: a snake that is coiled would be considered to be "sitting," as would presumably a large ruminant that places its rump on the ground (supported by its forelimbs or with them raised off the ground); any quadruped or bird that is lying on its side or has lowered itself onto its belly would be marked as "lying" (see example 1); similarly, a quadruped that has raised itself up on only its hind legs would be said to "stand."

The classification system is even more apparent with inanimate objects, though the dominant trend of most objects "sitting" still holds. Long, relatively slender or flat objects "lie," such as a broom or bow on the ground, a fallen tree, or a piece of paper (example 7). Long relatively slender objects that are standing unrooted on a base will be said to "stand," such as a bottle, a floor lamp, and so on. More idiosyncratic to Caddoan culture, stars and other celestial bodies also are considered to "stand" in the heavens (example 8). Objects that are blocky, boxy, round, or small will be said to "sit" (9), as in a ball, a box, a car, a book, a pencil (which could also "lie" given its shape, but typically "sits" given its small size). However, non-animates also have available to them yet more posture verbs. For example, an object that is rooted in the ground will make use of a "planted" verbs, including trees or other plants growing out of the ground or an arrow or other sharp object jabbed into a surface. Immense objects such as buildings or landscape features typically make use of yet other verbs that are reserved only for large spaces and times. There are also distinct verbs used for plural entities sitting and lying.

(7) iraása   ráktahkawarikuskucu' ásku   tíkita   ráwa   he
    ii-ra-**sa**
    that-PRT-**lie**.SB big.spear   one   it.extends   well   and
    tiráhaak**ca**   rikutútaaku'
    ti-ra-haak-**sa**
    this-PRT-wood- the.stick.is.like.this
    lie.SB

    "that long spear [**lying**] extends out one length; this stick [**lying**] is about so long."

    South Band Pawnee (Effie Blaine in Weltfish 1937, "Spear Games," 44)

(8) šohnuutapeerikú sákaa'A   t'nawaa**waaríčI**, áxkU   nootiwaáko':
                              ti-na-waa-**waariči**
    while.they.were   star   this-PRT-DST-   one   then.said
    looking   **stand**.PL.SB
    "anuuna**aríčI** sákaa'A nootat'nisté'."
    anuu-na-**ariči**
    that.far-PRT-   star   then.I.like
    stand.SB

    "while they were looking at the various stars [**standing**], one said, 'I like that [**standing**] star over there'"

    Arikara (Dan Howling Wolf in Parks 1991, vol. 2, "Star Husband," 1029)

(9) Ahuutaahkaraahwiítit   tíraa**ku**   taáwirus
                           ti-ra-**ku**
    he.clenched.it.in.his. this-PRT-**sit** hoop
    mouth

    "He clenched this hoop [**sitting**] in his mouth."

    Skiri Pawnee (Roaming Scout in Murie n.d., "Lucky Man")

However, Parks (1991, 1:xviii) also remarks, "In contemporary Arikara speech this classification has begun to give way to a simplified system in which most objects are denoted as sitting. Although younger speakers in particular have neutralized the older distinctions in most contexts, the shift to the simpler system does not entirely follow generational lines among speakers but also occurs within the speech of many individuals, both older and younger." Although I think that the generalizations given in this chapter are accurate—reflecting the wide patterns observed across the Arikara and Pawnee language data—Parks's observation of change in the speech of some late speakers may result in some exceptions to the rules.

There is a second classificatory system at play in Caddoan languages that is largely orthogonal to the posture verbs, namely *classificatory noun incorporation*. Marianne Mithun (1984, 863) defines this as when "a relatively general [noun] stem is incorporated to narrow the scope of the [verb]"[7] ... but the compound stem can be accompanied by a more specific external [noun phrase] which identifies the argument implied by the [incorporated noun]." Often, for certain types of references, a combination of both of these classificatory systems is at play to properly express the predicate. For example, liquids most often "sit" or "lie," but the verb will almost always be accompanied by an incorporated stem specifying that it refers to a liquid (liquid in a free state, Pawnee *kiic-* or Arikara *čis-~ ts-*, or liquid in a container, Pawnee *kirar-* or Arikara *čiran-*). Likewise, many objects made of wood or long, slender objects (that historically were often made of wood) will often require the verb to incorporate the noun stem *haak-* "wood, stick" (the same form in Arikara and Pawnee). There are many examples of incorporation throughout this chapter—whether classificatory or other types (see Mithun 1984 for an overview of incorporation constructions).

One construction that extends the use of the classificatory posture verbs in combination with such incorporation expresses landscape features and other features that may occur singly or distributed across a larger surface. When asserting a singular or dual occurrence of such a feature, the noun stem for the feature itself is incorporated into the "sit" verb. However, when multiple instances of one of these features is distributed across the landscape or surface, instead of using the usual plural "sit/lie" stem *roos* (A) or *ruuc* (P), the singular form of the "stand" verb *arik* is used instead. Some examples of such "sit—stand" pairs from Arikara from the dictionary database (Parks n.d.a) are shown in example 10.

(10)
Singular		Plural	
haahtet**kux**	"grove of trees"	haahteet**arik**	"groves of trees"
čiwahaah**kux**	"lake"	čiwahaan**arik**	"lakes"
kanihaah**kux**	"garden, patch"	kanihaan**arik**	"gardens, patches"
pira**kux**	"curve, bend"	pira**arik**	"curves, bends"
tahnah**kux**	"clump of stalks"	tahnaan**arik**	"clumps of stalks"
ta**kux**	"patch"	ta**arik**	"patches"
raapiišta**kux**	"price tag"	raapiišta**arik**	"price tags"
ut-raanusta**kux**	"rusty spot"	ut-raanusta**arik**	"rusty spots"
in-kanahkaaskata**kux**	"white spot on the belly"	in-kanahkaaskata**arik**	"white spots on the belly"
hunaata**kux**	"patch of snow"	hunaata**arik**	"patches of snow"

Examples 11 and 12 illustrate some of these pairings within context in both Arikara and Pawnee: compare the singular (a) sentences with the plural, distributed (b) sentences.

(11a) noowitiitAhnáh**kUx**, hawá   tuuhé'   hawá   uukaríkAt.
noo-witi-i-tat-ran-**kux**
there-QT.3-AUX-plant-PL-**sit**   also   there   also   in.the.middle
"There was a clump of stalks [**sitting**] there, as well as over there and also in between."
Arikara (Alfred Morsette in Parks 1991, vol. 1, "Corn Woman," 123)

(11b)   wah   kanawituxtaačeéʼA   noowitiitAhnaanáRIt...
                                       noo-witi-i-tat-ran-**arik**
         well   it.was.not.long   there-QT.3-AUX-plant-PL-
                                       stand

"And it was not long before clump**s** grew [**standing**] here and there."
Arikara (Alfred Morsette in Parks 1991, vol. 1, "Corn Woman," 125)

(12a) Ráhiira'   ríhuksu'   raahkuhaásiki   ihi   háskaatit
      some   only   being.ropes   uh   black.rope

raruuhuúruʼ   kíriku' raahkúc**taku**.
              kíriku-raahku-ut-**ta-ku**

meteorite   something-maybe-
              DAT-**hanging-sit**

"They only being some black ropes, perhaps some kind of meteorite hung [**sitting**] from it."
Skiri Pawnee (Roaming Scout in Murie n.d., "Animal Spirits")

(12b)   Káʼuktu'   **títaarit**   tíraaku   haákaʼu'   isiriíriku.
                    ti-**ta-arik**

        plume   IND.3-   this.sitting   drum   that.they.sat.
                    hang-   holding
                    stand

"Down feather**s** hung [**standing**] on this drum that they sat holding."
Skiri Pawnee (Roaming Scout in Murie n.d., "Doctors' Dances")

To my knowledge, this is a cross-linguistically idiosyncratic use of "stand" versus "sit": there is nothing in the wider linguistic world landscape that would suggest the occurrence of such a construction. But a comparable pattern is found in Siouan, which is returned to below.

FURTHER DISTRIBUTION OF CLASSIFICATORY POSTURE VERBS

Asserting the location of someone or something is not the only context of use for these classificatory posture verbs. Another primary use of the posture verbs, a use with particularly high frequency of occurrence, is their involvement in demonstrative constructions, that is, the expression of "this" and "that." In Arikara and Pawnee there are no independent words, as such, that have such meanings as "this" or "that"; instead, these concepts are expressed by prefixes that are always appended to a verb form.[8] Effectively any verb expressing an action or state may be accompanied by one of these demonstrative prefixes; a most literal English translation would be realized as a relative clause: "this one that...," as seen in examples 13 and 14.

(13) Axtóh   sčíiri   niitʼnuutaánu   tʼnatakuraahnuuwaʼaanu
     kaakunaahé

                           nii=ti-na-ut-aan-hu   ti-na-taku-raak-
                                                   ruuwaʼaan-hu

     Surely.it.is Pawnee that=this-PRT-DAT-   this-PRT-INCL.O-PL-
     not.good   do-IPF.SB   hurt-IPF.SB

"This that the Pawnees are doing is not good, **this their hurting us."**

Arikara (Alfred Morsette in Parks 1991, vol. 1, "Arikara Separation," 468)

(14) witatatíraktaru   **tirastiraattaraaha.**
                        ti-ra-s-tiraak-rar-raaha

     now.I.give.bows.   this-PRT-2S-bow-PL-have.SB
     to.you

     "Now I am giving you **these bow and arrows that you have.**"

     Skiri Pawnee (Roaming Scout in Murie n.d., "Medicine Robe")

However, the most basic and common demonstrative constructions that are used consist of the prefixes attached to a form of the posture verbs. In this usage, the classificatory system described above becomes even more prevalent: it is always necessary to specify an entity as "this one sitting/standing/lying" and so forth. For example, "this man" and "these men" may be expressed in one of several ways, depending on the man's position and other contextual factors.[9]

(15) Pawnee Classificatory Determiners

tíraa**ku**	pií*ta*	"this man (**sitting**)"
tíraa**riki**		"this man (**standing**)"
tíraa**sa**		"this man (**lying**)"
tíra**wihat**		"these men (**sitting**)"
tíra**waariki**		"these men (**standing**)"

Recall also example 1, where the classificatory assertion of the coyote lying is (seemingly redundantly) also reflected in the demonstrative, expressing the coyote's position: *t’naáxA t’neešá nuxtaanoóku* "Here **lies** this **lying** coyote that had been singing."

This use of the posture verbs with the demonstrative prefixes is well enough entrenched in Arikara and Pawnee and fits in with general verb patterns of relative clauses and verbal modifiers in Caddoan languages. However, and notably, no other Caddoan language has a similar demonstrative construction. Demonstrative elements in Wichita (example 16), Kitsai (example 17), and Caddo (example 18) appear as autonomous words without the obligatory accompaniment by a verbal construction, let alone a posture verb. Moreover, posture verbs do not seem to be as prominent in these languages in specifications of location, existence, or possession.

(16) tatí:’i:khiya’a **ti’i**   ’aras   hatakiccare:hih.
     I want   **this**   meat   to put mine on top
     "I want to put **this** meat of mine on top."
     Wichita (Bertha Provost in Rood 1977, "Turtle, Buffalo, and Coyote," 93)

(17) **ti’i**   kírika   iríasu   kírika   á:cak   kocakwahá:ti
     this person   first   person   shoot   red.bird
     "This person was the first person to shoot a red bird."
     K (KaiKai in Lesser 1929–31, "Flint Boy")

(18) *Kaytcí:bah   hikat'a'nihah,   kúyt'adihah **dí:**   dahay'*
     I.will.see   what.he.does   where.   **this**   brother.
                                    he.goes   in.law

dúhya'   nasa'yah.
now   when.he.goes

"I will see what he does, where **this** brother-in-law goes now when he goes."

C (Sadie Bedoka Weller in Chafe 2018, "Transformed Husband and Elf," 106)

Thus, the extended use of posture verbs in Arikara and Pawnee that is described above is suggested here to be an innovation within that branch of the Caddoan language family. In and of itself, this is an interesting but largely unremarkable development: the use of posture verbs as classificatory demonstratives seems a natural extension of wider Caddoan patterns of verbal constructions used as modifiers plus the loose classificatory patterns already found with posture verbs. However, we see below that there are suggestions that this development may have also been encouraged by contact with neighboring Siouan languages.

Classifiers in Siouan

Compared to Caddoan, Siouan is a large, widespread, and relatively diversified family. Within that diversity, however, the loose classificatory use of posture verbs is a common occurrence and has been reconstructed to Proto-Siouan (Rankin 2004). This includes, first and foremost, their use in locative constructions. Again, this itself is unremarkable from a linguistic typological perspective. As in Caddoan, the system revolves around at least three core verbs expressing "sitting," "standing," and "lying."

Another frequent use of these posture verbs is as auxiliaries loosely bound to a main verb in order to express grammatical features—such as continuative aspect or resulting state—a usage not paralleled by Caddoan, but one that Rankin (2004) also suggests may have been preserved from Proto-Siouan, the reconstructed ancestor of all Siouan languages. This shows how old classificatory posture verbs are within Siouan.

(19) Téék   háá **nakiní**   Kinúma'kshis paréxa hąąka't
      So   look **sitting**. Old.Man.   that. getting.angry
                  and   Coyote   moving

"So Old Man Coyote was [**sitting**] look**ing** at him and getting mad."

Mandan (Otter Sage in Hollow 1964–73, "Coyote Races Buffalo," author's transcription: audio time stamp 538.49s)

(20) Hána'ra   rokąąkaxihseena   onápoomaks hįį
      maká
      sleeping   the.old.woman   she.found. uh
      lying.while   him.they.say

*While he was [**lying**] sleep**ing**, the old woman found him.*

Mandan (Otter Sage in Hollow 1964–73, "Coyote Races Buffalo," audio time stamp 1692.54s)

But one use found in some Siouan languages that is comparable to Caddoan usage is the combination of the posture verbs with a nominal reference as a demonstrative determiner. In some constructions the posture verbs are combined with a deictic element, as in Mandan (example 21, exemplified in context in examples 22 and 23) and Omaha (examples 24a and 24b).

(21) Mandan Classificatory Determiners
      ré-**ma'k**   "this (**lying**)"
      ré-**na'k**   "this (**sitting**)"
      ré-**hą'k**   "this (**lying**)"

(Watkins 1976, 30; also cited in Aikhenvald 2000, 177)

(22) kóópųseena   ááhuuni,   "Ré-**ma'k**   íni'minix-ta!"
      striped.   brought.and   this-**lying** play.with.it!
      squashed

"she brought a striped squash and [said], 'Play with this one [**lying**]!'"

Mandan (Annie Eagle in Hollow 1964–73, "Forked Feather," audio time stamp 697.57s)

(23) koníkseena rushááni róó manátkas. "Watéwe- ré-**na'k**?"
  'na
  her.son took.and here the.heart. what-Q.F this-**sitting**
  shape

"Her son took it and (found) the heart (necklace). 'What is this [**sitting**]?'"

Mandan (Annie Eagle in Hollow 1964–73, "Forked Feather," audio time stamp 345.13s)

(24a) ú'e ðé-**khe** šnáhni ttaí ha
  field this-**lying** you. IRR IMPER
  swallow

"You shall devour this field [**lying**]."

(24b) wa'ú ðįkhé šé-**ðįkhe** agíkkąbða-xti-mą
  woman the that-**sitting** I.want.mine-very-I.do

"I do want my woman back, that one [**sitting**] near you."

Omaha (Rankin 2004, 215)

In other constructions, the posture verb by itself serves as the determiner, as seen in examples 25 and 26 from Mandan and contrastively with the same type of object in examples 27a, 27b, and 27c from Osage.

(25) Tataxihéé, nihų́p-**hą'k** owáátaani
  Grandfather.ADDR your. I.wear.on.my.feet.and
  shoe-**this.**
  standing

  wááx=**na'ke** ími'sąąpaa warááhiniitekt-o'sh.
  cottonwood=**this.** I.go.around I'll.go.quickly-IND.M
  sitting

"Grandfather, I want to wear these shoes of yours [**standing**] and go quickly around that stand of cottonwoods [**sitting**]."

Mandan (Annie Eagle in Hollow 1964–73, "Speckled Arrow II," time stamp 664.14s)

(26) Hiré   ráske=**ma'k**   karúxų'ha makų're mikák,
     now   summer=**this.**   none.plows.for.me
                 lying

"This summer [**lying**] there was no one to plow for me"

Mandan (Annie Eagle in Hollow 1964–73, "Annie's Garden," time stamp 19.27s)

(27a) Žą́ą   **įkšé**   ą́ą-họọ
      tree   sit   I.like

"I like that [**sitting**] tree."

Osage (Quintero 2004, 376)

(27b) Žą́ą   **kxą**   ą́ą-họọ
      tree   stand.ANIM   I.like

"I like that [**standing**] tree"

Osage (Quintero 2004, 377)

(27c) Žą́ą   **kše**   ą́ą-họọ
      tree   lie   I.like

"I like that [**lying**] tree"

Osage (Quintero 2004, 379)

This use of posture verbs as determiners is found in Mandan, Dhegiha, and Chiwere-Winnebago languages (Helmbrecht 2017), and only marginally in Missouri River (Crow-Hidatsa), but not in Dakotan or—as far as I can tell—the Ohio River languages.

Broadly speaking, the generalizations of the Siouan classificatory systems are comparable to the Caddoan systems: long and slender or flat entities "lie," long and upright entities "stand," and blocky and round entities "sit." Though, the finer details show more divergences, demonstrating the cultural relativity of the linguistic systems: celestial bodies in Siouan tend to "sit" (where they "stand" in Caddoan); anything with legs or a base, including most midsized or larger quadrupeds, will "stand" in Hidatsa and Mandan, even if not otherwise vertically oriented (where they would "sit" in Caddoan).

Notably, in Dhegiha languages we also find a pattern that is idiosyncratic—but reminiscent of one mentioned for Caddoan above—wherein a singular entity is classified as "sitting" but plural entities are marked as "standing." Unlike in Caddoan, this is not limited to features on a landscape or surface, but rather applies to referents that form a collective of some kind. This can be seen in examples 28a and 28b from Osage (Quintero 2004, 387):

(28a) htóožu **įkšé** wíhta
meat.pie **sit** mine
"this [**sitting**] meat pie is mine"

(28b) ðe htóožu **che** wíhta
that meat.pie **stand** mine
"these [**standing**] meat pies are mine"
Osage (Quintero 2004, 387)

The Dhegiha pattern appears to be more elaborated as well: for those entities that are classified as "lying" in the singular are marked as "sitting" in the plural.[10] Quintero (2004, 384–88) also suggests in Osage that an entity classed as "standing" in the singular will "lie" in the plural, though she gives no examples to support this. Boas (1907, 319–21) and Rankin (2004, 211–12) also describe such a system for other Dhegiha languages, the Omaha-Ponca pattern summarized in example 29.

(29) singular | | collective plural |
| --- | --- | --- | --- |
| ðą | "sitting" | t^he | "standing" |
| k^he | "lying" | ðą | "sitting" |
| t^he | "standing" | k^he | "lying" |

The plural usage only refers to *collective plurals* (plural entities conceptualized as a set in some way); individuated plurals are marked by a different word entirely: *ge* in Omaha-Ponca (Rankin 2004, 214). Unfortunately these discussions come with few compiled examples in the published literature. Rankin (2004) includes a pair from Omaha-Ponca (213–14), seen in example 30, as well as some individual examples of collective plural uses from Quapaw (212, citing Dorsey 1890–94), seen in examples 31a, 31b, and 31c.

(30a) *ttí*   **the**
dwelling   **stand**
"the house, lodge, tent"

(30b) *ttí*   **khe**
dwelling   **lie**
"the lodges"

(31a) *hǫbé*   **the**
shoe   **stand**
"the (pair of) moccasins"

(31b) *ttí-kde-kde*   **khe**   *a-kdé*
house-stood-stood   **lie**   I-return
"I go home to the (line of) lodges."

(31c) *é*   *zaˑní*   *žą́*   *įké*
DEM   all   **lie**   **sit**
"they are all reclining."

Note in examples 31b and 31c that even though another posture verb is present illustrating the default posture being expressed—"standing" in example 31b; "lying" in example 31c—the corresponding plural posture verb ("lying" and "sitting," respectively) is added to express the collective plural sense. Such a pattern of number-associated alternating positionals has not been reported for any other branch of the Siouan language family (Rankin 2004).

Comparison of Classifiers

Based on the summary descriptions above, it may be observed that Caddoan and Siouan languages show comparable uses of posture verbs in two main constructions: locative predications and classificatory determiners. Their use in the former is typologically common and would not suggest any connection, but the latter use is more notable. The semantics of the classificatory systems largely follow cross-linguistic trends with finer categorizations being culturally and linguistically distinctive between the two families.

However, one particular similarity is a subset of referents that show a typologically unique pattern, referring to collective concepts in Dhegiha Siouan and to features relative to a surface in Caddoan. In this pattern a singular entity that is in one posture in the singular is marked as being in a different posture in the plural, where it is only the difference in posture that marks the distinction in number. In Caddoan, the only contrast seems to be between singular "sitting" features and "plural" standing features. In Dhegiha Siouan, on the other hand, there is greater systemization, different classes of entities alternating different postures, as described above: "sitting" singular objects "stand" in the plural, as in Caddoan, but "standing" and "lying" singular objects also respectively "lie" and "sit" in the plural.

These posture alternations do not reflect any known cross-linguistic typological patterns: the metaphors are too idiosyncratic to have evolved independently in both Siouan and Caddoan, suggesting that one group of languages may have adopted these patterns from the other. Given how deeply entrenched the classificatory use of posture verbs is throughout Siouan, including their use as determiners, compared to the fact that such use—as determiners and adopting the posture-contrastive number marking—is limited in Caddoan to just Pawnee and Arikara, this would suggest that the directionality was from Siouan to just these northernmost Caddoan languages.

Under this proposal the posture-based number marking almost certainly must have been adopted into Arikara-Pawnee from some Dhegiha language, being the only Siouan branch in which that usage is found. However, that does not necessarily mean that the prevalent use of classificatory posture verbs (particularly as determiners) also stems from Dhegiha contact. Although the full classificatory posture verb "package" may have been adopted under a single contact situation, it is also possible that posture verbs had already been incorporated into Caddoan grammar from an earlier contact with Siouan—or possibly as an independent development—and that it was only through a later or secondary contact situation that the Dhegiha posture-number metaphor was incorporated.

Alternatively, one could suggest that the classificatory and determiner use of posture verbs developed independently in Arikara-Pawnee as a natural extension of preexisting relative clause structures within Caddoan and that this usage was at most reinforced by contact with Siouan. Even under this proposal, though, Siouan contact would still have been necessary to share the posture-number metaphor. One could then suggest that the metaphor may have originated in Arikara-Pawnee before being transferred to and elaborated in Dhegiha Siouan. However, this seems a nonstarter: the pattern is found across all Dhegiha languages, which first separated from each other in the Ohio Valley region well before significant contact with Caddoan seems probable.

Although no resolution to this question can be offered at present, the next section discusses some of the known geographical and temporal venues where such contact may have occurred.

Historical Population Movements

Considering the distribution of Caddoan-speaking peoples, the Caddoan languages have had most regular geographic proximity—and thus the potential for linguistic contact effects—with many language families, such as the Muskogean languages and language isolates of the Southeast, with the language isolates and small families of central and southern Texas, with Algonquian languages, , and with various eastern outliers of language families located farther to the west and southwest, such as Kiowa (Tanoan), Plains Apache (Athabaskan), Numic languages, and Montana Salish.

However, more than any of these, the Siouan languages appear to have been a constant eastern neighbor to the Caddoan villages from at least the mid-seventeenth century on, from the Quapaw encroaching on the Caddo villages in the Arkansas region and north to the eventual settlement of the Arikaras among the Hidatsas and Mandans in present-day North Dakota, as well as the almost continuous warfare by the Arikaras and Pawnees with many of the Lakȟóta- and Dakȟóta-speaking tribes throughout the nineteenth century.

But in considering the possibility of contact phenomena with Arikara and Pawnee, specifically in regard to certain classificatory uses of posture verbs, we might narrow down the relevant points of contact. The range of uses of posture verbs in the documented modern variety of Arikara and in both Skiri and South Band Pawnee appears to be virtually identical. This suggests that the constructions developed at a time when Arikara and Pawnee existed in an effectively undifferentiated speech community, either before they had separated or after separation but still with significant and frequent interactions. This would have placed these Northern Caddoan communities in the vicinity of modern-day eastern and central Nebraska and Kansas. The most geographically proximal Siouan groups would most likely thus have been Dhegiha-speaking groups, such as the ancestors of the Omaha-Poncas.

Alice C. Fletcher and Francis La Flesche ([1911] 1992, 75–78) describe intimate relations between the Omahas and the Arikaras, including a tale of how the Arikaras introduced maize cultivation to the Omahas—although the writers interpret the story as apocryphal—and mention how the Arikaras taught the Omahas to build earth lodges. They also recount an Omaha-Ponca tradition of having warred with the Arikaras and driven them from the land along the Missouri River that the Omahas would settle before European contact.

W. P. Clark ([1885] 1982, 286–87), citing an 1880 article by John B. Dunbar published in the *Magazine of American History*, recounts how the (South Band) Pawnees report that they originally conquered their historical land in Nebraska from the Otoes, Omahas, Poncas, and Skiri Pawnees. (Dunbar conjectures that the Skiri, along with the Arikaras, preceded the South Bands north into the Nebraska territory by about a century.) Within this account, Dunbar says the Pawnees spoke of the Otoes, Omahas, and Poncas as "subjugated" tribes and "dependents" and that, despite much contention between the bands, the Skiri too occupied a "subordinate" position to the other Pawnee bands.[11]

While such accounts must be interpreted cautiously, they do suggest close contact between Arikara-Pawnee-speaking peoples and at least the Omaha-Poncas, if not also other Siouan-speaking groups, probably between the mid-seventeenth and early nineteenth centuries. This seems like the most promising point of contact for the introduction of the classificatory patterns from Siouan into Caddoan. However, more than simple geographic proximity is typically required for such linguistic transference; there must also be a significant amount of bilingualism. In this case, for Siouan semantic patterns to enter into Caddoan languages, first-language Siouan speakers would probably have had to be incorporated into Caddoan-speaking communities, learning the Caddoan speech as a second language, but retaining and transferring patterns from their first language. Such subtle Siouan grammatical patterns may have gradually disseminated among the wider Arikara-Pawnee speech population. Although the exact time, place, and circumstances of this Siouan integration into Caddoan remains unclear, this study suggests at least that it may have happened.

Conclusion

This chapter briefly describes some grammatical patterns in Arikara and Pawnee that show marked similarity to patterns also found in Siouan languages, suggesting linguistic acculturation through contact. The distribution and details of the patterns imply a transfer of traits from Siouan languages—most likely from Dhegiha Siouan—into Northern Caddoan, which must have occurred before the Arikara and Pawnee speech communities had fully separated from each other, given that they share these apparently borrowed features. While the classificatory patterns are fascinating in and of themselves, and deserving of more study, they also raise the question of what other features may have been shared, in either direction, across the long period of contact between Caddoan and Siouan languages.

Notes

1. Abbreviations used in language examples in this chapter: ADDR = address form; ANIM = animate reference; ASR = assertive mode; AUX = auxiliary element; DAT = dative-benefactive prefix; DEM = demonstrative; DST = distributive number; DU = dual number; EV = evidential mode; F = female addressee; IMPER = imperative mode; INCL = inclusive first person; IND = indicative mode; IPF = imperfective aspect; IRR = irrealis mood; M = male addressee; O = direct object; PAST = past tense; PL = plural; PRT = participial mode; Q = question mode; QT = quotative indicative mode; S = subject; SB = subordinate clause; 1, 2, 3 = first, second, third person. For more information on Arikara and Pawnee grammar, see Parks 1976; Parks, Beltran, and Waters 1979; Parks and Pratt 2008.

2. Though PISL may have contributed to the diffusion of semantic forms, the meaning expressed via sign being translated into spoken languages. This is suggested, for instance, by synonymy among different languages' names for other tribes (e.g., Parks 2001a, 389–90).

3. This overview does not include historically under- or undocumented languages that have received greater or lesser speculation to have been affiliated with Caddoan, such as Adai (Powell 1891; Lesser and Weltfish 1932; Taylor 1963a, 1963b; Chafe 1979) or Jumano (Hickerson 1994).

4. For more information on the Caddoan-speaking peoples, see the appropriate chapters in DeMallie (2001), particularly Parks (2001a, 2001c) for Arikara and Pawnee. See also van de Logt (2011, 2020, 2023) for more recent treatments on the history of Caddoan peoples.

5. Stassen's sample, as a well-constructed typological study, attempts to be "distributed fairly evenly among the genetic and areal conglomerations in the world" (Stassen 1997, 8). The generalizations made from such large and balanced samples thus contend to reflect general patterns of human language overall.

6. The Arikara and Pawnee text corpora comprise almost all known monologic texts transcribed to date, consisting of narratives of various genres. All analyses of the texts are my own. A handful of texts for all three varieties were published in Parks (1977). For Arikara, the corpus is largely built of the narratives published in Parks (1991) as well as a number of texts that are unpublished or of limited distribution. For South Band Pawnee, the corpus comprises the texts of Weltfish (1937) as well as a fairly large collection of texts that were recorded by Parks from a number of speakers but that remain unpublished. For Skiri, the

mainstay of the corpus is composed of the accounts of Roaming Scout (Murie n.d.), augmented by narratives from two speakers recorded by Parks in the 1960s (Parks n.d.b).

7. "Incorporation" refers to a noun stem being compounded with a verb stem to form a single word. This is a construction that exists in numerous languages in one form or another, particularly among Indigenous American languages.

8. These same prefixes may refer more directly to spatial location (translating "here" and "there") or to temporal location ("now" and "then"). Context and other affixes involved in the constructions will typically clarify how the demonstrative/deictic prefixes are being used.

9. Verbs of motion such as "go" and "come" and certain other number distinctions may expand this list at least fourfold.

10. It appears that this last pattern, the use of "sitting" for collective plural of objects that are "lying," is not well documented, so far as I could find in the literature. Boas (1907) and Quintero (2004) give no examples for Ponca or Osage, respectively, and Rankin (2004, 212) marks this form with a question mark for both Kansa and Omaha-Ponca in his table.

11. However, Dunbar's description cannot be entirely taken at face value. Whatever the validity of any of the migrations and historical tribal interactions, his assertion that the Skiri dialect "forms an intermediate link between the pure Pawnee [South Band dialect] and the Arikara" (qtd. in Clark [1885] 1982, 287) seems inaccurate (see Parks 1979). Arikara shows just as many similarities to South Band Pawnee, and its divergence suggests an earlier separation from both Pawnee dialects than is suggested by the differences between Skiri and South Band. It is not clear what features of Skiri Pawnee could be interpreted as "intermediate" between Arikara and South Band.

References

Aikhenvald, Alexandra. 2000. *Classifiers: A Typology of Noun Categorization Devices*. Oxford: Oxford University Press.

Allan, Keith. 1977. "Classifiers." *Language* 53, no. 2: 285–311.

Boas, Franz. 1907. "Notes on the Ponka Language." In *Congrès International des Américanistes*, vol. 15, 317–37. Quebec: Dussault and Proulx.

Brown, Cecil H. 1996. "Lexical Acculturation, Areal Diffusion, Lingua Francas, and Bilingualism." *Language in Society* 25, no. 2: 261–82.

Chafe, Wallace L. 1979. "Caddoan." In *The Languages of Native America: Historical and Comparative Assessment*, edited by Lyle Campbell and Marianne Mithun, 213–35. Austin: University of Texas Press.

———. 2018. *The Caddo Language: A Grammar, Texts, and Dictionary Based on Materials Collected by the Author in Oklahoma between 1960 and 1970*. Petoskey MI: Mundart Press.

Clark, W. P. (1885) 1982. *The Indian Sign Language*. Philadelphia: L. R. Hamersly. Reprint, Lincoln: University of Nebraska Press.

Croft, William. 2000. *Explaining Language Change: An Evolutionary Approach*. Essex, UK: Pearson Education Limited.

Davis, Jeffrey E. 2007. "A Historical Linguistic Account of Sign Language among North American Indians." In *Multilingualism and Sign Languages*, edited by Ceil Lucas, 3–35. Washington DC: Gallaudet University Press.

———. 2010. *Hand Talk: Sign Language among American Indian Nations*. New York: Cambridge University Press.

DeMallie, Raymond J., ed. 2001. *Handbook of North American Indians*. Vol. 13, *Plains*. Washington DC: Smithsonian Institution.

Dorsey, George A. 1890–94. Quapaw dictionary and texts. MS 4800, National Anthropological Archives, Smithsonian Institution, Washington DC.

Fletcher, Alice C., and Francis La Flesche. (1911) 1992. *The Omaha Tribe*. Vol. 1. Twenty-Seventh Annual Report of the Bureau of American Ethnology to the Secretary of the Smithsonian Institution, 1905–1906. Washington DC: Government Printing Press. Reprint, Lincoln: University of Nebraska Press.

Goddard, Ives. 2001. "The Algonquian Languages of the Plains." In *Handbook of North American Indians*, vol. 13, *Plains*, edited by Raymond J. DeMallie, 71–79. Washington DC: Smithsonian Institution.

Helmbrecht, Johannes. 2017. "On the Grammaticalization of Demonstratives in Hoocąk and Other Siouan Languages." In *Unity and Diversity in Grammaticalization Scenarios*, edited by Walter Bisang and Andrej Malchukov, 137–72. Berlin: Language Science Press.

Hickerson, Nancy Parrott. 1994. *The Jumanos: Hunters and Traders of the South Plains*. Austin: University of Texas Press.

Hollow, Robert C. 1964–73. Mandan narrative texts. Robert C. Hollow Papers, North Dakota State Historical Society, Bismarck.

Kroskrity, Paul V. 1982. "Language Contact and Linguistic Diffusion: The Arizona Tewa Speech Community." In *Bilingualism and Language Contact in the Borderlands: Spanish, English, and Native American Languages*, edited by Florence Barkin,

Elizabeth A. Brandt, and Jacob Ornstein-Galicia, 51–72. Bilingual Education Series. New York: Teachers College Press.

———. 1993. *Language, History, and Identity: Ethnolinguistic Studies of the Arizona Tewa*. Tucson: University of Arizona Press.

———. 1998. "Discursive Convergence with a Tewa Evidential." In *The Life of Language: Papers in Linguistics in Honor of William Bright*, edited by Jane H. Hill, P. J. Mistry, and Lyle Campbell, 25–34. Trends in Linguistics Studies and Monographs 108. Berlin: Mouton de Gruyter.

Lesser, Alexander. 1929–31. Kitsai language field notes and texts. Unpublished field notes housed at the American Indian Studies Research Institute, Indiana University, Bloomington.

Lesser, Alexander, and Gene Weltfish. 1932. *Composition of the Caddoan Linguistic Stock*. Smithsonian Miscellaneous Collections 87, no. 6. Washington DC: Smithsonian Institution.

Mithun, Marianne. 1984. "The Evolution of Noun Incorporation." *Language* 60, no. 4: 847–94.

———. 1999. *The Languages of Native North America*. Cambridge: Cambridge University Press.

———. 2020. "Contact and North American Languages." In *The Handbook of Language Contact*, 2nd ed., edited by Raymond Hickey, 593–612. Hoboken NJ: Wiley-Blackwell.

Murie, James. n.d. "The Roaming Scout Narratives: Teachings of a Pawnee Priest." Edited and translated by Douglas R. Parks. Unpublished manuscript, American Indian Studies Research Institute, Indiana University, Bloomington. Also in part available online: Roaming Scout Collection, Indiana University, http://zia.aisri.indiana.edu/~corpora/RoamingScout.php.

Newman, John, ed. 2002. *The Linguistics of Sitting, Standing, and Lying*. Amsterdam: John Benjamins.

Parks, Douglas R. 1976. *A Grammar of Pawnee*. New York: Garland.

———, ed. 1977. *Caddoan Texts. International Journal of American Linguistics*, Native American Text Series, vol. 2. Chicago: University of Chicago Press.

———. 1979. "The Northern Caddoan Languages: Their Subgrouping and Time Depths." *Nebraska History* 60: 197–213.

———. 1991. *Traditional Narratives of the Arikara Indians*. 4 vols. Lincoln: University of Nebraska Press.

———. 2001a. "Arikara." In DeMallie 2001, 365–90.

———. 2001b. "Caddoan Languages." In DeMallie 2001, 80–93.

———. 2001c. "Pawnee." In DeMallie 2001, 515–47.

———, ed. n.d.a. Arikara, Skiri Pawnee, and South Band Pawnee dictionary databases. Unpublished Field Works Language Explorer (FLEX) database files, American Indian Studies Research Institute, Indiana University, Bloomington. Also in part available online: AISRI Dictionary Portal, AISRI Research Projects, Indiana University, http://zia.aisri.indiana.edu/~dictsearch/.

———, ed. n.d.b. Skiri Pawnee narratives of Harry Mad Bear and Sam Allen. Unpublished recordings, transcripts, and database, American Indian Studies Research Institute, Indiana University, Bloomington. Also in part available online: Harry Mad Bear Collection, Indiana University, http://zia.aisri.indiana.edu/~corpora/ParksSkiri.php.

Parks, Douglas R., Janet Beltran, and Ella P. Waters. 1979. *Introduction to the Arikara Language*. Bismarck ND: Mary College.

Parks, Douglas R., and Lula Nora Pratt. 2008. *A Dictionary of Skiri Pawnee*. Lincoln: University of Nebraska Press.

Parks, Douglas R., and Robert L. Rankin. 2001. "Siouan Languages." In DeMallie 2001, 94–114.

Powell, J. W. 1891. *Indian Linguistic Families of America North of Mexico*. Seventh Annual Report of the Bureau of American Ethnology to the Secretary of the Smithsonian Institution, 1885–1886. Washington DC: Government Printing Office.

Quintero, Carolynn. 2004. *Osage Grammar*. Lincoln: University of Nebraska Press.

Rankin, Robert L. 2004. "The History and Development of Siouan Positionals with Special Attention to Polygrammaticalization in Dhegiha." *Sprachtypologie und Universalienforschung* 57, no. 2/3: 202–27.

Rood, David. 1977. "Wichita Texts." In *Caddoan Texts*, edited by Douglas R. Parks, 91–128. *International Journal of American Linguistics*, Native American Text Series, vol. 2. Chicago: University of Chicago Press.

Sherzer, Joel. 1976. *An Areal-Typological Study of American Indian Languages North of Mexico*. Amsterdam: North-Holland.

Stassen, Leon. 1997. *Intransitive Predication*. Oxford: Oxford University Press.

Taylor, Alan R. 1963a. "The Classification of the Caddoan Languages." *Proceedings of the American Philosophical Society* 107, no. 1: 51–59.

———. 1963b. "Comparative Caddoan." *International Journal of American Linguistics* 29, no. 2: 113–31.

van de Logt, Mark. 2011. *War Party in Blue: Pawnee Scouts in the U.S. Army*. Norman: University of Oklahoma Press.

———. 2020. *Monsters of Contact: Historical Trauma in Caddoan Oral Traditions*. Norman: University of Oklahoma Press.

———. 2023. *Between the Floods: A History of the Arikaras*. Norman: University of Oklahoma Press.

Watkins, Laurel J. 1976. "Position in Grammar: Sit, Stand, Lie." *Kansas Working Papers in Linguistics* 1: 16–41.

Weltfish, Gene. 1937. *Caddoan Texts, Pawnee, South Band Dialect*. Publications of the American Ethnological Society, vol. 17. New York: G. E. Stechert.

Wooden Boatmen, Spirits, and Bushy Eyebrows

13

American Indian Names for the French in North America

DOUGLAS R. PARKS

An overlooked topic in the history of North America is systematic study of the names that American Indians first gave to Europeans colonizers that have survived into the twentieth century. As this chapter shows, many of those ethnonyms were created on the basis of Native perceptions of the white newcomers, while others were borrowed from other, generally linguistically related tribes. What nearly all tribes in the eastern half of the continent had in common were terms that distinguished the three nationalities—French, English, and Americans—and frequently by the late nineteenth or early twentieth century an earlier name for one Euro-American group was generalized to all white people.[1]

This chapter focuses on the names that Native peoples in the area east of the Rocky Mountains gave to the French, who were generally the first Europeans they came to know and with whom they developed close relations through trade and intermarriage. It also gives some tangential attention to the names designating the English and Americans, especially since, among a few tribes, those ethnonyms changed referents as social relationships with Euro-Americans changed over time.

Categories of Names

American Indian ethnonyms for the French fall into a small number of semantic types or categories:

The first and largest type comprises a name, or name type, that is widespread in a geographical area and generally coincides with a language family, a group of historically related languages. Thus, most tribes speaking Algonquian languages—that is, members of the Algonquian language family—have a common name for the French, as do, similarly, speakers of Siouan and Muskogean languages, two other widespread linguistic families.

An overlapping group comprises tribes that borrowed the English designation "French" and adapted its pronunciation to their own languages.

Another category comprises names that are geographical descriptors, specifying the location or direction of the French "homeland," either the Saint Lawrence River valley or St. Louis in the Illinois country, relative to the location of the tribe itself.

There are, in addition, at least two names that describe a prominent physical or cultural feature that distinguished the early French traders.

Finally, there is a small group of names that originally designated the Americans or the British and later shifted their designation to the French.

WOODEN BOATMAN

Eastern Algonquian tribes who interacted with the French first designated them by a name that meant, approximately, "wooden boat owner," derived from the canoes that early French traders and coureurs de bois used to ply the waterways of the St. Lawrence valley, and later other rivers, in the course of their trade with the Native populations. The Plains Cree term *weemistikoosiw* provides a clear example of how the word is derived in these languages. It is based on two nouns, *mistik* "wood; log" and *oosi* "canoe; boat," yielding the base form of the name. Ownership of this noun is then formed by adding an initial *o-* and a final *-I*, resulting in an animate intransitive verb *omistikoosi*—meaning "to own a wooden boat." The addition of the suffix *-w* nominalizes the verb and results in "wooden boat owner."

Later, after tribes became acquainted with other Europeans, the name given to the French was sometimes extended to the English and other white people as well, as seen in Shawnee and Plains Cree (see table 3). In the early 1800s Thomas Forsyth, Indian agent to the Sauk and Fox, remarked that the Algonquian-language-speaking Great Lakes

Indians called the French "Wem-ty-goush," a short form of "Wa-bay-mish-e-tome," which he mistakenly said meant literally "white person with a beard" and which apparently had become a folk etymology among one or more tribes (Forsyth 1912, 240n95). Prince Maximilian zu Wied-Neuwied also cited the same name, spelled differently as "wemstegosó," as a designation for "Frenchman" (Maximilian [1843] 1906, 24:253).

Table 3 presents the variants of the common name that most Algonquian tribes gave to the French.

TABLE 3. Variant forms of the name "French" in Algonquian languages

Tribe	Modern recording(s)	Historical recording(s)
Montagnais	məstukuušu 'Frenchman' (C)	Meshtukushu (Lm)
Ojibwa	wemtigoozhii 'Frenchman' (R); wemitigoozhi (NN)	Uämestihóhsch 'Frenchman' (M)
Plains Cree	weemistikoosiw 'Frenchman; white person' (var.) (C); mistikoosiw 'Frenchman' (W); 'Frenchman; white person; HBC manager' (WA)	Wemstegosó 'Frenchman' (M); wemistikojiw 'un français, un canadien, un blanc, un homme civilisé' (LC)
Miami-Illinois	meehtikoošia 'Frenchman' (C)	mamistig8chia (prob. *maamihtikoošia); 8emistig8chia (prob. *weemihtikoošia) (C)
Potawatomi	wemtəgoži (C)	
Menominee	wɛɛmɛhtikoosew (lit. dugout canoe) 'Frenchman' (loan from Ojibwe); cf. mɛʔtekoos 'dugout canoe' (C)	

Tribe	Modern recording(s)	Historical recording(s)
Sauk	*meemehtekooŝiiha ~ weemehtekooŝiiha* 'Frenchman' (C)	Mith-o-cosh (F)
Fox	*meemehtekooŝiiha* 'Frenchman' (C)	
Kickapoo	*eemehtekoosiiha* (C)	
Shawnee	*(m)tekohsiya* 'white man' (prob. loan from Kickapoo) (C)	

Note: Most of the Algonquian words in this table, modern and historical, along with their original sources, were provided by David Costa (= C) in personal communication, April 6, 8, 2009; January 9, 14, 24, 2011: for modern Montagnais, Costa cites Drapeau (1991, 316); for modern Plains Cree, Costa gives the first form citing no other source; for Miami-Illinois, Gravier (1700) and Le Boullenger (1725, 90) for the historical forms, with the phonemic reconstructions (marked by asterisks) and modern form provided by Costa himself; for Potawatomi, he cites an unpublished lexicon given to him by Laura Buszard-Welcher; for Menominee, Bloomfield (1975, 269), as well as the word for "dugout canoe" (119); for modern Sauk, Whittaker (2005, 70); for Fox, Costa cites a personal communication from Ives Goddard; for Kickapoo, Voorhis (1988, 25); for Shawnee, Voegelin (1938–40, 140) and Edgar (1891, 377). Sources for other forms: historical Montagnais (Lm = Lemoine 1901, 132); modern Ojibwa (R = Rhodes 1985, 357, 482; NN = Nichols and Nyholm 1995, 118, 184); historical Ojibwa (M = Maximilian 1843, 261); modern Plains Cree (WA = Wolfart and Ahenakew 1998, 95; W = Wolvengrey 2001, 107); historical Plains Cree (Maximilian 1843, 253; Lc = Lacombe 1874, 645); historical Sauk (F = Forsyth 1912, 240).

SPIRITS

In the period of early contact with Europeans, many of the Native inhabitants in the eastern part of North America referred to the white intruders as spirits because the Europeans were able to do so many things that the Natives could not do. The priest Louie Hennepin, for example, wrote that Hurons, in speaking of the French discoveries in America, told him that "they [Hurons] were men but we Frenchmen were spirits, because if they had gone as far as we had[,] strange tribes would have killed them, while we went everywhere without fear" (1938, 109).

On another occasion, when staying with the Santee in what is now Minnesota, Hennepin also quoted a Santee man who was watching him examining his own papers as saying, "When we question Father Louis . . . , he does not answer until he has looked at what is white (they have no word for paper). He answers us and makes us know his thoughts. It must be that this white thing [paper] is a spirit that explains to Father Louis all that we say to him" (123).

Later Hennepin recounts the return of a hunting party, one member of which tells the villagers that "while hunting near the head of Lake Superior some of the people had met five spirits, as they call Frenchmen" (128).

In the eighteenth century, when the first French traders ascended the Missouri River and encountered the Siouan tribes living along its course from present-day Nebraska up to Montana, those peoples marveled at the mysterious cultural and technological items that the white men had. The gun, in particular, inspired awe, and the Sioux gave it the name *mázawakhaŋ*, literally "holy iron." Similarly, many other introduced items were designated *wakháŋ* "holy, mysterious, awesome": the horse, for example, was called *šúŋkawakhaŋ* "holy dog," and whiskey was called *mníwakhaŋ* "holy water." Such designations reflected the mysterious powers that most of those tribes ascribed to the French traders, whom they designated as "spirits."

In 1795 the St. Louis trader Jean-Baptiste Truteau remarked in his notebook:

> The Arikaras <Panis Ricaras> are of a rather gentle nature. They respect <and defer to all> white men. I will use this name in the continuation of these memoirs to designate all civilized nations, because none of the Indians of any of these regions understand how to distinguish among the nations of the Spanish, French, English, &c., and they call them all white men or spirits indifferently. It is said that formerly they had such great veneration for us that they honored us with a kind of worship, giving feasts in which they threw the first morsels into the fire as an offering to the white men, and they also threw painted

robes and dressed skins decorated with feathers into the water as a sacrifice to us. Several old men have recounted these facts to me as true, or they have assured me that the Cheyennes and the other peoples farther away still practice these customs. As for the Arikara nation, the great intercourse that they have had for some years with the Sioux and the Skiri Pawnees has brought a notable change to the ideas that their ancestors had formed of the white men, whom they regarded as divinities. Now they think of us simply in connection with the merchandise that we bring them that is so necessary to them, and above all with the firearms that they receive from us that protect them from the incursions of the many formidable enemies who often used to steal their women and children. (Truteau 2017, 171)

Later, when he accompanied a large party of Arikaras who visited a Cheyenne village to dance the Calumet for them, a Cheyenne couple adopted Truteau.[2] He described graphically their beliefs about white men:

As for the man's action of stripping me nude and leading me thus into the center of the dance ground to dress me with other clothing, I knew very well that this is an act of generosity and bravery very common among them, but the woman's actions and her purpose were unknown to me. I made inquiries of some, who told me that the young man and the young woman, having like all those of their nation great veneration for white men and great faith in their power, believed that by touching me, and then rubbing herself, as I described above, the children she would bear would be exempt from illness and would live a very long time. If these poor ignorant people have these absurd prejudices, what would you have me to do about it? (Truteau 2017, 331)

The Middle Missouri Siouan Tribes

The historical life of the name "Spirit" that the middle Missouri River peoples gave to the first French traders varies with each tribe. Perhaps the most interesting is the term that occurs among the various Sioux groups. The earliest name that they used was *wašícu* or *wašícuŋ*, which still means "spirit" in ritual contexts but is now more commonly restricted to "whiteman" in a generic sense. The generalization of the term to Europeans and Americans began early in the nineteenth century, but among the Eastern Sioux (or Dakota) in the late nineteenth century it still primarily designated the French, albeit often with a modifier. One of the two major dictionaries of Dakota—that of the Presbyterian missionary Stephen Return Riggs from the mid-nineteenth century—defines *wašicu* as "French (in particular); white person (generically)" but states that the word is nearly synonymous with *wakháŋ* "holy, mysterious" and that in the Teton dialect it means "a familiar spirit; some mysterious forces or beings which are supposed to communicate with men," essentially the same gloss that Buechel gives in his Teton dictionary. Riggs cites the form *Wašicu xiŋca* as meaning "Frenchman from France" (lit. "real, or original, whiteman") and *Wašicu hokšidaŋ* as "a French boy, a common name for Canadians in Dakota country; anyone who labors," the latter usually a reference to Frenchmen (Riggs 1890, 536; Buechel 1970, 551). John P. Williamson, another missionary among the Eastern Sioux who published an English—Dakota dictionary at the turn of the twentieth century, gives the word for "French" as *wašicu-ikceka*, which is literally "common spirit" or "common whiteman." In Sioux the modifier "common" is used to derive a noun that designates an older, or original, form of a class of objects—in this case describing the French as the original, or more familiar, variety of whitemen. For the English he gives first the older designation, *sagdaša* and then glosses *wašicu* as "English; whiteman" (Williamson [1902] 1938, 59, 71).

In Western Sioux (Lakȟóta) in the early twentieth century, Father Eugene Buechel, the most prominent Jesuit missionary among the Lakȟóta, translated *wašicuŋ-ikceka* as "Frenchman" in his dictionary (Buechel 1970, 551). In 1833 the German traveler Prince Maximilian recorded the Yanktonai Sioux name for Frenchman as "Uaschidjo" (modern *wašicu*) (Maximilian [1843] 1906, 215). He recorded the same name, Uaschidju "Frenchman," in the related Assiniboine language

(223), but in 1908 Edward Curtis cites the same term as "wa-shí-chu^n," meaning "whiteman" (Curtis 1908, 3:158).

A name for "Frenchman" that appears to be a cognate form of *wašicu* appears in several other Siouan languages. In 1819–20 Thomas Say, the zoologist on Major Stephen Harriman Long's expedition to the Rocky Mountains, collected vocabularies of the Indian tribes they encountered on their route. In the Min-ne-ta-re, or Hidatsa, vocabulary list he recorded "bo-she" as the Hidatsa name for the French (Say 1905, 304). Over a decade later Maximilian ([1843] 1906) recorded the same name in Omaha as "uáchä" (239) and in Mandan and Hidatsa as "waschi" and "uaschi" (266), which are contemporary Mandan *waší/mąší* and Hidatsa *wašíi/mašíi*. He also gave it as the Crow term, which he wrote "ma-schí-di," with a suffix "-di" (282).³ Today the Mandan term means "white person" and has been folk-etymologized as "nice, pretty," putatively because of the nice clothes that whites wear, while the Hidatsa name has no known etymology or other meaning.⁴ In the late nineteenth century, however, the U.S. Army physician Washington Matthews noted in his Hidatsa dictionary that the word originally applied only to the French and to Canadians, but that when he was stationed at Fort Berthold in the 1870s, the French and Canadians were sometimes designated "mašika'ti" (modern *mašíigaadi*) "true whitemen" (1877, 188). In the early twentieth century Curtis stated that the Hidatsa word "ma-shí" meant "white man" (1909, 4:196). So here again the original Hidatsa name *wašíi/mašíi* "spirit" that was first given to the French was later generalized to mean any whiteman, and then a modifier, usually "true" or "real" (*gáádi* in Hidatsa, the equivalent of *xiŋca* and *ikceka* in the Sioux dialects), was added to designate the French specifically among whitemen.

The Winnebago, a Siouan tribe closely related linguistically to the Oto (see below) and who lived in present-day Wisconsin in the nineteenth century, also called the French spirits. The term *waxopįnį* means both "spirit" and "Frenchman, French person," and, as in Sioux, the cognate enclitic *xjį* "real" is sometimes suffixed to the term when speaking of the French (Helmbrecht and Lehmann 2010, 205).

The Algonquian-Speaking Tribes of the Northwestern Plains

Another regional subtype of the name "spirit" occurs among the Algonquian-speaking tribes of the northwestern plains: the Arapahos, Gros Ventres (Atsina), Blackfoot, and Cheyennes. After meeting the first French traders, and later other Europeans, these tribes extended the meaning of the name for their creator-trickster to include the white newcomers.

For each of these four tribes their trickster was a creator and one of their foremost supernatural beings. Although he was devious, as the designation "trickster" suggests, his defining attribute was his supernatural power, which was greater than that of most other beings. Hence their designation of the French as tricksters or, more accurately, supernatural beings was in effect the same as the downriver-Siouan tribes' designation of them as spirits. Those tribes also perceived the technological objects of the newcomers and the powers that they possessed as awesome, the attributes that only mysterious beings possessed.

Although the four Plains Algonquian tribes' name "spirit" originally designated Frenchmen, who were the first whites they met, it was later extended to designate all whitemen after the tribes became acquainted with other Europeans and Americans. And like the Siouan-speaking tribes, after generalizing the name to all whitemen, these Algonquian peoples designated the French as "real whitemen" in contrast to other, generic whitemen. Thus their naming pattern follows the same one as the middle Missouri Siouan tribes.

Other Possible Examples

The Natchez, a large confederation of tribes that lived in what is now southwestern Mississippi and were defeated by the French in the early eighteenth century, may represent groups in the southeastern United States that designated Frenchmen as spirits. In the early twentieth century there were several surviving Natchez who spoke their native language, and in the course of documenting it, the linguist Mary R.

Haas recorded the word *koyokop* for "white person." In the eighteenth century the term *koyokop šiil* (written then as Coyocopchill) is recorded as "great spirit," and in the twentieth century *tah koyokop* meant "powerful supernatural being."[5] This evidence strongly suggests that the Natchez, and perhaps other southeastern tribes as well, called the French "spirits," just as tribes on the central and northern plains did.

The Caddo, who formerly comprised a confederation of bands, or tribes, and lived in eastern Texas and western Louisiana, represent a type of borrowing that is seemingly different from the above names. Their word for Frenchman is *kaanush*, which seems to be the last two syllables of the word "Mexicanos," according to linguist Wallace Chafe, who has documented the language. Chafe also notes that the linguist Harry Hoijer, in his dictionary of Tonkawa, a language isolate spoken by the tribe of that name in southern Texas, cites *kaanos* as their name for "Mexican" and says that it came from Mexicanos (Hoijer 1949, 32).[6] Chafe suggests that the Caddo borrowed *kaanush* from Tonkawa and used it to designate any European. Later they narrowed its reference to Frenchman, when *ispayun* became their term for "Mexican."[7]

Chafe also notes the possibility that *kaanush* might be derived from Caddo *kahyuh* "ghost" but then dismisses that likelihood on the basis of sound correspondences. His argument is sound, but one must wonder if the Caddo actually did refer to the French, and later to other Europeans as well, as "spirits," like the Natchez and other tribes on the middle and upper Missouri River did.

CULTURAL AND PHYSICAL TRAITS

There are three names for the French of limited provenience that refer to cultural and physical traits that distinguished the newcomers.

Axe Makers

Among the merchandise of the early French traders that apparently impressed the Iroquois tribes most were the iron axes that the newcomers traded to Indians. An early recording of the name for the French as an ethnonym occurs in the seventeenth-century Mohawk dictionary of Jacques Bruyas (1863, 80, 84, 103), who cites the form "onseronni" as the name for "Les Francais." Today that name, *o'serón:ni'* continues among the Mohawk in Québec as the name for Frenchmen, and some speakers of the language there still understand it to mean literally "axe-makers." At Six Nations in Ontario, however, the term now means "white person."

In the United States the word was recorded in the seventeenth-century journal of Harmen Meyndertsz van den Bogaert as "kristoni asseroni" and given as the name for the Dutch (Gunther Michelson in Gehring and Starna 2013, 66). And in his late eighteenth-century *Indian Dictionary*, the Moravian missionary David Zeisberger gives the entry "asseróni" as the Onondaga name for "white(s)" (1887, 229). Today on the Six Nations Reserve *o'serón:ni'* means "white people." Seneca has a word for whites that is based on the root for "iron," and in Oneida the cognate of the preceding forms is *o'slu·ní·*, which means "white person," but speakers today no longer recognize the underlying meaning of the name.[8]

The data suggest that the Iroquoian peoples came into contact with the French first, and because of the newcomers' culturally distinctive iron axes, they gave them the name "axe makers." Later, after contact with other Europeans—English and Dutch—they extended the name to designate all white people. Because the white population in Québec is predominantly French, the name has continued to be used there specifically for the French, but because the population in New York is not predominantly French, the name has been generalized to all whites.

On the Great Plains an isolated instance of the name "iron worker" or "axe maker" occurs among the Oto, a Siouan-speaking tribe that is a member of the Chiwere subgroup that includes the Winnebago. In 1833 Maximilian recorded "masonkä-okannä," which in a modern orthography is *mąθ'ųkʰe okʰéñe* and literally means "common iron worker." The first element, *mąθ'ųkʰe*, means "works in iron," and in the nineteenth and twentieth centuries it has meant "white man," including anyone who is French, British, or Spanish. Since there was an earlier term for the British, "sanganash," and one for Americans, *mąhį xąje* "long knife," it appears that *mąθ'ųkʰe* was originally the term for Frenchmen since they were the earliest white people whom the Otos encountered, but that later, after Otos became acquainted with other Europeans, they generalized the term to designate all whitemen. Then, to designate Frenchmen specifically that form was modified by *okʰéñe* "common; original," becoming *mąθ'ųkʰe okʰéñe* "common (or original) whitemen." This scenario follows the familiar pattern illustrated above in the Sioux dialects, where *ikceka* "common; original" was added to *wašíču* "spirit; whiteman" to specify Frenchmen.

Poil aux Yeux

Apparently when members of several Dhegiha Siouan-speaking tribes first met the French, they were most impressed by their bushy eyebrows—a physical trait that contrasted sharply with their own plucked eyebrows. That distinguishing characteristic apparently prompted the name "eyebrow" as a designation for the French among three tribes that spoke dialects of a single language: the Osage, Kansa, and Quapaw. The earliest recordings of the name occur in the 1830s. Louis Cortambert, a French writer who settled in St. Louis in the early 1830s and who visited the Osages at that time, wrote in the account of his trip: "The Osage hate the Americans, whom they call Manhitanga (Big Knives). They like the French, to whom they give the name Ichertarin, meaning Poil aux yeux [Eye Hair], because we let our eyebrows grow out" (1837, 36).[9]

Prince Maximilian, a contemporary of Cortambert, recorded the same name for "Frenchman," writing it as "ischtáchä," which in a modern orthography would most likely be *ištáxe*, since the prince wrote the guttural sound *x* as *ch* (and he noted it as guttural) and generally wrote *ä* for the sound *e* (Maximilian [1843] 1906, 24:269). In 1840 Tixier, another French traveler who went up the Missouri and visited the Osages, gives the same name for the French, writing it as "Ishtajêh" (where he writes *j* for the guttural sound *x*) (McDermott 1940, 131, 148–49, 285).

Based on Cortambert's and Tixier's spellings of the name, the form appears to be Osage *ištáxį* or *ištáxe* or *ištáhe*, which in the twentieth century the Omaha anthropologist Francis La Flesche and the linguist Caroline Quintero say literally means "yellow eyes," but which they translate in their Osage dictionaries as "whiteman" (La Flesche 1932, 77; Quintero 2009, 107). However, Cortambert gave the literal translation "Poil aux yeux," which in contemporary Osage is *įįštáhį* "eyebrow." In the late nineteenth century the missionary linguist James Owen Dorsey recorded *ištáhi* as "eyebrows"; Quintero writes the word as *įįštáhįį* (variant *iištáhii*). She also cites a nearly identical forms *įįštáxį* (variant *iištáxį*) for "white person, French person, Canadian; British person (later) whiteman" and translates it literally as "light/yellow eyes." Dorsey translates the form *ištáxį* as "Frenchman, a Canadian; a white man, white men in general as distinguished from Indians" (Quintero 2009, 107, citing Dorsey 1883). In Kansa and Quapaw the cognate term is *ištáxe* "Frenchman; whiteman" and literally means "eyebrows."[10]

Although the preceding Osage data are somewhat confused, one must bear in mind that a literal translation "yellow eyes" does not seem likely, given the fact that most Frenchmen they encountered would have had dark eyes.[11] Cortambert's translation, in contrast, draws attention to a physical trait, "(long, bushy) eyebrows," that does distinguish Frenchmen and other Europeans physically from Indian people, who characteristically lack long eyebrows. Moreover, the forms in Kansa and Quapaw are not as problematic and suggest that Cortambert's information is correct.[12]

Cheveux noirs

An anomalous name for the French is Pawnee *pakskaatiit*, literally "black head," that is, "black hair," which came into use at an unknown time. The origin of this name is not known, although the reference is to a common French physical trait. In the nineteenth century the Pawnee term for French was recorded as South Band Pawnee *reecikucu'*, literally "long knife," the common term in North America for an American.[13]

GEOGRAPHICAL DESCRIPTORS

A less frequently occurring name type for the French is a geographical designator that specifies the direction of the French traders' homeland, which in the early contact period would be either the St. Lawrence River valley or, perhaps more likely, St. Louis, the eighteenth- and early nineteenth-century entrepôt of the fur trade that flourished on the middle and upper Missouri River.

One directional name is Nez Percé *'alláyma* "Frenchman" that literally means "from downriver." For the Nez Percé, who lived in Idaho but sometimes crossed the Bitter Root Mountains to the headwaters of the Missouri River, that term undoubtedly referred to the eastward flow of the Missouri across northern Montana and down through central North and South Dakota, eventually entering the Mississippi River at St. Louis.

Documentation of Nez Percé contact with French traders is scant. However, one account tells of a Nez Percé woman who in the late eighteenth century was the first of her people to see a white man. She was captured by Blackfeet or Atsinas, taken to Canada, sold again, and finally purchased by a white man, probably French Canadian. Eventually she ran away and returned to her people. The explorers Lewis and Clark recorded an account of three Nez Percé who made a daring expedition to the Hidatsa villages on the Missouri River in North Dakota to trade horses for corn and guns. During their stay with the Hidatsas, the men heard of an expedition of white men that had already gone upriver to the western mountains to trade "powerful goods." The Nez Percé secured six guns from the Hidatsas and then returned home with them, the first guns that the Nez Percé ever owned. These two incidents clearly exposed the Nez Percé to French Canadians, the first one to a man probably from French Canada and the second one to French traders from St. Louis (Josephy 1965, 37–38).

A similar name is Kiowa *t'óók'yààhyò* "French (people)," which literally means "north people" (Laurel Watkins, personal communication, 2010). This ethnonym seemingly describes the direction of French Canada, since St. Louis is actually southeast of Kiowa territory, which in the late eighteenth century was west of the Black Hills in southwestern South Dakota. Here their earliest contact with the French might have been with the La Vérendryes's exploring expedition in the 1740s. The Kiowas were still living there when Jean-Baptiste Truteau visited the Arikaras in central South Dakota in 1795–96, and they, with other nomadic western tribes, came to the Arikara villages to trade. Early in the nineteenth century, however, the Cheyennes and Sioux pushed the Kiowas from the northern to the southern plains, where they lost contact with French traders.

Shifts in Names for Europeans

An interesting development in the history of ethnonyms among several tribes is the reassignment of a common name for one Euro-American nationality to another one. Most of those changes occurred during the second half of the nineteenth century or somewhat later, after the need to differentiate among nationalities became less relevant to tribal life. The most notable occurrence of this type of change is in a small area on the northern plains among the Arikaras and Hidatsas in North Dakota and the Gros Ventres (Atsina) in north central Montana.

In 1833 Maximilian recorded two Arikara names for whitemen. One was *neesikúsu'* "American," which meant literally "long knife" and was the common name for Americans among tribes throughout the eastern half of North America. The other name was *sahNIštaaká* "Frenchman; whiteman," which meant literally "white human/person." In the twentieth century the term "long knife" continued as the designation for "American" in most languages of the eastern half of North America. However, in Arikara the term had become the name for "Frenchman"—and remained that until the end of the twentieth century when there were no longer any fluent speakers of the language—and the term "white human" retained its generic meaning "white person" for any Caucasian.

Maximilian also recorded two Hidatsa names for whitemen: one, *mé'chi-ihdíà*, literally meant "big knife" and designated Americans, while the other, *mašíì*, meant "Frenchman; whiteman" (see the section above titled Spirits for the significance of this term). In Matthews's 1877 dictionary of Hidatsa, he cites *mašíì* as meaning "whiteman [generically]," but says, "The word was originally applied only to the French and Canadians, who are now sometimes designated as maši-ka'ti [*mašíìgaadi*], the true whites" (188). Matthews also gives the form "maétsiicti'a" "Big Knives" as the name for Americans and notes that it "is probably translated from the language of some tribe farther east" (183).

In the latter half of the nineteenth century, however, those designations changed, at least for some Hidatsas, just as they had in Arikara. Wolf Chief, a literate Hidatsa, dictated to Gilbert L. Wilson in the early twentieth century:

> I was born at Like-a-Fishhook village [in 1849] a little after Christmas time.... There were two white men living in the village who observed Christmas season that year, and by I know what time of the year I was born.
>
> One of those whitemen had come to us from the north and sold whiskey to my people. After the whiskey was all sold he still remained in the village. My people called him Big Knife. He was a Frenchman, and at that time my tribe called all Frenchmen Big Knives. He ... lived in our village for many years. He was always called Big Knife, Meetsio-ixoti-ac. (Wilson 1914, 157)

It is significant to note that of the three tribes that have lived together on the Fort Berthold Reservation, the Mandans, who were allies of the Hidatsas, never changed their name for the French.

A third tribe that shifted the name Long Knives for Americans to designate Frenchmen is the Gros Ventres (Atsina), who live on the Fort Belknap Reservation in north-central Montana. During the twentieth century this Algonquian-speaking tribe called the French baːaswɔːɔθah, literally "big knife," according to Allan Taylor, who has documented the language and whose primary informant was in her nineties in the late twentieth century. This informant insisted that the name referred to Frenchmen and to no one else. This shift in designation is interesting since the Assiniboines, who share the Fort Belknap Reservation with the Gros Ventres, still call Americans "Big Knives," as do the Blackfoot tribe, which was allied with the Gros Ventres in the nineteenth century and lives immediately west of them (Allan R. Taylor, personal communication, 2009).

Another term that has experienced a change in its referent is "sagadasha," which occurs in many variant forms and which is the usual term for British. Use of the ethnonym, which is a borrowing of French *les Anglois*, extends from tribes on the East Coast of the United States to those on the plains. Among nearly all of those tribes the word has survived as the term for "British," but in two communities on the northern plains it has shifted referents.

Among the Yanktonai Sioux on the Standing Rock Reservation in south-central North Dakota, the term *sagdaša* now designates the Turtle Mountain people, that is, the Métis who live on the Turtle Mountain Reservation in north central North Dakota. In northern Montana the Assiniboine on the Fort Belknap Reservation also use the term—there it is *sakná*—for Métis and mixed-bloods in general.

Borrowings of the English Term "French"

A final type of ethnonym that has been used to designate the French is a borrowing of the English term "French." In some languages the English source is transparent and immediately recognizable because it and the Native name are nearly identical in form, but in several other languages it is less obvious.

The English loanword, in nearly identical form, is prevalent among Muskogean languages that are distributed throughout the southeastern United States. Because the French were not trading in the area of those tribes in the eighteenth century, the use of an English name probably occurred relatively late historically, and after entering one or more of the Muskogean languages in the late eighteenth or early nineteenth century, it then spread to the others. There are recordings of the name in four languages: *Falànchi* in Alabama (Sylestine, Hardy, and Montler 1993, 97), *Falánchi* in Creek (Martin and Mauldin 2000, 241), *Falanci'* in Chickasaw (Munro and Willmond 1994, 420), and *Filanchí* in Choctaw (Byington 1915, 456).

Similar to the preceding borrowings are two that occur in the northeastern Algonquian languages Penobscot and Passamaquoddy, whose speakers live in Maine and New Brunswick. These names, however, are not as obviously transparent as the southeastern forms. They are Penobscot *pəléčəman* "Frenchman" (Siebert 1996, 370) and nearly identical Passamaquoddy *polécomon*, pronounced [pəlécəmən] (Philip S. Lesourd, personal communication, 2009).

Parallel with the preceding borrowings is Munsee Delaware *pŭlanzhŭmaan* "Frenchman," which is a borrowing from Dutch (cf. modern Dutch *Fransman*; O'Meara 1996, 262).

Conclusion

The overview of American Indian ethnonyms presented here reveals that in the eighteenth and early nineteenth centuries there were two widely distributed names for the French in North America. One, translating as "wooden boatmen," based on the canoes that French voyageurs and coureurs de bois used to take trade to Indian villages, became the standard name among most Algonquian tribes except for several living on the East Coast and four on the northwestern plains. Although the name survived into the twentieth century some speakers of those languages have generalized it to designate Englishmen and whites more generally.

The other widespread ethnonym, "spirit," arose during the period of first contact when tribes in the Missouri River basin and elsewhere first met French explorers and traders. Based on the Frenchmen's technological possessions and awesome abilities, the Native populations perceived the intruders as spirits who controlled supernatural power and inspired awe.

Most tribes in the areas of the American Midwest and the American and Canadian plains met the French before they met the British and Americans, and so the name "spirit" initially designated the French. Later, however, as the Native population became acquainted with other Euro-American nationalities, most of them generalized the designation "spirit" to other white people of European origin and later Americans. Although the term "spirit" itself became a generic term for all whites, some tribes distinguished the French as "real, or original, spirits."

Although some tribes have had other names for the French—borrowings of the English name "French" and names that specify a physical trait or a geographical term of origin—only the two preceding names, "wooden boatmen" and "spirit," were widely used to designate French people and thus parallel a similar single ethnonym for the British and another for Americans.

Notes

Acknowledgments: The author wishes to express his gratitude to the following linguists who contributed data for this chapter: Wallace Chafe, David Costa, Linda Cumberland, Ives Goddard, Jimm Good Tracks, Geoffrey Kimball, Philip LeSourd, Justin McBride, Karin Michelson, Marianne Mithun, Mauricio Mixco, Indrek Park, Robert L. Rankin, Allan R. Taylor, Laurel Watkins, and Arok Wolvengrey. It is also a pleasure to acknowledge Raymond DeMallie and Gilles Havard for drawing my attention to several obscure historical sources and Havard for translating this chapter into French.

1. Spaniards were also distinguished, but names for them are outside the scope of this paper.

2. The Calumet, or Pipe, Dance was an adoption ceremony among many tribes in eastern North America. The rite served to cement relations between two social groups, such as bands of a tribe or even tribes. During the eighteenth and early nineteenth centuries, chiefs would commonly adopt traders in order to establish strong ties to them and thereby gain control over the distribution of trade goods (see Fletcher 1904 for details and interpretation of a Pawnee Calumet Ceremony).

3. Modern Hidatsa spelling provided by Indrek Park. Curtis (1909, 4:196) states that Crow "ma-shí-di" is "a corruption of maishta-shídi 'yellow eyes,'" an interpretation that seems unlikely.

4. Mauricio Mixco and Indrek Park, personal communications, 2010. [Editor's addendum: the folk-etymology in Mandan is probably driven by the interpretation of the syllable ší in waší/mą́ší as being derived from the root ší "good, pretty" (Logan Sutton, June 2023).]

5. The Natchez data presented here was recorded by Mary R. Haas and was provided by Geoffrey Kimball, who is editing Haas's field materials.

6. A language isolate is one that is not closely related genetically to any other language(s).

7. This account of the Caddo name is based on a description by Wallace Chafe in two contributions, one dated July 29, 2002, and the other August

22, 2006, in the Siouan List. See https://listserv.linguistlist.org/pipermail/siouan/. [The Siouan List is now run through the University of Nebraska, SIOUAN@LISTSERV.UNL.EDU.] See also Chafe (2018, 233).

8. The Iroquoian data presented here come from Michelson (2000), as well as from Wallace Chafe and Marianne Mithun (personal communications, 2010).

9. "Les Osages détestent les Américains, qu'ils appellent Manhitanga (Grand couteaux). Ils aiment les Français, auxquels ils donnent le nom d'Ichertarin, c'est-à-dire Poil aux yeux, parce que nous laissons croitre nos sourcils." English translation by Logan Sutton.

10. Kansa and Quapaw forms provided by Justin McBride and Robert L. Rankin, respectively (personal communications, n.d.).

11. In his Indian vocabularies from 1819 to 1820, Say (1905, 299) gives the name for white people as "mash-te-se-re," literally "yellow eyes." Leforge (1928, 185–86) also states that the Crow called a white person "Mah-ish-ta-schee-da" "yellow eyes." This name may have been a confusion with the term for "spirit" that occurs in Omaha, Mandan, Hidatsa, and Sioux, but more likely it refers to the light eyes of many northern and central Europeans. See also note 3 above.

12. The question is in part whether there is an actual phonemic distinction between h and x in Osage (Robert L. Rankin, personal communication, 2010).

13. Data come from the author's Pawnee field materials, collected 1965–2001.

References

Bloomfield, Leonard. 1975. *Menomini Lexicon*. Edited by Charles F. Hockett. Milwaukee Public Museum Publications in Anthropology and History 3. Milwaukee: Milwaukee Public Museum Press.

Bruyas, Rev. James, S.J. 1863. *Radices Verborum Iroquæorum: Radical Words of the Mohawk Language with Their Derivatives*. Shea's Library of American Linguistics, vol. 10. New York: Cramoisy Press.

Buechel, Eugene, S.J. 1970. *A Dictionary of the Teton Dakota Sioux Language: Lakota–English, English–Lakota*. Edited by Paul Manhart, S.J. Pine Ridge SD: Holy Rosary Mission.

Byington, Cyrus. 1915. *A Dictionary of the Choctaw Language*. Edited by John R. Swanton and Henry S. Halbert. Bureau of American Ethnology Bulletin 46. Washington DC: Government Printing Press.

Chafe, Wallace L. 2018. *The Caddo Language: A Grammar, Texts, and Dictionary Based on Materials Collected by the Author in Oklahoma between 1960 and 1970*. Petoskey MI: Mundart Press.

Cortambert, Louis. 1837. *Voyage au pays des Osages. Un tour en Sicile*. Paris: Chez Arthus-Bertrand, Libraire.

Curtis, Edward S. (1907-30) 1970. *The North American Indian*. 20 vols. Edited by Frederick W. Hodge. Norwood MA: Plimpton. Reprint, New York: Johnson Reprint.

Dorsey, James Owen. 1883. Osage-English vocabulary. Manuscript no. 4800/268. Dorsey Papers, National Anthropological Archives, Smithsonian Institution, Suitland MD.

Drapeau, Lynn. 1991. *Dictionnaire Montagnais-Français*. Québec City: Presses de l'Université du Québec.

Edgar, Matilda. 1891. *Ten Years of Upper Canada in Peace and War, 1805-1815; Being the Ridout Letters*. London: T. Fisher Unwin.

Fletcher, Alice C. (1904) 1996. *The Hako: Song, Pipe, and Unity in a Pawnee Calumet Ceremony*. With the assistance of James R. Murie. Music transcribed by Edwin S. Tracy. Bureau of American Ethnology Annual Report 22. Washington DC: Government Printing Office. Reprint, Lincoln: University of Nebraska Press.

Forsyth, Thomas. 1912. "An Account of the Manners and Customs of the Sauk and Fox Nations of Indians Tradition." In *The Indian Tribes of the Upper Mississippi Valley and Region of the Great Lakes, as Described by Nicolas Perrot, French Commandant in the Northwest; Bacqueville de la Potherie, French Royal Commissioner to Canada; Morrell Marston, American Army Officer; and Thomas Forsyth, United States Agent at Fort Armstrong*, vol. 2, translated, edited, annotated, and with bibliography and index by Emma Helen Blair, 183-245. Cleveland OH: Arthur H. Clark.

Gehring, Charles T., and William A. Starna, eds. 2013. *A Journey into Mohawk and Oneida Country, 1634-1635: The Journal of Harmen Meyndertsz van den Bogaert*. Rev. ed. Translated from the Dutch by Charles T. Gehring and William A. Starna. Wordlist and linguistic notes by Gunther Michelson. Syracuse NY: Syracuse University Press.

Gravier, Jacques. [ca. 1700]. "Dictionary of the Illinois Language." Manuscript in Watkinson Library, Trinity College, Hartford CT. Photocopy, Manuscript no. 4871, National Anthropological Archives, Smithsonian Institution, Washington DC.

Helmbrecht, Johannes, and Christian Lehmann, eds. 2010. *Hocąk Teaching Materials*. Vol. 1, *Elements of Grammar/Learner's Dictionary*. Albany: State University of New York Press.

Hennepin, Father Louis. 1938. *Father Louis Hennepin's Description of Louisiana; Newly Discovered to the Southwest of New France by Order of the King*. Translated by Marion E. Cross. Published for the Minnesota Society of the Colonial Dames of America. Minneapolis: University of Minnesota Press.

Hoijer, Harry H. 1949. *Analytical Dictionary of the Tonkawa Language*. University of California Publications in Linguistics 5, no. 1. Berkeley: University of California Press.

Josephy, Alvin M., Jr. 1965. *The Nez Perce Indians and the Opening of the Pacific Northwest*. New Haven CT: Yale University Press.

Lacombe, Père Alb[ert]. 1874. *Dictionnaire de la Langue des Cris*. Montreal: C. O. Beauchemin & Valois.

La Flesche, Francis. 1932. *A Dictionary of the Osage Language*. Bureau of American Ethnology Bulletin 59. Washington DC: Government Printing Press.

Le Boullenger, Jean-Baptiste. [ca. 1725]. "French–Illinois Dictionary." Manuscript in the John Carter Brown Library, Brown University, Providence RI.

Leforge, Thomas H. (1928) 1974. *Memoirs of a White Crow Indian*. As told by Thomas B. Marquis. New York: Century. Reprint, Lincoln: University of Nebraska Press.

Lemoine, Georges. 1901. *Dictionnaire français—montagnais avec un vocabulaire montagnais—anglais, une courte liste de noms geographiques et une grammaire montagnaise*. Boston: W. B. Cabot and P. Cabot.

Martin, Jack B., and Margaret McKane Mauldin. 2000. *A Dictionary of Creek / Muskogee*. Lincoln: University of Nebraska Press.

Matthews, Washington. 1877. *Ethnography and Philology of the Hidatsa Indians*. Department of the Interior, U.S. Geological and Geographical Survey, Miscellaneous Publications 7. Washington DC: Government Printing Office.

Maximilian, Prince of Wied-Neuwied. (1843) 1906. *Travels in the Interior of North America, 1832-1834*. Translated by Hannibal Evans Lloyd. 2 vols. London: Ackermann. Originally published in German as *Reise in das innere Nord-America in den Jahren 1832 bis 1834*. 2 vols. Coblenz: J. Hoelscher, 1839–41. Reprint in *Early Western Travels, 1748-1846*, vols. 22–24, edited by Reuben G. Thwaites. Cleveland OH: Arthur H. Clark.

McDermott, John Francis, ed. 1940. *Tixier's Travels on the Osage Prairies*. Translated by Albert J. Salvan. Norman: University of Oklahoma Press.

Michelson, Gunther. 2000. "Notes for a Mohawk Dictionary." Manuscript in possession of Karin Michelson.

Munro, Pamela, and Catherine Willmond. 1994. *Chickasaw: An Analytical Dictionary*. Norman: University of Oklahoma Press.

Nichols, John D., and Earl Nyholm. 1995. *A Concise Dictionary of Minnesota Ojibwe*. St. Paul: University of Minnesota Press.

O'Meara, John. 1996. *Delaware-English, English-Delaware Dictionary*. Toronto: University of Toronto Press.

Parks, Douglas R. 2013. "Personnes au bateau de bois, Esprits, Faiseurs de haches, Poil-aux-yeux... Ou comment les Indiens d'Amérique du Nord appelaient les Français." In *Un continent en partage: Cinq siècles de rencontres entre Amérindiens et Français*, edited by Gilles Havard and Mickaël Augeron, 233–50. Paris: Les Indes savantes, Rivages des Xantons.

Quintero, Caroline. 2009. *Osage Dictionary*. Norman: University of Oklahoma Press.

Rhodes, Richard. 1985. *Eastern Ojibwa-Chippewa-Ottawa Dictionary*. Trends in Linguistics, Documentation 3. Berlin: Mouton.

Riggs, Stephen Return. 1890. *Dakota-English Dictionary*. Edited by James Owen Dorsey. Contributions to North American Ethnology 7. Washington DC: Smithsonian Institution.

Say, Thomas. (1905) 1906. "Vocabularies of Indian Languages." In *Account of an Expedition from Pittsburgh to the Rocky Mountains, Performed in the Years 1819, 1820. By Order of the Honorable J. C. Calhoun, Secretary of War, under the Command of Maj. S. H. Long, of the U.S. Top. Engineers*, vol. 4, 289–308. Reprint in *Early Western Travels, 1748–1846*, vol. 17, edited by Reuben G. Thwaites. Cleveland OH: Arthur H. Clark.

Siebert, Frank T. 1996. "Penobscot Dictionary." Manuscript, Ms. Coll. 97, box 27-29, American Philosophical Society, Philadelphia.

Sylestine, Cora, Heather K. Hardy, and Timothy Montler. 1993. *Dictionary of the Alabama Language*. Austin: University of Texas Press.

Truteau, Jean-Baptiste. 2017. *A Fur Trader on the Upper Missouri: The Journal and Description of Jean-Baptiste Truteau, 1794–1796*. Edited by Raymond J. DeMallie, Douglas R. Parks, and Robert Vézina. Translated by Mildred Mott Wedel, Raymond J. DeMallie, and Robert Vézina. Lincoln: University of Nebraska Press.

Voegelin, Carl F. 1938–40. *Shawnee Stems and the Jacob P. Dunn Miami Dictionary*. Indiana Historical Society Prehistory Research Series 1: 63–108, 135–67, 289–323, 345–406, 409–78. Indianapolis: Indiana Historical Society.

Voorhis, Paul H. 1988. *Kickapoo Vocabulary*. Algonquian and Iroquoian Linguistics, Memoir 6. Winnipeg: University of Manitoba Press.

Whittaker, Gordon. 2005. *A Concise Dictionary of the Sauk Language*. Stroud OK: Sac & Fox National Public Library.

Williamson, John. (1902) 1938. *English–Dakota Dictionary*. New York: American Tract Society. Reprint, Yankton SD: Pioneer Press.

Wilson, Gilbert L. 1914. Field Report [Summer 1914], vol. 16, Wilson Papers, Minnesota Historical Society, Minneapolis.

Wolfart, H. C., and Freda Ahenakew, comps. and eds. 1998. *The Student's Dictionary of Literary Plains Cree*. Algonquian and Iroquoian Linguistics Memoir 15. Winnipeg: University of Manitoba.

Wolvengrey, Arok, comp. 2001. *nēhiýawēwin: itwēwina. Cree: Words*. 2 vols. Regina SK: University of Regina Press.

Zeisberger, David. 1887. *Indian Dictionary: English, German, Iroquois — the Onondaga and Algonquin — the Delaware*. Printed from the original manuscript in Harvard College Library. Cambridge: John Wilson and Son.

Afterword

PHILIP J. DELORIA

In the spring of 1988, in shock that I'd been admitted to graduate study, I contemplated two paths: American studies at Yale or ethnohistory at Indiana University. I chose the former, in large part because New Haven proved a better fit for my wife's career possibilities, but I have always wondered about how differently things would have looked had I ended up in Bloomington as one of Raymond DeMallie's and Douglas Parks's students at the American Indian Studies Research Institute and the Department of Anthropology.

I would have engaged with distinctly different forms of interdisciplinarity. Rather than the watered-down high school Spanish I used to pass a translation test at Yale, Lakȟóta language and linguistics would have been a critical part of my makeup, as it was for so many Indiana students. Community-engaged scholarship—"fieldwork" as it might then have been called—would have been a requirement as well. And while I would have missed the literary and media analysis that centered American studies in those years, I would certainly have engaged in serious research in historical archives. Indeed, when I made my first trip to the National Archives in 1989, it was an Indiana student who kindly walked me through the basics and intricacies of Record Group 75, with its confusing room full of finding aids. These things made up the "ethno" and the "history" that constituted the field as it was practiced in Bloomington. As Joanna C. Scherer and Thierry Veyrie point out in their opening essay, Ray DeMallie's practice of ethnohistory—while always open to diverse approaches—can nonetheless be defined by that triangulation: meticulous archival research, elaborated upon and corrected through community engagement, epistemologically enlightened through expertise in Native languages. In this linguistic component, of course, one can also see the constant influence of Douglas Parks.

This volume serves as a tribute to the lasting contributions of DeMallie and Parks, and it does so by putting those grounding principles into practice, while also following in their footsteps in being open to new questions, methods, and possibilities. Sebastian Braun reminds us of the contingency of historical narration and temporality, Mark van de Logt looks with a critical eye at the ways gender fluidity and sexuality may have worked in the pre-reservation period, and Sarah Quick rejoins sound studies and ethnohistory in ways that evoke the constant overlaps—so visceral at Indiana—between ethnography, folklore, and ethnomusicology. Gilles Havard dives into an analysis of ritual behavior, Logan Sutton puts linguistic evidence to work answering historical questions, and—always having the last word—Douglas Parks traces colonial encounters through the language chosen to represent the French. All of these, as well as the other essays in this book, demonstrate the distinctive brand of rigor, creativity, and accountability that was the hallmark of the work of DeMallie, Parks, and the scholarly community clustered around the American Indian Studies Research Institute.

Of course, Doug Parks may have the final essay, but he doesn't get the last word. It turns out that I do, and for that I want to turn back to one of the opening essays, Ray DeMallie's consideration of my own family history. It may be that I chose Yale American studies to continue my longstanding efforts to put a bit of distance between myself and my father, Vine Deloria Jr. I'd tried music and public school teaching, both of which succeeded in pulling me out of his orbit. Graduate school, however, would put me in a more perilous proximity. (Indeed, at my first academic job, at the University of Colorado, my father and I shared an office for a year!) Ray, who had been mentored by a seemingly endless roster of brilliant archivists and classic anthropologists, was generously willing to return the favor in my direction.

The mentoring was nothing formal, in large part because it did not need to be formalized. As Rani-Henrik Andersson, Logan Sutton, and Thierry Veyrie observe in their introduction, Raymond DeMallie was "virtually a member of the Deloria family." I first met him in 1975, when he helped my mother retrieve me from the Colorado mountains after I'd collapsed with a serious, undiagnosed case of mononucleosis. As anthropologists sometimes do, he was just hanging around our house for some part of that summer, acting with a purpose I never quite figured out. When my parents moved to Tucson in 1978, I'd come to visit at the holidays, and Ray—and occasionally Doug—would be there too. We'd go for hikes in the mountains and chat about all manner of things. We circumnavigated the city's used bookstores and art galleries. A decade later, as I was finishing a master's degree in journalism, Ray and Doug invited me to Fort Berthold to serve as a videographer. I gathered footage of elders Rose Weasel and Jim Earthboy for their student Brenda Farnell, putting on videotape plains landscapes and the pounding of chokecherries. They made sure I had read the poetry of James Welch, and they took me to the Earthboy 40.

This kind of mentoring and engagement, I've been assured, was familiar to Indiana students, and it produced cohorts of people who, in effect, sought to redeem anthropology from the critiques of those like my father. Indeed, at the 2017 conference honoring Ray DeMallie, I was struck by the significant number of former and current students able not simply to speak but also to craft jokes in the Lakȟóta language, who had worked on language preservation, taught in Native schools, or collaborated with tribal intellectuals and leaders. All these things testify to the triangulation of language, engagement, and scholarship that Ray and Doug developed at Indiana.

Ray DeMallie's entanglement with our family crossed three living generations and extended at least three generations back into the past. He met my great-aunt Ella in 1965, when he was nineteen, and again in 1969, when she corrected his pronunciation of the Lakȟóta language that had been gifted by my grandfather earlier that year. My father came next, in 1970, and their collaboration—funny, generous, affectionate—lasted until my dad's death in 2005. Somewhere in there,

Ray and Doug met my mom, to whom they were always gracious and decent—something that cannot be said about many of my father's collaborators. All the while, Ray was trying to figure out the "who" and "where" of a French-speaking man who showed up on the Missouri in the late eighteenth century while simultaneously offering a few bits of sage advice to the youngest generation.

How could my family not feel honored? Among all the other Indian people Ray DeMallie worked with over the years, my relatives served as his first language teachers, as one of his historical archives, and as one of his longest-lived communities. Ray never failed to give back to us, just as he always gave back to students, colleagues, collaborators, and communities. Doug, of course, had his own set of families, collaborators, and friends, often overlapping. All of us—writers and readers alike—can feel honored to be present here with Raymond DeMallie and Douglas Parks in the form of this book, celebrating their memory, methods, ethics, achievements, and legacies. The writers here, all touched by Ray and Doug, are giving back in the most literal and heartfelt way, with the scholarly rigor that defined their careers and their lives.

CONTRIBUTORS

JEFFREY D. ANDERSON (PhD, University of Chicago) is a professor of anthropology at Hobart and William Smith Colleges. For the past thirty-two years he has conducted or collaborated in fieldwork, archival studies, and applied research on the language, culture, and history of the Northern Arapaho Nation of Wyoming. He is author of *The Four Hills of Life: Northern Arapaho Knowledge and Life Movement* (2001), *One Hundred Years of Old Man Sage: An Arapaho Life* (2003), *Arapaho Women's Quillwork: Motion, Life, and Creativity* (2013), and various articles and chapters on language shift, language ideology, ethnohistory, temporality, knowledge systems, human development, ethnopoetics, and art.

DR. RANI-HENRIK ANDERSSON is an associate professor and senior lecturer of North American studies at the University of Helsinki. He has served as the interim McDonnell Douglas Chair, professor of American studies at the University of Helsinki Finland during 2014–16, and a CORE Fellow at the Helsinki Collegium for Advanced Studies. He is the author or editor of ten books, including *The Lakota Ghost Dance of 1890* (2008) and *Whirlwind Passed through Our Country: Lakota Voices of the Ghost Dance* (2018). One of his recent books edited with Boyd Cothran and Saara Kekki is *Bridging Cultural Concepts of Nature: Indigenous People and Protected Spaces of Nature* (2021). His newest books are *Lakȟóta: An Indigenous History* with David Posthumus (2022) and an edited volume with Janne Lahti, *Finnish Settler Colonialism in North America: Rethinking Finnish Experiences in Transimperial Places* (2022).

SEBASTIAN F. BRAUN is director of the American Indian Studies Program and associate professor of anthropology at Iowa State University. After earning a Lic.phil.I from Universitaet Basel in ethnology, history, and philosophy, he took his PhD from Indiana University in anthropology. He then taught for over a decade in the Department of American Indian Studies at the University of North Dakota, for which he also acted as chair. Among other publications, he is the author of *Buffalo Inc.: American Indians and Economic Development* (2008) and editor of *Transforming Ethnohistories: Narrative, Meaning, and Community* (2013). He has coauthored several textbooks on Native American studies, most recently *Introduction to American Indian Studies: Histories, Policies, and Contemporary Issues* (2021). He has also contributed the chapters on the United States to the yearbook of the International Work Group for Indigenous Affairs (IWGIA) since 2004. His current research project deals with the consequences of oil extraction on the northern plains.

PHILIP J. DELORIA is the Leverett Saltonstall Professor of History at Harvard University and the author of *Playing Indian*, *Indians in Unexpected Places*, and *Becoming Mary Sully: Toward an American Indian Abstract*. Deloria received a PhD in American studies from Yale University and has taught at the University of Colorado and the University of Michigan. He has been a long-serving trustee of the Smithsonian Institution's National Museum of the American Indian, president of the American Studies Association and the Organization of American Historians, and is an elected member of the American Philosophical Society and the American Academy of Arts and Sciences.

FRANCIS FLAVIN received his PhD at Indiana University, where he majored in history and minored in cultural anthropology. While at Indiana University, he studied the Lakȟóta language with Raymond DeMallie and Douglas Parks. Under the direction of DeMallie and Parks, Flavin was a graduate research assistant at the university's American Indian Studies Research Institute, where he worked on projects related to Plains Indian history, culture, and language. He taught history for several years at the University of Texas at Dallas and now works as a historian for the assistant secretary of Indian affairs in the U.S. Department of the Interior.

GILLES HAVARD, a French historian, is head of research at the Centre National de la Recherche Scientifique (CNRS) in Paris. Specializing in the history of New France and in the history of American Indians, he is the author of *The Great Peace of Montreal: French-Native Diplomacy in the Seventeenth Century* (2001), *Empire et métissages: Indiens et Français dans le Pays d'en Haut, 1660–1715* (2003), *Histoire des coureurs de bois* (2016; to be translated and published in 2025 as *Coureurs de bois: A Social History of the Fur Trade, 1600–1840*), *L'Amérique fantôme: Les aventuriers francophones du Nouveau Monde* (2019), and *Les Natchez: Une histoire coloniale de la violence* (2024). He is also coeditor of *Un continent en partage: Cinq siècles de rencontres entre Amérindiens et Français* (2013) and *Eros et tabou: Sexualité et genre chez les Amérindiens et les Inuit* (2014). These two edited volumes include articles by Raymond DeMallie and Douglas Parks. Havard has also cowritten one article with DeMallie for the *Journal de la Société des Américanistes*: "Writing the History of North America from Indian Country: The View from the North-central Plains, 1800–1870" (2019).

THOMAS W. KAVANAGH is a retired professor of anthropology and museum curator. He has written numerous books and articles on Comanche history and culture. His current project is "Degrees of Resistance: Actors and Actions in Comanche Indian Politics, 1867–1966. A Social and Political History."

BRAD KUUNUX TEERIT KROUPA, an enrolled Arikara member of the Mandan-Hidatsa-Arikara (MHA) Nation of the Fort Berthold Reservation, earned his doctoral degree in anthropology and the history of education from Indiana University. Dr. Kroupa then began work at the Arikara Cultural Center located in White Shield, North Dakota. From 2013 to 2017, he led cultural, language, historical, educational, and community advancement efforts in this role. Currently Dr. Kroupa is the executive director of Spotted Eagle, Inc. and research associate with the American Indian Studies Research Institute at Indiana

University. His work focuses on engagement with decolonized research methodologies (i.e., community-based participatory research, youth participatory research, methods in language revitalization), Arikara history, Indigenous language activism, and a commitment to critical collective action within Indigenous communities.

SARAH QUICK is an associate professor of anthropology at Cottey College, a small women's college in southwest Missouri. There she teaches cultural anthropology courses, qualitative research methods, interdisciplinary courses overlapping with environmental studies, and Cottey's first-semester writing course. She has also co-led an "excursion" course on Osage history and culture. Dr. Quick trained in sociocultural anthropology and ethnomusicology at Indiana University, and it was through her doctoral field research on Indigenous fiddle dance performance in Western Canada that she began to really delve into archival source materials in conjunction with ethnohistorical methods and topics. Her research interests span into more contemporary Indigenous music/dance performances, farm-oriented youth groups, and food movements. She is also in the process of collaborating and contributing her own digital recordings to a digital archive on the fiddle dances she and others have documented.

JOANNA C. SCHERER is an emeritus anthropologist at the Smithsonian Institution's National Museum of Natural History. She is an authority on photographs of Native Americans and was a key researcher for fourteen volumes of the *Handbook of North American Indians*, an encyclopedia on the history and the cultures of all Indigenous peoples of North America, published between 1978 and 2006. As a result of her research she amassed a collection of over one hundred thousand historical and contemporary photographs of Native Americans, currently housed at the Smithsonian's National Anthropological Archives. She also authored several articles on *Handbook* history for the *Introduction* (volume 1) of the *Handbook of North American Indians*, published in 2022. She has written a number of books, including *A Danish Photographer of Idaho Indians: Benedicte Wrensted* on returning family photographs to the Northern Shoshone and Bannock families at the Fort Hall Reservation. This book won three national awards: Idaho Book of the Year 2006 by the Idaho Library Association; Secretary's Research Prize, Smithsonian Institution, 2008; and Collier Prize for Still Photography Research, Society for Visual Anthropology, a unit of the American Anthropological Association, 2008.

LOGAN SUTTON holds a PhD in linguistics from the University of New Mexico (2014). As a linguist, he specializes in particular in the Caddoan and Kiowa-Tanoan language families as well as the Siouan languages Mandan and Hidatsa. He has worked on language documentation and revitalization projects among the Tanoan Pueblos of New Mexico since 2006, completing a comparative-historical study of that language family for his doctoral dissertation. Sutton also worked on Arikara and Pawnee language projects as a research associate under Douglas R. Parks at the American Indian Studies Research Institute (AISRI), Indiana University from 2005 to 2019. At the time of this writing, he has continued his affiliation with AISRI, currently also serving on the advisory board, and has lived and worked since 2019 on the Fort Berthold Indian Reservation, under the MHA Nation's Culture and Language Department, where he assists in the revitalization of the Arikara, Hidatsa, and Mandan languages.

MARK VAN DE LOGT earned an MA in American studies from Utrecht University, the Netherlands (1995), and a PhD in American history from Oklahoma State University (2002). He was a research fellow under Douglas R. Parks and Raymond J. DeMallie at the American Indian Studies Research Institute at Indiana University. He was also a fellow at the United States Military Academy at West Point, New York, before joining the history department at Benedictine College, Atchison, Kansas. He is currently an associate professor of history at Texas A&M University at Qatar and specializes in Native American history, U.S. military history, Mexican history, and the American West. He previously published *War Party in Blue: Pawnee Scouts in the U.S. Army* (2010) and *Monsters of Contact: Historical Trauma in Caddoan Oral Traditions* (2018). His most recent book, *Between the Floods: A History of the Arikaras* (2023), largely relies on oral traditions and oral history.

His articles have appeared in the *Journal of Military History, American Indian Quarterly, American Indian Culture and Research Journal,* and *Wicazo Sa Review.* In his spare time he has written a yet unpublished historical novel set among the Pawnee people titled "The Witch and the Scarecrows." Currently he is completing a work on the 1586 siege of his hometown of Grave, the Netherlands, during the Eighty Years' War. The recipient of seven teaching awards, Dr. van de Logt lives with his wife and daughter in Doha, Qatar.

THIERRY VEYRIÉ is an anthropologist and ethnohistorian specializing in Northern Paiute and Lakȟóta cultures and languages. Trained at the American Indian Studies Research Institute at Indiana University with Raymond J. DeMallie and Douglas Parks, he also is versed in the French anthropological tradition. With DeMallie, Veyrié edited *The Dakota Way of Life* (2022) by Ella Deloria and continues to prepare primary sources relative to Native peoples of the plains for publication. Veyrié's doctoral dissertation, "A Historical Ethnography of the Fort McDermitt Paiute-Shoshone" (2021), weaves together oral traditions of the Paiute-Shoshone people and military correspondence to compose a multicultural history of this community. Veyrié also works toward the maintenance of the Northern Paiute language, and he currently serves as Language Program director for the Fort McDermitt Paiute-Shoshone Tribe. He was awarded several large federal grants to support his efforts in McDermitt, the last sizable community of speakers of the Northern Paiute language.

INDEX

Page numbers in italics refer to illustrations.

Adai, 338n3
Alabama (language), 361
Alberta, 142, 143–46, 149, 151–53, 158n1, 318
Algonquian (languages), 199–200, 228–29, 316, 335, 346–48, 353, 360, 361–62
allotment of lands, 43
American Anthropological Association, 38, 40, 44, 45, 59
American Fur Company, 73
American Horse (Wašíču Thašúŋka), 94, 97, 98, 106
American Indian Studies Research Institute, xv, 1–2, 38, 41, 87
American Society for Ethnohistory, 8
androgyne, 116
anthropology, 4, 10–11, 23, 26, 27, 39, 44, 59, 89, 138–39, 154, 193, 196, 227, 231
Apache(s), 202, 225, 238; languages, 335
Arapahos, 14, 132, 170–71, 221–40, 353
archives, 2, 4, 9, 23, 25–29, 31–35, 39, 140, 196
Arikara(s) (*sáhniš*), 1, 3, 12, 40, 113–34, 335–37, 349–50; ceremonialism, 14, 243–62; language, 16, 315–28, 334–35, 338n6, 339n11; words, 116, 211, 359
Assiniboines (Nakodas), 64, 203, 318, 351–52, 360, 361

at^{i}ná' neéšu' (Mother Corn), 243, 244, 246, 248–50, 254, 256
At-sa-wi, 131
Attocknie (man and branch of Ketahto), 302–3, 304, 307
Attocknie, Francis J. ("Joe A"), 293, 298–99
Bakken oil boom, 96
Bantu (Nguni), 316
Bear (Medicine) Society, 257–59
Beaver-Foot, 235–36
Beede, Aaron McGaffey, 123
Beesowuunenno', 229
Benedict, Ruth, 59, 124
berdache, 116, 125, 133
Big Foot (Sí Tȟáŋka), 103, 178–79, 181
bilateral kinship, 294, 296
Bird-Nester, 193
Black Bear (Arapaho chief), 235
Blackbird, 208–11
Black Elk (Heháka Sápa), 61, 178–80, 265
Blackfoot (Blackfeet), 202, 203, 228–29, 353, 358, 360
Black Fox (Šuŋgmánitu Sápa), 97–98
Black Hills, 63, 269, 282
Blaine, Garland, 121–22, 124
Blaker, Margaret, 25, 29, 30–36, 48
Blindy (Arapaho tribal historian), 232

Boas, Franz, 4, 38, 59
Boon, James, 35, 37
Bozeman Trail War (Red Cloud's War), 102
Buffalo Bill (William Cody), 165, 269–70
bundles ("bird case"). See *karuúxu'* (Arikara village sacred bundle)
Bushotter, George, 29
bushy eyebrows, 356–57
butch, 116

Caddo (Southern Caddoan), 317, 327–28, 335, 354
Caddoan (languages), 2–3, 16, 201, 244, 315–28, 333–37
cairns (*ʒi'eyoono'*), 236–37, 238
Callihoo, Victoria, 144
Catawba, 318
Center for the Study of Man, 39, 49n8
Cheevers, 300–303, 304, 307
Cheyenne River Reservation, 38, 59, 87, 103, 107
Cheyennes, 118, 132, 170–71, 173–74, 204, 210, 222–23, 225–27, 234, 239, 350, 353, 359
Chickasaws, 361
Chief Above (Arikara), 245, 248, 254, 256, 257
Chipps, 98
Chiwere-Winnebago (languages), 318, 331, 355–56
Choctaws, 204–5, 361
Christianity, 60, 62–65, 69–73, 80, 114–15, 122, 182–83, 269–71, 275, 278, 281, 286
ckúsaat, 114, 116–17, 121, 124, 133, 134. See also two-spirit
Clark, William P., 223–24, 227, 234
classifiers, 315–16; in Caddoan, 319–28; comparison, 333–35; in Siouan, 328–33
collective plural, 332–33, 334, 339n10
Colombia, 141
Columbia University, 59
Comanches, 171, 293–310

communities, 4, 8, 9, 23, 42
composite (kinship type), 296, 297, 299, 306, 307
Cook, Joseph W., 70–71, 73, 74
coureurs de bois, 57, 73, 82, 198, 207, 346
Crazy Horse (Tȟašúŋke Witkó), 24, 88, 89, 91, 93, 94, 97–99, 100, 101, 102, 104, 108, 168, 174–77, 181–83
Crazy Thunder, 103
Creeks, 205, 361
Crees, 143, 149–50, 153, 346, 347t
Crow Dog (Kȟaŋǧí Šúŋka), 88, 90, 91, 99, 100, 108
Crows, 171, 228, 319, 331, 352, 363n3, 364n11
cultural relativism, 43
Curtis, Edward S., 244, 261n8, 310n8, 352, 363n3
Custer, George A., 165, 168, 174

Dakota(s), 3, 6, 29, 46, 62, 65; languages, 318–19, 331, 351
Dakota Access Pipeline, 87
Damas, David, 41
D'Azevedo, Warren, 41
decolonial listening, 12, 139–42, 154–57
Deloria, Ella C., 3, 44, 45–46, 58, 59, 62, 73
Deloria, Philip J., 82, 142
Deloria, Philip J. (Thípi Sápa), 58, 60, 70–78
Deloria, Vine Jr., 2, 7, 27, 38, 58, 59, 79–82
Deloria, Vine Sr., 37, 58, 59–62, 71–72, 78–79
Deloria family, 11, 46, 57–82
DeMallie, Ramond J., xv, 1–10, 16, 23–51, 59, 87, 115, 137, 138, 154–55, 180, 193, 211, 221–22, 224, 265
Deslauriers, François (Saswé), 58, 61–78
Dhegiha (Siouan languages), 318, 331–36, 356
Dion, Joseph Francis, 149–53, 156
Dorsey, George Amos, 120, 126
Dorsey, James Owen, 27–29, 60, 125

Ducheneaux, Frank, 107–8
Dunbar, John Brown, 120
Dutch, 355, 362
earth-diver, 231
Echo-Hawk, Roger, 122
Eggan, Fred, 24, 26
Elliott, Noel P., 45
endogamy, 294, 296, 305
ethnoethnohistory, 221, 226
ethnohistory, 4–9, 23, 38, 40, 46, 48, 87, 92, 95, 106, 107, 108, 114, 117, 137–39, 155, 193, 196, 208, 221, 226, 231, 265–66, 286
ethnomusicology, 139–41
ethnonyms, 294, 298, 300, 304, 310n8, 345
Evans, Clifford, 39, 44, 51
Evarts, Mark, 121
Evening Star, 116, 128
Ewers, Ezra P., 26–27
Ewers, John Canfield, 26–27, 39–40, 44, 48
exogamy, 294, 295, 302, 305, 309n7

field, 27, 39
Field Museum of Natural History, 36
Flandreau, 95
Flat-Pipe (*se'eicoo*), 231, 233, 235
Fletcher, Alice, 42–44
Fogelson, Raymond, 5, 7, 38, 41, 42
Forsyth, Thomas, 346–47
Fort Berthold Indian Reservation, 96
Fort Robinson, 94
Found-in-Grass, 237
Four Old Men, 232–33
Four Rings (Ščiskoóku'u' Čiití'Iš), 248, 253, 256
Fox tribe, 348t
French, 57, 61–74, 82, 150–54, 156, 194–95, 198–205, 345–64

Gall (Pȟizí), 101, 102, 104, 105, 174
Garnett, William, 94, 103
Gast, John, 170
gender, 116–17, 122–24, 125

gender-fluid, 116
Ghost Dance, 36, 101, 176–79, 182, 236, 265–66, 268–70, 274–79, 281–82, 284–86
Gilmore, Melvin R., 124, 243, 248, 251, 253
Goodman, Cheryl Rae, 31
Good Thunder (Wakiŋyan Wašte), 282
Grass, John (Pheží), 101, 104, 105
Great Sioux Reservation, 104, 266
Gros Ventres (Atsinas), 224, 229, 353, 358, 359, 360

Haas, Mary, 2
Halq'eméylem (Halkomelem), 140
Haŋbléčheyapi (Crying for a Vision), 66, 267
Handbook of North American Indians, 2, 23, 41–43, 50
Harkin, Michael, 6
Harvest Ceremony (Arikara), 249, 250
Heзebóoó (Dog Trail), 230–31
Heart River, 203
Helm, June, 41
Hennepin, Louie ("Father Louis"), 348–49
hermaphrodites, 116, 126
heyókȟa (thunder dreamer, contrarian), 273–74
Hidatsas, 318, 319, 331, 336, 352, 358, 359–60, 364n11
hiiteeni, 233, 237. *See also* Four Old Men
Hinman, Samuel, 69–70
history, 25, 31, 39, 59, 87–110, 138, 193, 196–97, 228, 230, 233, 236
Ho-Chunk. *See* Winnebago
Hoebel, E. Adamson, 294, 295–97, 305–6
Hoho'nookeenno' (Rock People), 229
holy men, 76
Hughte, Phil, 44
Hump (Miniconjou Sioux chief), 26
hungry listening, 140
Hurons, 348

Idaho State University, 2
Incas, 206

incorporation, noun, 323, 339n7
Indiana University, xv, 2, 39, 40–41, 45
Indian Claims Commission, 5–6
Indian Council Fire of Chicago, 58
Indian Peace Commission, 74
Indian police, 103–4, 107
Indian rights, 2
Iníkağapi (Making New Life), 66
interdisciplinarity, 4–9, 23
intersexuals, 116
iron, 171, 198, 200, 349, 354–55
Iroquois, 24, 194, 354–55

Jahner, Elaine A., 2
Jumano, 338n3

Kansa, 201, 339n10, 356, 357
karuúxu' (Arikara village sacred bundle), 243, 246, 247, 248, 249–53, 254, 257, 261nn3–6
Kavanagh, Thomas, 31
Ketahto, 293–94, 298, 300–307
Khoesan (languages), 316
kicahúruksu' ("scalped people"), 119
Kickapoo tribe, 348t
Kicking Bear (Mathó Wanáȟtaka), 183
kinship, 1, 24, 26, 31, 38, 40, 47, 48, 282–83
Kiowas, 36, 37, 171, 335, 358–59
Kipling family, 145–47
Kitkehahki, 113, 122. *See also* Pawnee(s)
Kitsai, 317, 327
knife, big or long (moniker for Europeans), 355, 357, 359–60
kunaananá (Arikara doctor, medicine man), 243, 246, 248, 254–56, 257, 259, 261n4, 261n7, 262n9
kunaá'u' NAhkaaWIhíni' (Arikara Medicine Lodge), 243, 246, 248, 250, 254, 255, 256–59, 261n8
kunahUxwaarúxti' (Arikara priest, holy man), 243, 246, 247, 248, 252, 253–54, 255, 256, 262n8
kúsaat, 114. *See also* two-spirit

kUxát, 116–17. *See also* two-spirit

La Flesche, Francis, 43, 51
Lake Sakakawea, 96–97
Lakȟóta, 1, 23, 29, 31, 37–38, 40, 46, 47, 48, 57–83, 88–108, 118, 138, 165, 168, 170, 179, 180, 181, 185, 222, 230, 234, 265–87; gender roles, 115–16; words, 351
ledger drawings, 37
legacy, 44, 46
Lewis, Oscar, 44, 51
Lewis and Clark Expedition, 204
Liberty, Margot, 40
listening, 137–42, 154–57
Little Big Horn battle, 165, 182, 266
Little Big Man (Wičháša Tȟáŋkala), 88, 91, 93, 108
Lurie, Nancy, 5

Mandans, 203, 318, 319, 329–31, 336, 352, 360, 363n4
Manifest Destiny, 168, 169
Manitoba, 49n6, 147–48, 157–58
manuscripts, 25, 27–28, 39, 41, 42, 44, 59
Mary College, 2, 40, 60
Mascoutens, 199–200, 207
Maximilian zu Wied-Neuwied, 252–53, 347, 351, 352, 355, 356, 359
Mazakutemani, Paul, 69, 70
Medicine Lodge (Arikara). See *kunaá'u' NAhkaaWIhíni'* (Arikara Medicine Lodge)
medicine wheels, 239
Meggers, Betty, 44, 51
Menominee tribe, 347t
Métis, 73, 137, 140–41, 142, 143–44, 145–46, 147–54, 157n1, 158n5
Miami-Illinois tribe, 347t
Miamis, 199–200
Missouri River Siouan. *See* Crows; Hidatsas
Mízhi^n, 204, 205

382 Index

modernity, 95–96, 97, 100–101, 103, 104, 105–8, 109n11, 142
Mohawks, 354–55
Montagnais tribe, 347t
moon, 116, 121, 124–25, 128, 131, 133, 207
Mooney, James, 36, 223, 236, 239, 294, 310
Morgan, Lewis Henry, 24
Morning Star, 116, 128
Mother Corn. See *at*^{i}*ná' neéšu'* (Mother Corn)
Munsee Delaware (language), 362
Murie, James R., 3, 113, 117, 120, 243
music, 139–49
Muskogean (languages), 335, 346, 361

Natani, Mary, 38
Natchez, 205–8, 209, 210, 353–54
National Archives, 25, 30–36, 48
National Congress of American Indians, 80
National Endowment for the Humanities, 2, 40
National Museum of Natural History, 25, 31, 36
National Science Foundation, 2, 26, 30
Native American Church, 36
Native American studies, 2
neešaánu' (Arikara chief), 244, 247, 251, 252
Neihardt, John G., 61, 165–87, 265–66, 271–73, 278, 280–81
Nez Percé, 358
Nih'oo3oo (Arapaho Creator), 232
noble savage, 166–67
Numic (languages), 335

Oglalas, 61, 97, 107, 265, 273
Ohio River Valley Siouan (languages), 318, 331
Ojibwes (Ojibwas), 200, 213n13, 347t
Old Timers (musical association), 142, 143–49, 153, 156, 158n2, 158n4
Omaha-Poncas, 332, 337, 339n10

Omahas, 43, 121, 208, 210, 245, 330, 336, 352, 356
One Horn (Hewáŋžiča), 28
oral traditions, 46, 58–76, 113, 114–34, 222–23, 226
Osages, 204, 205–6, 207, 213n13, 329, 331, 332, 356–57
Otoes, 336, 352, 355–56

Padoucas, 201–2
Pahuk, 129
Parks, Douglas, xv, 1–5, 16, 40–48, 60–61, 244
participant observation, 43
Passamaquoddy, 361–62
patrilocal, 296, 306, 307
Pawnee(s), 1–4, 12, 40, 113–34, 244, 336–37, 350; ceremonialism, 247, 251–52, 256, 261n3, 363n2; language, 16, 317–18, 319–28, 334–35, 338n6, 339n11; Skiri, 3, 4, 116, 120, 122, 128, 336–37, 350; words, 114, 357
Pawnee Rock, 114, 131
Penobscot, 361–62
Perrot, Nicolas, 198–200, 207
photographs, 27, 31, 35, 40, 74
Pine Ridge Reservation, 30, 37, 39, 59, 90, 107, 268, 269, 271, 274, 277–78
Plains Indian Sign Language, 227–28, 317
Poncas, 336, 339n10
posture verbs, 315–16, 319–20, 336
Potawatomi, 198, 199, 347t
Powder River, 173
Pratt, Nora, 3–4
priest (Arikara). See *kunahUxwaarúxti'* (Arikara priest, holy man)
primary sources, 4, 6, 10, 23–24, 38, 40, 44, 46, 47
Proto-Algic, 228–29
Proto-Algonquian, 228–29
Proto-Siouan, 328–29

Quapaw, 332–33, 335, 356, 357
queer, 116

Rattle Snake, 210
Red Cloud (Maȟpíya Lúta), *33, 34, 35,* 98, 100, 106, 172–73, 176, 183, 234
Red Horse the Storm-maker, 37
Red River Jig, 143–49, 150, 151, 152, 155–56, 158n3
Red Tomahawk (Tȟačhaŋȟpí Lúta), 88, 89, 91, 93, 108
rematriation, 141
Rigdon, Susan, 44
Rising Eagle (NéetAhkas TiirwátAt, aka Frank Hart), 256
ritual, 193, 198–211
Ritwan (languages), 228
Roaming Scout, 3, 113, 120, 122, 125, 130, 133
Rocky Mountains, 14, 63, 225, 230, 237, 345, 352
Rosebud Reservation, 77, 268
Rowlodge, Jesse, 239

Sage, Sherman, 230, 238
Salish, 335
Sand Creek, 239
Santees, 28, 67, 69, 74–75, 349
Saskatchewan, 149
Sauk and Fox, 346–47
Sauk tribe, 348t
Say, Thomas, 352, 364n11
Scabby-Bull, 126–29
Scheiber, Laura, xv
Scherer, Joanna, 10, 23, 30–48, 50
Schneider, David, 25, 38
Schurz, Carl, 99
Seaman, Ted, 44
sexism, 41–42, 43–44
Sharp Nose, 223
Shawnees, 346, 348t
Shoshones, 225, 234–35, 294, 295–96, 307–8
Sičháŋǧu, 99
Siouan (languages), 27, 60, 318–19, 328–33, 334–35, 336

Sioux, 1, 24, 26, 29, 38, 43, 57, 124, 169, 170–75, 178, 181–85, 349, 350–51, 352, 356, 359
Sioux religion, 40, 60–61
sirawari ("they go together"), 120
Sitting Bull (Tȟatȟáŋka Íyotake), 88, 89, 91, 93, 97, 99, 101, 102–5, 108, 168, 173–74, 176–77, 182–83
Six Nations, 355
Skiri Pawnee dialect. *See* Pawnee(s)
skUxát, 116–17. *See also* two-spirit
Sky Bull (Maȟpíya Tȟatȟáŋka), 104
Smithsonian Institution, 2, 23, 25, 30, 31–41, 45, 47, 48, 60
social organization, 46
South Band Pawnee dialect. *See* Pawnee(s)
Spider Woman, 113–14, 126
spirit (moniker for French), 348–54, 362
Spotted Tail (Siŋté Glešká), 88, 90, 91, 93, 98, 99–100, 105–6, 108, 172–74, 182–83
Standing Rock Reservation, 58, 77, 101, 103, 104
Standing Soldier, 103
Stanley, Sam, 39, 49
St. Elizabeth's Mission, 61, 77
Steward, Julian H., 294, 295–97, 306, 307–8
Stó:lō, 140
Stoneys, 318, 338
Sturtevant, William C., 38, 41–42, 47–48, 49
sun, 116, 128, 193, 198–201, 205–7, 211
Sun Dance, 279
Swift Bear (Matȟó Lúzahaŋ), 98
Sword, George, 59–60

Táhipirus, 113–14, 118, 130–33, 134
Tanoan. *See* Kiowas; Tewa
Tax, Sol, 39
Ten Bears, 293, 300–302, 304, 309n2
Teton Dakotas, 27
Tewa, 317
thiyóšpaye (extended family), 283
Three Affiliated Tribes, 96

Thunder Ceremony (Renewal Ceremony), 249–50
Toll expedition (1914), 230–31, 237, 238
Tonkawa, 354
Touch the Clouds (Maȟpíya Ičáȟtagya), 93, 98
transgender, 116
transmotion, 14, 222, 227, 231–33, 236, 240
Treaty of Fort Laramie, 225–26
Truteau, Jean-Baptiste, 3, 44, 208–9, 349–50, 358–59
tshunúxu' ("scalped people"), 119
Tuhiwai Smith, Linda, 7
Turner, Frederick Jackson, 183
Turtle Mountain (Métis), 361
two-spirit, 114–15, 116–17, 118

University of California, Berkeley, 1
University of Chicago, 1, 5, 24, 25, 35, 38–39
University of Wyoming, 1, 39
U.S. Army, 67–68, 276
U.S. Census Bureau, 184
uxorilocality, 301, 302, 306–7

VanStone, James W., 36
Veyrié, Thierry, 3, 45
Vézina, Robert, 3, 45
virilocality, 297, 302, 305, 306, 307, 308
visions, 61, 65–68, 80, 106, 114, 118, 236, 265–87
Voorhis, Paul, 36, 37, 48, 49

waaruksti (spiritual power), 119
wakȟáŋ (holy), 116, 266–86
Wakíŋyaŋ (thunder beings), 65–68, 71, 272–73, 277–78
Walker, James R., 2
Walking Sun, Tom, 122

Warrior (Skiri Pawnee), 127, 128
Weasel Bear, 233–35
Wedel, Mildred, 5–6, 39, 44, 46, 48, 49–50, 51
Wedel, Waldo, 5–6, 44, 48, 50, 51
Weltfish, Gene, 120, 121–22, 131–32
Wheeler-Voegelin, Erminie, 5
White Antelope, 239
White Sun, 113, 129
Wichita (language), 317, 327
Will, George F., 243, 257, 262n8
Wilson, Dick, 107
Wind River Indian Reservation, 234–35
wiŋktés, 115. *See also* two-spirit
Winnebago, 38, 352, 355
winter counts, 64
Wolf Chief (Hidatsa), 360
women in academia, 41–42, 43–44, 47
Wonderful-Sun, 126
Wood, Raymond, 6, 40
wooden boatmen, 346, 362
Wounded Knee, 80, 91, 95, 102, 103, 166, 170, 178, 181–82, 184, 270, 277–78
Wovoka, 176, 178, 181, 268

Yamparika, 293–94, 298–99, 300–303, 304, 305–6
Yanktonai, 64–65, 88, 100, 110n12, 351, 361
Yanktons, 60, 63–65, 67, 69, 75, 100
Yellow Bear (Matozhi), 31, 32
Yellow Bird (Ziŋtkázi), 177–79, 183
Young Eagle, Frank, 122
yuwípi (divination), 67, 69

Zeisberger, David, 355
Zuni, 44

IN THE STUDIES IN THE ANTHROPOLOGY OF
NORTH AMERICAN INDIANS SERIES

The Four Hills of Life: Northern Arapaho Knowledge and Life Movement
By Jeffrey D. Anderson

One Hundred Years of Old Man Sage: An Arapaho Life
By Jeffrey D. Anderson

Great Plains Ethnohistory: New Interdisciplinary Approaches
Edited by Rani-Henrik Andersson, Logan Sutton, and Thierry Veyrié

The Semantics of Time: Aspectual Categorization in Koyukon Athabaskan
By Melissa Axelrod

Lushootseed Texts: An Introduction to Puget Salish Narrative Aesthetics
Edited by Crisca Bierwert

People of The Dalles: The Indians of Wascopam Mission
By Robert Boyd

A Choctaw Reference Grammar
By George Aaron Broadwell

War Paintings of the Tsuu T'ina Nation
By Arni Brownstone

The Lakota Ritual of the Sweat Lodge: History and Contemporary Practice
By Raymond A. Bucko

From the Sands to the Mountain: Change and Persistence in a Southern Paiute Community
By Pamela A. Bunte and Robert J. Franklin

A Grammar of Comanche
By Jean Ormsbee Charney

New Voices for Old Words: Algonquian Oral Literatures
Edited by David J. Costa

The Dakota Way of Life
By Ella Cara Deloria
Edited by Raymond J. DeMallie and Thierry Veyrié
Afterword by Philip J. Deloria

Reserve Memories: The Power of the Past in a Chilcotin Community
By David W. Dinwoodie

Haida Syntax (2 vols.)
By John Enrico

Northern Haida Songs
By John Enrico and Wendy Bross Stuart

Life among the Indians: First Fieldwork among the Sioux and Omahas
By Alice C. Fletcher
Edited and with an introduction by Joanna C. Scherer and Raymond J. DeMallie

Powhatan's World and Colonial Virginia: A Conflict of Cultures
By Frederic W. Gleach

Native Languages and Language Families of North America
(folded study map and wall display map)
Compiled by Ives Goddard

Native Languages of the Southeastern United States
Edited by Heather K. Hardy and Janine Scancarelli

The Heiltsuks: Dialogues of Culture and History on the Northwest Coast
By Michael E. Harkin

Prophecy and Power among the Dogrib Indians
By June Helm

A Totem Pole History: The Work of Lummi Carver Joe Hillaire
By Pauline Hillaire
Edited by Gregory P. Fields

Corbett Mack: The Life of a Northern Paiute
As told by Michael Hittman

The Spirit and the Sky: Lakota Visions of the Cosmos
By Mark Hollabaugh

The Canadian Sioux
By James H. Howard

The Canadian Sioux, Second Edition
By James H. Howard, with a new foreword by Raymond J. DeMallie and Douglas R. Parks

Clackamas Chinook Performance Art: Verse Form Interpretations
By Victoria Howard
Transcription by Melville Jacobs
Edited by Catharine Mason

Yuchi Ceremonial Life: Performance, Meaning, and Tradition in a Contemporary American Indian Community
By Jason Baird Jackson

Comanche Ethnography: Field Notes of E. Adamson Hoebel, Waldo R. Wedel, Gustav G. Carlson, and Robert H. Lowie
Compiled and edited by Thomas W. Kavanagh

The Comanches: A History, 1706–1875
By Thomas W. Kavanagh

Koasati Dictionary
By Geoffrey D. Kimball with the assistance of Bel Abbey, Martha John, and Ruth Poncho

Koasati Grammar
By Geoffrey D. Kimball with the assistance of Bel Abbey, Nora Abbey, Martha John, Ed John, and Ruth Poncho

Koasati Traditional Narratives
By Geoffrey D. Kimball

Kiowa Belief and Ritual
By Benjamin Kracht

The Salish Language Family: Reconstructing Syntax
By Paul D. Kroeber

Tales from Maliseet Country: The Maliseet Texts of Karl V. Teeter
Translated and edited by Philip S. LeSourd

The Medicine Men: Oglala Sioux Ceremony and Healing
By Thomas H. Lewis

A Grammar of Creek (Muskogee)
By Jack B. Martin

A Dictionary of Creek / Muskogee
By Jack B. Martin and Margaret McKane Mauldin

The Red Road and Other Narratives of the Dakota Sioux
By Samuel Minyo and Robert Goodvoice
Edited by Daniel M. Beveridge

Wolverine Myths and Visions: Dene Traditions from Northern Alberta
Edited by Patrick Moore and Angela Wheelock

Ceremonies of the Pawnee
By James R. Murie
Edited by Douglas R. Parks

Households and Families of the Longhouse Iroquois at Six Nations Reserve
By Merlin G. Myers
Foreword by Fred Eggan
Afterword by M. Sam Cronk

Archaeology and Ethnohistory of the Omaha Indians: The Big Village Site
By John M. O'Shea and John Ludwickson

Traditional Narratives of the Arikara Indians (4 vols.)
By Douglas R. Parks

A Dictionary of Skiri Pawnee
By Douglas R. Parks and Lula Nora Pratt

Lakota Texts: Narratives of Lakota Life and Culture in the Twentieth Century
Translated and analyzed by Regina Pustet

Osage Grammar
By Carolyn Quintero

A Fur Trader on the Upper Missouri: The Journal and Description of Jean-Baptiste Truteau, 1794–1796
By Jean-Baptiste Truteau
Edited by Raymond J. DeMallie, Douglas R. Parks, and Robert Vézina
Translated by Mildred Mott Wedel, Raymond J. DeMallie, and Robert Vézina

They Treated Us Just Like Indians: The Worlds of Bennett County, South Dakota
By Paula L. Wagoner

A Grammar of Kiowa
By Laurel J. Watkins with the assistance of Parker McKenzie

To order or obtain more information on these or other University of Nebraska Press titles, visit nebraskapress.unl.edu.

www.ingramcontent.com/pod-product-compliance
Lightning Source LLC
Chambersburg PA
CBHW020837020526
44114CB00040B/1283